Witnessing Suburbia

# Witnessing Suburbia

*Conservatives and
Christian Youth Culture*

Eileen Luhr

UNIVERSITY OF CALIFORNIA PRESS
*Berkeley · Los Angeles · London*

University of California Press, one of the most distinguished university presses in the United States, enriches lives around the world by advancing scholarship in the humanities, social sciences, and natural sciences. Its activities are supported by the UC Press Foundation and by philanthropic contributions from individuals and institutions. For more information, visit www.ucpress.edu.

University of California Press
Berkeley and Los Angeles, California

University of California Press, Ltd.
London, England

Chapter 3 contains a slightly revised version of "Metal Missionaries to the Nation: Christian Heavy Metal Music, 'Family Values,' and Youth Culture, 1984–1994." *American Quarterly* 57, no. 1 (March 2005): 103–28. Reprinted with permission of *American Quarterly*.

Lyrics to "Planned Parenthood" and "Operation Rescue" appear courtesy of Lust Control (Captive Thought/ASCAP).

All verses of the Bible not taken from quotations are derived from the New Revised Standard Version Bible, copyright 1989, Division of Christian Education of the National Council of Churches of Christ in the United States of America. Used by permission. All rights reserved.

Library of Congress Cataloging-in-Publication Data

Luhr, Eileen, 1972–.
    Witnessing Suburbia : Conservatives and Christian youth culture / Eileen Luhr.
        p.    cm.
    Includes bibliographical references and index.
    ISBN 978–0–520–25594–4 (cloth : alk. paper)
    ISBN 978–0–520–25596–8 (pbk. : alk. paper)
    1. Evangelicalism—United States—History—20th century.    2. Christianity and culture—United States—History—20th century.    3. Christian youth—Religious life—United States—History—20th century.    4. Suburbs—United States—History—20th century.    I. Title.
BR1642.U5L84    2009
261.0973'09049—dc22                                        2008017178

Manufactured in the United States of America

18  17  16  15  14  13  12  11  10  09
10  9  8  7  6  5  4  3  2  1

*For my parents: John Paul Luhr,*
*George L. Snyder, Leah Luhr Snyder*

# Contents

# Illustrations

# Introduction

The popular mythology of youth rebellion features two major types of teen idol: the maverick outsider and the nonthreatening square. As the story is told, the teen rebel—always a male—poses a threat to social conformity, traditional authority structures, and civic peace; his antagonists include parents, the preacher, and the magistrate. The square, while not quite an antidote to the rebel, nonetheless offers a palatable alternative for adults disturbed by his counterpart's impact on impressionable teenagers. More role model than heartthrob, the square cultivates a public image that values education, hard work, and respect for authority.

This was the narrative *Life* magazine drew on in its August 1956 story "Elvis—A Different Kind of Idol." Detailing the "fans, fads—and fears" generated by a series of concerts Elvis Presley gave in Florida, the article described "a town all worked up." The objections to Elvis raised by Jacksonville's elders included those of a judge who attended an afternoon show and was preparing to charge Elvis with "impairing the morals of minors" if subsequent performances were not toned down. Elvis's concerts also drew the concern of the city's religious community: a local Baptist congregation prayed for his soul, and a Methodist congregation held a church social for teenagers preceded by a sermon entitled "Hotrods, Reefers and Rock'n'Roll."[1] To drive home the difference between sacred and profane reactions to this rebel, the magazine juxtaposed photographs of pious teens at the Baptist church contemplating the state of Elvis's soul with pictures of hysterical female fans.

Figures 1a and 1b. A 1956 *Life* photo spread of Elvis juxtaposed fanatical teens sent into "frenzies of schreeching and wailing" during performances (above) with pious teens praying for the icon's soul at a Baptist service (opposite). Robert W. Kelley/*Time* & *Life* Pictures/Getty Images.

The binary between dangerous and domesticated youth persisted months later when *Collier's* tried to persuade its audience that teens had begun to abandon Elvis in favor of Pat Boone, his clean-cut rival. The article highlighted each performer's attitude toward middle-class norms. Whereas Elvis "scorn[ed] marriage as a waste of time for a young idol with thousands of admiring girls beating at the stage door," Boone had been married for over three years. Whereas Elvis had ended his education after high school, Boone continued to sing while maintaining "a straight A average" at Columbia. And while Elvis's style was criticized for emphasizing the "roll," Pat's reputation was "solid as a rock." The accompanying photographs underscored the message that Pat Boone was the idol more acceptable according to middle-class sensibilities. One photograph, with a caption that noted Elvis's reputation for "one night stands," showed the star shirtless and in bed in a hotel room; in another, he was relaxing on a couch with a female fan. In contrast, Boone was shown visiting with his sisters and playing on the floor with his three daughters as his wife watched approvingly.[2]

According to the conventional narrative of youth rebellion, conservative religious believers identified with bland paragons like Pat Boone. This appeared to still hold true in 1978, when the first issue of *Contemporary Christian Music* magazine *(CCM)* hit the stands with a lead story on Pat Boone's daughters: his youngest child, Debby, had reached the top of the charts a year earlier with the single "You Light Up My Life."[3] However, another piece in the magazine undermined the expectation that evangelicals would identify only with the culturally vapid. Columnist Don Cusic argued that *His Hand in Mine,* recorded after Elvis was discharged from the army in 1960, was the first contemporary gospel record. Cusic lamented that the "religious establishment" of the day had condemned Elvis for his forays into inspirational recordings, even as stories about him had "emphasized a clean-cut, wholesome youth who openly admitted his love for gospel music, his parents and Christianity."[4] Cusic's piece redefined Elvis as a sincere, pious youth who had been misrepresented by modern-day Pharisees. The real Elvis, Cusic argued, was raised in the conservative Pentecostal religious tradition and had frequented gospel concerts in Memphis as a youth.

Cusic had a valid point. While Elvis's more domesticated image was attributable in part to the maneuvering of his clever manager, the influence of the Deep South's religious environment on his style had always been clear. The Jordanaires, his backup vocalists beginning in 1956, were a well-established gospel quartet. Within six months of his near-arrest in Jacksonville, Elvis ended his third and final performance on *The Ed Sullivan Show* with "Peace in the Valley," a popular spiritual composed by Thomas A. Dorsey that he recorded for an inspirational album a few weeks later. After being discharged from the army in 1960, Elvis released *His Hand in Mine,* a gospel collection that included the songs "Known Only to Him" and "Jesus Knows What I Need."[5] In fact, when it came to selecting a cultural lineage of rock musicians, Cusic had a range of options. A number of 1950s-era white southern music stars, including Jerry Lee Lewis and Johnny Cash, came from Pentecostal backgrounds; after Elvis, Lewis, Cash, and Carl Perkins kicked around at the Sun Records studio in early 1956, a resulting recording, known as the Million Dollar Quartet, included several traditional gospel numbers familiar to each artist. The link between gospel and rhythm and blues was even stronger among African American artists: Sam Cooke had been a member of the legendary gospel group the Soul Stirrers; Little Richard and Curtis Mayfield had crossed over from gospel; and Ray Charles and James Brown drew heavily on the call-and-response tradition of black churches.[6] Yet Cusic selected Elvis, the white "King of Rock'n'Roll" who had stirred the most controversy and achieved the greatest notoriety, as the pioneer of Christian rock.

By emphasizing Elvis's religious influences, Cusic reframed the false god of popular culture as the founding father of Christian recording—an interpretation embraced by other evangelicals as they appropriated "youth culture" in their conversion mission to American society. Cusic's piece was emblematic of a broader shift in Christian conservatives' attitudes toward secular culture from one of condemnation to one of engagement. Those who had once shunned youth culture or who had sought bland alternatives to it were creating a usable past within—rather than separate from—the cutting edge of American culture. Evangelicals may not have controlled popular culture, but they helped shape discourses surrounding popular culture and youth. These evangelicals sought to fit within, rather than react to, suburban consumer culture. By inserting their moralistic vision into popular culture, they participated more fully in the competitive cultural and consumer marketplace of the late twentieth century. Just as important, young believers would be players, not pariahs, in the moral and cultural "war of position" waged by white religious conservatives.

This book is a history of the suburbanization of evangelicalism and the "Christianization" of popular culture—twin pillars of the conservative shift in national politics during the Reagan-Bush era. The emergence of a politicized evangelical youth culture ranks as one of the major achievements of "third wave" conservatism in the late twentieth century. This book contrasts the old Christian Right—with its dogmatic resistance to youth culture per se—and the new "rock" evangelicalism, which embraced cutting-edge cultural forms and media in order to institute moral reform and broaden the impact of its proselytizing efforts. These processes, in turn, abetted a hegemonic conservative politics grounded in uniting possessive individualism with home-centered "traditional values."

The key to conservative ideological politics during the Cold War era—whether in the form of anti-communism, law and order, anti-feminism, or culture war—was the protection of the white middle-class home and family. Discourses about youth and the home dominated the American political, social, and cultural landscape, then defined by such issues as juvenile delinquency, the Moynihan Report, campus protests, the draft, the counterculture, the legalization of abortion, school prayer, and the taxpayers' revolt. At the same time, "folk devils" provided an accessible example of the challenges that youth subculture posed to traditional authority and normative values.[7] As an antidote to the perceived turmoil of the era, Christian conservatives nurtured a suburban

ethos that valued "self-reliance," "personal responsibility," and
"family values." Yet conservative evangelicals did not seek to excise
consumer entertainments from their values utopia. On the contrary,
family-oriented media became key components of the campaign to protect the economic and cultural prerogatives of the suburban evangelical
home. This amalgamation produced a cultural activism that was, in
fact, more innovative and widespread than the better-known political
protests of the Christian Right. Media coverage of the Moral Majority,
Family Research Council, or Christian Coalition often suggests that
religious conservatives' political efforts were fundamentally motivated
by a backlash against American culture. White evangelical Christians'
cultural practices, in contrast, demonstrate that conservative believers
were also engaged in a values-based suburban activism expressed in a
consumer vernacular.[8]

Evangelical cultural activism illuminates the convergence of suburbanization, conservatism, and youth culture during the late twentieth
century. The concern for family heightened during a period when the
balance of power in American politics and culture shifted from the
Northeast to the South and West, from the city to the suburb, and from
the poor and (often) nonwhite to the middle class and white. Drawn by
the populist rhetoric of suburban political culture that emphasized
"meritocratic individualism" while it ignored structural inequalities in
American society, suburbanites gradually became increasingly
Republican during the late twentieth century.[9] While the suburban vote in
1960 slightly favored Republicans, by 1988, suburbanites—constituting
48 percent of the electorate—favored Republicans over Democrats 28
percent to 20 percent.[10] In 2004, Republican George W. Bush dominated the outer suburbs—often known as the "exurbs"—by winning
ninety-seven of the nation's one hundred fastest-growing counties. These
areas, where Bush received 63 percent of votes cast, were located in the
Midwest as well as the South and Far West.[11] Christian conservatism,
ensconced in exurbs and suburbs, played an important role in creating
this differential.

This book explains how the suburban home came to be viewed both
as the sentimental repository of established values and economic success and as the source for a dynamic culture of resistance during the
late-twentieth-century conservative era. Other studies have focused on
the political culture of middle-class suburbanites, but this work explains
the cultural politics of emerging evangelical middle-class consumers.
White evangelicals' concerns about the influence of popular culture on

children meshed perfectly with other conservative movements that defended the sanctity of the home through language that emphasized individual rights and responsibilities. The taxpayer and anti-busing revolts of the late 1970s crystallized the social concerns of middle- and working-class white suburbanites who viewed the American home as the embodiment of the American dream. Christian conservatives viewed themselves as the guardians of "family values," a concept that invoked white, suburban, middle-class, patriarchal, and heterosexual authority. They contrasted these values to those of the identity movements of the late twentieth century.

Evangelicals' contribution to this process was significant because, as a result of the migrations of the postwar era, many conservative Christians now resided in the politically, culturally, and demographically dominant suburbs of the Sunbelt. Just as commercial culture and urban identity had altered the religious identities of Jewish and Catholic immigrants in the nineteenth-century metropolis, the suburban sensibilities and culture of the late twentieth century affected the beliefs and practices of conservative Protestants. Suburban megachurches, often associated with nonsectarian Protestant faiths, attracted new members with nonthreatening architecture that mimicked suburban designs, pastors who wore casual clothes and preached about everyday issues, and a contemporary worship style that featured up-to-date music.[12] The relaxed atmosphere of these churches often belied a worldview that might be described as Hawaiian-shirt conservatism: beneath these signifiers of suburban ease remained a deeply conservative message about personal responsibility, respect for authority, and traditional gender roles. With evangelicals' emphasis on the importance of changing hearts (a cultural issue) rather than votes (a political issue), popular culture provided an appealing way to intervene in American public life. By analyzing both the content and the impact of white evangelical Christian cultural forms—particularly popular music aimed at youths—this book demonstrates that the cultural activism of evangelicals aided the conservative political surge by facilitating their entrance into national discussions about public morality and values.

If conservatives sentimentalized the middle-class home, progressives romanticized the revolutionary potential of youth rebellion. In the wake of the 1960s, there was a sense that cutting-edge youth cultures had always been a destabilizing force against authority and therefore would always serve the interests of the Left. Since the passage of the Twenty-sixth Amendment, voters age eighteen to twenty-four—a group with notoriously low turnout historically—have tended to be more sympathetic to left-leaning candidates. Conservatives, however, have tried to minimize this advantage by establishing conservative get-out-the-vote networks and by promoting among young people both conservative values and the habit of voting.[13] They often borrowed from progressive innovations. Therefore, while it is generally assumed that conservative Christians spearheaded the "backlash" against the sixties, the decade actually influenced believers' rhetoric and practices. As the initial outrage at Elvis indicates, conservatives had a tradition of involvement with youth culture, even if it was to serve as killjoy foils for the latest fad. The Christian youth culture of the post-1960s era, however, was not necessarily just a latter-day manifestation of the sentiment in Pat Boone's (white) family-friendly (and grammatically correct) cover of Fats Domino's "Ain't It a Shame." Conservative Christians believed that the behavior of young people reflected the state of American values and thus viewed "youth" as a critical ideological battleground. Rather than simply trying to reverse the changes the sixties had wrought, these prototypical activists of the culture wars believed that the 1960s provided a blueprint for the cultural revolution they wished to achieve in the 1980s and 1990s. Christian youth culture became a form of activism for Christ.

## THE SUBURBAN HOME IS WHERE THE HEART IS

The suburbanization of the American middle class transformed both the content and form of traditional evangelicalism. During the post–World War II era, the suburb became the new demographic center of gravity in the United States. In retrospect, the hegemony of the American city proved fleeting; the U.S. census reveals that the majority of Americans lived in cities for less than half a century. By 1920 Americans who lived in urban areas outnumbered rural residents for the first time. By 1960, however, Americans were split evenly among rural, urban, and suburban areas. In the 1970s the American suburban population increased by 22 million, much of this suburban growth occurring in formerly rural areas surrounding the Sunbelt cities of Atlanta, Dallas, and Houston.[14] By 1990 only 31 percent of Americans lived in urban areas, while almost half lived in the suburbs.[15] The suburb even outstripped its name, as planners and critics coined new terms such as "edge city," "postsuburbia," "metroplex," "exopolis," and "exurbia" to describe growth that obviated an urban core by shifting functions (government centers, office buildings, retail complexes, white-collar employment, even the daily commute) to suburbs that acquired high-rise nodes distributed in a polycentric pattern. The exodus to the suburbs occurred as the overall population shifted to the South and West, with California (48%), Texas (24%), Florida (78%), Arizona (73%), and Nevada (78%) experiencing enormous growth between 1940 and 1980.

The demographic shifts had significant social and political consequences. In 1969, Republican political strategist Kevin Phillips predicted an era of GOP dominance hastened by migrations to the "sunbelt," a term he coined to describe the American South and West. The influx of young "blue-collar and middle-level white-collar families" from northern cities, combined with the concentration of African Americans in the urban core, had created a "new settlement frontier."[16] The departure from the cities, often described as "white flight," polarized the nation along racial and class lines as government policy subsidized racially zoned suburbanization. Although many had assumed that all Americans would reap the rewards of the Fordist era of rising wages, that consensus became unglued during the social turmoil of the 1960s, then collapsed during the economic downturn of the 1970s and 1980s and the accompanying postindustrial restructuring of the economy. In the wake of urban riots, heightened middle-class concerns about security resulted in a "militarization of city life" through repressive architecture, urban planning, and law enforcement. The result was an "increased spatial and social insulation" between cities and impoverished minorities on one hand and suburbs and the sentimentalized white family on the other.[17] The Moynihan Report, published in 1965, became the ruling paradigm of Nixon-era welfare reforms as politicians and social scientists increasingly attributed the disparities in social and economic life to a perceived moral crisis among African American families. As historian Robin D. G. Kelley explains, while some posited "the 'ghetto'" as the source of a "vibrant culture of resistance," others designated it as "the Achilles' heel in American society" and "the repository of bad values and economic failure."[18] By blaming values rather than structural racism, conservatism located poverty in culture and behavior: "immoral" populations were deemed parasites that needed to alter their values to improve their station.[19] These sentiments were typified by Dan Quayle's famous 1992 speech after the Los Angeles riots in which he blamed a "poverty of values," rather than the conditions of poverty, for social unrest.

While the ghetto was pathologized as a locus of "bad values" and "economic failure," the suburban home was apotheosized as the epitome of American virtue. Historian Lizabeth Cohen has noted that American citizenship became tied to consumerism during the Cold War era; this consumer identity, in turn, became closely tied to the private home and, moreover, the entire suburban landscape.[20] As historian Elaine Tyler May has explained, during the 1950s, the domestic ideology of the Cold War promised personal fulfillment through a consumer-oriented family life in the suburbs: consumerism was heralded as a "means for achieving individuality, leisure, and upward mobility."[21] These assumptions were apparent in 1959 when Vice President Richard M. Nixon engaged Soviet Premier Nikita Khrushchev in the famed "Kitchen Debate," which framed the Cold War conflict in terms of access to consumer durables.[22] Consumer identity altered political affinities. Historian Peter La Chapelle has traced the cultural and political transformation of Dust Bowl migrants from producer-based identities rooted in the New Deal coalition to a "property-based" and "consumer-based" political culture in the 1960s and 1970s.[23] The taxpayer and anti-busing movements of the 1970s are often viewed as efforts to protect the consumerist prerogatives of middle-class home owners from the encroachments of inflation, stagnated income, and tax-funded government programs for the poor.[24]

The connection between consumerism and the suburban home led to fears that society would become atomized as Americans increasingly valued home life above community life. As early as the 1940s, the celebration of privatization led critic Lewis Mumford to remark, "Suburbia is a collective effort to lead a private life."[25] Critics mourned the "isolation en masse" and the loss of a "sense of common purpose" symbolized by one-family homes built on identically sized lots; they also noted the tendency of housing markets to become segmented by race and class through zoning laws, discriminatory government loan policies, and racial covenants.[26] Nevertheless, the bewildering sense of danger that prevailed in the suburbs led some home owners to seek ever-greater levels of exclusivity. Gated communities represented a new degree of isolation and withdrawal from the larger community. By the 1990s, 20,000 such communities contained 3 million housing units in the United States. Gated communities were particularly popular in Southern California, where a 1990 survey of home shoppers showed that 54 percent wanted to live in a "gated, walled development."[27]

The predominance of the middle-class family extended to all aspects of American culture. Historian Eric Avila has described how the racial polarization of city and suburb created a "new spatial culture of suburbia" based on "homogeneity, containment, and predictability" and exemplified in film and by freeways, ballparks, and theme parks.[28] In the 1980s, critics such as Barbara Ehrenreich worried about the "tendency to see the middle class as a universal class," a trend manifested in, for example, the disappearance of working-class Americans from American television programs in favor of people with white-collar jobs.[29] Mike Davis noted that the drive for "personal insulation" shaped the built environment of the inner city as well as those of shopping malls and office centers. To protect the affluent from pariah groups, designers installed video surveillance cameras and limited both pedestrian access and street frontage. As a result, activity was transferred to a sumptuary core behind the barricade-like walls of office buildings and shopping malls.[30] The concern for family safety extended to the vast network of roads built to ease the exurban commute from the cul-de-sac to the office park. According to journalist Keith Bradsher, the surge in sport utility vehicle (SUV) sales during the 1980s and 1990s—years after suburban sprawl had become commonplace—represented another step in the deterioration of the nation's communal ethos. With their intentionally menacing designs (one industry designer was quoted as joking, "If you put a machine gun on the top [of SUVs], you will sell them better") and with their high kill rates in accidents with motorists in smaller cars, SUVs demonstrated a ruthless drive to protect oneself and one's family even at the cost of others' safety.[31]

Given the supersized sense of besiegement in the suburbs, it was perhaps no surprise that the protection of the home became the pivotal political issue of the late-twentieth-century conservative revolution. Beginning in the 1960s, conservatives mobilized suburbanites around a set of "gut-level" issues centered on the sanctity of middle-class white family life.[32] As Kevin Phillips had predicted in 1969, it was this "populist revolt" of the middle strata, rather than the antiwar movement, that would have the greater long-term impact on American politics.[33] As the emerging historiography of suburban conservatism has shown, a thriving grassroots political culture arose during the 1960s and 1970s, based on a discourse of home-owner "rights." Writing shortly after Ronald Reagan's 1966 gubernatorial victory, political scientist James Q. Wilson argued that the conservative's victory rested in Southern California's culture of single-family homes.[34] The federal government had heavily subsidized suburban development, but campaigns in defense of (white) middle-class entitlements nonetheless used the rhetoric of the dispossessed. Although concerned with a range of issues, suburban activism may have reached its greatest notoriety during the so-called taxpayer revolt of the late 1970s, which first appeared in California. To critics of "local control," the taxpayer revolt represented another step in the devolution of community into fragmentary suburban lots. Journalist Peter Schrag argues that California's Proposition 13 represented a shift in the idea of government services from a "communitarian ethic" to a "fee ethic" in which the immediate beneficiary alone pays for his or her share of government-provided service.[35] In supporting these anti-government measures, home owners argued that their status was the result of individual merit rather than the consequence of Cold War Keynesian policies that channeled substantial government resources into Sunbelt suburbs.

Popular media accounts tend to cast the conservative movement as negative, reactionary, or delusional—that is, as backlash or false consciousness—rather than as a social movement with a persuasive ideological core.[36] Thomas Edsall suggests that the "rebellion of the haves," as some have called the taxpayer revolt, "provided conservatism with a powerful internal coherence."[37] But this coherence derived from moral as well as economic imperatives to protect the home. Christian conservatives provided critical groundwork in this area through their programmatic dedication to organizing around the defense of home and youth. Conservatives have demonstrated a consistent ideological commitment to a value system—any value system—that critics have found missing from the Left.[38] As historian Lisa McGirr has shown, normative and fiscal conservatives' spirited grassroots political activism in Orange County, California, in the 1960s contributed to a historic rightward shift in American political life, portended by Ronald Reagan's election as governor of the state and fulfilled in his successful bid for the presidency in 1980.[39] The "suburban warriors" whom McGirr describes provided an early glimpse of the motivational power inherent in a campaign centered on nationalism, individualism, and traditional values.

In fact, regulation of the home—a site that unified nationalism, individualism, and traditional values—provided the moral as well as economic core of the conservative movement. In the 1830s, Alexis de Tocqueville—a historical observer often quoted by modern conservatives—explained the flow of order between public and private realms in the United States: "Religion exercises but little influence upon the laws and upon the details of public opinion; but it directs the customs of the community, and, by regulating domestic life, it regulates the state."[40] But what would happen if regulating domestic life became the point of

departure for political debate? Tocqueville warned against such an over-
lap between politics and religion. The discourses of the Reagan era,
however, turned concerns about the home inside out, and personal
morality became an essential part of public life. In the words of critic
Lauren Berlant, positions on pornography, abortion, sexuality, personal
morality, and family values became "key to debates about what
'America' stands for" and "how citizens should act."[41] In this environment, Barbara Ehrenreich notes, "permissiveness"—a word that evoked
liberalized postwar child-rearing techniques—was "the most indispensable word in the New Right vocabulary," as it could be used to describe
abortion, homosexuality, promiscuity, pornography, drug abuse, and
feminism as well as allegedly overindulgent anti-poverty programs.[42]
On the other hand, as Paul Apostolidis argues, organizations such as
James Dobson's Focus on the Family made the "straight family" into the
"highest ethical obligation" in American society.[43] Indeed, secular and
religious activists came to identify themselves regularly not just as taxpayers or home owners but also as parents. These sentiments continued
during the Clinton administration, as the confrontations over gay rights,
abortion, and welfare reform centered on threats posed to the family.
During the 2000 election, pollsters suggested that differences in voters'
attitudes about sexual norms were becoming the "key variable" in
American politics.[44] Taken together, these discourses fused the categories of citizenship with parenthood and established "youth" as a category of innocence in need of parental protection from a hostile world.

## A SUBURBAN STRATEGY:
### EVANGELICAL CHRISTIANITY IN THE POSTWAR ERA

The valorization of the middle-class white family required that emotional themes such as nation, duty, authority, and tradition be linked
with neoconservative economic themes such as competitive individualism and opposition to taxation and government.[45] Conservative evangelicals were integral to the process of domestic sanctification.
Historically, evangelicals have at times emphasized progressive values,
but the dominant religious conservatives of suburbia were often economic individualists who saw a causal relationship between moral
laxity and economic misfortune. To conservative suburbanites, the protection of the white middle class entailed not just home values but
values in the home. Their views reflected the suburbanization of
American evangelicalism, a belief system well equipped to address

within a consumer idiom the private concerns and emotional needs of families. Consumer culture promised the economic agent personal transformation through the choices offered by liberated markets; similarly, evangelicalism offered the moral agent an intensely emotional religious experience if only he or she chose to be saved.[46] Beneath the suburban signifiers, however, remained a conservative message about the responsibilities of the liberal subject.

Earlier periods of American history saw similar claims made for a special connection between religion and domestic life. During the Second Great Awakening, which accompanied the shifting social relations of the Market Revolution, reformers fixated on establishing personal piety through familial (especially maternal) nurture. Religious belief provided a means for establishing social order in both the market economy and the middle-class home in the bustling "burned-over district" of western New York.[47] Educator and domestic commentator Catharine Beecher, the older sister of Harriet Beecher Stowe, opined that family was "the home church of Jesus Christ."[48] In the South, where the agricultural economy limited the emergence of public and private spheres, evangelical religion and family nonetheless converged to order society.[49] According to historian Donald G. Mathews, southern evangelicals wanted the "economic, biological, affective, and socializing functions of the family to be simultaneously transformed by and supportive of" their efforts to live a "disciplined, holy life."[50]

Shortly after the Civil War, moral crusader Anthony Comstock established the New York Society for the Suppression of Vice and, as a special agent of the post office, began a forty-year effort to enforce the federal anti-obscenity law of 1873. In his book *Traps for the Young*, Comstock declared that there was "no more active agent employed by Satan in civilized communities to ruin the human family and subject the nations than evil reading"—that is, the newspaper serials and "half-dime" novels available to youth in the emerging urban mass markets.[51]

Over time, media and cultural representations associated religious conservatism with so-called rural values. At the end of the nineteenth century, conservative Protestants, destined to be outnumbered by urban majorities in the Northeast and Midwest, were linked to the small towns of the Old South and Great Plains. In this environment, economic radicalism and evangelical pietism combined to form a ruggedly anti-institutional worldview in the Jeffersonian tradition. As both Thomas Frank and Michael Kazin have commented, the populists of the late nineteenth century, embodied by Nebraskan William Jennings Bryan, found their greatest support among rural Protestant "producers" who resented the concentration of wealth among a few corporations and wanted the federal government to counter these powers.[52] In 1909 Bryan, a Democrat and Social Gospel advocate, publicly joined the ranks of prohibitionists—including the socialist Upton Sinclair—who called for the abolition of the "liquor trust" because of the damage it had inflicted on workers and the nation's social fabric.[53] Even when religious conservatives were urbanized, they defiantly identified themselves with such "country" values as thrift, sobriety, and producerism. The Iowa-born revivalist Billy Sunday, who referred to himself as "a rube of the rubes," fulminated against big-city vices like the theater, dance hall, and saloon as he conducted urban revivals attended by recent transplants; similarly, Aimee Semple McPherson, born in rural Ontario, routinely established a rapport with her Los Angeles audiences by asking how many of them had been born on a farm.[54]

Even as Bryan delivered his "Cross of Gold" speech in 1896, he and other conservative Protestants were already becoming identified more with cultural backwardness than with populist monetary policy. Clever scribes soaked their descriptions of religious conservatives in citified cynicism and sought to confine fundamentalists to an "anti-modern" time and distant, "separatist" space. The army of temperance advocates that gathered in Southern California in 1895 was enough to lead novelist Mrs. Charles Stewart Daggett to deadpan, "I am told that the millennium has already begun in Pasadena, and that even now there are more sanctified cranks to the acre than in any other town in America."[55] The writer of a 1906 article in the Los Angeles Times, perhaps concerned that an increase in the number of "sanctified cranks" suggested a primitive recidivism incongruent with boosters' imagination of the "City of the Future," expressed disgust at the "weird babel of tongues" emanating from the Azusa Street mission, a crucible of the burgeoning Pentecostal movement.[56] In 1912 the preponderance of rural-bred sensibilities among recent migrants to Los Angeles led critic Willard Huntington Wright to grumble in the Smart Set that the city was "overrun with militant moralists, connoisseurs of sin, experts of biological purity" from the Midwest who "brought with them a complete stock of rural beliefs, pieties, superstitions, and habits." The irritating remnants of ruralism included "the Middle West bed hours, the Middle West love of corned beef, the church bells, Munsey's magazine, union suits and missionary societies," as well as a "complacent and intransigent aversion to late dinners, malt liquors, grand opera and hussies."[57] Bryan's prosecutorial efforts at the Scopes Trial in 1925 provided cosmopolitan writers with additional fodder.[58] "Heave an egg out of a Pullman window," humorist H. L. Mencken famously sneered in an obituary for Bryan shortly after the trial, "and you will hit a Fundamentalist almost anywhere in the United States today." Not content merely to note the geographic pervasiveness of religious conservatives, Mencken delighted in assigning a stagnated cultural evolution to Bryan's fundamentalist followers, whom he labeled *"Homo neandertalensis,"* "gaping primates," and "anthropoid rabble."[59] Writing two years later (and dedicating his work to H. L. Mencken), novelist Sinclair Lewis set his novel *Elmer Gantry* in fictional lesser-light midwestern towns with absurd names such as Banjo Crossing and Gritzmacher Springs, Kansas.[60]

In time, the notion that religious conservatism was locked in a perpetual state of provincialism became an intractable cultural image. The Gantry-esque hypocrite and the wowser served as the first fundamentalist archetypes; the god of this pair, to use Wright's dismissive description of transplanted midwesterners in Los Angeles, resembled "a combination of [John] Calvin and Anthony Comstock—with Comstock predominating."[61] In the minds of secular liberals and satirists of the late twentieth century, contemporary conservative Protestants continued to inhabit a distant space and time. As anthropologist Susan Harding has shown, the Scopes Trial served an important role in shaping modernity's understanding of itself. Harding notes that the trial helped establish "an escalating string of oppositions between Fundamentalist and Modern—between supernaturalist and reasoning, backward and progressive, ignorant and educated, rural and cosmopolitan, anti-intellectual and intellectual, superstitious and scientific, duped and skeptical, bigoted and tolerant, dogmatic and thinking, absolutist and questioning, authoritarian and democratic."[62] These dualities reflected ignorance of a long history in which conservative Protestantism demonstrated a remarkable adaptability to change. As Martin E. Marty has explained, evangelicalism emerged in the eighteenth century alongside Adam Smith and modern economic theory. It adapted to modernity by helping believers cope with the "chopping up" of life and functions (home and work, church and state), by focusing on the "private dimensions of life" through voluntarism, and by emphasizing moral free agency and "choice" in open economic markets.[63] These attributes made evangelicalism the perfect belief system for suburbia.

Many evangelical Protestant sects had traditions of radical communitarianism dating to the eighteenth and nineteenth centuries, but suburban evangelicalism developed a mono-emphasis on capitalist values.[64] Neoliberal and consumerist rhetoric reflected the belief that American society valued individual choice and affiliation, not ascription. Similarly, evangelical beliefs emphasized the importance of agency in personal and religious matters. In fact, the description of southern evangelicals offered by historian David Edwin Harrell Jr. in 1981 resembles the platform of the modern Republican Party: "[They] have been more individualistic, less confident in social reform, more literal in their views of the Bible," and "more moved by personal religious experience" than other Americans.[65] Likewise, many evangelical Christian leaders of the late twentieth century favored free markets and limited government. According to Pat Robertson, government could do little to assist the disadvantaged because "the problems of poverty, inequality, and injustice are problems of the human spirit" that could not be solved by government intervention since "no massive federal program can force upon us what does not come from within." Alluding to the federal anti-poverty programs of the Johnson administration, Robertson remarked, "the great society begins in the transformed hearts of the people, and it spreads one by one among us until the entire world is transformed."[66] A Reagan administration official told attendees at a Financial Success Seminar in Anaheim, "Economic salvation and spiritual salvation go side by side."[67] This individualistic outlook, which predicated economic redemption on personal conversion, precluded progressive government economic policy.

Despite evangelicalism's proven flexibility, its secular critics assumed (or perhaps hoped) that conservative religion would be marginalized before disappearing altogether. To some, this inference certainly seemed to be confirmed by U.S. Supreme Court decisions on school prayer, evolution, and abortion during the 1960s and 1970s. Even though personal belief in God remained high and evangelist Billy Graham ranked as one of the most admired Americans, 75 percent of Americans surveyed in March 1970 said they thought religion's influence on American life was decreasing.[68] Nonetheless, declaring an end to religion still provoked a furor, as when the publication of Harvey Cox's *The Secular City* led *Time* magazine to pose the judiciously restrained question "IS GOD DEAD?" on the cover of its early April 1966 issue—just in time for Good Friday.[69] Religious conservatives rose again to challenge these pronouncements: it took just over five years before the magazine resurrected Jesus on its cover under a banner proclaiming "The Jesus Revolution."[70] The perceived importance of religion in America also rebounded: in 1976, 39 percent of Americans reported that religion's influence in society was increasing.[71]

Whatever its perceived influence in American life, religion remained a buyer's market, especially in the suburbs. Mass consumerism fostered an environment where, according to sociologist Christian Smith, believers "become spiritual consumers uniquely authorized as autonomous individuals to pick and choose in the religious market whatever products they may find satisfying or fulfilling at the moment."[72] Secularists may have assumed that conservative religious beliefs were doomed, but growth rates in the number of conservative Protestant churches and in their membership dramatically exceeded those of mainline Protestant and Catholic churches in the postwar era. In fact, religious studies scholars Roger Finke and Rodney Stark have suggested that churches thrived most in pluralistic areas where "religious entrepreneurs" had to compete to win "market shares" among "religious consumers."[73]

During the postwar housing boom, an abundance of new markets emerged for religious entrepreneurs. Statistics from the early postwar period show that new church membership grew faster than the population. A church construction boom tracked the growth of residential building: Americans spent $4 billion building new churches, many of them in the suburbs, between 1945 and 1955.[74] This environment provoked concerns that churches focused on the social aspects of their congregation to the detriment of doctrine and theology. As historian James Hudnut-Beumler has explained, suburbanites wanted a "de facto community center," with child-friendly amenities, extensive programming, and coffee hours. This form of "popular religion" focused more on morals and patriotism than on "ecclesiastical religion," which adhered to rigorous institution building, traditional rites, and formalized doctrine.[75]

What was good for church growth was not always conducive to social justice causes, as new congregations were affected by the racially zoned suburbanization policies of the federal government. As the government poured money into suburban mortgages and infrastructure projects, many churches followed the money trail out of the cities. The market-driven religious environment raised fears among critics that suburban church growth was leading churches to renege on their moral obligation to address social justice in the urban core. In a condemnation that paralleled the attacks of social critics William Whyte and David Riesman on the conformist white middle class, Gibson Winter, a Unitarian minister and divinity professor at the University of Chicago, criticized the complacency of mainline Protestantism.[76] Noting Martin Luther King

Jr.'s lament that "eleven o'clock on Sunday morning is the most segregated hour in the United States," Winter condemned religion's complicity with residential segregation and wondered how the "inclusive message" of faith could be "mediated through an exclusive group" based on social-class identity. By dwelling too much on congregational and parochial life at the fringes of metropolitan centers, churches had become "mere refuges for the fleeing middle classes."[77] In this interpretation, churches were overidentified with the private concerns and emotional needs of the middle class.

Although Winter aimed his criticism at liberal mainline churches, the more conservative and evangelical churches that focused on the private and emotional aspects of life won the battle for market share in the Sunbelt suburbs. While the success of old-time religion in the newest subdivisions in American society may seem counterintuitive, sociologist Christian Smith has argued that "evangelicalism maintains its religious strength in modern America precisely because of the diversity it confronts. American evangelicalism is strong . . . because it is—or at least perceives itself to be—embattled with forces that seem to oppose or threaten it."[78] Far from dooming conservative beliefs, the cultural and demographic changes of the postwar era positioned evangelicals to emerge as resident critics—the Jeremiahs of the consumer suburbs.

Conservative religious traditions, though associated in the American mind with the rural South, excelled at attracting suburban adherents across the country.[79] Denominations such as the Southern Baptists and the Assemblies of God were particularly successful—especially in California after Dust Bowl migrants established new churches.[80] Sociologist Mark Shibley has argued that the efforts of southern evangelicalism drove the growth in American Protestantism during the late twentieth century. Between 1971 and 1990, when the U.S. population grew by almost 20 percent, evangelical churches grew by 26 percent as mainline churches declined in adherents by 8.5 percent; the increase in the number of southern-style evangelical church adherents was particularly impressive, rising 31.3 percent in the South and 88.7 percent in the West.[81] The Southern Baptist Convention (SBC) had a church in every state by the 1960s and a convention in every state by 1986 (compared to nineteen states in 1931 and twenty-nine in 1961); moreover, between 1926 and 1981, the rural SBC membership, once the convention's dominant constituency, declined from 72 percent of members to 25.3 percent. In 1990, SBC membership was nearly 19 million. The Assemblies of God, established in 1914 during the Pentecostal movement, expanded into every state and into more than 2,500 counties across the country and reached a membership of over 2.1 million in 1990.[82] Of course, sometimes evangelicalism became suburbanized merely by standing in place, as vast expanses of the South were transformed from backwoods to suburban backyards in a matter of years. In a 1981 profile of Jerry Falwell's Liberty Baptist Church, Frances Fitzgerald noted the transformation of southern mill towns like Lynchburg into corporate headquarters surrounded by a decentralized patchwork of suburban developments and shopping plazas. As Fitzgerald observed, Lynchburg's location between urban Washington, D.C., and rural Appalachia represented the "transfer point" between the Old South and the New South—between the "underdeveloped countryside" and "the city"—and, despite the continued conflation of conservative Christianity with rural areas, Falwell's parishioners represented a new suburban middle class.[83]

Even as evangelical churches seemed to accommodate the demands of suburban culture, a sense of antagonism helped propel growth in this environment. Conservative evangelical churches thrived in part because their traditions had long incorporated a hostility to mainstream authority. The success of these churches counteracted larger late-twentieth-century trends that challenged the authority of many American institutions—government, the military, universities, even the family. Religious institutions faced changes as well. During the postwar era, Christian believers divided along liberal-conservative rather than denominational lines; this schism had the effect of weakening differences on doctrine while strengthening concerns about personal morality.[84] The change benefited evangelicalism. As Christian Smith notes, evangelicalism offered a fluid tradition that drew from several traditions and required no central organization or core region but still maintained a distinct sense of its mission in the world.[85]

Just as the suburbs outgrew the need for an urban core, evangelicalism thrived without a vertically organized institutional core. Typical postwar evangelical organizations were either "parachurch" groups like Youth for Christ, which supported a web of independent ministries including Billy Graham's, or, later, "special purpose groups" like the Moral Majority that were oriented around objectives rather than institutions.[86] Emerging new denominations eschewed categorization. California-based churches that appeared during the 1960s and 1970s, such as Calvary Chapel and Vineyard, emphasized the localness of their organization; meanwhile, Rick Warren's Saddleback Community

Church, affiliated with the Southern Baptist Convention, omitted mention of the denomination's name.

When journalists and sociologists poured into the suburbs in the late twentieth century to explain the nature of community in a culture of sprawl, they turned to the megachurch, represented by usually Protestant churches with large congregations (between 2,000 and 10,000+ members) and a full calendar of programs.[87] According to sociologist Robert Putnam, who analyzed the decline of American social networks in his best-selling book *Bowling Alone,* by the late twentieth century evangelicals had become a model for grassroots social movement in a political and cultural environment characterized by perpetual anti-government revolt. Putnam's work showed that frequent churchgoers were more likely to be engaged in some kind of civic activity, much of which focused on the church itself. In examining how Americans were reshaping community in the suburbs, Putnam focused on Rick Warren's 15,000-member megachurch in Orange County, California, which turned the weekend "crowd" attending its services into a dedicated "congregation" through small groups that forged bonds among churchgoers, many of whom lived in gated communities.[88]

Ensconced in the suburbs, evangelicals engaged in cultural as well as political reform. Evangelical beliefs often—but not always—overlapped with conservative political goals. As they embarked on activist projects, many evangelicals invoked the work of theologian Francis A. Schaeffer, who called on Christians to become more involved in the arts and culture while carefully maintaining a Christian message and worldview. Schaeffer intended these activities to serve as a counterweight to the dominant humanistic worldview: Reformation Christianity needed to compete in the "marketplace of ideas" rather than willingly participate in the "hidden censorship" of separatism.[89] Evangelicals were, as Christian Smith explains, prepared to promote their traditional belief systems while "becoming confidently and proactively engaged in the intellectual, cultural, social, and political life of the nation."[90] Ninety-two percent of American evangelicals—a higher proportion than among other Christian subgroups—believed that Christians should try to change America to reflect God's will. Similarly, compared with other Christian subgroups, evangelicals more frequently agreed that people are obligated to do more for the world than raise a good family. When questioned about how to improve the world, evangelicals agreed on a variety of strategies: 91 percent believed they could convert people to belief in Jesus, 81 percent believed they could live a radically different way of life, 69 percent believed they could work for political reform, 63 percent believed they could defend a biblical worldview in intellectual circles, and 77 percent believed they could volunteer for local community organizations.[91]

Although evangelicals may have felt a personal responsibility to change society, not everyone became a grassroots political activist. If evangelicals were to be active in an industrial society that valued consumption rather than self-denial, they needed to broaden their witnessing practices to help believers achieve self-realization through therapeutic means.[92] Nineteenth-century revivalists had weakened the connection between Protestantism and concepts such as work, thrift, and sobriety by incorporating commercial entertainment styles that featured intense emotion and theatricality.[93] Services conducted by Aimee Semple McPherson and Billy Sunday exemplified this tradition: attendees arrived at revival meetings expecting to be entertained and were seldom disappointed.[94] McPherson's services included Sunday-night "illustrated sermons," performed using special effects and costumes borrowed from nearby Hollywood studios. A contemporary observer marveled at "a brass band bigger and louder than Sousa's, an organ worthy of any movie cathedral, a female choir bigger and more beautiful than the Metropolitan chorus, and a costume wardrobe comparable to Ziegfried's."[95] The strategy behind such epic theatrics was best expressed by the fictional Elmer Gantry's revivalist colleague Dr. Binch, who explained, "My motto as a soul-saver . . . is that one should use every method that, in the vernacular, will sell the goods."[96] Some revivalists reached audiences more efficiently than others: Billy Sunday's conversion rates hovered around $2.00 per soul, and a contemporary economist ranked Sunday's operation as one of the nation's five most successful businesses, alongside Standard Oil and United States Steel.[97] The line between selling the sacred and the profane was not always clear, as when an obscure African American gospel group in the 1920s changed its name to the Nugrape Twins and recorded two jingles hawking NuGrape, a popular southern beverage. "I Got Your Ice Cold Nugrape" and "Nugrape—A Flavor You Can't Forget" were recorded about the same time as their redemptive effort, "Pray Child if You Want to Go to Heaven."[98] In a consumer economy, deliverance had earthly as well as eternal meanings.

In addition to adapting to a consumer idiom, evangelicals adjusted their witnessing practices to a suburban landscape where civic life increasingly occurred in commercially owned spaces. As the center of

American culture shifted away from the city, evangelicals tailored their message for the spaces of suburbia: store, car, school, highway, and home. In these environments, witnessing—not picketing or protesting—was the preferred mode of evangelical activism.[99] As Susan Harding explains, witnessing is "an argument in conversation form" that allows evangelicals to create a new reality in a listener without resorting to preaching.[100] Of course, in the United States many cultural conversations were conducted in the midst of commercial transactions, and it was important for religious conservatives to affirm both their religious beliefs and their middle-class status via participation in mass culture.[101] In this respect, conflation of Christian consumerism with the Christian Right reifies the assumption that evangelicalism is monolithic. But Christian consumerism should not be ignored: in the year 2000, Christian merchandise produced $4 billion in sales, including $747 million in music merchandise (music sales reached $920 million in 2001).[102] Christian consumerism promised to deliver evangelicals from evil *and* mark their deliverance from Bible Belt to Sunbelt Christianity.

By making the middle-class home the moral—not just economic—center of American life, evangelicalism provided late-twentieth-century conservative ideology with internal coherence. Resurgent evangelicalism's privatization of religion reinforced the profound emphasis on the sanctity of family life. To claim otherwise is to misunderstand the extent to which privatization became a part of the nation's dominant ethos during the Reagan era.

## MORE POPULAR THAN THE BEATLES: CHRISTIAN CONSERVATIVES AND YOUTH REBELLION

Christian conservatives attached significant symbolic value to the souls of young people and worried about the impact mainstream culture had on adolescents' morals. Both youth innocence and youth agency became important tactics for advancing the evangelical cause. Although some conservative believers maintained that youth culture contributed to the loosening of American morals, other—typically young—evangelicals argued that American culture could support traditional values. Each side used a language of rebellion to describe its fight against the prevailing cultural mood. In the aftermath of the 1960s, a cohort of young evangelicals sought to be counted as innovators rather than mimickers in the highly politicized environs of American youth culture. In short, they sought to emulate Elvis rather than Pat Boone.

Christian consumer culture encompassed styles ranging from praise music to adult contemporary tunes to boy bands, but the evangelicals who wanted to occupy the cutting edge of youth culture—first the counterculture and later the punk movement and heavy metal scene—discomfited those who conflated either youth culture with progressive politics or conservative religious belief with rebellion. To be sure, at times, evangelicals' efforts could, by any measure, be deemed derivative, farcical, or even pathetic—no more successful than an aging Pat Boone's late-1990s effort to croon heavy metal standards such as "Crazy Train" and "Smoke on the Water." But these efforts also upset the sentimentalized view of youth rebellion held by many secular liberals in the wake of the 1960s. For while Christian recording artists often remained the "safe" alternative to non-Christian options, they were frequently at odds with their elders, and more important, they consistently attempted to turn the idea of rebellion on its head.

It is a testament to the fluidity of evangelicalism that believers could simultaneously embrace and critique forms of youth culture. On the one hand, Christian adults and parents worried about the messages sent by American youth culture and its corruption of their children. Evangelical parents during the late twentieth century were eager to ensure that their children retained their faith. To this end, born-again Christians cheerfully invested in summer camps, vacation Bible schools, Christian videos and fiction, and Christian music, as well as such youth-oriented groups as InterVarsity, the Navigators, and Campus Crusade for Christ.[103] As Heather Hendershot has explained, one of the primary appeals of Christian popular culture was that it offered moral guidance about teenage issues while remaining legible to parents.[104] On the other hand, evangelicalism also found a fervent audience among reform-minded middle-class suburban youth. Although some young people joined groups such as Students for a Democratic Society to protest the lack of meaning in American suburban culture, others saw a society that had become secular, sexually permissive, and nihilist and determined to change American culture—but from a different ideological standpoint. This stance did not make young evangelicals the minions of Pat Robertson or Jerry Falwell, although political organizations certainly endeavored to enlist them.

For its part, the Left, seemingly content to assume it had cornered the market on innovative youth culture, underestimated the connections between conservatism and youth culture. This was particularly true within the early historiography of the 1960s, which, as Rick Perlstein has written, tended to highlight the student movements of the Left through the memoirs of its former activists.[105] In contrast, younger historians have argued that the campus youth movement of the sixties should be viewed primarily as an existentialist search for self-meaning and only secondarily as a leftist attempt at structural change.[106] In this view, conservative ideals could appeal to the same set of sentiments, even if they offered different solutions. In the early 1960s, both Young Americans for Freedom and Barry Goldwater fashioned themselves as counterinsurgents against a liberal establishment. Madison Avenue marketers, insisting that capitalism was just as dynamic a force for transformation as the counterculture, similarly sought to be counted among the era's revolutionary forces.[107] And when the home-owner movements of the 1970s and 1980s adamantly demanded "community control," "neighborhood power," and "slow growth" development, conservative George Will warned of a growing "Sunbelt Bolshevism."[108]

The Christian youth culture that emerged out of the 1960s shared many of the ideals of more widely known non-Christian subcultures. Although some might suggest that the counterculture was antithetical to religion, the decade actually saw growth in evangelical Christianity as a result of the Jesus Movement, a West Coast youth revival. Affinities of the Jesus Movement and later Christian youth cultures with other youth movements included a preference for peer cohorts and the authority of one's own generation, a desire for individual experience and self-expression, anxiety about the future, a critique of adults' vision of the world, a tendency to express rebellion through personal style and consumption, and occasionally, a belief that direct action is the best way to change the world. If the sixties are recast this way, it is easy to see how conservative churches stood with anti-tax home owners as the biggest beneficiaries of the decade's language of dissent, authenticity, and anti-institutionalism; in fact, many of the young converts considered themselves to be the true inheritors of the 1960s.[109] Just as corporate marketers found much to admire in the counterculture, some religious leaders seized on the era's desire for self-realization—even if they did not agree with its methods.

When evangelicals joined national conversations about culture, they benefited from the changes of the 1960s. For many people the decade saw a re-imagination of ways to organize life. New terms of public discourse validated social criticism based in experience, including spirituality and morality, rather than in objectivity and rationality.[110] By emphasizing personal piety and the importance of religious experience in their lives,

Christian conservatives adapted to postmodern public debates in which the personal became the political. Historian Leonard Sweet has argued that much of the ecclesiastical authority lost by mainline churches in the 1960s was simply redistributed as cultural authority.[111] Evangelical churches that benefited from the era's anti-institutionalism also embraced the antinomian cultural styles of the 1960s: after all, Reinhold Niebuhr had once described sectarian evangelical churches as representing "Christ against culture." Calvary Chapel, Vineyard, and other similar California-based churches—dubbed "new paradigm churches" by sociologist Donald Miller—excelled at "mediating the sacred" by incorporating cultural forms such as contemporary music and dress in religious practices while also emphasizing a "therapeutic, individualistic, and anti-establishment" religious experience.[112]

To proselytize within the dominant culture, young Christians did not have to invent a new vocabulary or co-opt secular culture. Rather, they drew upon a longer history of believers who had adapted outsider rhetoric. The Judeo-Christian tradition of apocalyptic prophecy, dissent, and deliverance articulated by a "righteous remnant" stretches all the way to the creation of the Book of Daniel circa 165 B.C.[113] As R. Laurence Moore suggests in his analysis of American sects, evangelicals' sense of dispossession from and antagonism toward the dominant culture has historically allowed them to approach American life as disfranchised populists.[114] Consider the degree to which the language of resistance is tied to religious terminology: Protestantism, reform, antinomianism, dissent, nonconformity, heresy, blasphemy. Even the populism of the 1890s was tinged with "moral revivalism."[115] In his history of twentieth-century punk movements, music critic Greil Marcus offers German religious revolutionaries Thomas Müntzer and John of Leyden (whose name bears a serendipitous similarity to John Lydon of punk rock's Sex Pistols) as antecedents to the musical genre. Sixties-era agitators the Situationists, in search of revolutionary inspiration, rummaged through historian Norman Cohn's examination of religious anarchist and millenarian movements.[116] The religious themes of resistance and rebellion, in turn, meshed perfectly with sentiments of outsiderdom in youth culture—not to mention the dominant political rhetoric of the era. These rants and riffs gave young Christian believers the feeling that they were engaged in their own kind of subversive "culture jamming"— a term coined by the band Negativland in 1984 to describe the practice of altering advertisements and billboards to create new meanings.[117]

Christian youth drew on existing rhetorical traditions of dissent to rein-terpret the meaning of popular music themes.

Evangelicals' desire to participate in cutting-edge youth culture speaks to ideas about American cultural contestation. Christian interest in the countercultural fringe of youth culture also provides insights into traditions of opposition in American society. Much of the scholarship on youth culture (particularly on its working-class counterpart) has emphasized its potential as a source of resistance to dominant ideolo-gies, but the cultural work of evangelicals proves that concepts such as rebellion and alienation have no fixed meaning.[118] The Christian punk and metal scenes often offered contradictory messages that illuminate the contested nature of Christian and rock culture and that defy attempts to oversimplify what "conservatism" offered to young people. Christian youths in the late twentieth century redefined true rebellion in a post-Christian (and post-1960s) world as obedience to biblical authority and resistance to a sinful world. In this interpretation, reli-gious devotion and personal holiness allowed Christians to lay claim to being the mavericks of popular culture.

This book traces the rise of Christian conservative cultural activism at the end of the twentieth century through two approaches. First, I show how different groups of evangelical conservatives—including ministers, educators, and parents as well as young adults and Christian musicians—justified their actions as a defense of general categories such as "youth," "nation," and "family." Second, in each chapter I show the ways in which evangelicals' race, class, gender, and religious identities converged within consumer culture, allowing Christian conservative activists to deliver a religious message to suburbia in its own idiom.

Chapter 1 shows how the 1970s and 1980s—an era already known for taxpayer revolts, the New Right, the backlash against feminism, and demands for "law and order"—witnessed the origins of a parents' movement that aggressively sought to reclaim the category of youth from the movements of the 1960s and restore "traditional" authority in both public and private spaces. The chapter demonstrates that Christian conservatives' coalescence around categories such as "youth" and "family" allowed them to forge alliances with nonreligious organiza-tions to launch public morality campaigns against pornography, heavy metal music, and drug use. Parental cultural activism localized politics by removing issues from Washington corridors and placing them in everyday contexts such as the home, neighborhoods, and airwaves.

Although evangelicals considered youth as needing protection, they relied considerably on youth initiative and agency in cultural and political conversations. Chapters 2 and 3 demonstrate how evangelical Christians fused elements of their populist religious tradition to suburban cultural forms that valued rebellion and authenticity. The two chapters challenge romanticized notions about the subversive nature of countercultural youth movements while offering insights into the expansion of evangelical Christianity into the Sunbelt suburbs. The chapters also document how Christian youth culture provided young people with spaces, including fan magazines as well as youth groups, in which to develop their identities as Christians.

Chapter 2 explains how youth religiosity intersected with and furthered the cause of conservative ideas about the reformation of society through transformation of the self. Having sharpened their religious identities within the confines of the Christian subculture, young evangelicals became agents in public debates about morals, school prayer, and abortion. Chapter 3, by analyzing the Christian heavy metal scene, provides a case study on evangelical participation in cultural discussions. Between 1984 and 1994, Christian heavy metal bands attempted to reform their corner of American culture by cultivating a secular audience, playing on bills with secular bands, and occasionally signing with secular labels, all in an attempt to increase their influence and fan base in the mainstream music world. Even as they sought acceptance from the secular world, Christian metal bands embraced themes of spiritual warfare that echoed the rhetorical strategies of Christian political leaders such as Jerry Falwell and Pat Robertson.

The final chapter draws the major themes together through an examination of Orange County's annual Harvest Crusade, an annual revival concert established during critical years of the nation's culture wars. Although critics have lamented the demise of civic life in American suburbs, this chapter shows how evangelicals adapted to and politicized the public spaces and consumer culture of Orange County during the 1990s. The Harvest Crusade, founded by former members of the Jesus Movement, attempted to unite families while addressing young people through forms of popular culture, especially contemporary Christian bands. While celebrating the emotionally powerful categories of "family" and "nation," the Crusade avoided mentioning mundane ones such as "government." As a result, the event offered a glimpse of what Christian conservatives believed civic life in a culture of "family values" would look like.

By tracing the rise of Christian popular culture at a time when American conservatives sought to roll back the programs of the Great Society and link the nation's fate to the survival of patriarchal authority, this book shows the ways by which white evangelicals' cultural activism complemented their newfound political voice. Christian conservatives were among the first to embrace doctrines such as self-reliance, personal responsibility, and family values. These phrases had significant economic and cultural implications, since Christians believed that observance of these values obviated the need for government welfare programs. By expressing their beliefs in popular music and print culture, Christian conservatives sought to establish control over the home as well to influence national conversations on values. Through this kind of activism, youth culture became the basis for Christian conservatives' mission to restore "family values" to American society.

# CHAPTER I

# Home Improvement

*Christian Cultural Criticism and the*
*Defense of "Traditional" Authority*

On November 24, 1979, brothers Steve and Jim Peters hosted their first-ever record burning at the campgrounds of Zion Christian Life Center, their church in St. Paul, Minnesota. Describing the "burning celebration" a few years later, the brothers fondly recalled how cheers erupted as some four hundred youths "began to heap their once-prized rock albums onto the fire, nearly choking it with sheer weight."[1] In that single evening, participants burned an estimated $15,000 worth of records, tapes, books, and other items associated with teen culture (in compliance with fire codes, vinyl was smashed, not burned). Steve Peters explained to the *St. Paul Pioneer Press* that the event was intended not to "censor" rock groups but rather to break youth culture's hold on young people. As he put it, "These records encourage kids to rebel against their home and their parents, and we want that to stop." The event provided young believers with the opportunity to "[align] their lifestyles with their Christian commitments."[2] The brothers continued to hold the events regularly for the next several years, and by 1984 they claimed to have destroyed over $10 million worth of secular records and tapes.[3] Critics compared the event to Nazi book burnings, but the brothers claimed that the burnings were patterned after an episode in the New Testament in which converts burned their idols to show the sincerity of their Christian belief.[4] Given that the event functioned as a radical disavowal—a cultural exorcism of sorts—it might also have summoned memories of the student antiwar protests and draft card burnings of the 1960s. In this case, however, the brothers encouraged teenagers to burn items as a means of reestablishing, rather than severing, their ties to religious and parental authority.

Public bonfires like those hosted by the Peters brothers had long been part of the Christian anti-rock movement's symbolic repertoire, but by the 1980s some evangelical educators specifically avoided avowedly "Christian" denunciations of youth culture.[5] Although alarmed by the influence of popular culture on young people, these devout educators advised readers that activists who identified themselves as parents would be taken more seriously than those who were identifiably Christians. Al Menconi, who staged a record burning at a Christian school in Southern California in the 1970s, had come to believe that Christian threats of hellfire frequently backfired: patently Christian pickets and record burnings simply served to make an artist "more acceptable in the eyes of the rock audience."[6] Menconi recommended that a Christian who wanted to protest concerts or rock stars approach the responsible parties as "a moral, concerned parent—but not as a Christian."[7]

The disparity between a church-sponsored record burning for youth and a family-centered moral critique reveals the self-conscious "modernization" project undertaken by some conservative Christians in the late twentieth century. In both instances, music provided an entry point to debates about cultural reform. Both strategies demonstrate how conservative Christians linked youth culture and social problems and how they aggressively sought to reestablish "youth" as a category of innocence in need of adult protection during the late-twentieth-century culture wars. In both formulations of the reform agenda, culture, rather than socioeconomic structure, was the catalyst for change. In the 1960s, youth culture, particularly rock music, became linked to "countercultural" practices—with attendant links to the New Left and to African American vernacular culture—practices that valued leisure, consumption, and personal freedom at the expense of "traditional" authority structures and beliefs that encouraged obedience, order, and industriousness.[8] Conservatives like the Peters brothers and Al Menconi used the category of youth as a way of articulating a morality-based social criticism, but they disagreed over how best to protect young believers. The evangelical literature about youth culture produced between the 1970s and the 1990s included magazine articles, pamphlets, and an extensive array of full-length monographs—almost all of them written by believers who were white and male. The authors of this material identified entertainment forms as either enemies or allies. Some conservative

Christians assailed youth culture as the vanguard of a broader assault on traditional authority structures, while others saw a battleground for cultural and moral reform. The latter group believed that its ability to control and critique youth culture reflected its success in reasserting adult dominion over home and society.[9]

Evangelicals' cultural interventions reflected a critical shift in conservative religious affinities from Old Right to New Right as evangelicals developed "modern" middle-class suburban sensibilities and consumer habits. In both old and new mindsets, the family provided a critical building block of Christian society, and believers worried that a secular worldview encroached on familial authority. Proponents of both views feared that popular culture had replaced parents and church as the primary source of children's socialization. Strict fundamentalists avoided contamination of the Christian worldview by swearing off secular culture—at least in name. Conversely, suburbanized evangelicals like Menconi cautiously accepted television and music into the domestic circle but attempted to maintain careful adult guidance over message and interpretation. Moreover, these evangelicals optimistically believed they could maintain a proactive stand on culture.

At the precise moment that suburban evangelicals mobilized to protect parental prerogatives, other white suburbanites were organizing to protect "local" interests. As historian Lisa McGirr has shown, beginning in the 1950s, conservatives in Sunbelt suburbs such as Orange County, California, became involved in local political campaigns that challenged sex education, abortion, obscenity laws, and school busing and urged a return to "law and order."[10] Historian Matthew Lassiter has argued that the grassroots partisanship of suburban voters mattered less than their "populist identifications" as "homeowners, taxpayers, and schoolparents."[11] These identities merged with consumerism and evangelicalism to form what literary critic Lauren Berlant has called the "national sentimentality" of the Reagan era, defined by "a politics that abjures politics, made on behalf of a private life protected from the harsh realities of power."[12] Berlant argues that groups such as the Parents' Music Resource Center sought to make parenting, rather than citizenship, the identity necessary to enter into public debates. Christian conservatives were at the forefront of this effort to create a "nation controlled by a local, public, community matrix of parental public spheres." As Berlant explains, conservative activists believed that parenting should be considered a "public profession" and maintained that the "core context of politics should be the sphere of private life."[13]

Identification with youth and family issues allowed conservatives to forge alliances with nonreligious organizations in public morality campaigns. The 1970s and 1980s—an era of taxpayer revolts, anti-busing protests, the rise of the New Right, campaigns against the Equal Rights Amendment, and demands for "law and order"—witnessed the origins of a parents' movement that aggressively sought to reclaim the category of youth from the movements of the 1960s and to restore "traditional" authority in both public and private spaces.

The era's "parents movement" intersected with what has become known as the culture wars. The political battles of the culture wars are well known, but many of these struggles also involved popular culture, especially since entertainment provided a ready example of the challenges posed to parental authority. Evangelical Christians provided both rhetorical and organizational groundwork in this cultural endeavor. Christian conservatives viewed themselves as guardians of "family values" and believed that the erosion of "law and order" had its roots in challenges to parental authority. They contrasted "family values," with that term's positive invocation of white, suburban, middle-class, patriarchal, and heterosexual authority, to the notion of rioting urban minorities, rebellious white youths associated with the student movement, "emancipated" women associated with the feminist movement, uncloseted homosexuals associated with the gay rights movement, and godless secularists intent on removing religious symbols from the public sphere.[14] In the minds of Christian parents, the identity movements of the 1960s, in alliance with the consumer marketplace, had used youth culture to undermine traditional authority.

Evangelical activists viewed themselves as important historical agents in guiding America's destiny, but they did not view the nuclear family or youth as historically specific ways of organizing social relationships. On the contrary, conservative Christians found a biblical origin for both the form and authority structure of the family and tied this unit to the fate of the nation. Conservative Christians therefore identified with what British sociologist Errol Lawrence describes as the "common sense" construction of the family during the period. Within this ideology, the nuclear family was deemed "the crucial site for the reproduction of those correct social mores, attitudes and behaviours that are thought to be essential to maintaining a 'civilized' society" as well as the site where "'primary socialization' takes place and where 'culture' is reproduced." As Lawrence further explains, the family was "the site in which self-discipline and self-control are 'knocked into' children's heads and in which relations of authority and power are internalized."[15] Within the logic of the culture wars, secular culture disrupted familial sovereignty as it encouraged disobedience and, at times, outright rebellion among young people. Because conservative Christians believed that youthful behavior provided insight into the state of American values, teenagers held important symbolic value for them. An article in the evangelical Christian magazine *Moody Monthly* named the American adolescent "one of the world's critical mission fields" because "adolescents are the future of our country and the future of our churches."[16] In other words, the cultural and ideological category of youth signified a generational cohort as well as an imagination of America.[17]

Perceptions of youth changed between the 1960s and the 1980s. Beginning in the late 1970s, youth came to be viewed as endangered, rather than dangerous. While the paradigmatic youth of the 1960s was a young hippie or student protester, that of the 1980s was a younger, innocent white child capable of devout belief but in need of parental guidance and protection.[18] The transformation occurred through the efforts of organizations established to represent parental interests, including the well-known Parents' Music Resource Center (PMRC, 1985) as well as antidrug groups such as the Parents' Resource Institute for Drug Education (PRIDE, 1978), the National Federation of Parents for a Drug Free Youth (NFP, 1980), and Mothers Against Drunk Driving (MADD, 1980).[19] While white women usually headed these secular groups, several white male–headed evangelical Christian groups that invoked "family values"—including the American Family Association (AFA, 1976), Focus on the Family (FOF, 1977), and the Family Research Council (FRC, 1980)—also formed during this period. In addition, Anita Bryant, a former Miss America and Florida Citrus Commission spokeswoman, formed Save Our Children in 1977 as part of her successful effort to repeal a gay rights ordinance in Dade County, and Beverly LaHaye, the wife of Left Behind series author Tim LaHaye, established Concerned Women of America (CWA, 1979) to counterbalance organizations such as the National Organization of Women and causes such as the Equal Rights Amendment.[20] Perhaps no program captured the spirit of these groups better than the Back in Control Center, an Orange County–based "family training center" aimed at helping parents establish rules "to de-punk and de-metal" their teenagers.[21]

Political posturing and popular culture helped heighten parental fears about targeted attacks on young people. As sociologist Barry

Glassner has noted, public panics about juvenile crime, teenage suicides, drug addiction, ritual abuse, and kidnappings of children dominated congressional hearings and news cycles. Such concerns further shifted national attention toward issues dear to the suburban middle class and away from antipoverty and child welfare programs.[22] In 1985 members of the Parents' Music Resource Center appeared before the U.S. Senate Committee on Commerce, Science, and Transportation to discuss labeling for music recordings, particularly heavy metal music. President Reagan soon joined the fray when he noted:

> I often think the real heroes of today are the parents, trying to raise their children in an environment that seems to have grown more and more hostile to family life. Music and the media flood their children's world with glorifications of drugs and violence and perversity—and there's nothing they can do about it, they're told, because of the First Amendment. . . . I don't believe that our Founding Fathers ever intended to create a nation where the rights of pornographers would take precedence over the rights of parents, and the violent and malevolent would be given free rein to prey on our children.[23]

The speech created a decisive binary between the rights of parents and those of "pornographers." In 1986 the Attorney General's Commission on Pornography (also known as the Meese Commission), which included James C. Dobson of Focus on the Family, described the impact of pornography on American culture, urged strict enforcement of federal obscenity laws, and endorsed protests, pickets, and boycotts of companies and stores that sold pornographic materials. The findings were announced just after Southland Corporation, the parent company of 7-Eleven stores, announced the beginning of a self-imposed ban on the adult magazines *Playboy, Penthouse,* and *Forum.* (Christian groups, claiming that children frequented the stores, had boycotted the stores for months.)[24]

The media incited further public panic with breathless commentary about the ruinous consequences of an untamed contemporary culture. A few weeks after the PMRC hearings, *U.S. News and World Report* ran a cover story that asked "Do You Know What Your Children Are Listening To?" Echoing Reagan's earlier speech, the article answered with the warning, "Day and night, America's youth are enticed by electronic visions of a world so violent, sensual and narcotic that childhood itself appears to be under siege."[25] In 1988 a Geraldo Rivera special about satanic cults became the highest-rated two-hour documentary to air on television.[26] A similar pattern developed among conservative intellectuals. Picking up the PMRC's denunciation of "porn rock," conservative columnist George Will asked readers, "Would you want to live in a world in which no one, not even the young, blushed?" Like other conservatives, Will linked the content of music to the fate of the nation. One's taste in popular music—"porn rock" versus classical music or even classic rock—demonstrated one's propensity for "discretion" and "self-restraint," he argued. "An individual incapable of shame and embarrassment is probably incapable of the governance of the self. A public incapable of shame and embarrassment about public vulgarity is unsuited to self-government."[27] The debate over popular music thus provided a means for demonstrating self-control, one of the fundamental tenets of the conservative revolution. Allan Bloom continued these criticisms in a chapter of his 1987 best seller, *The Closing of the American Mind,* when he lamented that rock music and television had "assaulted and overturned the privacy of the home," resulting in "nothing less than parents' loss of control over their children's moral education at a time when no one else is seriously concerned with it."[28] Reflecting the era's shift away from economic amelioration for the poor, each account demonstrated a preoccupation with children's moral, rather than material, well-being.

Not for the first time were Americans debating the proper role of youth culture in children's lives. Over the course of the post–World War II era, teenagers, many of whom earned disposable income from part-time jobs while still enrolled in school, became such an important market for consumer products that advertisers began to attribute adult buying power to them.[29] Teens' newly acquired (and newly identified) buying power accelerated the commodification of youth culture and raised questions about the merits and consequences of children's entry into the consumer marketplace at an earlier age.[30] From time to time, parents worried about the challenges peer culture posed to their authority. Historian James Gilbert calls this concern an "episodic notion" and notes that fears about the impact of youth culture arose about movies in the 1930s and about comic books in the 1950s.[31] While conservative Christians formed a core constituency of anti-rock movements, evangelicals frequently tapped into modern media techniques and trends in order to establish church-sponsored youth groups that would, in Elmer Gantry's words, "take the *wreck* out of recreation and make it re-creation."[32] The convergence of styles was evident in Billy Graham's Youth for Christ stadium crusades in the 1940s.[33] Years prior to the PMRC hearings, the Reverend Jesse Jackson and Operation PUSH (People

United to Save Humanity) cited the impact of music on young people as the basis for their campaign in 1976 to persuade the music industry to remove "sexy songs" from the nation's airwaves.[34] When set alongside the PMRC, the efforts of Operation PUSH reveal the bipartisan nature of parents' movements.

Conservative Christians disagreed about what constituted a "biblical" or "Christian" stance on rock music, yet they concurred that youth culture exerted tremendous influence over young people. Rather than examining the campaigns as efforts at either censorship or co-optation, this study explores Christian conservatives' shifting attitudes toward youth culture to provide insight into how religious conservatives attempted to reenter public conversations about culture at the end of the twentieth century. Many Christian conservatives did, in fact, abhor the content of popular culture. The anti-rock literature generated between the late-1960s and the 1980s featured writers with backgrounds ranging from the anti-communist Right to fundamentalist Christianity to secular youth culture itself. Although each group articulated a slightly different stand on youth culture, most agreed that rock music—whether it represented a communist, countercultural, or Satanic threat—posed a grave danger to the modern Christian church and home. Because rock exerted tremendous mental, spiritual, and physical power over young people, these anti-rock critics believed that youth culture had no role to play in Christians' lives.

Yet as rock music became more engrained in American culture, other Christian conservatives, especially parents, became convinced that the genre could not be spurned entirely. While still suspicious of a secular world that scoffed at their concerns, these Christian conservatives self-consciously honed modern media protest techniques. Rather than protest on the basis of faith alone, this group of Christians became part of the parents' movement to reform the moral content of American culture: the family-based focus of these media experts overlapped with the "secular" guides endorsed by groups such as the Parents Music Resource Center. In the wake of the student movement and counterculture of the 1960s, these believers thought they could redomesticate youth by first taming rock 'n' roll. Instead of characterizing youth as agents (knowing or not) in the destruction of American values, these critics suggested that "innocent" young people needed parental guidance and protection. Parents' multipronged endeavor required vigilance and activism inside and outside the home. First, with the help of media experts, they began to approach youth ministry as they would a mission in a foreign country: by learning the culture. Second, Christians attempted to offer an alternative to secular music through Christian rock, which they believed offered a similar sound and appeal but with a "positive" Christian message. Finally, having secured their authority in the home, parents took one final step: they engaged in consumer and political campaigns against secular rock music in an attempt to cleanse its content.

Christian attitudes toward popular music reveal the contradictions created by the category of youth. The language of popular music, which frequently embraced themes not often associated with the Christian life—sensory satisfaction, personal freedom, rebellion—offered a way for Christians to delineate the boundaries that separated their Bible-believing values from those of the "world." At the same time, many Christians believed they could help the nation re-establish "traditional" authority by exerting greater control over youth culture at home and in public. The sustained alarm over children and media, in turn, demonstrates a narrowed American political discourse concerned with moral, not material, home improvement.

## "DANTE'S INFERNO IS COMING TO YOUR HOMETOWN": ANTI-ROCK CRITICS

During much of the post-1945 period, popular music provided conservative Christians with a catchall explanation for everything that was geopolitically threatening, physically perilous, or spiritually sinister. Even as moderate evangelicals like Billy Graham hosted wildly successful revivals that openly appealed to young people with finely calibrated marketing campaigns and contemporary-style gospel music, conservatives sought to avoid the stain of contemporary music. Their fears intensified in the 1960s. Assertions about rock music differed as to its precise sins, but conservatives generally agreed that the genre was a pernicious force in American society. Held to be synonymous with the counterculture and the 1960s, rock 'n' roll was thought to have conspired with communist and satanic groups, encouraged miscegenation, altered sexual mores, and incited sustained social unrest. Beginning in the late 1960s, however, the critique of rock 'n' roll increasingly shifted away from its reputed association with world communism toward its influence on domestic institutions. Critics suggested that the music posed a special danger to the Christian church and Christian home. This rhetorical shift suggests that consumer affluence and parent-child generational dissidence had crept into the lives of conservative Christians. Critics argued that rock music seduced "good kids" from "good homes" into sinful behavior, undermining parental efforts to instill self-discipline and morality into children and creating a "generation gap" within the home.

Some anti-rock activists with connections to the anti-communist movement insisted that rock music held geopolitical significance: the genre was part of the larger domestic communist threat. Just as there could be no neutral ground in the global battle against communism, popular music was strictly divided between the "free" and "unfree." And, as in the Cold War, there were wars of liberation. For a brief time, one of the great lights of the anti-communist movement in the United States, Australian-born physician Fred Schwarz of the Christian Anti-Communism Crusade (CACC), embraced the most quintessentially communistic form of auditory expression: folk music. In 1961 Schwarz helped stir the anti-communist awakening in Los Angeles and Orange County with his School of Anti-Communism, which featured "student day" and "youth nite" with appearances by such performers as Ronald Reagan, Pat Boone, Roy Rogers, and Dale Evans. Despite the presence of pop and country music performers, the movement began maximizing its use of music as an anti-Bolshevik pedagogical aid only in 1964. In the organization's newsletter, Schwarz noted that "every great movement throughout history has expressed its inspiration in music" and lamented that anti-communists had underutilized the medium, especially in contrast to the Reds' deployment of singers such as Paul Robeson and Pete Seeger.[35] In the mounting cultural arms race, Schwarz intended to fight fire with fire. He therefore hired Janet Greene, a television personality from Columbus, Ohio, to set his raging diatribes to music. Greene soon became known as the anti-communist movement's "anti–Joan Baez" for her arsenal of freedom-loving songs, including "Commie Lies," "Poor Left Winger," "Comrade's Lament," and "Fascist Threat" (the last a song set to a jarring calypso beat that might well have evoked concerns about voodoo from other religious conservatives). In the CACC newsletter item announcing her hiring, Greene noted the important role women and mothers could play in fighting domestic communism. The CACC emphatically agreed and suggested that Greene's program was "ideal for meetings of PTA's, Womens Clubs [sic]," "church groups," and "gatherings in the home."[36] Through Greene's activism, the anti-communist message could extend into female-dominated civil organizations such as the school, church, and home.

Despite Schwarz's foray into popular music production, other conservatives continued to believe that Christians would be wise to avoid youth culture—even Christian incarnations of popular music—altogether. The connection to communism was simply too great. For these conservative Christians, separation, not engagement, was the solution to defusing rock's potency. The most prolific and impassioned opponent of rock music was David Noebel, a Tulsa-based conservative who began his career working for radio preacher Billy James Hargis's virulently anti-communist Christian Crusade. Shortly after the British rock invasion of the 1960s, Noebel began to insist that contemporary music—including folk as well as rock—was a key component in communism's "mind warfare" against American society. The opening salvo in his rhetorical war against popular music was a twenty-six-page diatribe against the recently arrived lads from Liverpool. Entitled *Communism, Hypnotism, and the Beatles* (1965), the manifesto was published a year before John Lennon described Jesus' disciples as "thick and ordinary" and declared, in an interview with the London *Evening Standard*, that the Beatles were more popular than Jesus.[37]

Noebel's pamphlet also attacked the recordings produced by Young People's Records and the Children's Record Guild. YPR and CRG taught children about folk music and folklore, as well as classical and modern composers, while employing progressive pedagogical theories of music instruction such as active participation and performance. The record companies' ties to left-leaning cultural figures of the 1930s folk scene and their leftist politics had led a HUAC witness in 1947, the Hearst newspaper *New York Journal-American* in 1949, and *Red Channels* (a 1950 publication of the FBI front group the American Business Consultants) to charge that they formed a communist cultural front. Nonetheless, the records were staples of classroom and children's collections and had secured seals of approval from *Good Housekeeping* and *Parents' Magazine*. Noebel, however, revived charges of communist links. Whereas earlier red-baiting charges had complained of some of the music's proletarian lyrical affinities, Noebel now attacked the music as well. He alleged that communism had "contrived an elaborate and scientific technique directed at rendering a generation of American youth useless through nerve-jamming, mental deterioration and retardation." Although mainstream media accounts openly mocked Noebel's efforts, his pamphlet nevertheless persuaded parents in Torrance, California, to form an advocacy group, Torrance Committee of Parents Concerned About Communist Records, to demand the removal of nursery records from classrooms. The group, which had ties to the John Birch Society, ultimately failed: while the school board initially voted to cancel the district's subscriptions and to consider removing the records from classrooms, district trustees eventually voted to keep the records in classrooms and, further, to continue purchasing records.[38]

In subsequent works such as *Rhythm, Riots, and Revolution* (1966) and *The Beatles: A Study in Drugs, Sex, and Revolution* (1969), Noebel continued his crusade against the "hidden dangers of rock 'n' roll." According to Noebel, the genre undermined the emotional, psychological, spiritual, and moral strength of the nation's populace.[39] He consistently linked rock 'n' roll with social unrest. In *The Marxist Minstrels* (1973) Noebel once again suggested that communists deliberately targeted young people, who were induced to commit "menticide," defined as a "lethal psychological process that produces a literal suicide of the mind."[40] Although he claimed that "menticide" indicated an epidemic of youth self-destruction, Noebel also argued that the young people so manipulated would not just fade away: communists, having used rock music to destroy "youths' ability to relax, reflect, study and meditate," thereby prepared youths "for riot, civil disobedience and revolution."[41]

Noebel reserved a special hatred for Bob Dylan and the Beatles, deeming them emblematic of a generation that embraced promiscuous attitudes toward drugs and sex while shamelessly ignoring religious and moral authority. He argued that Dylan's synthesis of rock and folk styles spelled the doom of the United States. "No nation can long endure," Noebel wrote, "with its younger generation singing itself into defeatism, pessimism, a peace-at-any-price mentality, disarmament, appeasement, surrender, fear of death, hatred toward the South, atheism, immorality, drugs, revolution and negation of patriotism."[42] While Noebel associated Dylan and folk music with political causes such as the antiwar and civil rights movements, he associated the Beatles with drug experimentation and the sexual revolution, which together fed youths' desire for further rebellion. Noebel believed that the Beatles, though not necessarily communists themselves, were certainly serving the ends of communism in general and the New Left in particular.[43] Communism's use of cultural intermediaries to destroy the United States underscored the seductive power of music: Noebel reminded readers that the Soviet Union, no doubt aware of rock's psychological powers, had wisely banned the genre in the early 1960s.

In books about rock music that David Noebel published until well into the 1980s, he continued to link the growth of rock to internal subversion by communists. He was joined by the Movement to Restore Decency (MOTOREDE), the anti–sex education wing of the anti-communist John Birch Society. During the late 1960s, MOTOREDE dabbled in cultural criticism through anti-counterculture pamphlets such as *The De-Generation Gap* and *The Pied Pipers: Pot, Rock, and Revolution.* While MOTOREDE focused on drugs and opposition to sex education in schools, other conservatives focused on the degenerative effect of counterculture fashion on the national body. In a pamphlet entitled *Skimpy Skirts and Hippie Hair,* Dr. Hugh F. Pyle, pastor of the Central Baptist Church in Panama City, Florida, proclaimed, "Schools are being disrupted, homes divided, churches confused, and society itself embroiled over the issue of 'hair'!" More interested in endearing himself to parents than to children, Pyle dismissed the religious counterculture's portrayal of Jesus as a "skid-row welfare case who looked like a shiftless hippie," and he demanded that youths "[shift] your bubble gum, [turn] down your transistor, and [push] your locks back out of your eyes" long enough to consider the detrimental impact of long hair on American society. Long hair among young men was part of a "planned, calculated trend" of "Commie Goals" that would "break down the manliness of American men" and develop a "'unisex' population of weaklings."[44] External communism was the ultimate cause of degradation, but conservative hostility increasingly focused on counter-cultural youth.

Critics who could divine geopolitical threats from trends in music, dress, and hair styles were a vanishing breed by the early 1970s. Anti-rock critics continued to use aspects of anti-communists' arguments, but the dearth of additional voices that linked rock music with the Soviet threat reflected a larger trend in rhetorical strategies among conservatives. As historian David Bennett has explained, Protestant fundamentalists may have warned about the threat of domestic collectivism and Soviet expansion abroad after the 1970s, but they seldom issued accusations of internal communism.[45] Concerned about the changes brought about by the 1960s, conservative Christians instead attacked intellectual elites, the federal government, and countercultural youths for seizing power at the expense of "traditional" morality and authority structures such as the family and church.

During the 1970s, many conservative Christians focused on political issues such as educational curriculum and school prayer that held symbolic importance for reproducing values in young people.[46] Criticism of youth culture, given its (somewhat contradictory) associations with

the entertainment industry, the New Left, and African American vernacular culture, offered conservatives a way to express their displeasure
with the cultural and religious changes wrought by both the counterculture and the Great Society, which conservatives believed encouraged
personal freedom and centralized government at the expense of traditional authority structures and beliefs. For example, in 1970 evangelist
Bob Larson, a self-described former rock musician, surveyed the
national landscape and assessed the consequences of the sustained popularity of rock 'n' roll since the 1950s. Americans had recently witnessed some of the decade's most violent expressions of individual and
collective anger: riots in Detroit and Newark, the assassinations of
Robert Kennedy and Martin Luther King Jr., the Democratic national
convention in Chicago, and campus antiwar protests. Larson found a
common link among these events. "Rock music," he declared, "has . . .
taken over the role of the major influence upon youth. It has given them
a national sense of identification." More than giving youths a sense of
peer identity, however, music had also "replaced the traditional institution [sic] of society such as the church, school, and family unit." Rock
had, he suggested, "unified the voice of the teenage bloc and given solidarity to their rebellion."[47]

While rock music provided a source of peer identity for a rebellious
generation, it also provided an alarming index of the state of American
morality. According to Bob Larson, "music is an expression and indica
tor of the values of the society or portion of that society which has produced it. Observe this barometer in a particular era and it is possible to
discern the minds of men during that era. Rock music seems to express
the shifting values of our society and the hectic, confused speed of the
times."[48] In an attempt to "discern the minds" of the generation that
produced rock music during the late 1960s and early 1970s, Christian
anti-rock critics evaluated not just music but also its consequences and
the trends with which it was associated.

The suggestion that rock music reflected American values represented an important shift in conservative Christians' thinking about the
genre: whereas Noebel had suggested that a foreign enemy targeted the
young, the following generation of fundamentalist separatists asserted
that the young—or at least those youth associated with the counterculture or identity movements—were the enemy. In the estimation of fundamentalist critics, the rock music of the 1960s was a promiscuous
genre associated with a wide range of radical social causes and immoral
cultural phenomena. Frank Garlock, a music professor at Bob Jones

University, a fundamentalist school in South Carolina, offered an inventory of what he termed the "associates" of rock in 1971:

> drug addicts, revolutionaries, rioters, Satan worshippers, drop-outs, draft-dodgers, homosexuals and other sex deviates, rebels, juvenile criminals, Black Panthers and white panthers, motorcycle gangs, blasphemers, suicides; heathenism, voodooism, phallixism [sic], Communism in the United States . . . paganism, lesbianism; immorality, demonology, promiscuity, free love, free sex, disobedience (civil and uncivil), sodomy, venereal disease; discotheques, brothels, orgies of all kinds, night clubs, dives, strip joints, filthy musicals such as "Hair" and "Uncle Meat"; and on and on the list could go almost indefinitely.[49]

Garlock's litany included "Communism in the United States," but it was simply one co-conspirator amidst a cast of thousands. More prominent among rock's associates were signifiers of the antiwar, civil rights, gay rights, and women's movements and the sexual revolution, which were grouped with Satan worshippers, heathens, blasphemers, and other longtime spiritual nemeses of fundamentalists.

In addition to linking rock with an array of immoral causes, Garlock and other fundamentalists also attempted to assess the damage the 1960s had inflicted on the church. According to these critics, one of the key consequences of rock's popularity was that the generation gap had lodged itself in the church as well as in society at large. This was problematic for fundamentalists who sought to follow the advice of 2 Corinthians 6:17 to "come out from them, and be separate from them . . . and touch nothing unclean."[50] At the end of his list of rock's associates, Garlock regretfully added "powerless Christianity," as "churches and so-called Christian groups who have lost their spiritual power have adopted rock music as a way of reaching teenagers, but what a cheap substitute for spirituality it turns out to be."[51] Another critic concurred, concluding that rock music was "creating a crisis in the church" between those who eschewed rock (usually adults) and those who embraced it (usually the young).[52]

Agreeing with Garlock, in 1972 Bob Jones III published the pamphlet *Look Again at the Jesus People,* in which he criticized the most visible Christian youth movement in the nation. Jones argued that the Jesus Movement, in allowing young Christian converts in the late 1960s and 1970s to keep their countercultural styles after conversion, was "unbiblical," its leaders having failed to direct youthful believers into "spiritual obedience and spiritual maturity."[53] By permitting young people to retain styles associated with disrespect and rebellion, leaders were essentially inviting the problems of the world into the church. Moreover, since "countercultural" youth did not renounce their worldly accoutrements, Jones doubted the sincerity of their conversions. "Revival is God-given; it is not man-generated," he wrote. "Revival is not spawned in pot parties, love-ins, hippie pads, dens of iniquity, and rock orgies; but that is where the Jesus Movement was spawned."[54] Rather than accepting the counterculture into the church, Jones urged separation. Garlock found a biblical precedent to address the contemporary crisis: he urged believers to follow the path of Abraham, who settled in Canaan and entered into a covenant with the Lord, rather than with Lot, Abraham's nephew who settled among the sinners of Sodom.[55]

Although fundamentalist critics like Garlock and Jones did not link rock to communism, they asserted that rock threatened to introduce alien practices and beliefs into American culture. Rock 'n' roll had emerged from African American vernacular culture, and anti-rock literature written by conservative whites was rife with references to rock's African roots. Traditionalists in the 1920s had lodged similar complaints against "unspeakable jazz," with one critic decrying dances intensified by "the wriggling movement and sensuous stimulation of the abominable jazz orchestra with its voodoo-born minors and its direct appeal to the sensory center."[56] In a similar vein, Frank Garlock in the early 1970s pointed to the "voodoo rituals, sex orgies, human sacrifice, and devil worship" of rock 'n' roll.[57] At least two critics recounted an apocryphal tale about an American missionary in Africa whose children played rock music, only to have the natives ask him why he allowed his children to play music "that was used to call up demons during voodoo rituals."[58]

Even before gangsta rap became popular among white youths in the late 1980s and early 1990s—and became reviled by politicians for its embrace of a criminal lifestyle as exemplified in songs such as "Fuck tha Police" and "Cop Killer"—the rhetoric about rock's origins and form reflected concerns about law and order. According to critics, in addition to containing immoral lyrical content, rock violated basic aesthetic standards that promoted social order. Garlock, a music professor, explained that whereas "good" music carried the characteristics of coherence, dignity, variety, and balance between intellect and emotion, rock distracted youths from their devotions.[59] Another critic offered a visual representation of the split between the music of the Christian Reformation and that of slavery. One side of the chart this critic drew was a genealogy of "traditional music of the Church," said to appeal to "the spirit and the new nature." This music's lineage followed a path from early hymns to the Reformation—the chart making no mention of the Catholic Church—through chorales, anthems, and gospel songs. The other side of the chart reinforced earlier fears about African American vernacular culture by listing the "music of the world," which appealed to "the flesh and the old nature"; its lineage began with African drums, continued with slavery, and quickly morphed through several popular incarnations: blues, ragtime, jazz, swing, boogie-woogie, bop, and rock 'n' roll. According to this critic, "contemporary Christian music" had its origins in the world, not in the church.[60] The classification system typified fundamentalists' assertion that, just as expanded federal power defied "natural" laws of property and the free market, the youth culture of the 1960s violated the organic balance achieved through the lineage of Western culture.

While Frank Garlock, Bob Jones III, and like critics focused on rock and the counterculture's impact on social institutions such as the church, another kind of fundamentalist Christian anti-rock critic also emerged during the 1970s and 1980s. While these critics agreed wholeheartedly with Garlock and Jones on the need to avoid rock music, they based their authority not in the church but rather in their firsthand experimentation with rock music as either musicians or fans. Their eyewitness authority, which emphasized rock's assault on teenagers' emotions and senses, attempted to lend some credibility to the separatist impulse. Viewing themselves as latter-day Pauls, these critics guided concerned readers through the underworld of rock beats, behaviors, and events in an attempt to convince believers and nonbelievers alike to rid themselves of worldly music. Like the moral sensationalists of the nineteenth century who condemned novels yet dwelled on the grotesque retribution exacted upon the villains of their "true tales," these critics offered testimony that could simultaneously titillate and revolt Christian audiences.[61] In doing so, they engaged in a cultural conversation about the power and meaning of rock music.

What is most surprising about these critics is not their opposition to youth culture but rather their sincere belief in its authority. They attributed tremendous cultural, spiritual, and even political power to youth culture, suggesting that rock musicians were "secular gods" who represented "the avante-garde [sic] of cultural change," making it imperative for Christian conservatives to monitor their work.[62] Beyond associating rock with evil in general, these conservative critics suggested that rock—especially heavy metal—inspired serial killers such as Richard Ramirez to commit murder and encouraged teenagers to commit suicide.[63] Moreover, these native informants recounted how rock music seduced "good kids" from "good homes" into sinful (or even suicidal) behavior, undermining parental efforts to instill self-discipline and morality in their children. They based these concerns in biblical text: according to I Samuel 15:23, for example, rebellion amounted to witchcraft.[64]

The anti-rock "native informants" went to great lengths to establish their credibility as rock experts who had defected to Christianity's cause. In one book, Bob Larson, who conducted anti-rock seminars for parents and students across the country and hosted a long-running nationally syndicated call-in show, included a picture of himself holding his Fender guitar. His biography informed readers that he had his own rock band, the Rebels, by the time he was fifteen years old.[65] Other critics claimed to have been devoted rock fans who had witnessed the genre at its worst. For example, Jeff Godwin testified to readers that, when he attended the infamous 1979 concert by The Who in which eleven fans were crushed to death, he "saw with my own eyes thousands of teenagers driven insane with the Rock obsession." If his description of the Cincinnati concert did not persuade his audience of rock's madness, Godwin perhaps convinced them with a detailed account of a "typical" rock concert that compared the event to a heathen ritual.[66] Jimmy Swaggart laid claim to insider knowledge as well, using his cousin Jerry Lee Lewis's tortured life as an opportunity to expound against the rock 'n' roll lifestyle.[67]

Blaming rock music for subverting values, the former rock fans were concerned with both the physical and spiritual ramifications of exposure to the genre. Critic Jeff Godwin suggested that rock music emphasized "sexual lust" in order to "fire up teenage imaginations and hormones." But such manipulation served no foreign power. Writing during the early years of the AIDS crisis, Godwin ranted about the consequences of the sexual revolution and suggested that sexual activity among young people "serves a specific purpose—to spread demons. Demons are a venereal disease in the truest sense."[68] When not spreading disease, rock introduced non-Christian religious influences into the home; Eric Barger argued that secular rock music was "the single largest cult the world has ever seen."[69] Indeed, Bob Larson suggested, it was no longer enough for parents to worry about the introduction of African religious rites, for young people were now being introduced to Eastern religions through their bedroom record players.[70]

In addition to indoctrinating young people into belief systems that contradicted Christianity, rock threatened to introduce contemporary social problems into the home. Like Frank Garlock and Bob Jones III, former fans worried about a "generation gap" in the home that would pit rock's rebellion against the Bible's demand for submission to authority. Writing in 1970, Larson reported that parents all over the country had told him they were unable to communicate with their children. Larson then asked, "Could it be that their children are tuned in to a medium that is purposely seeking to alienate them from their parents?"[71] In a book published a decade later, Larson began each chapter with a description of the belief systems and practices introduced into the home through youth culture, including homosexuality, religious cults, the occult, and disco. Rock's invasive power concerned other critics as well. During the 1980s, Jeff Godwin argued that rebellion was the sole aim of the genre: "The purpose of rock music is to split, splinter, and destroy your home. While you are working to mend broken bridges between you and your children, the sleazy rock monsters are doing everything they can to tear those bridges to shreds and widen the gap."[72] These critics argued that rock's impact was local rather than global.

As if rock's attacks on the home were not enough, the genre's message could affect some groups more than others. The literature reflects conservative concerns about the student, feminist, gay rights, and civil rights movements, which challenged traditional authority structures and social norms. Writing at the height of the feminist movement, Bob Larson suggested that rock represented a particular threat to young women, who were imperiled by the relaxed behavioral norms offered by the rock 'n' roll lifestyle. Larson feared that girls—always presumed to be fans rather than performers—would succumb to pressure and become sex-crazed groupies. He also located a revolutionary feminist threat in popular dance styles. According to Larson, the separation of dance partners in the dance known as the twist represented a critical step in the degeneration of dance moves, as it signaled a decline in male authority and control. Prior to the separation, "the male led in the appropriate steps of the dance and the female followed," but the new dance allowed the female "to gesticulate her body in whatever manner the rhythm dictated without the leading of her male partner." The new moves were particularly troublesome because the mode of expression shifted from "hands and feet" to "the hips and shoulders, drawing attention to the chest and abdominal regions."[73] Larson also attributed fashion changes among young people to the shift in dance roles, asserting that the "look-alike neuter styles" and "role-reversing styles" were "partially an outgrowth of today's dances in which the male abrogates his traditional role as leader."[74] Larson's anti-feminism persisted: in 1989 he linked witchcraft to radical feminism.[75]

Other critics agreed that musicians intentionally attacked gender norms in American society. Jeff Godwin worried that gender-bending rock musicians like David Bowie and Elton John threatened "the God-given line between the sexes," and he claimed that, without action, young people would have "no proper sexual legacy" to inherit.[76] Others were more concerned that the gay rights movement would rob sons as well as fathers of their masculinity if sons decided to frequent gay discos rather than football fields.[77] In fact, the father's role was much under siege by the devil, who sought to destroy fathers and fatherhood alike.[78] To combat the devil, fathers needed to reclaim their authority over wives and children as well as music.

Whereas earlier critics had drawn the line between self and world around the church, younger critics now drew the line around the besieged suburban home; the home, in turn, fit into an eternal order. In contrast to their sixties-era predecessors, who viewed hippies and student protesters as conspirators with evil, the younger critics believed that (younger) children were victims of satanic predation. Since parents, especially the besieged father, were responsible for ensuring that their families served God, they needed to serve as gatekeepers between home and world. Godwin wrote, "YOU the parent draw the line! You decide the scope of the Rock problem within your own house!"[79] If parents neglected their responsibilities, they risked serving the wrong master, and children could become pawns in the battle between good and evil. In 1980 Larson asked readers (presumed to be parents): "Is it possible that while you proclaim your house is the Lord's, other gods are being extolled under your very roof? Is the stereo in your child's room an altar to darkness that dispenses the devil's liturgy?"[80] The pitched battle over rock music in the home became yet another way in which politics became localized for concerned suburban parents.

Concerned about the social and cultural changes wrought by music, Christian anti-rock critics located the root of rock's power in a supernatural force: Satan. Yet critics were cautious not to concede too much power to the devil. After all, the Bible—particularly the Old Testament, which includes the Book of Psalms—was filled with music and musical instruments used in worship. Instead, critics suggested that music possessed dual powers. They attributed the spiritual elements of music to God's creative power, and music's material elements to satanic subversion. Televangelist Jimmy Swaggart described the duality of music when he suggested in a 1986 anti-rock tract that music was either a force for Jesus or a force for Satan.[81] Because God and Satan were so clearly waging a fierce battle on the field of music, critics argued, music could never be neutral: it was by nature either productive or destructive.

Christians who wished to guard children from the evils of rock had a difficult task ahead of them, since musicians displayed tremendous ingenuity in delivering immoral messages to audiences through lyrics, lifestyles, and the objectionable beat of rock. Critics pointed to "morally degenerative lyrics" as the main cause of "the tidal wave of promiscuity, venereal disease, illegitimate births and political upheaval" that had swept the nation in the 1960s.[82] Musicians' lifestyles—particularly their drug use—also swayed the personal decisions of audience members. Concerts represented a particular peril for young people because they allowed the destructive tendencies of degenerate performers and demented fans to converge, if only for a few hours. Performances created an emotional atmosphere through drugs, alcohol, loud music, and other stimulants, leading one guide to warn parents, "Dante's Inferno Is Coming to Your Home Town."[83]

Anti-rock critics were appalled to learn that bands' satanic posturing might be related to the profit motive. In the mid-1980s, Bob Guccione Jr., publisher of the music magazine *Spin*, offered to send Bob Larson on the European leg of a tour by Slayer, a "satanic" metal band from the United States; in return for full access to the band, Larson was asked to write a cover story for the magazine. Reflecting on the trip, Larson later concluded, "If Slayer's soul was sold to Satan, they did so at the bank, not at a black mass. The forbidden brew Slayer sipped isn't the drink of lyrical death and despair. It's the elixir of fame. In the Garden of Rock 'n' Roll, they ate the apple of image over ingenuity, hype over integrity."[84] The fact that Slayer's stage act was a gimmick undertaken for theatrical and commercial reasons rather than out of conviction enraged the evangelist, who stopped just short of complaining that the band was not satanic. Larson argued that Slayer needed to convince fans to renounce Satanism, since the band had ostensibly led them into false worship. However, according to Larson, rabid fans instead repudiated Slayer for betraying (or selling out) the satanic faith.[85]

Although some Christian conservatives experienced spirit-filled worship, the anti-rock critics were highly critical of both the emotional and physical pull exhibited in rock music. Jimmy Swaggart acknowledged rock 'n' roll's debt to gospel music and Pentecostal worship but argued that rhythm appealed to man's flesh at the expense of the spirit and soul, causing an imbalance between man's senses and his worship patterns.[86] Other critics agreed, arguing that rock music was simply more powerful than other genres: its viscerality appealed to man's sinful nature. While praising "good music" for balancing intellect and emotion, critics accused rock of manipulating human emotions through a dominant beat. Specifically, they claimed that the "syncopated" beat matched the rate of the human heart.[87] Jeff Godwin wrote, "Rock music hits ALL listeners right in the guts, oozing its way like a ravenous leech into the most basic systems of the human body."[88] Other critics expounded on the physical dependencies caused by rock through its apparent ability to stimulate and release hormones.[89]

Critics also believed that rock affected the mind by creating critical lapses of judgment even in young people who had been trained to dissect religious texts rather than visceral beats and subliminal messages. According to Larson, "Music can exercise its influence over the body without meeting any intellectual resistance from the higher nervous centers," because rock music was "written to be *felt* rather than heard." Whereas the "spoken word" passed through "the master brain to be interpreted, translated, and screened for moral content," rock's "pounding fury" bypassed this "protective screen," causing youths to make no "value judgment" on the material.[90] Rock's ability to circumvent the intellect represented a particular threat to Christian children for it effectively subverted the moral groundwork their parents and ministers had so carefully tried to establish. "Backmasking," the practice of inserting a subliminal message into a recording, proved a particular concern for critics as well. According to Jacob Aranza, backmasking provided performers with a means of conveying "satanic and drug-related messages to the subconscious."[91] Teenagers who listened to rock music were therefore vulnerable to a two-pronged, physical and psychological attack.

Despite the sustained objections of anti-rock critics, who warned that contemporary music appealed to young people for all the wrong reasons, Christian rock exploded as a genre during the 1970s and 1980s. Proponents of Christian rock argued that the genre provided a tool for evangelism and a way for believers to enjoy contemporary entertainment while enhancing their faith. For preachers like Jimmy Swaggart, however, the sound was just one more example of worldliness invading the church.[92] While the Bible includes hundreds of examples of music making, Swaggart could find no scriptural reference that tied evangelism with music.[93] Christian anti-rock critics also saw rock music as antithetical to religiosity. They believed that lyrics should assume primacy in music and that rock's beat disrupted religious contemplation, distorted religious instruction, and generally fostered an environment devoid of spirituality.[94] Christian music, according to Bob Larson, should touch the "head and the heart," not the "hip and the heel."[95] Christian rock had the wrong goals, Larson argued, because "the Gospel is not intended to *please* men but to *warn* them."[96] Another critic echoed this sentiment about the valuelessness of Christian rock, claiming that listening to Christian music was akin to "trying to get my meals from the garbage can."[97]

Even if Christian music proved an effective tool for evangelism, critics worried that rock-inspired conversions would be the result of conditioning rather than conviction.[98] Doubters also worried that Christian rock offered a false representation of Christian dedication. They insisted that whereas evangelistic rock should emphasize lyrics, the music might actually hinder evangelism by making the message impossible to hear.[99] Likewise, because the music emphasized feelings rather than obligations, listeners might not realize that they should focus on obedience and "a holy fear of God."[100] Christian rock emphasized the sentiment of religiosity without naming the problem (sinfulness) or the solution (salvation). Years earlier, Bob Larson captured critics' misgivings about rock when he noted, "Great men of the faith have been martyrs, not swingers."[101]

As if rock's own traits were not troubling enough, Christians also worried that the genre's contexts and associations would always prevail over any positive message believers might insert into lyrics. Critic James Chute noted that

> contemporary Christian musicians would have us believe that changing the words changes the music's very nature, as if the power of music resides in the words alone; as if music can be completely severed from its cultural and social context and suddenly take on meanings not only removed but contradictory to those contexts.[102]

Chute disagreed with Christian performers who argued that they could use rock music to bring nonbelievers to Christianity. "In the struggle between the words and the music," Chute concluded, "music most often has the upper hand."[103] The genre was irredeemable—beyond even God's grasp—for several reasons. To begin with, regardless of Christian musicians' good intentions, the genre would continue to be associated with immorality, especially promiscuity and rebelliousness. Critics frequently noted that because "rock 'n' roll" was originally a euphemism for sex, believers should find the phrase "Christian rock" alarming.[104] Similarly, critics worried that rock's anti-authoritarianism would seep into the church. Swaggart reasoned that if Christian performers proved more acceptable to believers based on a "comparison test" with secular artists, it merely proved that the church had started to use the world, not the Word, as its standard.[105]

## "IS LEATHER 'OF THE LORD'?": CHRISTIAN PARENTS AND EDUCATORS

Critics who advocated complete avoidance of popular music were fighting a losing battle. By the 1980s, evangelicals were too middle class and too suburban—and consumption-based youth culture too pervasive—for separation to remain a tenable solution. Christian parents, including Christian media experts who sought to assist parents during the 1980s, represented a new thread of late-twentieth-century evangelical Christian thought about youth culture. In contrast to their anti-rock counterparts, who asserted that the debased state of youth culture demonstrated the need to avoid the secular world's wickedness, these experts and parents believed that youth culture's influence should be met by Christian activism at home and in public. In favoring Christian rock, these activists tended to emphasize moral concerns over doctrinal or institutional interests, and the earthly order of the family over an eternal order. To some extent they scorned the public campaigns undertaken by their fundamentalist predecessors and instead sought to advance their cause by deploying "modern" techniques for engaging popular culture.

Parents pursued a number of strategies as they attempted to understand, influence, and ultimately, limit kids' consumer choices. First, with the help of media experts, parents concluded that they needed to approach youth ministry in a manner similar to that of a ministry to a foreign country: by learning the culture. Rather than preventing children from indulging in youth culture, parents needed to manage its flow into their homes. Second, media experts recommended that parents encourage their children to listen to Christian rock, an emerging industry that sold more than 20 million albums in 1984, outsold jazz and classical music by 1985, and received increased airplay on religious stations that featured Christian rock or had switched to a Christian rock format.[106] While religious rock music incorporated aspects of youth culture, parents believed that the medium was redeemable if filtered through a Christian worldview. Third, media experts urged believers to step into the public sphere on behalf of their children through consumer and political campaigns against rock music. These solutions resembled the actions prescribed by nominally secular parent groups such as the PMRC (Parents' Music Resource Center), rather than the blanket denunciations of fundamentalist church leaders.

In order for parents to teach children morals and reestablish their authority, Christian media experts believed they first needed to possess a commanding knowledge of youth culture. Although wary of secular culture, these critics acknowledged that it played a vital—perhaps even defining—role in young people's lives. One writer for *Youthworker* magazine reflected that rock's critics had "burned it, banned it, damned it, defamed it, labeled it, legislated it, picketed it, protested it, petitioned against it, and prayed hellfire down upon it. They've called it lewd, rude, crude, racist, sexist, demonic, pornographic, and communistic"; they had not, he said, tried to debate it.[107] Experts on youth ministries recommended that Christians familiarize themselves with youth culture through a "cultural reconnaissance" mission; one educator dubbed this tactic "relational ministries."[108] Another suggested that parents' lack of familiarity with popular culture could actually impede youths' spiritual growth. "Even among Christian parents, who take fathering and mothering seriously," this expert explained, "cultural ignorance blocks family growth and spiritual maturing of youths."[109] Knowledge of youth culture thus became an imperative for "serious" parents who did not want to inhibit their children's religiosity.

As a result of the commercialization of youth culture during the 1970s, critics no longer associated rock music with the counterculture. While thus loosened from its seeming connection to alternative lifestyles, rock music—particularly heavy metal and punk rock—was still viewed as a tremendous threat to the American home. Whereas earlier critics had worried about the generation gap in American society and the church, conservative Christian parents now agonized over the generation gap at home, a breach intensified by popular music.[110] Unlike earlier critics, however, the new generation of Christian educators recommended a critical engagement with popular culture.

To help parents become "students of teenage culture" who understood both rock's appeal and its latest trends, Christian educators began to offer parents an array of books, magazines, and pamphlets that promised to keep them informed about the lives and beliefs of current secular performers.[111] Billy Graham was perhaps the first figure to foster peace between the generations when, in 1971, he published *The Jesus Generation,* an analysis that he explained was "*to* the young, *about* the young, and *for* the young," but also "for the older generation to help them in bridging the generation gap."[112] The genre of Christian parenting advice did not flourish, however, until the 1980s, when critics produced a formidable array of titles including *The Heart of Rock and Roll, It's All Rock and Roll to Me, Lord! Why Is My Child a Rebel?* and *Why Knock Rock?* In addition to evangelical magazines such as *Moody Monthly* and *Charisma,* specialized newsletters such as *Media Update,* established in 1982 by Christian educator Al Menconi, furnished parents with ways to address the issue of youth culture in the home. Christian media analysts were not out to seize the primary nurturing responsibility from parents; rather, they intended to facilitate relationships between parents and children by helping parents become conversant with youth culture. This kind of youth work, in which adults entered youth culture and spoke its language, was termed "incarnational youth ministry," as it mimicked God's decision to send Jesus to save humanity.[113] Discussing youth workers, one author reminded readers that the mission of youth workers remained "to help support and strengthen families."[114] These educators offered Christian parenting advice in an authoritative, professional tone that emphasized the importance of maintaining Christian values in the American home.

Evangelical parents linked the growing influence of popular culture to other changes in social norms and cultural authority. Like Christian political activists of the era, many evangelical writers decried the decline of "family values." In this view, the home became a repository of white middle-class economic security, female domesticity, and heterosexual male authority. Jacob Aranza reminisced about the way he and, presumedly, his audience had been reared: "Most of us were raised in families where Dad went to work and Mom stayed home to take care of us. When we got off of the school bus, Mom was there to meet us, hear about what happened that day, and sit us down with a good snack before we did our homework."[115] Aranza lamented that this "traditional family" had nearly disappeared due to divorce rates and working parents.

Other authors struck a similarly nostalgic tone about changes in American society as they idealized the nuclear family of an earlier era. In a March 1992 article in *Moody Monthly,* a professional educator pointed to the "rootlessness" among teenagers: "Only a couple of generations ago it would have been common for a person to spend the first 18 years of his life in the house where he was born. He knew where home was. And it was a symbol of stability. Now, such a symbol is a luxury." More important, the author continued, instability had spread to the nuclear family and had confused gender roles. "Only a couple of generations ago, it would have been common for a teenager to have his biological mom at home and his biological father at work during the day. Now that is a luxury of a mere 4 percent." The author suggested that the "ideal" family organization, in which a mother stayed at home to attend to the household while the father went to work, was nearly extinct; and by specifying "biological" parents, the author alluded to divorce rates. Even the kids who grew up in "traditional families" could not escape the ill effects of social disarray, since they were bound to have friends who were "bruised and disoriented."[116]

Conservative Christians believed that a decline in cultural standards accompanied these social changes. As a result, Christians who wished to maintain their faith needed to be aware of the dangers presented by secular culture. One author, Al Menconi, explained the perils posed to Christians in an article that framed the "spiritual war" in contemporary American culture in terms of the seductive powers of consumer desire. One of the "weapons" in this conflict—entertainment—remained extremely dangerous to the Christian belief system, yet some Christians continued "to treat this journey like a stroll through a shopping mall" rather than "a race through a battlefield!" Instead of focusing on their faith, Christians "wander around casually window shopping at the enemy's stores!"[117] In an earlier article entitled "A Wake Up Call for America!" Menconi asked parents, "Do you know what post-Christian America is teaching your children through their entertainment?"[118] While Menconi indicated Christians' alienation from mainstream culture by referring to a "post-Christian America," he also reclaimed the category of America by issuing a "wake up call" to the nation, whose parents needed to lay claim to entertainment in order to protect children. In this logic, parenting became an endeavor linked to the nation's cultural fate.

Whereas stricter contemporaries such as Jeff Godwin viewed children as victims of predatory cultural practices, Christian parent activists viewed children as agents *and* potential allies in efforts to discern immorality in culture. One author-parent lamented that adolescents were "growing up in an R-rated world" in which they had to "process more garbage and make more moral decisions in a week than some of us made during our entire adolescence." However, in contrast to the anti-rock critics, this educator did not expect parents to withdraw from popular culture. As much as parents might have wished for "some kind of protective shield," he instead advised parents to arm their children with moral answers before they were forced to choose. In fact, he claimed, kids wanted parents to help them with the answers because they were so besieged by choices. "Adolescents," the author suggested, "live in a relative world, and they come to church to find that which is absolute." He warned that if children's stress was not lessened, parents should prepare for "a '90s version of the '60s student protests," which to this author stood as the ultimate assault on adult authority.[119]

Before parents expunged the vilest secular artists from their children's collections, they were told, they should examine their own consumer habits. Ministers informed parents that to become Christian role models, they needed to purge their homes of country-and-western music, "mellow lust" pop music, romance novels, and soap operas.[120] By getting rid of their own secular vices, Christian families could present a united front against outside influences.

While their anti-rock predecessors had attributed rock's popularity to the devil's scheming, educational critics took a therapeutic approach to breaking rock's spell in the home. As they began to research youth culture, parents needed to understand why young people listened to music in the first place. One media expert wrote that, contrary to some pastors' belief that the elimination of rock 'n' roll would end "teen epidemics" such as pregnancy, violence, and drug abuse, music was "not the problem": the real core of the problem was, naturally, sin.[121] The same critic emphasized that peer pressure, emotion, and independence played an important role in listening habits. Rather than prohibiting the music, the writer suggested, parents should use it as a springboard for conversations about Christian values.[122] Another Christian media analyst theorized that children listened to rock music because it offered "unqualified acceptance" and "understanding" that parents were perhaps not providing. Even if parents viewed rock music as "a problem," the analyst cautioned that their teenager may view it as "a solution and a friend."[123] Parents could learn how to be both "solution and friend" by understanding how rock music fulfilled this role.[124] By understanding rock music, parents could better insert themselves into the world of young people—and thus close the generation gap.

Christian media educators believed that, besides understanding rock's persistent appeal, parents should familiarize themselves with the latest trends in secular music. The literature reveals a concern with the lifestyles of rock musicians rather than a belief that the music was intrinsically evil. The publishers of *Media Update* prided themselves on keeping parents up-to-date on shifting patterns of youth culture. About once a year *Media Update* published its "Hot 100," which profiled the most popular musical acts in the nation and usually attempted to damn the artists with their own words and actions. The editors boasted to readers, "We read, clip and file articles from every credible rock magazine and major newspaper each month as well as take notes from music video programs such as MTV, 'Entertainment Tonight,' and 'Rock and Roll Evening News.'"[125] Perhaps because of their research, the editors disapproved of anti-rock critics like Jeff Godwin, whose book *The Devil's Disciples* they dismissed for being "riddled with mistakes, wild conjecture, little biblical scholarship, poor historical research and a free-form style."[126] Although they criticized Godwin, the *Media Update* editors also disapproved of rock music and musicians. However, the editors insisted they were not "carrying out an angry, opinionated vendetta against rock music." Their profiles were "a matter of public record"—and a public service to parents who could not otherwise navigate the complex channels of youth culture.[127]

Concerning other issues, *Media Update* highlighted emerging trends in the music industry and explained their moral implications. For example, the May–June 1986 issue featured a special article on New Wave music that warned parents not to be fooled by the genre's "milder, more melodic sound" as compared to heavy metal. Informed parents would instead be disturbed by the genre's lyrical themes, "often depressing, dark, macabre, and full of despair." While the sound was not as discordant as that of metal, it was "a prime example of a third generation punk message teaching kids to be happy about being hopeless." The lifestyles and political identities of band members were also deemed unsatisfactory. The article included warnings about bands such as Everything but the Girl ("avowed Socialists"), the Jesus and Mary Chain ("anarchy seems to be at the heart of their message"), Scritti Politti (the band leader "spent most of his time reading about Marxism and leading the Young Communist League in Wales"), and Dead or Alive ("fronted by androgyny king/queen Peter Burns").[128]

Dave Hart, a *Media Update* editor who wrote about popular music trends, found secular music to be fertile ground for biblically based moral lessons in his book of profiles about the contemporary music scene. Hart noted that the female punk band L7, founders of the pro-abortion organization Rock for Choice, "have become a voice for women who feel they need to be tougher and cruder than men in order to protect themselves in an abusive world. But becoming just like the men they hate is no solution. Women can't become all that God created them to be if they keep trying to be something they're not."[129] Hart used the example of L7 to insist that rock 'n' roll defied divinely ordained gender roles: God had not designed women to be "tough" or "crude," though Hart left unclear how (or if) the women in L7, who were presumed to "hate" men, should "protect" themselves. In another entry, Hart expressed admiration for the work ethic of former Black Flag singer Henry Rollins, but he argued that the singer's rage forestalled resolution. "Unless Rollins reconciles with the Father and forgives his father," Hart concluded, "he will carry the fire of his anger and alienation into the most fiery and alienated place in the universe—the ultimate mosh pit of Hell."[130] While demonstrating his knowledge of punk vocabulary ("mosh pit"), Hart maintained that punk alienation could not ameliorate rage but that religious conversion would. In a sense, the lessons modeled arguments that parents could present to youths who listened to secular music. In fact, following most of his profiles, Hart offered a "music exchange" that provided parents with a Christian musician whose style, but not message, approximated that of the particular secular artist.

Other Christian educators offered resource materials for parents that, like *Media Update,* were more concerned with cataloging rock's immorality than with detecting any secret (or satanic) messages in music. The Peters brothers, whose "Truth about Rock" seminars were aimed at parents and children, published *Rock Music Research,* a "rock dictionary" that featured minibiographies of popular bands from AC/DC to ZZ Top, with additional categories for rock associates such as "deaths" (subdivided into "suicide," "accidents," "killed," or "drug-induced"), "drugs," and "sex and rock." Writing about the potentially backmasked messages in a song by Prince, the Peters brothers asked, "Why look for secret messages in the music when there is so much garbage blatantly displayed up front?"[131] The brothers also urged parents to conduct ethnographic research by visiting record stores and magazine shops that catered to the youth market, as well as by speaking directly to young people about the lifestyles and values advocated in rock music.[132]

Another minister, Eric Barger, developed an elaborate rock rating system based on ten immoral or blasphemous themes frequently found in rock music. Created when most Christian critics were concerned with heavy metal rather than rap music, the categories included the occult, drug use, cultic influences, sexual overtones or hedonism, rebellion and violence, Satanism, nihilism and escapism, murder/-suicide, and subliminal messages. Barger's ratings tended to penalize (or reward, depending on one's perspective) career longevity and breadth of lyrical focus. In his system, a perfect 10—a negative rating in every category—proved difficult to achieve: out of a list that included, among others, Led Zeppelin, the Beatles, the Sex Pistols, AC/DC, and Van Halen, only Mick Jagger and the Rolling Stones achieved a perfect score. Of course, if performers were to be deemed unacceptable by the number of notches earned alone, a fictional band like Spinal Tap (sexual overtones, Satanism, and blasphemy) or an aging folk singer like James Taylor (drugs, rebellion, nihilism, murder/suicide) might be judged more objectionable than rappers Public Enemy (sexual overtones/hedonism, rebellion) or the Village People (sexual overtones, rebellion), whose members were rather overt about their homosexuality.[133]

Although educational materials were generally written for an assumed parental audience, authors occasionally addressed young people directly. In such cases, the authors emphasized obedience. Young people were urged to "closely examine" their albums and play their "favorite songs for Mom and Dad," taking care to "explain the lyrics they probably can't hear." If a young person's parents did not approve of the albums, he or she should ask parents for suggestions as to contemporary artists who advocated "wholesome values" using a "contemporary sound."[134] Children were told to live by their parents' rules and forego their favorite music if their parents so asked. Through such encouragement, the parent activists attempted to foster family unity.

Because parent activists placed blame for immorality squarely on the shoulders of rock stars, they did not believe that rock music was intrinsically evil. As a "creative force," rock music was "God-given" and therefore not "bad" (or evil) by nature; rather, both man and Satan had perverted musical creation, and the rotten fruits of this collaboration were evident throughout the secular music catalog.[135] Although rock conveyed immorality through lyrics, album graphics, lifestyles, and goals, there was no reason that Christian musicians could not create an even more powerful force by communicating "positive" beliefs using the same cultural materials. As a result, media educators were confident that Christian musicians could "redeem the music marketplace" with their work, making "the world of rock music a safer place for young people's ears."[136] Believers hoped to externalize the values of the home through the cultural work of Christian rock. When challenged, educators argued that modern media did not contradict biblical values as long

as they were "Christ-centered."[137] Responding to criticism from conservatives, Al Menconi published a defense of Christian rock that justified the contemporary sound:

> Since the basis of Christian music is to be Scripture and scriptural princi-
> ples set to music (an idea upon which we all agree), then Christian music
> should have the same purpose as Scripture. II Timothy 3:16 clearly teaches
> us that Scripture is profitable for doctrine, for reproof, for correction, and
> for instruction in righteousness. Therefore, Christian music should also
> teach, reprove, correct, and encourage the believer to righteousness.[138]

According to Menconi, while Christian rock did not derive its lyrics
directly from the Bible, it drew on biblical principles and was therefore
acceptable.

Media educators and activists believed that Christian music, like educational materials, should attempt to foster religious and moral beliefs
and strengthen the home. The Peters brothers outlined the goals of
music in one of their first books. The brothers did not object to the
influence the music industry had on young people: they disagreed not
with the medium but with the message.[139] According to the brothers,
the music industry needed "to become less concerned with rhyme,
rhythm, and songs that sell," and instead focus on creating "music that
is uplifting and inspiriting" for young people. The brothers specified the
values that music should convey:

> There should be songs that build strong morals in young people and teach
> them to be good citizens; music that will help stem the divorce rate by
> teaching about real love, not lust; tunes that will help end child abuse and
> wife battering by showing how men can be men and not bullies; melodies
> that derail the tendency toward teenage rebellion, and advocate respect,
> communication and character.[140]

This outline for musical activism demonstrates Christians' supreme
faith in the cultural authority of music. According to the Peters brothers,
music could and should instill the values of citizenship, calm adolescent
hormones, solve social problems, and quell generational rebellion.

Music as conceived by Christian parental activists was not an
artistic—or even commercial—endeavor but something closer to Lauren
Berlant's understanding of "social parenthood" in which adults self-
censor to safeguard the impressionable minds of children. This was particularly true regarding artist lifestyles. Christians, perceived by activists
as "sheep among wolves," needed to maintain "Christian witness in an
ever-darkening environment."[141] Christian performers were expected to

be "teachers" who "bear responsibility for what they teach—not only with their words and music, but also with their lives."[142]

Christian educators believed that Christian rock music would help unify homes, but they worried that Christian rock musicians' appearances and sounds would repulse most parents. As a result, educators attempted to teach parents how to "read" the intentions of Christian musicians. They told parents not to base conclusions about sinfulness on outward appearance: fashion, like music, was neutral—part of the everyday vernacular of youth culture. Even though Christian rock looked as if it was conforming to the world, conformity was a matter of the heart, not of appearances.[143] The media experts instructed parents to look beyond surface appearances such as fashion and to recall biblical nonconformists such as John the Baptist. The Peters brothers captured this effort to reconcile Christianity and the world when they asked in a headline, "Is Leather 'of the Lord?'"[144]

Even as support for Christian recording artists grew, a few critics asserted that believers should erase the boundary separating "sacred" and "secular" culture. This step involved some risk for Christians since they could no longer be assured that young fans would understand which music contained a Christian message and which music did not. Christian media analysts addressed this concern by counseling believers to develop "discernment," which worked in two ways. First, critics acknowledged that mainstream culture had sharpened kids' ability to detect inferior products. Evangelical youths were skilled consumers who demanded "quality recordings, not just religious ones." Consumerism empowered Christian teenagers, who simply would not buy music of an "inauthentic" quality.[145] Second, "discernment" meant religious criticality—that is, Christians' relationship to culture at large and their desire to be "*in* the world, but not *of* the world." In this sense, "discernment" meant learning how to consume the products of an unchurched culture selectively—a religious form of reception theory. Christian bands already practiced "discernment" by appropriating secular music for Christian ends, but Christian consumers had to hone their interpretive skills as well. As one writer explained,

> "Sacred" and "secular" are not qualities of things; they are qualities of relationship orientation. For example, one cannot paint a Christian landscape, but one can view it in a Christian way, for what the beholder brings to the encounter determines its sacred or secular quality. Thus the terms sacred and secular are better used in conjunction with a mode of existence—namely one's basic orientation is either sacred or secular.[146]

Once confident in their ability to "discern," Christians could use the terms "sacred" and "secular" to describe their orientation to things, not the things themselves.

Before they could deploy this strategy, Christians had to learn how to separate the biblical "truth" of an artist's work from his or her lifestyle. One article argued that believers should scrutinize secular music for Christian—not satanic—content. It asked,

> Does Elton John's biblically inconsistent homosexuality make his biblically consistent song "Healing Hand" any less true? Should Madonna's repulsive ideals and behavior invalidate the profoundly anti-abortion message of "Papa Don't Preach?" Do Janet Jackson's recent sleazy videos make her bold song urging sexual restraint, "Let's Wait Awhile," any less true?
>
> We think not. Those who follow Christ and live by His Word must be discerning enough to be able to separate truth from the imperfect vessels who come bearing that truth.[147]

Music's "imperfect" creators, according to this article, did not determine the final meaning of their products; instead, believers could extract Christian values out of non-Christian commodities. The authors clearly viewed this as an oppositional cultural tactic; once Christians knew how to read secular culture, their interpretations could be transgressive. Indeed, the article quoted another Christian author who suggested,

> We will be more effective when we penetrate behind enemy lines . . . how does an army fight behind enemy lines? It doesn't move its forces *en masse*, it can't. Rather, it infiltrates small units to disrupt the enemy's communication and attack strategic targets. And that's exactly what Christians must do in a post-Christian culture.[148]

In this view, living in a closed Christian subculture simply signified acceptance of Christians' exile from popular culture. Instead of withdrawing from that culture, Christians had to learn how to subvert mainstream commodities for Christian purposes. This strategy was not without its dangers, as "subversive" consumption—actions as simple as rewriting the words to a favorite secular band's song or listening to a band because it had a "Christian" member—could lead to greater thirst for secular culture. There were limits to what Christians could consume. "Sinful" products still existed—John Styll maintained that Christian pornography could never exist—but Christians had to be mindful of their opportunity to become cultural leaders through discernment.[149]

Christian parents aimed their efforts at mitigating the effects of a hostile culture once it had entered the home, encouraging the consumption of "Christian" culture, or exercising Christian "discernment" in examining secular culture. These activities formed only one part of a campaign that also extended outside the home. This dual quality of the campaign reflected Christians' belief in social solutions: before parents could become activists in the world, they first needed to become activists in their own homes. That is, as the Peters brothers concluded, Christians needed to "take out the garbage" in their homes before they could criticize their "neighbor's trash heap."[150] And yet, because they believed that rock music was moving "away from the principles that build strong character, produce good citizens and unify families," parents needed to take action in both local and national settings.[151] Defending the home from home was not enough: Christians needed to defend "traditional" authority by moving into public space.

Christians believed that they had important roles as moral stewards for the nation's culture and that they needed to carry their activism outside the home to protect children. The Peters brothers typified this sentiment when they spoke of the need to defend American culture:

> Ultimately, we have to ask ourselves what kind of society—what kind of culture—we want for ourselves and our children. More and more, our culture displays an irreconcilable pull away from the Judeo-Christian ethic, and our vulnerable youth are often too immature or too inexperienced in their faith to fight this irresistible force. If we Christian parents are contented doing nothing to help guide our children—as well as to struggle against the forces seeking to destroy our culture—then we are promoting the reign of the devil—the status quo.[152]

In the Christian activists' estimation, children were vulnerable—"too immature" or "too inexperienced" to fight the pull away from Judeo-Christian values—so parents must join the struggle against the "irresistible" force of contemporary culture. Whereas the youth described by the fundamentalist anti-rock critics had been viewed as dangerously independent and potentially volatile, the generation coming of age in the 1980s needed parental support. The shift from sixties-era dangerous youth to eighties-era endangered youth marked one of the critical shifts in evangelical cultural activism, as it allowed devout parents to enter national debates on behalf of children. The culture of the 1960s may have become the "reign of the devil," but Christian parents were determined to reestablish control over American culture.

While Christian music provided a line of defense in the home for parents, political activism on behalf of children mounted a Christian counterattack in the culture wars. Although Christian leaders such as Jerry

Falwell and Pat Robertson attempted to mobilize heretofore world-wary conservative Christians to get involved in local and national politics, evangelical Christians like the Peters brothers were also involved in community morality campaigns. And while activists supported legislative efforts to rein in popular culture, they also proposed several consumer-based solutions. Ted Baehr, founder of the Christian Film and Television Commission, demonstrated the parity that consumer solutions had reached with voting rights when he told readers that Christians needed to "reject the bad and choose the good on television, at the theater, and in the voting booth."[153] By suggesting that musicians were corrupting young American consumers through their lyrics and lifestyles, activists framed the debate not as an issue of artistic expression but rather as an issue of consumer safety.

To improve social mores, parents engaged in the dialog about contemporary culture. This did not necessarily mean that activists identified themselves as Christians to other community members. Al Menconi was among educators who suggested that believers frame their critiques as concerned parents rather than as devout Christians. Another writer advised parents who planned to communicate with local radio stations and sponsors not to lace their letter with "Christian jargon and scriptures": after all, he continued, Christians "need not sound as though we just graduated from 'The University of Fire and Brimstone' to be effective."[154] Parents were advised to retain their Christian motives but subordinate them to achieve their desired outcome.

Leaders also urged parents to use their consumption habits to press for changes at the local level. Groups in earlier eras had positioned themselves as national moral stewards, as when the Catholic Church's Legion of Decency sought to influence film content through a rating system and boycotts.[155] Now James Dobson and Gary Bauer recommended boycotts of popular culture, including television and music—a tactic also advocated by Donald Wildmon of the television watchdog group American Family Association and by Ted Baehr of the Christian Film and Television Commission. Parents who wanted to encourage performers to record "positive, wholesome music" needed to stop buying secular records and remember that their "pocketbook votes count!"[156]

Beyond consumer-based solutions, Christian leaders urged parents to get involved in campaigns to persuade municipal or state governments to ban or regulate rock music. Expressing no reservations about legislating morality, parents catalogued grievances against rock, such as the health hazards posed by loud music and the nuisance of large concerts.

As evidence of successful campaigns, they pointed to efforts in cities such as San Antonio, Texas, where the activist municipal organizations Community Families in Action and Parents against Subliminal Seduction (PASS) helped lobby for a city ordinance that restricted attendance of youth under age fourteen at "obscene" rock concerts.[157] Media experts also claimed victories at the state level, as in April 1982, when Assemblyman Phillip Wyman conducted hearings in the California Assembly's Committee on Consumer Protection and Toxic Materials to determine whether records allegedly containing subliminal information should carry warning labels. The proposal died in committee, but the hearings nonetheless generated publicity for the cause.[158]

Christian activists also supported national efforts at regulating rock music to protect young consumers. In general, they favored the actions of the PMRC—perhaps because a Christian minister, Jeff Ling, served as an adviser to the organization. Some activists, however, noted that they would have pressed for legislation.[159] In fact, long before the PMRC hearings in 1985, the Peters brothers circulated a national petition asking for a record ratings system; a ban on "obscene, indecent, or profane records" from public airwaves; and a prohibition on sales of "indecent or profane records" to minors under the age of seventeen except by parental consent. The petition asked "all branches of government" to "stop innocent children from being immorally influenced by pornography disseminated through music sold to minors or played over the public airwaves."[160] The brothers also included a form letter for parents who wished to register complaints with the Federal Communications Commission. Conservative Christians who held appointed office also contributed to the cause. In 1983, Ronald Reagan's secretary of the interior, James Watt, an evangelical Christian, decided to ban rock music from the annual Fourth of July celebration on the national mall. Watt explained that rock groups drew "the wrong element" and that Independence Day would be "for the family and solid, clean American lives."[161] Watt replaced the rock lineup, which the previous year had included the Beach Boys, with Wayne Newton and the Army Blues Band.

The battle over rock music in the home provided a way to talk about domesticity, "family values," and the loss of "law and order" in American society. Parents' ability to assert control over rock music in the home became a metaphor for adults' ability to exert discipline and order throughout society in the years after the 1960s. The parents movement of the mid-1980s demanded, in the words of a PMRC pamphlet, an environment in which artists and industry exercised "social responsibility and self-restraint when dealing with young people's minds."[162] Secular and religious organizations as well as lawmakers called on secular artists such as Twisted Sister (whose lead singer, Dee Snider, testified at the PMRC hearings in 1985) and 2 Live Crew (whose lead singer, Luther Campbell, was arrested on obscenity charges in 1990 for performing songs from the group's album *As Nasty As They Wanna Be*) to self-censor their work for the benefit of children.[163]

Earlier fundamentalist criticism of rock for its alleged dalliance with communism and Satanism had placed conservative believers at the margins of public discourse on the impact of music on youth. When conservative believers reframed their critique to reflect concerns about the impact on home and morality, however, they reentered public conversations about "values" in American culture. A PMRC pamphlet, "Let's Talk Rock," demonstrated this intersection of interests in its "Recommended Reading" section, which listed sources by David Noebel and the Peters brothers alongside addresses for National PTA publications and secular parenting guides.

The intersection of parental interests brought closure to the notion of the "dangerous" (middle-class white) youth of the 1960s. The record burning hosted by the Peters brothers in 1979 sought to provide young evangelicals with a symbolic disavowal of dangerous culture. Both secular and evangelical parenting guides presented children as victims of rock musicians, thus restoring "youth" as a category of innocence in need of parental protection. Young people were savvy consumers, to be sure, but in this aspect of the debate, they needed parental guidance to be agents. Yet it turned out that youth rebellion might have a useful moral purpose after all. In the mid-1980s, evangelicals began to see young people as potential allies in the effort to insert Christianity in the public spaces of suburbia. Like the twelve-year-old Jesus quoting scripture in the temple of Jerusalem, these modern-day religious prodigies would amaze their elders by seeking to enact a radical reformation of American values.

# Rebel with a Cross

*The Creation of a Christian Youth Culture*

In conservative demonology, the hippie and the student protester rank among the most despised nemeses of American society. Each sixties-era archetype represents a distinct affront to conservative principles: while the hippie flouted the work ethic and personal responsibility, the student protester defied deference and law and order. In early 1970—about the time the Chicago Seven conspiracy trial ended but just before the Kent State tragedy—conservative historian of religion Will Herberg, drawing on these archetypes, condemned the "student anarchist assault on civilization" being staged on the nation's university campuses. Herberg argued that "lawless violence" was rapidly wiping out "moral restraints" and predicted that there would soon be no difference between violent agitators and hippies: the degeneracy would make associations "increasingly murky," causing "the line between the student radical and the underworld hippie" to "fade away."[1]

Herberg soon changed his mind about at least one segment of the counterculture. In a November 1971 article in the *New Guard*, the magazine of the conservative campus organization Young Americans for Freedom (YAF), Herberg fondly profiled the "Jesus freaks," members of a youth-led revival that glowed with particular intensity on the West Coast. He found that the difference between YAF straights and hippies had receded, offering hope that the counterculture could yet be reintegrated into "the continuing American consensus." While acknowledging that the "cultic uniforms" of the young converts might arouse hostility from "middle America," Herberg directed readers' attention to areas where the freaks diverged from the hippie subculture: morality and religion. According to Herberg, "Not only do [the freaks] strive to lead sober, disciplined lives, but they campaign actively against the moral laxity and putrid permissiveness that have gone so far in corrupting American middle-class, especially suburban middle-class, society." Eschewing "vague, meaningless hippie-religiosity," the Jesus freaks represented a movement "from within the counter-culture . . . to dissolve the counter-culture and restore sanity and sobriety." For conservatives this development could have only positive political implications. Herberg therefore urged his conservative readers to "affirm [the movement] and wish it well."[2]

Herberg was one of many observers who noted the discrepancy between young believers' countercultural aesthetic and what he described as "moral and religious earnestness." Unlike journalists for popular magazines such as *Look* and *Time,* who treated young converts as cultural novelties, Herberg saw the potential for a moral-political alliance between political and moral conservative activists.[3] The Young Americans for Freedom—along with their founder, William F. Buckley Jr.—knew how to cultivate a subversive edge within a conservative belief system for political gain: the YAF had simultaneously bucked the old guard of the GOP's Protestant core and battled against the "liberal establishment." In a similar manner, the youthful converts of the Jesus Movement challenged both the mainstream Protestant church and permissive secular culture. Just as neoconservatism moved the balance of power in the Republican Party from its midwestern base to Sunbelt states such as Arizona and California, where public figures like Barry Goldwater and Ronald Reagan dominated politics, the advent of the Jesus Movement affirmed that evangelicalism was a Sunbelt—not just a Bible Belt—phenomenon.

Beginning in the 1960s, youth religiosity intersected with and furthered the cause of the conservative reformation of society through transformation of the self. While some young people protested the lack of meaning in consumer culture by joining campus demonstrations, others saw a society that had become secular, sexually permissive, and nihilist and were determined to reform it through religion. Even as Christian parents and educators considered youth to be in need of protection, some young adults made inroads into "Christianizing" American culture and society. In a political and cultural climate dominated by the actions of parents, home owners, and taxpayers, young evangelicals achieved two significant innovations: they fused popular religious traditions to middle-class cultural forms that valued authenticity; and they carried this message into the dominant spaces of suburbia—store, car, highway, home, and school—through their proselytizing. Such efforts proved that young adults could be agents rather than victims in the moral and cultural "war of position" waged by white evangelicals.

Earlier revivals in American history also sought to enlist young people. Enthusiastic religions offered young people an intense religious experience, personal salvation, and a strict moral code that were often combined with anti-institutional rhetoric. During the Great Awakening of the mid-eighteenth century, revival religions found broad support among ethnically and economically diverse populations—and among young people. Historian Patricia Bonomi suggests that the rhetoric of these revivals may, in turn, have provided a model for Revolutionary-era political battles.[4] Similarly, Christine Leigh Heyrman argues that eighteenth- and early-nineteenth-century southern evangelical clergy recognized the power of peer pressure and the dearth of outlets for youthful imagination. Religious leaders consequently targeted young people in their conversion efforts.[5] As industrialization drew more Americans into the cities in the late nineteenth century, organizations such as the YMCA and the Salvation Army sought to establish a clear moral order for young people.[6] Moreover, early Pentecostal periodicals recounted tales of children between the ages of ten and twelve who were moved by the Holy Spirit—and permitted by adults—to offer exhortations and speak in tongues at services and, in a few cases, on the revival circuit.[7]

Concern for the state of young souls continued throughout the twentieth century, as religious conservatives voiced a general concern over attacks on homes, schools, and churches alike. The Scopes Trial, of course, centered on the issue of what children could be taught as part of their school curriculum, and in subsequent years fundamentalists were so apprehensive about the impact of modern culture on young people that they established an impressive network of nondenominational organizations dedicated to fostering religiosity among young people. In the wake of World War II, groups such as Youth for Christ held rallies that drew hundreds of thousands of young people to concerts all over the nation during a period of heightened anxiety over juvenile delinquency.[8] In this light, the youth-driven Jesus Movement signaled a continuation of evangelical interest in the state of young people's souls.

Although Protestantism tended to be linked to concepts such as work, thrift, and sobriety, revivalists had begun long before to incorporate commercial entertainment styles that featured intense emotion and theatricality.[9] Historian Colleen McDannell has suggested that sustained interaction with cultural artifacts such as magazines, books, and music helped young Protestants learn the "values, norms, behaviors, and attitudes" so important to their faith.[10] During the post–World War II era, these values and practices fostered a booming industry composed of independent Christian bookstores catering to a growing evangelical population that believed Christianity was a lifestyle as well as a belief system. This trend was driven in part by the Jesus Movement. The number of independent Christian bookstores grew from 725 to 1,850 between 1965 and 1975, and average store sales grew at a rate of 16 percent annually between 1975 and 1979. The proportion of merchandise sold at stores changed from nearly 70 percent print materials (including Bibles), 12 percent music, and 20 percent nonprint goods (including gifts, jewelry, and films) in 1978, to 49 percent books, 15 percent music, and 36 percent nonprint goods in 1993. As sales increased, the merchandise became more emphatically "Christian" and less theological and denominational.[11] With the increased variety and quality of Christian cultural products, the evangelical consumer also became more solidly middle class.[12] Teenagers proved to be an ready market for these commodities. A study by the National Survey of Youth and Religion found that conservative Protestant teenagers (ages 13–17) reported having attended a religious concert (51%), worn jewelry or clothing expressing religious or spiritual meaning (49%), shared their religious faith with someone not of the faith (56%), or listened to a religious music recording (70%) at much higher rates than the average adolescent in their cohort.[13]

The enthusiasm for cultural goods coincided with a critical shift in American religious practices and institutions during the postwar era. As James Davison Hunter argues, the lines of cultural conflict in the late twentieth century were drawn around the issue of "moral authority."[14] In addition, as William Connolly suggests, the 1960s opened up new terms of public discourse that validated social criticism based in experience—including spirituality and morality—rather than in objectivity and rationality.[15] Rather than marginalizing religion, this experiential shift resulted in a new configuration of public religiosity in which, according to anthropologist Susan Harding, "power and authority are less centered."[16] In this new order, "born-again Christians" maintained their separate theological identities but focused their Bible-based supernaturalist rhetoric on moral, social, and political issues such as the Equal Rights Amendment, school busing, pornography, abortion, homosexuality, public school curricula, and popular culture.[17]

Harding's work offers a way to understand how youth culture allowed young believers to avoid being mere casualties of cultural fallout. Harding, who conducted fieldwork at Jerry Falwell's Thomas Road Baptist Church in Virginia, argues fundamentalist Christians use preaching and witnessing as two primary linguistic strategies to "reproduce their cultural modes of interpretation through encountering, reconfiguring, and incorporating specimens of alien, worldly culture."[18] In both strategies, conservative Protestants "speak the Gospel" in order to convert nonbelievers. It is through these forms that nonbelievers acquire the "specific religious language" of believers. Although Harding's insights pertained to one-on-one witnessing, the kinds of testimony offered in Christian cultural forms represent further adaptations that evangelical Christians made to encounter, reconfigure, and incorporate popular culture in order to reproduce their worldview in others. The ultimate goal remained the same: to transform nonbelievers—including children and young adults—into "speakers."

Not every evangelical Christian teenager lived by the exact tenets set forth by conservative religious leaders. Indeed, many young Christians expressed feelings of alienation from "establishment" conservatives such as Pat Robertson and the normative religious values they professed to defend. According to a 2005 study of youth religiosity by Christian Smith, American teenagers, despite tremendous resources devoted to fostering their piety, very often hold an instrumental and relativistic view of religion that privileges individual benefits and use value over institutionalized doctrinal demands. Nonetheless, conservative Protestants and Mormons have excelled at retaining young people within their traditions, and most religiously devoted teenagers who passionately adhere to their faith derive from these traditions.[19] These teenagers powered a grassroots Christian fan culture that abetted conservative political ideologies by believing in the reformation of society through transformation of the self.

The history of Christian fan culture reveals three characteristics that helped young evangelicals disseminate their message. First, Christian youth culture emphasized the messages of personal salvation and morality, minimizing denominational differences and allowing young evangelicals to unite behind a simplified version of Christianity. Beyond discussions about specific religious beliefs, the culture emphasized that social change could occur only through individual regeneration and thus prized personal piety. Second, Christian youth culture offered young people certainty and empowerment, often with a "rebellious" edge—even while the culture attempted to inculcate young people in "traditional" beliefs. Young evangelicals had spaces, including newspapers, fan magazines, and concerts, in which they could develop their identities as Christians. Third, by expressing beliefs within the vernacular of contemporary culture, evangelical youth culture reflected the savvy of cultural activists who sought to make it easier for young people to witness to their peers. Yet Christian cultural products amounted to more than appropriation or co-optation of secular styles: rather, they demonstrate the genuine passion many young people felt for both their music and beliefs. They also provided young people with the opportunity to become active "speakers" in the cultural debate on values and beliefs. In this third step, devout youths became agents for reintroducing public religiosity into public spaces, including schools.

At the beginning of the Jesus Movement, Will Herberg expressed hope that the "moral and religious earnestness" that young converts brought to their witnessing would benefit conservative politics.[20] In the thirty years following Herberg's article, young Christians perfected a language that blended religiosity with current trends in youth culture. This religious worldview, in turn, meshed with neoliberal demands for personal responsibility, self-control, and "family values" that intensified during the conservative revolution of the 1980s and 1990s.

## THE JESUS MOVEMENT: THE COUNTER TO THE COUNTERCULTURE

The emergence of the Jesus Movement in the late 1960s signaled that political progressives held no monopoly on youth or rebellion. In previous periods of American history, enthusiastic religion's focus on individual salvation and the "self-validating nature" of spiritual experience provided a challenge to established hierarchies.[21] Moreover, as historian R. Laurence Moore has shown, evangelicals' long-standing sense of dispossession vis-à-vis the dominant culture has allowed them to portray themselves as disfranchised populists.[22] The evangelical nonconformist was, in other words, a rebel with a cross. This outlook blended with the alienation expressed in the 1960s, when white middle-class American youths of the New Left drew on their feelings of marginality to articulate a vision of democracy that vowed to restore "authenticity" through radical social change. Commenting on the importance of "authenticity" to the young people who populated the YMCA conferences and civil rights and feminist groups at the University of Texas, historian Doug Rossinow has argued that the campus youth movement of the sixties should be viewed primarily as an existentialist search for self-meaning and only secondarily as a leftist attempt at structural change.[23] If the sixties are recast this way, the Jesus Movement's embrace of authenticity and marginality—and the individualistic and moralistic turn of its young religious converts—becomes a critical part of the decade rather than an aberration.

Although Christian anti-rock critics viewed both youth culture and the social movements of the 1960s as potentially dangerous forces, the decade saw growth in evangelical Christianity as a result of the Jesus Movement, a youth revival that began in California. Many of the converts considered themselves the authentic inheritors of the spirit of the 1960s. As sociologist Stephen Kent has argued, at the end of the decade, many disillusioned youths turned from leftist political engagement to Christian and Eastern faiths that allowed them to shift the focus of transformation from social structures to the self.[24] Robert Ellwood, a sociologist who studied the Jesus Movement in the early 1970s, noted that while the counterculture and Jesus Movement differed in their methods for inducing experience, there was a continuity of feeling—especially the sense of individual protest and alienation.[25] Evangelical authors Ronald M. Enroth, Edward E. Ericson Jr., and C. Breckinridge Peters, who were critical of the Jesus Movement's excessive emphasis on experience and its devaluation of social engagement, noted affinities with the counterculture in both the youth revival's street ministries and the era's new churches.[26] In 1998 Christian rock critic Steve Rabey described the revival as a counter to the counterculture, observing that young people turned to Jesus when they realized that "free love could be costly, trips could be bad and cults could be expressways to the heart of spiritual darkness."[27]

Members of the Jesus Movement hoped to harness aspects of youth culture to express the emotional intensity of religion as well as the importance of personal salvation and self-control. Rock 'n' roll was a particularly important medium in the Jesus Movement, as young converts believed "God could redeem and use their music just the same as He had done with them." Christian activist Randy Matthews claimed, "For the masses today, the greatest medium for expressing the gospel is rock 'n' roll. . . . It's not even a musical form anymore; it's a culture, and it's a lifestyle. The pulpit of this generation and the next is the guitar."[28] Outside the organizational hierarchy of established churches, young converts established their own record labels (Calvary Chapel's Maranatha! Music in 1971), convened their own music festivals (Explo '72 in Dallas), and started their own music magazines (*CCM* in 1978). When musician Larry Norman recorded the song "Why Should the Devil Have All the Good Music?" in 1972, he captured the spirit of a youth movement unwilling to cede any terrain to secular culture.[29]

Some Christian authors, noting that rock music had originated in the gospel tradition, argued that their actions were not redemptive but were instead a reclamation project. Within this understanding of rock, the stories of Elvis Presley, Little Richard, Jerry Lee Lewis, and other legends who had been reared in Christian churches in the South were "cautionary parables" about the tensions between the world and the spirit. At the same time, critics were encouraged by references to God and Jesus as well as the "fascination with eternity" in the music of the 1950s, 1960s, and 1970s: for example, even if George Harrison's "My Sweet Lord" did not refer to Jesus, his song reflected a "journey of self-discovery."[30] The Jesus Movement also praised musicals such as *Jesus Christ Superstar* and *Godspell* that depicted figures from the New Testament. *Rock in Jesus,* a magazine created by Jesus Movement members to provide news of religious rock releases, reflected believers' simultaneous interests in secular and Christian music. The back cover of the first issue was a full-page advertisement for Joan Baez's folk album *Blessed Are . . . ,* which included songs written by Mick Jagger and John Lennon and Paul McCartney. Yet the magazine also profiled key figures from the Jesus Movement such as Larry Norman and Love Song; printed lyrics to Christian rock songs and advertisements for Christian rock radio shows, and attempted to create a narrative of the "Jesus Rock" movement.[31]

Christian rock was not the only cultural product of the era. The Jesus Movement spawned a wide range of religious groups that helped transform the practices of evangelical Christianity, including the Children of God, the Christian World Liberation Front, and the more mainstream Calvary Chapel.[32] Members of the Jesus Movement spurred sales of Hal Lindsey's *The Late Great Planet Earth* (1970), which prophesied the end of the world based on readings of current events and which had 9 million copies in print by 1978, and *The Living Bible* (1971), a paraphrased translation that sold over 3 million copies in its first year of publication alone.[33] By the late 1960s, a number of "Jesus papers," a variation on the theme of the underground papers established in the 1960s, appeared across the country.[34] The newspapers included the *Hollywood Free Paper* in Los Angeles, *Right On!* in Berkeley, and *The Truth* in Spokane.[35]

Along with the era's rock music and rock commentary, the print culture of the Jesus Movement demonstrates how young converts adapted the rhetoric of generational and social rebellion; this outsider's stance had long held a place within American evangelicalism. Although many attacks were aimed at elders within the church, young converts broadened their critique to include social institutions. However, converts did not put the language of rebellion in the service of structural change; on the contrary, they exalted personal holiness and condemned the counterculture as well as the antiwar, feminist, and other social movements. Within this language, rebellion became an individualized stance, and personal morality became the basis for reform.

Rather than downplaying the generation gap, members of this cohort highlighted its significance to the Jesus Movement. Paul Baker, a Christian disc jockey and the founder of the Jesus Movement magazine *Rock in Jesus,* has described the late 1960s in his history of Jesus music. Whereas anti-rock activists of the 1960s and 1970s tended to ignore context in their criticisms of youth, Baker located the causes of youth rebellion in social and cultural changes rather than in music. He recalled a generation angry about "wars, greediness, hypocrisy, pollution, bigotry, technology, and the Establishment in general." This generation sought answers in several avenues: there were "the radicals" whose solution was "to destroy"; the "less aggressive hippies" who coped with chaos by escaping "into the world of drugs"; and the "flower children" whose "desired world was one of peace, brotherhood, love, and understanding" but who "lacked the knowledge" necessary to live their ideals.[36]

But to Baker, blame for the crisis of the 1960s ultimately rested with the liberal Christian church's failure to minister to the generation that came of age during the decade. According to Baker, dissatisfied youths "were trying desperately to find answers which technology could not provide, and solutions which American Christianity had failed to convey to them," perhaps because they associated religion with parents and institutions rather than with Jesus Christ.[37] Baker presented the Jesus Movement, an "underground church," as a solution amidst the confusion whose participants hoped to "communicate Christ to millions of stranded and confused young people caught in the middle of a Generation Gap," as well as to instill "joy and excitement about true

Christian living" in youths who had grown up as Christians but who had "grown tired of church life."[38] Baker presented young people as victims of, rather than aggressors in, the national generation gap.

Other members of the Jesus Movement also believed their movement would revitalize Christianity without the help of the institutional church. They found a model for their actions in Jesus, whom they saw as a "rebel" who challenged "the tyrannical chains of religious tradition."[39] Many texts suggested parallels between the Jesus Movement's troubles with the institutional church and Jesus' confrontations with the Pharisees and Sadducees, the elders who opposed many of his teachings.[40] One author proudly labeled the Christians of the New Testament as "revolutionaries" and Jesus as a "rebel against the established order"; the same author speculated that Paul "probably caused more riots and arrests than any other person in his day."[41] Other writers adapted an anti-church stance as well as the vernacular of youth culture to describe Jesus' actions. In a *Hollywood Free Paper* article entitled "Can You Dig It?" Rich Schmidt criticized churches for presenting Jesus as "some kind of a prejudiced, middle-class materialist" or a "milk-toast [sic] character that wants to spoil your bag with a bunch of rules and regulations." Presenting his argument for belief, Schmidt told readers, "Jesus Christ is truly the Cool One because He took the rap for you and me on the cross, so that we could have life—the real down-inside kind of life that hits at the very core of your being."[42] Jesus became the rebel rather than the antidote to rebellion, providing the Jesus Movement with a subversive edge even as it rejected the transgressive behavior endorsed by the wider counterculture.

Young believers gave Jesus a visual makeover to help him attain wide acceptance within the counterculture. As historian Colleen McDannell has written, prior to the 1960s many Protestants favored the depiction of Jesus rendered in Werner Sallman's *Head of Christ* (1940), but critics complained that the painting made Jesus resemble a "bearded woman."[43] In contrast, the image of Jesus that proved to be most popular within the Jesus Movement was created by Richard Hook in 1964 and copyrighted by a Lutheran publishing house. In the painting, which differed from other postwar depictions of Jesus in its depiction of a "masculine" Christ, an Anglo-Saxon Jesus looks straight ahead and appears to be about to speak. He has long, unkempt hair, a beard, and a deep tan; even his clothes, which resemble a hooded sweatshirt made of rough-hewn fabric rather than robes made of finely spun cloth, created an aura of masculinity. Hook presciently painted a hippie Jesus who fit perfectly within the counterculture.[44]

The creators of *Right On!* the newspaper of the Berkeley-based Christian World Liberation Front, and the Los Angeles-based *Hollywood Free Paper* were among those who found a model of inspiration in Jesus.[45] In fashioning their image of Jesus, they seemed to draw directly from the drug culture. In 1969 both papers published a broadside that resembled a western-style "Wanted" poster. The poster's text repeated the anti-authoritarian, anti-institutional stance of the movement by providing aliases, an identity ("notorious leader of an underground liberation movement"), charges (including "practicing medicine, wine-making, and food distribution without a license" and "associating with known criminals, radicals, subversives, prostitutes, and street people"), an appearance ("hippie type"), and a generalized warning ("His insidiously inflammatory message is particularly dangerous to young people who haven't been taught to ignore him yet"). Yet the accompanying mug shot, a simple drawing that depicted Jesus looking to his left, was the most revealing part of the poster, as Jesus bore an uncanny resemblance to the man (a nineteenth-century French soldier) on the packaging for Zig-Zag cigarette papers, a popular product within the drug culture.[46] With this visual usurpation of a drug culture icon, the underground papers of the Jesus Movement demonstrated their desire to intervene in the counterculture by investing "secular" objects with religious meaning and redeploying them for evangelism.

Jesus' rebellious reputation inspired some young Christians to direct their critique at a range of social institutions, especially those that seemingly condoned sinfulness. In 1965 Arthur Blessitt, a Southern Baptist youth minister, carried the Jesus Movement's anti-authoritarian edge to the Sunset Strip in Los Angeles. Blessitt's genius for evangelism stemmed from his refusal to acknowledge a separation between sacred and secular spaces. He told young Christians that he wanted to teach them how to "revolutionize your neighborhood, your city, and the whole world" by witnessing in "bars, brothels, and pornographic bookstores, as well as on buses and airplanes and in schools."[47]

In the late 1960s, Blessitt turned the threat to the survival of his Christian coffeehouse, "His Place," into a referendum: "[Is] there room for Jesus Christ on the Sunset Strip?"[48] Jesus' success on the strip apparently hinged on Blessitt's ability to shut down the strip joints, adult bookstores, and drug dens. Blessitt argued that his work helped decrease the numbers of young people on the strip, as he urged converts to return home to their families. For this crusade, Blessitt again unsheathed his most powerful populist denunciations. Rather than

Figure 2. The depiction of Jesus printed in the Christian newspapers *Right On!* and the *Hollywood Free Paper* closely resembled that of the man on the package for Zig-Zag cigarette papers, a popular product of the sixties drug culture. Reprinted from the *Hollywood Free Paper* 1, no. 1 (October 1969).

working within the system to rid the strip of vice, Blessitt instead condemned "the four prongs of the Establishment" that controlled it: area
club owners, real estate brokers, the Sheriff's Department, and the West
Hollywood Chamber of Commerce. Not content to draw the line at
mere rhetoric, Blessitt also dabbled in symbolic action. When he was
evicted from his building in 1969 for having an illegal lease, he drew a
parallel between Jesus' crucifixion and his own legal problems by chain-
ing himself to a wooden cross on the sidewalk in protest. Blessitt later
recalled his decision to fight the establishment: "I was ready to go down
to the wire against the opposition. All they had was money, guns, influence, intimidation, and jails. I would have a New Testament in my hand,
a cross at my back, and Christ at my side. I couldn't lose."[49] By claiming
a piece of the Sunset Strip, Blessitt cast himself as a lonely religious
underdog who clashed with law enforcement and business interests. He
sealed his reputation as a maverick when the American Civil Liberties
Union defended him in his eviction case and in a loitering case that
resulted from his arrest by sheriffs for street witnessing.

Although in railing against "the Establishment," Blessitt and his fellow
believers echoed other social movements of the 1960s, they were concerned with personal morality and piety rather than with structural social
change. "One Way," the movement symbol that depicted an index finger
raised toward heaven, captures believers' approach to reform. Young conservative Christians viewed the counterculture as well as the antiwar and
feminist movements with skepticism. As sociologist Stephen Kent has
observed, the religious movements of the early 1970s promised a revolution, but one that was "fueled by the purified lives of the devout and spiritually trained" who could be integrated into society if they avoided drugs
and promiscuity and developed a strong work ethic. This promise directed
young converts away challenging social structures and institutions and
toward joining a mainstream society that emphasized self-reliance and
self-determination.[50] The revolution would be personal, not political.

Because the young converts viewed themselves as the authentic heirs of
the counterculture, they invested considerable time in attacking pre-
tenders to their throne. They inevitably called attention to the drug culture that developed during the 1960s, particularly the use of psychedelic
drugs and its connection to spirituality.[51] The critics were especially critical of the Grateful Dead, whose fans came to represent the countercultural search for spiritual power. They argued that the drug culture offered
empty religiosity, exposing religious experience to an array of spiritual
dabblers and dilettantes. LSD, for example, was said to reduce "the

religious impulse to a dissolving sugar cube on the tip of your tongue," making the "devotion, discipline, and self-deprivation" usually associated with spirituality into a "trip, maybe more accurately a holiday, eighteen hours long, embarking anytime, night or day."[52] The drug culture subordinated meaning to the senses of sight, sound, and touch.[53] By these Christians' accounts, authentic religion could be found only through faith in God and being "born again." Sociologist Robert Ellwood, noting this inseparable link between the drug culture and the Jesus Movement, argued that the cultures were bound "not only by feeling-oriented assumptions" but also by "the personal narratives of persons who have moved from one to the other. Like [Alcoholics Anonymous], the Jesus movement is tied to the psychology of its greatest enemy."[54]

Despite conservative believers' criticism of the drug culture, when Bob Dylan, the man who gave the Beatles their first taste of marijuana, became a born-again Christian and began attending Bible studies at Vineyard Fellowship in the late 1970s, evangelicals giddily welcomed him aboard.[55] CCM offered several reviews of and features on Dylan's Christian albums, which included Slow Train Coming, Saved, and Shot of Love. In a 1980 review the magazine remarked that Saved "relies not on subtleties or metaphors but rather on the composer's personal response to his relationship with the Lord." In the next month's issue, one feature on Dylan's conversion speculated about the expanded audience that might hear Christian rock; another article noted the symbolic import of the spiritual redemption of a sixties counterculture icon.[56] After 1983, when Dylan released Infidels and allegedly returned to Judaism, interest in his faith waned.

Members of the Jesus Movement believed that Christianity provided the true path out of the social, environmental, and political controversies that arose during the sixties. Jesus concerts provided a glimpse of how religious revival could transform the nation. Campus Crusade for Christ organized Explo '72, a multiday event in Dallas for young Christians that culminated in an assembly at the Cotton Bowl headlined by Billy Graham and followed by a Christian concert. In the wake of the concert, Frank M. Edmondson Jr., who also published under the name Paul Baker, reflected on the utopian possibilities of the concert. Admitting that a Dallas newspaper survey had identified the majority of concertgoers as "middle-class, conservative Christians," Edmondson argued that "regardless of whether the delegates were low-class, middle-class, upper-class or no-class; regardless of whether they were conservative or liberal, short or tall, tan or white, brown or black, young or old, one fact remains: they got along." He boasted about the absence of arrests, the courtesy shown to police, the patience exhibited by departing concertgoers—no angry bursts of horns or frustrated cursing from this crowd—and the care with which they stacked trash at designated receptacles. Edmondson contrasted this orderliness to a recent festival at a venue in Pennsylvania and another series of shows by the Rolling Stones in Washington (implicitly comparing the event to the band's tragic Altamont concert in 1969) and concluded that the young people and adults at Explo had been practicing "Christ-like living."

Edmondson saw something that went beyond an exhibition of Christian habits: he saw the Christian spirit as a prescription for the social problems that plagued the nation. Edmondson offered Explo '72 as an updated version of John Winthrop's vision of a city on a hill: by momentarily standing apart from society, the delegates offered a window on solutions made possible by lives dedicated to Christ. Edmondson suggested, for example, that the environment "could be saved by everyone being pollution conscious," because "it worked at Explo"—where concertgoers had picked up after themselves. Referring to the war in Vietnam, he speculated that wars would likewise cease "if all men aspired to the qualities of Christ" as they had at Explo; indeed, he predicted that the issues of "prejudice, over-population, abortion," and "every other problem to the last" could be overcome through devotion to Jesus. That was the reason for the crowd's "cold response" to antiwar protesters. In conclusion, Edmondson reduced social problems to individual sinfulness: antiwar activists were "working from the wrong end" by trying to change policies rather than hearts.[57]

As the members of the Jesus Movement aged and the first generation of contemporary Christian music faded, the 1960s remained a model for Christian critics. By the 1990s, Christian music had become a multimillion-dollar business, with a chart in *Billboard* magazine and non-Christian ownership of Christian record labels.[58] The Jesus Movement's view of social change persisted—that it could occur only through individual conversion and personal action. This remained the model for Christian punk and heavy metal fans who followed in their footsteps.

## "CHRISTIAN PUNK?": CHRISTIAN UNDERGROUND FAN MAGAZINES, 1984–2000

The network of Christian rock bands, labels, music festivals, and venues established by young believers during the Jesus Movement flourished in the 1970s. By the late 1980s, however, the contemporary

Christian music industry had a corporate feel: fueled by pop artists such as Amy Grant and Michael W. Smith, the genre's solid sales were beginning to attract secular investors. The Christian video market for children also expanded, as series such as Focus on the Family's McGee and Me and Big Ideas Productions' VeggieTales sold briskly after their debuts in the early 1990s. In her analysis of Christian media, Heather Hendershot suggests that evangelicals drew on heavily commodified forms of resistance identity intended to make kids feel "less alienated from American consumer culture." Hendershot links conservative Christians' acceptance of commercial culture to a growing desire for solid middle-class respectability that was expressed in consumerist terms: these products appealed to Christian parents because they were legible to adult interpretation.[59]

A number of church and parachurch organizations established publications aimed at safely integrating Christian teenagers into church, home, and society. These periodicals included *Brio*, a girls' magazine established by Focus on the Family in the early 1990s, and *Campus Life*, a teen magazine founded in 1942 and owned by the evangelical periodical *Christianity Today*. With a circulation of nearly 120,000 in 1994, *Campus Life* resembled a Christian version of teen-themed magazines like *Seventeen*. Like its secular counterparts, the glossy magazine covered a range of issues ostensibly of interest to teens, including dating, music, school, and family relationships. The magazine emphasized self-control and chastity among teenagers. Some features were written entirely in first-person from the perspective of a young, struggling Christian, while others began with questions from teenagers that were answered in the body of the article. To link the first-person accounts with "real" teenagers, the magazine illustrated articles with close-ups of adolescents. One article entitled "I Am What I Follow" appeared in the magazine's "Spark" section, which professed to offer "Help for Life's Hassles." In the article, a "new Christian" recounted both the experience of being born again and continued struggles over self-control, anger, and morality. Through the use of first-person narrative, the article subtly guided youths toward reflection on their lapses of self-control.[60] Another department, "Person to Person," provided religiously informed answers to questions reportedly posed by teenagers about grief, loneliness, and conflict with parents.[61] Another regular column, "Love, Sex, and the Whole Person," reinforced "God's perspective" on ideas about heterosexuality, personal chastity, and marriage by answering questions such as "Is it OK to pray for someone to go out with?"[62]

Yet there were also magazines in which young Christians developed their identities with a less direct adult filter. Just as the underground publications of the 1960s had inspired young converts to start their own papers, young evangelicals in the 1980s established an array of fan magazines that mimicked the style of the era's punk magazines. Zines, as they were called, were photocopied magazines created by fans from their homes. Amateur participation in the creative process was intended to democratize cultural production as part of a broader punk critique of a social ethic that had turned consumption into a passive act.[63] Like punk rock musicians who rejected the notion of "professionalism" in sound, zine proponents embraced a do-it-yourself aesthetic that spurned slick layouts, journalistic distance, and glossy paper in favor of cut-and-paste layouts, confrontational editorials and reviews, rough drawings, and photocopied pages. The language and layout of the original zines, such as *Sniffin Glue* and *Ripped and Torn,* suggested the urgency of "memos from the front line."[64] Young Christians, on the other hand, found the genre well suited to amateur (but not necessarily angry) evangelists who viewed themselves as soldiers on the moral front lines. The personal—often emotional—style of the genre, as well as its participatory nature, provided young Christians with a way to express their faith. With titles such as *Gospel Metal, Heaven's Metal,* and *White Throne,* the magazines were usually written by and for young believers interested in the Christian music scene; the magazines, in turn, helped build a grassroots network of fans. Some magazines, including *Heaven's Metal,* began as simple photocopied products but grew more professionalized in layout and writing style over time; others remained steadfastly simple—if they continued to be published at all. From 1980, when Chris Yambar started *The Activist,* through the late 1990s, when Internet access and personal websites became widespread, evangelical Christians established nearly two hundred fan magazines (not counting those that originated in the United Kingdom, the Netherlands, Brazil, and elsewhere outside the United States). A significant number of these publications began in Sunbelt states: of nearly 180 titles with known addresses, more than 25 originated in Southern California (with 2 more in Northern California), 14 in Florida, and 13 in Texas.[65] The strength of Christian fan culture in these areas reflected the shift in evangelicalism's balance of power toward Sunbelt suburbs.

Christian fan magazines betrayed their secular influence in layout style, tone, subject matter, and musical preference, but the zines also inverted punk so that they reflected a moralistic, not nihilistic, outlook.

# HEAVEN'S METAL

VOL.I
#1
July '85

What is it? It is the expression of love &
answers to problems from a Christian world-view.
This is the first issue of a bi-monthly newsletter
dedicated to hard rock in the Christian music world.
This newsletter welcomes all Christian bands and will
feature free promotion of all interested parties. If
you rock for Christ, send us some info on your band
and we'll print it. Although this newsletter is
called <u>Heaven's Metal</u>, from time to time it will
feature groups who some may not consider metal.
(ie: Arkangel, AD, Jimmy Hotz, Darrell Mansfield,
Vision, Avion, Dennis Welch, etc.) This is a mid-70's
definition of metal. When I was younger, anything
from Aerosmith-LedZep was considered heavy metal.

This issue's feature group: STRYPER

OZ FOX, of Stryper, with a lollipop in Austin, Texas.

Figure 3. The fanzine *Heaven's Metal* debuted as a six-page photocopied newsletter that used typewritten and handwritten text. The magazine evolved into
*HM*, by 2000 a glossy publication with over 15,000 subscribers. Reprinted by
permission from *Heaven's Metal/HM* Magazine (www.hmmag.com).

On one hand, many of these fanzines, like the media that Hendershot discusses, simply allowed kids to engage in mild rebellion that might, for example, poke fun at self-satisfied churchgoers and fundamentalist squares while otherwise attempting to integrate young people into church, home, and society. On the other hand, the youth culture's anti-institutional language also drew on the same long-standing evangelical rhetorical tradition of dissent that the Jesus Movement had tapped. Other magazines were determined to position themselves as heirs to both the come-outer religious tradition and such secular expressions of alienation as punk rock. Despite the contrast in rhetorical positions, the Christian fan magazines all shared the goal of creating a distinct Christian youth identity that advocated strict doctrinal and moral codes.

While some fan magazines attempted to attract non-Christians, most published under the assumption that their audience was composed of Christians.[66] The magazines' content offered models for religious inspiration, often through music reviews, band interviews, and alerts about upcoming concerts. *CCM*, a trade publication established in 1978 that evolved into the genre's definitive magazine, attempted to steer youths' interpretation of music through an occasional column entitled "Getting the Message." Organized around themes such as "Satan," "Sexual Temptation," and "Abortion," the column presented readers with the moral messages of a range of artists and styles.[67] One newsletter, *Take a Stand*, provided Bible study guides for topics such as "wisdom and discernment," "gossip," and "spiritual growth."[68] The newsletter also offered a "Correspondence Directory," which listed the names, ages, and musical influences of people who wanted to hear "from other Christian rockers."[69] *CCM* and its smaller relatives also regularly offered pieces on the "lifestyle Christianity." These articles featured artists—ranging from pop stars Amy Grant and Steven Curtis Chapman to metal groups such as Stryper and Barren Cross—testifying to the importance of faith in their lives and in the creation of their music. Readers who failed to draw inspiration from the stories of Christian musicians could focus instead on the personal testimonies of personal salvation published in zines like *Rizzen Roxx* and *The Narrow Path*. In these stories, converts spoke of how religion—usually in the figure of Jesus—guided them through difficult periods of their lives when, for example, they had considered suicide or developed a drug habit.[70]

The fan magazines also covered Cornerstone, a much-anticipated annual event that had come to define contemporary Christian music.

A descendent of Explo '72, Cornerstone was more narrowly cast than that earlier exemplar of Christianity: the event was clearly for believers—an affirmation of Christianity rather than a beacon for society. Jesus People USA, a residential religious community in Chicago, began Cornerstone at the Lake County, Illinois, fairgrounds in 1984. The community possessed ideal credentials for staging a Christian rock festival: it had a long history of outreach programs including a long-running magazine (*Cornerstone*) and a well-respected music ministry led by The Resurrection Band (Rez), one of the first Christian hard rock bands. By the late 1980s, the festival had established itself as an annual convention for young Christian rock fans. Advertisements for the event appeared in nearly every Christian music magazine, and enthusiastic first-person accounts of fans willing to endure interminable road trips, miserable camping accommodations, and adverse weather conditions for the opportunity to partake in three days of concerts by the genre's biggest acts became standard fare in fanzines.

Zine editors, like many revival preachers, outlined a shortened path to salvation and regeneration, leaving little need for doctrinal or theological disquisition. Most tended to equate Christianity with a personal relationship with Jesus. For example, in an issue of *Rizzen Roxx*, editor Judd Harper explained the basic requirements for a church to follow Jesus: salvation through Jesus, belief in the Bible's literal truth, and an emphasis on fellowship and community. Basic tenets like these made worship practices flexible, allowing music to assume a primary role in young Christians' faith.[71] Another zine, *Different Drummer*, published an essay that put forth a similarly straightforward path to salvation while dismissing religious sectarianism.[72]

One magazine that did emphasize doctrine and sermons, *The Pendragon*, had only a fleeting existence. While other magazines featured a music-intensive format, *The Pendragon* put doctrine first, literally. Rather than making a band interview or concert review the lead article, editor Jeff McCormack offered articles such as "Saving Faith?" and "A Brief and Untechnical Statement of Faith" that—titles notwithstanding—were loaded with complex doctrine and biblical proof texts more reminiscent of a Jonathan Edwards sermon than a fan magazine for teenagers.[73] McCormack explained that he founded the publication because he had seen "too many people who seem to base their whole salvation and Christianity on music or an experience in connection with music." He initially strove for balance, but by the final installment of the magazine's four-issue run, McCormack nearly ignored music altogether,

running twenty-five pages of sermons and doctrinal explication alongside one page of music news. The cover did warn readers of the issue's
contents: "A lot less music, a lot more Jesus."[74] Jesus Music founder
Larry Norman had sounded a similar alarm in 1968 when he tried to
name People!'s first album *We Need a Whole Lot More of Jesus and a
Lot Less Rock 'n' Roll,* but few other magazines saw a contradiction
between the two.[75]

Although salvation held an important place in young Christians'
belief system, the zines often distinguished their readers from the world
through adherence to a strict personal code of conduct rather than
through doctrine. The zines urged readers to exercise self-control and
assured them they would find an improved state of satisfaction through
religion; these behavioral norms mirrored the renunciatory tendencies
of the secular straight-edge movement viewed as a reaction to the
nihilism of early punk. The magazines often specified the kinds of temptation young people needed to resist. In an article titled "Eternal Life,"
*Rizzen Roxx* editor Judd Harper told readers that a convert needed to
"take control" of his or her life by repenting from sin and following
"righteousness" rather than "foolish desires of the flesh" such as "getting drunk, smoking dope, having sex outside marriage, cutting people
down, and being a jerk."[76] The magazine's regular comic strip also dealt
with sexual temptation.[77] Another zine, *Gospel Metal,* tried to
empathize directly with readers by offering situations—parents' divorce,
the end of a relationship, or a hangover after a party—and counseling
them to avoid "Misery, Opposition, Remorse, and Emptiness" by opening their hearts to Jesus, reading the Bible, talking to God, and going to
church.[78]

When the many zines that focused narrowly on the Christian subculture contained any satirical commentary, it tended to poke fun at sanc-
timonious church elders and at their more conservative Christian
brethren. The jabs resembled some of the Jesus Movement's complaints
about the "generation gap" in the church but used less confrontational
language. For example, *Rizzen Roxx* editor Judd Harper published a
picture of himself with long hair and sunglasses and joked about how he
had ventured into the bookstore at fundamentalist Bob Jones University
to get his publication on the magazine display shelf. On the same page,
Harper thanked the "underground short-haired metalheads" who
bought the magazine at a bookstore near Liberty University, the fundamentalist college in Virginia established by Jerry Falwell.[79] In another
issue, *Rizzen Roxx*'s resident comic strip artist, Shawn Finley, published

"A RAD guide to Church Members," in which he poked fun at stock church characters familiar to young Christians—preachers, choir directors, Sunday school teachers, and pastors' kids.[80] In another edition, Finley offered a humorous series of "Tips on Witnessing" that mocked evangelicals' perceived cultural deafness and backwardness while reassuring readers that they were among the stylish. Finley's characters in the strip recommended that would-be evangelists avoid wearing "a three-piece polyester suit that went out of style in 1974"; they should instead "dress like the kind of people you are witnessing to."[81] These rather mild examples exhibit mischief more than rebellion against church leadership and were more likely to produce nods of agreement than any action. In fact, the features seem likely to affirm existing religious beliefs by suggesting that readers were better equipped for evangelism than their stricter brethren.

Most Christian fan magazines devoted the bulk of their pages to delineating the path to salvation and dissecting the latest releases by Christian rock bands. While some magazines focused on Christian audiences and Christian cultural trends, others attempted to position themselves and their readers for engagement with secular audiences and music. Some tried to position themselves and their readers as outsiders.

Engagement with popular culture made Christians more aware of the interests of their non-Christian friends and neighbors. In addition to their coverage of evangelical groups, magazines such as *Cutting Edge* and *CCM* occasionally reviewed releases and concert performances of mainstream bands like U2 whose members included professed believers.[82] Although some readers complained that this inclusiveness watered down the message of Christian music, others applauded *CCM* for keeping them apprised of what music was popular among secular audiences. One reader suggested that by covering "secular artists who are singing songs with spiritual references," *CCM* was giving readers "information which may be used to break the ice and discuss spiritual matters with the unsaved on a level of their interest."[83]

*Heaven's Metal,* renamed *Hard Music (HM)* in the early 1990s, had an innovative strategy for engaging secular heavy metal artists in discussions about spirituality. Although the magazine primarily covered the Christian hard music scene, each issue offered a word-for-word transcript of an interview with a member of a secular band, such as Sammy Hagar, Kirk Hammett of Metallica, and Scott Rockenfield of Queensryche. The exchanges included questions about a band's projects or tours as well as its members' lifestyles. At some point in the session, the interviewer always asked two questions, "What do you think of Jesus Christ?" and "What do you think of [Jesus'] claims to be the way, the truth, and the life?"[84] *HM* twice interviewed members of Megadeth, a band singled out by some Christian conservatives for its irreverent lyrical content. Despite these criticisms, *HM* editor Doug Van Pelt conducted a lengthy discussion about values and spirituality with lead singer Dave Mustaine, a privately religious person who used religious metaphors and imagery in songs such as "Looking Down the Cross." Mustaine was initially a reluctant witness, telling Van Pelt, "I don't want to get heavy into religion in this interview." But Van Pelt patiently persisted and found that the two shared not just a common taste in metal music but also a similar value system:

> DM: . . . I've seen more stuff than you could possibly ever see in your lifetime. . . . My own pastor said that I could do more by living my life right, playing hard, and doing my gigs, than going around saying, "Hallelujah, Jesus loves you." And I know that God knows that too, so I don't do that shtick. . . . I'm a father, I'm a husband. I'm loyal to my wife and family, and that's the best thing that I can do for them.
> DVP: . . . The true definition is "Christ-like." . . .
> DM: . . . you know, me being in a 12-step program, one of the main tenets of this program is to treat people like you want to be treated. And that goes back to the Sermon on the Mount, where there are the two new commandments that Christ put down. One about, "love God with all your whole heart, soul, mind and body," and the other one about, "Love your neighbor as yourself." . . . Those are the two core things I live by.[85]

The column provided a model for Christian music fans who wished to witness to fans of popular music. Christian readers could learn that although mainstream bands may not preach the gospel in their music, band members might nonetheless share their "Christian" values; the only way to find out was to interact with them. Instead of judging unfamiliar artists by their appearances, youths were told, they should keep the faith by searching for the godly core in everything—even "black" metal.

In some instances, musicians were a bit more spiritually omnivorous than the interviewers expected. In 1997 *HM* interviewed Sammy Hagar, who enthusiastically embraced a broad spectrum of world religions and philosophies. Interviewer and garrulous musician bonded over parenthood (Hagar had three children, including a newborn girl) and over the theme of forgiveness before the interviewer, noting that the songs on the new album reflected a "Judeo-Christian outlook," inquired if Hagar had experienced a religious conversion. Hagar responded:

I'm not an organized religious guy at all. I don't go to church. . . . I believe in prayer. I believe in the power of it, that it has power if you pray and project positive thoughts, there is power there, and that's a good thing. The love side, about unconditional love, which is the Christ philosophy, that you give love unselfish love—forgiveness, amnesty, that kind of thing—but I have Buddhist philosophies and I have Zen philosophies, and I have Krishna philosophies. That's just me. . . . And what I try to do, is I try to take any great man that's ever walked this planet, that has had something good to say, then I read about him, it affects me, and I'm in. I'm going, "Hey, I'll take that philosophy and add it to mine and continue on in my life." I want to be good, and I want the world to be good. I want to share happiness and goodness with everyone.[86]

Although later in the same interview Hagar admitted to being "more of a Christian," his acceptance of multiple religious outlooks broadened the conversation beyond exclusively Christian truth. When asked directly what he thought about Jesus, Hagar responded, "He's one of the greatest men that ever walked the earth," but the artist also refused to settle on one true religion. He continued:

I think [Christianity is] one of the great religions of all time, but there are other religions. You can't just be confined to Christianity, like some organized Christian churches say, "You come to this church; you can't go to another church." That is wrong. That's like, "Hold it now." You can't go to another church? (Bleep!) You can do anything you want, as long as you don't hurt another person, you don't inflict your power on a person, you don't try to do evil to another person. There are certain rules you follow, and you can walk into any church, you know, Hinduism, and all those things, they have a lot to offer as well. All those men are like Jesus. They were a different avenue to God, and I do not believe that Christianity is the only avenue to God. . . . I believe you can be born onto this planet and be enlightened and understand God from birth, and never even hear the words "Jesus" or "Buddha." You could still understand God. There's a lot of different ways.[87]

The interview remained cordial, but Hagar's cheerfully promiscuous religiosity thwarted efforts to establish Christianity's monopoly on universal truth. By advocating the inclusion of all faiths in the dialogue, Hagar provided a rhetorical alternative to the binaries of Christianity/secularism and Christianity/Satanism often used in the broader cultural conversation.

Even as many young evangelicals settled into a comfortable Christian youth subculture, a sense of alienation—whether from the rest of the Christian church or the rest of the world—suffused young Christian identity in fan magazines. Some Christian cultural products were intended to make young believers feel less alienated from society, but many Christian zines took an outsider's stance. To mark their distance from the mainstream, these magazines embraced some of the conventions of the punk subculture. Punk had emerged from the historically specific conditions of late-1970s Britain, when race riots, heat waves, and an economic recession created a sense of angry nihilism among jobless working-class youths. To express their refusal to partake of mainstream norms and authority, punks mobilized a range of oppositional rhetorical practices, archetypes, and symbols. According to sociologist Dick Hebdige, the vulgar rhetoric of punk was "drenched in apocalypse" that matched the era's pervasive sense of crisis. Punk music, which emulated the rebellious sounds of the Rastafarian, represented the "white translation of black ethnicity." This sense of identification whereby alienated white working-class youths rejected "white" Britishness provided yet another incarnation of the ongoing friction between black and white Britain in the post–World War II era.[88]

Young evangelicals who embraced punk did so out of a desire to express an otherness from the so-called mainstream. Editors appropriated punk subculture's propensity for defiantly adapting derogatory labels and mimicking the language of crisis that permeated British media in the 1970s. Zine titles epitomized this attitude: *Take a Stand, Radicals for Christ, Baptized Rebellion, Radically Saved, The Nonconformist, Against the Grain, Different Drummer, Knights in Messiah's Bold Radical Army* (or *KIMBRA*), *Screams of Abel, Thieves and Prostitutes, Narrow Path,* and *Slaughter House.* The alienation that pervaded Christian punk, however, was not a refusal to assimilate into the capitalist parent culture. Whereas secular punks embraced negative labels out of a sense of irony and adopted the language of crisis out of a sense of nihilism, Christian zines signified their "otherness" out of a sense of moral righteousness.[89] The magazines that most thoroughly embraced the punk aesthetic, *Thieves and Prostitutes* and *Slaughter House,* affirmed strict religiosity among their young readers. Young evangelicals cited punk aesthetics and music as influences, but their demands also resembled elements of the come-outer tradition of Protestant sects that sought religious truth from outside establishment religious institutions: one editor described her group as a "community of faithful objectors."[90] Later in the decade, some youths solidified the connection to this tradition by poring over copies of *Jesus Freaks,* an updated version of *Foxe's Book of Martyrs,* the Reformation-era tome about religious persecution.[91]

Figure 4. Creators of the fan magazine *Thieves and Prostitutes* borrowed from the punk aesthetic to depict cultural outsiders. Illustration courtesy of *Thieves and Prostitutes* editors Alexis Neptune and John DiDonna.

Although young editors sought to proselytize among the unchurched, evangelical zines did not view their secular counterparts as allies, nor did they seek their good opinion. This was perhaps for good reason, as secular editors scoffed at the work of their Christian counterparts. In response, *Slaughter House* and *Thieves and Prostitutes* flaunted the negative reviews

Figure 5. The creator of the punk zine *Slaughter House* drew from punk aesthetics by using simple line drawings of punks. Illustration courtesy of Dave Simmons/*Slaughter House*.

given them by secular zines—and not necessarily in the Sex Pistols–era spirit of expressing appreciation or approval through expectoration. Even as Christian zines advocated personal rather than political revolution, Christian editors accused their counterparts of creating a normative standard for judging punk attitude. Rejections from secular punk merely bestowed greater authenticity on their efforts. Under a headline that read "The Reviews Are In!" *Slaughter House* editor David Simmons included a review by "Bad Newz" that described the zine as "[fifteen] pages of born-again Christian poser-punk conformity news. . . . When will these people ever give up and get the fuck out of a scene that was created to destroy everything they stand for?" A review from the revered punk zine *Maximum Rock 'n' Roll* was similarly dismissive: "More religious garbage disguised as punk . . . a sick joke?"[92] *Thieves and Prostitutes* likewise gloried in secular rejection, including dismissals from *Maximum Rock 'n' Roll* ("Lame Christian zine. Not punk.") and *The Unintelligencer* ("Looks like a zine, feels like a zine, reads like a . . . Yikes! Revival pamphlet"), though at least one reviewer concluded, "A Christian punk zine? I really don't mind."[93] In addition to the reviews, *Thieves and Prostitutes* ran magazine correspondence, including a bizarre (and dismissive) letter from GG Allin, a notoriously inflammatory and violent punk performer from the 1980s who was jailed for a time in the early 1990s for aggravated assault. The editors also took the opportunity to ridicule Glen Benton, the leader of the satanic metal band Deicide, who had mentioned *Thieves and Prostitutes* in a magazine interview.[94]

Despite their sarcastic tone, the editors of *Thieves and Prostitutes* put a great deal of thought into their assertion that they were the authentic rebels of American society. According to religious testimonials that appeared in the magazine, the publication's main contributors, John DiDonna ("the thief") and Alexis Levy Neptune ("the prostitute"), were recent converts to Christianity; DiDonna claimed to have been a drug dealer and user, while Neptune was from a nonobservant Jewish family and had dabbled in a number of religions and the occult. Unlike many fanzine creators, who seemed to publish primarily for Christian audiences and who criticized secular music and culture, DiDonna and Neptune Levy intended their publication to be used for evangelism (the magazine was free) and candidly expressed admiration for secular forms of culture. DiDonna and Neptune listed the Doors, the Damned, and Operation Ivy as their favorite bands and *Dune* and *Catcher in the Rye* as favorite novels.[95]

To establish its punk bona fides, *Thieves and Prostitutes* published a lengthy essay that traced a genealogy of punk showing the genre's cultural and dispositional parallels with Christianity. In her article "Christian Punk?" Alexis Levy Neptune outlined her response to the question "How can you be a Christian and be a punk at the same time?"

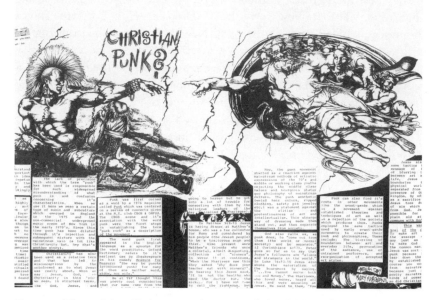

Figure 6. The article "Christian Punk?" argued that biblical figures provided models for modern punks and was accompanied by an illustration that played on Michelangelo's depiction of creation from the Sistine Chapel. Illustration courtesy of *Thieves and Prostitutes* editors Alexis Neptune and John DiDonna.

For Neptune, the stances of punk and radical Christianity were not so different; indeed, she suggested, "if Jesus were here today . . . punks would be just the people he would hang-out with and make disciples of." As described by Neptune, Christianity and punk were, at their roots, reactions to stale aesthetics: early Christians rejected the hierarchies of organized religion, while punk shunned the pretensions of art and the music industry.[96]

Neptune knew her punk history. She noted that "the punk movement started as a reaction against mainstream methods of artistic expressions of the 70's and middle or working class youths rejecting the middle class values and bourgeois status quo philosophy of mainstream culture." The "punk aesthetic," she added, helped punks separate themselves from society. Citing several New Testament verses—including one from Paul's second letter to the Corinthians that fundamentalists used to justify separation—Neptune argued that Christians are called upon to remain separate from the world. Referring to other members of the staff, all of whom were recent converts, Neptune observed, "As punks we were more willing to accept Jesus because we were already non-conformists so being accepted by the world didn't matter much to us." Neptune concluded her analysis with a series of analogies that elaborated punk rock's affinity with Christianity: as Jesus "sought to make God accessible to the common man," so punk tried "to make art accessible to the average working class guy"; just as Jesus used uneducated fishermen and shepherds to spread his message, so punk rock valued "untrained performers"; just as such biblical figures as John the Baptist and Samson used clothes and hair to highlight their devotion to God, so punks used clothes, hair, and jewelry to announce their stance toward the world.[97] In this formulation, Christian punks claimed a role in identity politics based on their marginalization vis-à-vis both the established Christian church and mainstream society.

Like the Jesus People before her, Neptune organized her understanding of religion around the figures of Jesus and a handful of iconoclastic (mostly New Testament) figures. The emphasis on the message of Jesus, rather than on a historical church, provided young people with a renewable inspiration for rebellion. Neptune ended her remarks with one final parallel: just as fanzines of the 1970s had "promoted the bands, propagated punk philosophy, and generated interest" in punk through their varied layouts and articles, so *Thieves and Prostitutes* hoped to herald the Christian punk movement through its pages and perspectives.[98]

As formulated by Neptune, both punk and Christianity provided a radical reorientation of the self through nonconformity. Whereas many punks embraced individualistic negation, Christian punks channeled their new religious code into a moral crusade that did little to challenge economic structures while attacking the perceived permissiveness of liberalism. The Christian punks echoed evangelical revivalists of the 1830s in the burned-over district, who concerned themselves with maintaining high standards of personal holiness and refused to acknowledge neutral ground in rooting out sin. Encouraged by the missionary efforts of benevolent organizations, believers tied personal religion to reform crusades such as temperance, leading to what historian Whitney Cross describes as "excessive individualism," which located evil in individual souls rather than in economic or social structures.[99] The outsider rhetoric proved an asset to Christian zine owners in the 1980s and 1990s in that it allowed them, like their predecessors in the Jesus Movement, to claim that they were the authentic exemplars of dissent in American culture.

While the staff of *Thieves and Prostitute* reveled in their disdain for secular society, others suggested that Christian distance was the result of exile from society rather than voluntary separation. In the article "What Is a Christian . . . Really?" *Gospel Metal* editor Keith Day addressed the issue of Christian identity in American society. Writing while televangelist scandals were making headlines, Day concluded that because Christendom was "under more attack than ever before," the world needed Christians to be vigilant. Day offered a moral code for believers: "Don't give in to the peer pressure around you that says that partying is all right, getting drunk and doped up is cool, that sex is o.k. before marriage and, if there's a mistake, to have an abortion." Day warned readers to be "ready for persecution and hardships." It also meant they might have to sacrifice "worldly entanglements," even give up non-Christian friends.[100]

Christian fan magazines helped young people develop boundaries for their religious identity through concepts such as salvation, fellowship, and personal morality. Fan magazine articles occasionally expressed a social gospel message more often identified with liberal than with evangelical Christianity. For example, in an interview commemorating his magazine's one-hundredth issue, *Cutting Edge* editor Dan Kennedy, who was older than most other zine publishers, lamented that his denomination, the Southern Baptist Convention, was controlled by the conservative contingent "opposed to the idea of a social gospel that says you need to be involved in changing the living conditions of people as well as their personal convictions, especially their relationship with Christ." Kennedy noted that he leaned toward the position of Jimmy Carter, another Southern Baptist, who had been criticized for emphasizing social justice over evangelism.[101] Jesus People USA was a religious community that offered church services and religiously based counseling as well as a soup kitchen and emergency shelter in Chicago.[102] While Christian punks emphasized their alienation from institutional and political Christianity, their beliefs at times intersected with conservative evangelical activists. The attitudes Christian fan magazines took regarding abortion demonstrate that a key component of Christian identity rested in one's relationship to the unregenerate world. The Christian punks at *Slaughter House* and *Thieves and Prostitutes* took the most extreme position, but other fan magazines voiced similar anti-abortion opinions.

Among all the beliefs cited in Christian magazines that distanced them from the world, the issue of abortion crystallized their personal sin and social behavior. They were united in their condemnation. *Heaven's Metal* printed an ad headlined "Abortion is murder!" that urged readers to take political action by contacting their representatives in Washington on the issue.[103] Some zines urged readers to tap into grassroots organizations that opposed abortion, as when *The Burning Bush* printed an invitation to a weekly Bible study and fellowship group in Kansas City that, besides reaching out to bands and concertgoers, included a "pro-life branch" as part of its mission.[104] One magazine editor's pro-life stance brought her into the orbit of Operation Rescue, the New York–based anti-abortion protest organization founded by Randall Terry. When a reader expressed pro-choice sentiments in a letter to *Different Drummer*, the editor asked, "Would Jesus do it?" and printed a letter from the Southern California office of Operation Rescue thanking the recipient for the editor's participation or support in the organization's three-day "Holy Week of Rescue" during Easter week in 1989. Reviewing the event, the letter documented both the number of women who had decided against having an abortion and the number of prisoners who had been born again after having heard activists' testimony while they were incarcerated.[105] Similarly, another Southern California–based publication, *Gospel Metal,* viewed the treatment of abortion protesters as evidence that "the world laughs at Christians" and that believers should be "ready for persecution and hardships." Citing protests in Cypress staged by Operation Rescue, the author complained that the "news media" had showed clips of protesters being removed from the clinics rather than depict them "boldly singing praise songs to the Lord."[106]

To show their opposition to abortion, fan magazines also printed pro-life advertisements, editorials, and articles. Other magazines believed that abortion lay only at the surface of a deeper problem. *Radically Saved* featured a pro-life article by guest columnist Rich Wilkerson. In "Abortion Is Not the #1 Problem" Wilkerson linked abortion to general sexual immorality in America, since "the sin of abortion is really a follow-up sin to the sin of fornication."[107] In 1988 *Rizzen Roxx* printed a short story by Mark Hodges about a young Christian woman who bypasses the male protesters outside an abortion clinic and, once inside, persuades a patient to forego an abortion.[108] *Slaughter House,* a free punk zine, worked its anti-abortion message into a collage on its title page. Amid text and other youth-oriented drawings pasted at odd angles is a drawing of an empty highchair on a slightly elevated platform; the chair is hooked up to electrical outlets, suggesting an executioner's chair. The drawing's caption reads, "A baby is a terrible thing to waste: Stop Abortion."[109]

*Slaughter House's* punk counterpart, *Thieves and Prostitutes,* went even further in graphically denouncing both abortion and pro-choice activists. A two-page spread at the end of one issue offered four separate condemnations of abortion. The first piece, titled "Surprise!!! More Hypocritical Facts on Abortion!!!" condemned abortion in China and Japan, denied any right to air pro-life ads in election-campaign television commercials, and—most important—decried efforts to restrain Operation Rescue activists. The piece's emotional, confrontational portrayals of the two sides—voiced with the immediacy of other punk zines—jump off the page. The article discussed a *Nightline* segment about a pro-life politician it identified (incorrectly) as Senator Bailey from Illinois; the piece labeled his debate opponent a "Femminazi." The piece also mistakenly accused the Federal Communications Commission (FCC) of "planning to ban" Bailey's pro-life ads.[110]

The final half of the article defended Operation Rescue, which in 1992 staged actions in Southern California and at the Republican National Convention in Houston, despite efforts to prevent demonstrations during the nomination meeting.[111] The authors depicted Operation Rescue in the most sympathetic tone possible, detailing how protesters' rights had been violated and damning the "leftist oppression" suffered by those who had tried "to go against the P.C. flow" and had paid with legal charges or police brutality. The piece ended with an open accusation against abortion rights advocates:

> Seems kinda sorta HYPOCRITICAL, all this fascism coming from the P.C. camp. Come on, admit it, you're as bad as the far right! You're nazis, and anyone who doesn't like your brand of liberalism or infanticide is a felon to be beaten, arrested and incarcerated. Take the plank out of those closed eyes.[112]

The article's extreme characterizations blended morality and politics. While referring to the Gospel of Luke (Luke 6:39–42), the article attacked "big government" (the FCC), political correctness, and the feminist movement and praised pro-life politicians and activists. Two of the visual condemnations of abortion were similarly strident. One targeted RU486, the so-called "abortion pill" that in 1992 was still banned in the United States. The final piece, "Runaway Fetus Meets the Feminists," was a reprint from another fanzine, *Wrong Conclusion.* In the strip, the "runaway fetus," having escaped abortion, surprises a meeting of feminists. The anatomically correct and rebellious male fetus offends the braless, buck-toothed, shorthaired feminists, who seek to silence the fetus for giving "false truth to the myth of the pre-born alive."

## MOBILIZING MORAL RIGHTEOUSNESS:
## YOUTH GROUPS AND SCHOOL PRAYER

The piety expressed in music zines had significant political value. Christian publications for youth reflected a spectrum of adult involvement ranging from adult-approved magazines such as *Brio* and *Campus Life* to self-published music zines such as *Slaughter House* and *Thieves and Prostitutes*. The latter publications signified a thriving Christian youth culture independent of any adult-influenced institutional or political structure. Christian youth groups likewise contained a range of adult involvement and influence. During the 1990s the youth religiosity expressed by school prayer groups became an important component of conservative efforts to "reclaim" suburban space for Christian values. These challenges to secularism's perceived monopoly on public space evoked the actions of earlier religious dissenters who had defied the established church by ignoring conventions that dictated when, where, and how services would be observed.[113]

Evangelical youths demonstrated agency in the cultural battles of the late twentieth century, but conservative adults helped orchestrate many of these confrontations by advising Bible study groups or offering legal advice to support Christian school activities. In addition to coordinating displays of religiosity, adult evangelical activists—in contrast to the church elders of the Old Right—discovered that they could either mobilize or co-opt young believers' moral righteousness to "restore" Christianity to the dominant spaces of suburbia. In this inverted incarnation of a moral panic, devout youths became renegade heroes and secular school administrators became the folk devils who provoked Christian outrage for their bureaucratic excesses. While the resulting confrontations and organizations may seem inorganic, it would be wrong to dismiss youths' motivations or the sense of agency they felt in witnessing. In both cases, youth piousness and alienation intersected with conservative political efforts to denounce the perceived rising tide of secularism and intolerance for religion. Young people's actions in these debates demonstrate that they became agents, not bystanders, in suburban battles over displays of religiosity. As Will Herberg had hoped in 1971, conservatives enlisted young people of faith in cultural and political causes.

Youthful religious demonstrations occurred within a new configuration of religiosity in which, in the words of Susan Harding, "power and authority are less centered."[114] Conservatives were responding in part to changes in American religious structures. As sociologist Robert

Wuthnow has shown, in the postwar era many of the sectarian divisions within Christianity receded, making distinctions between "liberal" and "conservative" Protestants more important than differences between denominations. In turn, conservative Protestant identity coalesced around issues that concerned government policy and personal morality such as abortion, pornography, homosexuality, and school prayer.[115] Although many conservatives undertook these campaigns in defense of youth, young people contributed to defining the terms and locations of the debate.

Evangelical Christians' reliance on youth religiosity coincided with both legislative lobbying efforts and legal claims intended to establish religion in public and civic spaces in the 1980s and 1990s.[116] It was the U.S. Supreme Court in the 1960s and 1970s that spurred religious conservatives like Jerry Falwell into action after it eliminated school prayer (*Engel v. Vitale*), extended the rights of criminal defendants (*Miranda v. Arizona*), and legalized abortion (*Roe v. Wade*). Many conservative Christian parents responded to these decisions, as well as those enforcing school busing, by home schooling their children or by sending them to one of the thousands of Christian private schools established during the 1970s and 1980s.[117]

But not all conservative Christians believed in educational separatism, and many Christian parents continued to try to restore religion to the nation's public schools through other means. As sociologist Christian Smith has explained, some evangelicals advocated a strategy of "engaged orthodoxy" that sought to uphold traditional theological views while seeking to transform the surrounding society and culture. These believers viewed public schools as the very places in need of evangelical influence. Sending their children to "secular" public schools, they believed, would solidify their children's religious identity through the personal interaction that proselytizing required.[118] This strategy coincided with conservative legal efforts to establish a place for prayer in the schools. While secularists based their arguments against mandated school prayer on the Establishment Clause in the Bill of Rights, some religious conservatives posited a First Amendment argument of their own: they maintained that prohibition of religious expression in schools and other public venues represented a violation of students' free speech. The new legal strategy offered religious conservatives a tactical advantage: whereas issues like school prayer and evolution instruction could be criticized as attempts to indoctrinate children into an adult-imposed set of sectarian beliefs, the free speech argument defended *student-initiated* and *student-led* displays of religiosity—even if students were encouraged or assisted by adults.

Student-led prayer liberated conservatives from the mantle of censor and frequently left secularists to defend heavy-handed school administrators and boards of education that tried to regulate the time and place for student prayer. This strategy put a premium on expressions of the kind of teen religiosity fostered by church youth groups, fan magazines, and concerts. These cultural forms tended, in turn, to emphasize morality over doctrine, allowing religious conservatives to sidestep divisive religious sectarianism. Thus, the Jesus papers and the Christian music magazines, which put so much effort into turning young people into "speakers," ultimately helped reopen public schools to religious intervention. The transformation of Christian youth culture perfectly complemented the legal arguments forwarded by Christian activists.

A series of U.S. Supreme Court decisions cleared the way for Christian youth culture to appear in public schools, although Christians initially had little reason for optimism. When in *Wallace v. Jaffree* (1985) the Court ruled against an Alabama law that allowed for a moment of silence in public schools, it dealt a severe blow to adult-sanctioned school prayer. For a few years, however, it appeared that the Court might be willing to accept student-initiated school prayer. The Court ruled in *Lee v. Weisman* (1992) that a public school could not allow a member of the clergy to offer a prayer at graduation ceremonies, as it represented an endorsement of religion by the state. The decision also vacated a decision (*Jones v. Clear Creek*) by the U.S. Fifth Circuit that had permitted "non-sectarian, non-proselytizing" prayers initiated and led by students, but the appellate court—with jurisdiction over Texas, Mississippi, and Louisiana—chose to stand by its initial ruling. The Court eventually declared this practice unconstitutional in 2000.[119]

Although religious conservatives were frustrated in their efforts to introduce organized prayer in public schools, they prevailed in a string of cases that affirmed the right of students to express their religious beliefs. In these cases, conservatives contended that religious viewpoints had been unconstitutionally excluded from the exchange of ideas in the educational system, a line of argument based on the Equal Access Act, a law dubbed "son of school prayer" by some members of Congress when it was passed in 1984.[120] According to the law, districts that allowed one "non-curriculum-related student group"—for example, a chess club—had to allow others to exist.[121] Christians considered the law a victory, but it also opened new confrontations over morally suitable campus groups as students used the same claims on access to establish gay clubs in the mid-1990s.[122]

The court again narrowly sided with religious conservatives in 1995, when, in *Rosenberger v. University of Virginia,* it ruled that the University of Virginia was obligated to provide money for student-run religious publications if it subsidized other student publications. The case centered on a request by a student, Ronald Rosenberger, who had been denied university funds for a magazine, *Wide Awake,* that offered a "Christian perspective" on contemporary issues. The Court majority found that the university could fund student publications, including those with a Christian viewpoint, on a neutral basis without promoting Christianity. The justices reasoned that the money was going not to a sectarian church but to a student group, and that the student group intended to use the funds for a publication rather than any explicitly religious activity.[123] Thus, the young plaintiff's development of a "Christian" viewpoint—as opposed to Presbyterian or Baptist—aided his case, as did the fact that Christian youth culture organized itself around cultural practices like music rather than the sacraments.

The Court's decision to uphold the Equal Access Act in *Westside Community Schools v. Mergens* (1990) provided the impetus for an explosion of student-led displays of religiosity in the nation's public schools during the 1990s as Christianity became a core identity for teens at both local and national levels. The fan magazines made the requirements placed on the young "Christian" clear: in addition to believing in salvation, teens needed to adhere to a code of personal piety and to "witness" to peers by establishing a Christian community. In the wake of the *Mergens* decision, Christian-oriented clubs became commonplace in high schools around the nation—even as some districts decided to prohibit extracurricular clubs of any kind.[124] While not the primary instigators of the Jesus Movement, interdenominational campus groups like InterVarsity (a British organization that arrived in the United States in 1938) and the newer Campus Crusade for Christ (established in 1951) benefited from the revival, as it raised awareness of religion and provided innovations for evangelizing. In 1994 the National Fellowship of Christian Athletes (NFCA) counted 5,278 school affiliates (largely in secondary schools), an increase of nearly 50 percent since 1992. The same year, Campus Crusade for Christ reported that it reached 250,000 junior and high school students across the country.[125] In 1998, Challenge 2000 Alliance, an umbrella group of Christian youth organizations, reported an estimated 10,000 Christian clubs in secondary schools across the nation; some newspaper accounts placed the number of such groups between 12,000 and 15,000.[126] The growth of Christian clubs was particularly pronounced in places like Orange County, California, where the NFCA grew from six chapters in 1998 to about thirty in 2001 and where the Christian club at Newport Harbor High School, established in 1996, was within five years the school's largest student organization.[127] These clubs were a call to service for many young Christians, who mobilized to develop a network of Christians committed to sacralizing a portion of their time at school, whether before or after the school day or during lunch.

Christian-themed clubs provided teenagers with regular opportunities to pray and socialize with other believers at their schools, and one organization created an annual religious crusade that linked young Christians across the nation and, later, around the world. The observances demonstrate young evangelicals' desire to join together in a larger faith movement, but it also reveals adult co-optation of youth religiosity. In 1990 a Southern Baptist minister organized a public prayer demonstration at approximately 1,000 school flagpoles—devotional substitutes for the cross—for 45,000 teenagers across Texas. Interest in the event, dubbed "See You at the Pole," grew quickly: by 1993 the annual event claimed over 2 million participants, and by 1996 it included 2.5 million students at all grade levels in twenty countries.[128] The demonstrations were billed as an opportunity for students to pray for world peace as well as for an end to the influences of "sexual immorality, drug and alcohol abuse, satanic cult influences and suicidal tendencies" at their schools.[129] But perhaps more important, the events offered students another chance to identify themselves as Christians before their peers, a concept confirmed by participants and event organizers: one student explained that he viewed the event as an opportunity to take "a stand for Christ." Sponsoring organizations were aware that adults did not have the same reach as young people. A spokesperson for the Baptist General Convention of Texas, for example, acknowledged, "Young people have opportunities for access (for evangelical work) that adults do not have in public schools."[130]

The new criteria for expressing religiosity proved controversial in some districts, even as Christian activist groups such as the Christian Coalition established organizations to inform students of the latest legal decisions and ensure that school districts complied with the changes. These confrontations offered Christian teenagers opportunities to draw on evangelicalism's rhetorical tradition of dissent. Here again, intense

youth religiosity intersected with broader evangelical cultural and political agendas.

Christian activists proved eager to test and protect student-initiated
expressions of religiosity at schools once the practice was affirmed by
the *Mergens* case. Many conservatives interpreted the ruling to mean
that students also had the right to distribute religious materials. As a
result, school districts and Christian legal activists struggled in the
1990s to define how young adults could express religious belief. Shortly
before the *Mergens* decision, students in Orange and Seminole counties
in Florida attempted to distribute a newspaper, *Caleb Issues and
Answers,* in local high schools as part of a weeklong evangelistic campaign by several churches. When school officials stopped the students,
their church's youth pastor enlisted the legal advocacy group Christian
Advocates Serving Evangelism (CASE) to defend the students. Aided by
the *Mergens* decision, students were eventually granted the right to distribute materials, once school principals reviewed them, before and
after school as well as during lunch.[131] Jay Sekulow, the students' attorney, who would go on to win several Supreme Court cases on public displays of religion, predicted that the right to distribute Christian
literature would become "the legal issue of the 1990s" and added,
"Students do not shed their constitutional rights to freedom of speech
when they enter the schoolhouse gate. And you cannot treat Christian
students as second-class citizens because their message is the gospel."[132]

Sekulow's strategy to reframe school prayer as a First Amendment
free speech issue highlighted the Right's desire to enlist young people in
its efforts to Christianize public space through proselytizing. In some
arenas, the confrontational styles of punk and metal remained a reli-
able public enemy of conservative parents. Here, however, devout students witnessed their faith using the signifiers of punk and heavy metal
culture, and conservative groups raised a collective howl when they
were not permitted to distribute the publications. The issue religious
literature distribution made news in Florida again in late 1991 when
Martino DeBenedetto, a Hollywood Hills High School student, received
a ten-day suspension for distributing the metal/punk fanzine *Thieves
and Prostitutes* without administrative approval. Although students
were entitled to distribute political or religious literature in Broward
County schools, principals had the authority to restrict the manner,
time, and place in which materials were distributed; officials were also
allowed to ban materials they deemed to be obscene, pornographic, or
libelous.

Although DeBenedetto argued that *Thieves and Prostitutes* had been prohibited because of its religious message, it is more likely that the magazine's punk signifiers confused the principal. The fanzine's editors intended their publication to be controversial. In addition to its provocative name—which, while inspired by a biblical verse,[133] was itself likely to raise red flags among lawsuit-wary school administrators—the illustration-intensive magazine drew heavily from the dark, exaggerated art found in metal and punk culture. The particular issue that DeBenedetto circulated contained particularly irreverent material. The creators of *Thieves and Prostitutes* belonged to a ministry headed by a messianic Jew named Marvin Pressman, and the issue's cover featured an illustration of Pressman sporting a Mohawk haircut and wearing combat boots and a tallith. Pressman stood in front of a wall with religious graffiti, including a star of David, a crucifix, an *icthus* fish, and the phrases, "God Rules! Satan sux." A caption at the bottom read, "Beware! It's the attack of the Punk Rabbi!" Newspaper accounts of the controversy also noted that the issue included "Satanic figures," an observation apparently based on a drawing of a "scantily clad woman with horns sprouting from her head."[134] In short, the magazine deployed art of a kind that had frequently been misinterpreted and criticized by religious conservatives as blasphemous or satanic. In this case, however, the magazine was attempting to put this style to use to convert heavy metal and punk fans.

School administrators maintained that discipline was the basis for the suspension; they noted that DeBenedetto had been warned once before about distributing religious materials that had not been submitted to the principal for review. They also expressed concern that the issue's cover could be interpreted as anti-Semitic.[135] In an editorial, the *Miami Herald* noted the school's right to restrict the time and place of distribution, urging that "the lobbies and courtyards be lively forums" for religious and political debate, but only "for those who willingly participate."[136]

DeBenedetto countered that the materials were censored for their religious content and that the principal had told him that "no religious material" could be distributed at the school.[137] One article quoted the student as saying that he got the idea to distribute religious materials after seeing Jay Sekulow, on his popular television show, explain the legal rights of students to distribute religious materials.[138] DeBenedetto became a folk hero among religious conservatives after he appeared in a December 1991 Christian Coalition newsletter and on an early January episode of the *700 Club*, with Pat Robertson, who urged

Figure 7. Christian groups reacted angrily after a school principal in Florida
suspended a student for distributing copies of issue no. 2 of *Thieves and
Prostitutes*. School officials asserted that the material had not been submitted
for review and expressed concern that the cover could be interpreted as being
anti-Semitic. Illustration courtesy of *Thieves and Prostitutes* editors Alexis
Neptune and John DiDonna.

viewers to contact the school's principal. Moreover, Robertson's non-profit legal foundation, the American Center for Law and Justice (ACLJ), provided free counsel to DeBenedetto in a pending lawsuit against the school board.[139] DeBenedetto's attorneys eventually agreed to drop that suit against in exchange for a revision of policy as to what could be distributed on campus; the school board also expunged the suspension from the student's record and, in an exception to its policy, allowed him to make up missed work.[140] DeBenedetto's attorney, Keith Fournier, executive director of the ACLJ, proudly noted that DeBenedetto had been "completely vindicated" by the settlement: "Rather than [being] seen as a kid who disobeyed authority, he has been seen for what he is: a very good kid with a lot of courage who said what was in his heart and was punished wrongly for it."[141] By casting the episode in this light, religious conservatives found a way to merge a populist youth culture into a David versus Goliath narrative.

The controversy at Hollywood Hills High School brought *Thieves and Prostitutes* onto the front lines of the culture wars, but traces of evangelical punk rage remained in its reaction to the controversy. John DiDonna, the zine's primary artist, observed that DeBenedetto had been "a little overzealous," handing out copies "to practically everybody."[142] Yet in a subsequent issue, the zine's creators packed an entire page with news of the controversy, including a collage of media coverage entitled "The Censorship of Fascist Liberalism," a reproduction of the controversial issue's front cover as well as that of the first issue, and a copy of a flyer entitled "Students' Bill of Rights on a Public School Campus." In an unsigned article, the authors assumed a tone of surprise that their magazine had been "censored" by established churches—thus linking the zine to the anti-institutional stance of the old Jesus newspapers—as well as by the "Liberal Left," whose refusal to read or distribute the magazine proved that "the Right" did not "hold exclusive rights to censorship." The article then tied the distribution issue to other disputes over "free speech" by adding bitterly, "Just try praying in a public school or [talking] about life near an abortion clinic. Gotta love that free speech!"[143] Even as schools and courts affirmed students' ability to express their religiosity at schools, Christian youths' rage at secular institutions and culture continued, demonstrating once more the perfect coalescence of punk anger and evangelical Christianity's outsider identity.

The emergence of student-led school prayer groups in the 1990s allowed young believers to sacralize the public school, an institution that many Christian conservatives had considered to be hopelessly secular and humanist. While adults debated about the schools, young Christian conservatives took the debate about faith and values into the schools. In this realigned version of public religiosity, young believers' desire to witness their faith to their classmates in the vernacular of youth culture bolstered other efforts conducted at PTA meetings and in congressional hearings, consumer boycotts, and even Supreme Court cases.

Many anti-rock critics of the late 1960s and early 1970s viewed Christian youth culture as an insidious means for dividing generations within the church as well as within the home. Christian parents and educators, on the other hand, had an instrumental view of Christian youth culture as providing an alternative to what they perceived to be destructive secular forms. For the most part, these contrasting views presented youth as either aggressive agitators who had internalized secular values or as passive vessels in need of protection from the hostile world. Observers like Will Herberg, however, saw the potential for alliances with enthusiastic young converts who critiqued youth culture from within. Instead of an adversarial relationship with cutting-edge subcultures, older conservatives believed they could put popular culture to religious use.

Years after Herberg's editorials, Christian writers saw hope in extending the decade's cultural activism into the music industry. In a 1991 article, CCM's editor and publisher, John Styll, told readers, "Your world today is different because of a major cultural revolution that began in [the 1960s]."[144] Styll then challenged "songwriters, artists, record industry executives and those in related fields" to undertake a similar mission. These groups, he wrote, needed "to think in terms no smaller than starting a new revolution in popular culture. It happened in the '60s when some musicians captured the spirit of the age and led the way to a new reality. It's time for a new revolution, and followers of Christ are to lead it. Isn't that the essence of the Great Commission?"[145] Rather than reversing the changes of the sixties, leaders of the new "cultural revolution for Christ"—as one reader called it—believed that the 1960s provided the blueprint for what they might accomplish.[146] This plan required religious conservatives to intervene in musical discourses by calling on the rock 'n' roll singer to glorify God. This time around, Jesus would be bigger than the Beatles.

# CHAPTER 3

# Metal Missionaries to the Nation

*Christian Heavy Metal Music, 1984–1994*

On June 26, 1987, members of the Christian metal band Stryken attended a Motley Crüe concert in San Antonio, Texas. It was not uncommon for Christian bands to attend secular concerts; many bands did so, they said, to keep current on musical trends. But Stryken arrived at the show ready for confrontation. According to the Christian metal magazine *White Throne*, the band, "wearing full suits of armor . . . and bearing a 14 × 8 foot wooden cross," "stormed the doors of the arena, pushing through the crowds of teenagers and television cameras down the corridor towards the inlet to the main stage." At this point, the "boys in armor" erected the cross and "began to preach to the masse[s] of kids who were gathering all around." The authorities quickly intervened, and, "ordered to remove 'the cross' or face arrest, the members of Stryken continued to speak openly about Jesus Christ, and were one by one hand-cuffed and forcibly removed from the arena."[1] Stryken's actions—which invoked the persecuted early Christians described in the Acts of the Apostles—offer insights into Christian metal during the 1980s. Motley Crüe's music and the lifestyle of its members were designed to shock middle America, but the band had become one of the most successful acts of the 1980s. By upstaging Motley Crüe's over-the-top behavior with their own bold act, Stryken attempted to claim heavy metal's reputation for outrageousness for Christianity. By getting removed from the concert, the band positioned itself as the persecuted minority—the authentic outlaws of American music in the 1980s.

During the 1980s and early 1990s, Christian heavy metal bands like Stryken conducted a campaign across the United States to promote Christian values. Christian heavy metal bands offer an ideal case study for examining the cultural activism of conservative Christians during the 1980s. Along with their secular metal counterparts, and with such activists as the members of the Parents' Music Resource Center, they helped to politicize youth as a category linked to the "family values" debate in national politics. Evangelicals' involvement with heavy metal partook of the renewal of their reformist impulse as it coincided with the high tide of the nation's "culture wars." Many of the battles in this sustained fight centered on competing discourses about youth conducted by secular and evangelical culture. At the same time that the harmful effects of youth culture, including heavy metal, were loudly criticized, evangelical Christians, ever attuned to the social forces that affected young people, were acutely aware that consumer culture offered young people an ever-expanding range of choices. They used popular music as a way of introducing young people to their conception of morality while fulfilling youths' desire to stay abreast of contemporary music styles. Bands, arguing that parental power had disintegrated and kids relied on peer authority, hoped to empower kids through religious knowledge that would lead them to live moral lives.

Recent scholarship has revealed the long-standing connections between consumer culture and American Christianity, noting that revivalists such as Dwight Moody employed modern business techniques and that Salvation Army converts adapted the styles of contemporary parades, music, and street shows during the late nineteenth century.[2] In the 1960s and 1970s, white evangelical Christians adapted popular music forms as thousands of young people participated in the grassroots Jesus Movement.[3] While successful, the Christian music scene offered an alternative oasis, rather than a share in the mainstream musical universe. Christian metal bands, in contrast, represented a break with tradition because they cultivated a secular audience, played on bills with secular bands, and occasionally signed with secular labels, all in an attempt to increase their influence and fan base in the mainstream music world. Christian heavy metal bands thus constituted an attempt at "cultural reform" among Christians. As anthropologist Susan Harding has noted, during the 1980s, religious leaders like Jerry Falwell tried to transform their flock from "fundamentalists," who limited their engagement with and commitments to secular society, into "'conservative Christians,' who would fight worldly battles and who sought worldly power and influence in the name of 'Christian values.'"[4] Rather than continue to promote a separate space for Christian culture— thereby surrendering most public space to the world—Christian heavy metal bands sought to engage with the world by inserting their work into the cultural conversation.

The increased efforts at Christian cultural activism mirrored white evangelicals' contemporaneous political mobilization. At the same time that Stryken was storming the gates of the arena in San Antonio, other evangelical Christians were demanding entry into the political arena. White Christian conservatives, once considered political novices, were by 1994 deemed political activists savvy about the political process, mobilized at the local level, and vocal in promoting their national agenda. They had also established themselves as one of the GOP's core constituencies: over 70 percent of white evangelicals voted for winning candidates Ronald Reagan or George H. W. Bush in the presidential campaigns of 1984 and 1988, and Christian leaders claimed to have played a vital role in bringing about the "Republican Revolution" that swept the first Republican majority since the early 1950s into Congress in the 1994 election.[5]

Heavy metal emerged during the 1970s, when such bands as Black Sabbath, Led Zeppelin, and Judas Priest fused elements of blues, rock, and psychedelic music. Although scorned by critics, the genre exploded during the 1980s, when it fragmented into subgenres such as melodic metal and speed or thrash metal. Conservative Christian critics, of course, denounced all metal subgenres, but some devout musicians saw an opportunity. Whereas punk appealed to young evangelicals' right- eous renunciatory tendencies, metal's emphasis on theatrics, along with its use (or desecration) of sacred symbols, gave Christians a perfect opportunity to engage in a dialogue with popular culture. The music featured powerful and loud vocals and guitar work that, in contrast to punk music, prized virtuosity and control.[6] The genre emphasized visu- ality through logos, album covers, music videos, and other band mer- chandise, as well as through costumes, lighting, and choreography in live performances.[7] According to sociologist Deena Weinstein, heavy metal fell into two basic categories, both of which questioned estab- lished power and authority: Dionysian metal, which celebrated hedo- nism in realms such as sex and drugs, and chaotic metal, which dwelt on emotional issues such as injustice, death, and rebellion, often using imagery drawn from Judeo-Christian traditions.[8] Because of these themes, the genre drew fire from parental and religious groups during

the 1980s. But some Christians responded to what they saw as a per-
version of American values by trying to co-opt the sonic, visual, and
verbal elements of heavy metal for their own purposes.

In their analysis of the contemporary Christian music community,
Jay R. Howard and John M. Streck suggest that Christian artists, fans,
critics, and distributors disagreed on the goals of the music: should it be
considered ministry, entertainment, or art?[9] Unlike some of their fellow
believers, Christian metal bands viewed their music as a critical intervention toward improving the damaged morals of the secular world.
Their efforts involved a combination of symbolic and rhetorical actions
and battles.

To begin with, Christian metal bands considered the clubs, coffeehouses, and arenas where they played—and to a lesser degree, the pop
charts—as so many spiritual battlegrounds with secular and Christian
bands the combatants. The rhetoric of spiritual warfare thus reinforced
Christians' sense of disfranchisement from American society while
announcing their intention to reclaim their vital role as spiritual
guardians. Christians' continued suspicion of the world affected artists:
some believers worried that Christian bands might compromise their
message in exchange for mainstream acceptance, while others predicted
that uncompromising Christian bands were doomed to failure in the
hostile secular world.

Although born-again Christian bands sought to reform the music
industry, they did not want to undermine the authority of heavy metal
music. Christians believed that music—and the people who created it—
influenced what young people thought and how they acted. Young
people who listened to immoral music created by immoral artists were
thereby tempted to sin and rebel against authority. Rather than simply
condemn music for contributing to what they saw as an assault on adult
authority (though they did plenty of this), Christian metal bands used
youth culture as a starting point to return biblical values to American
society.

Because Christian bands also wished to avoid listener confusion, they
had to be clear about what constituted "biblical values." Although their
tactics differed slightly from those of the political leaders of religious
conservatism, Christian bands delivered a similar message to young
people: in addition to singing about strictly religious themes such as
God's love and the need for conversion, bands addressed social issues
ranging from abortion and "family values" to drugs and capital
punishment—issues that conservative Christian political activists kept

alive throughout the 1980s and 1990s. As evangelicals, the bands believed that the nation's problems could be solved only through religious commitment. Unlike many of their anti-rock counterparts, however, they believed that the music of youth culture was neutral and encompassed lyrics and lifestyles open to Christian messages. Christian musicians wanted young people to know the "Christian point of view" on topics like abortion and premarital sex and therefore addressed these themes in songs. In addition to addressing specific topics, Christian bands broached the subject of authority in American society. Although Christians blamed youth culture for contributing to the loss of stability in American society, these bands expressed confidence that youth culture could be used to restore it.

Finally, Christian bands constructed a rhetorical justification for metal music to defend themselves against older Christians who remained skeptical of the moral power of music. Although Christian bands claimed a number of victories in the secular music world, appropriation ultimately proved controversial among evangelicals, as some critics wondered whether it was possible to suture the seeming disjunction between "secular" style and "sacred" content. Tension existed in Christian rock music between the desire to evangelize among nonbelievers and the fear that the secular world would compromise the Christian church and its message. Bands and fans alike wondered whether the Bible provided a firm basis for adapting secular practices ranging from dance styles like moshing, to musical styles like punk and heavy metal, to clothing styles that featured leather, spandex, and fishnet stockings. Worse still, despite assurances that band members lived by "conventional" gender norms, critics fretted that metal fashions and practices routinely contradicted Christian doctrine. In attempting to reaffiliate middle- and working-class youths with family, marriage, and "traditional" gender roles, Christian heavy metal bands may have unintentionally further destabilized the cultural authority structures they had set out to restore.

American youth became a critical battleground in late-twentieth-century American culture, and the trajectory of Christian metal shows how conservatives participated in the debate. In *Resistance through Rituals*, Stuart Hall and his colleagues describe the connections between affluence, consensus, and youth culture and emphasize that youth became an important focus for social anxiety as both symptom and scapegoat during the post–World War II era.[10] Whereas Hall's British cultural studies group has pointed primarily to working-class subcultures as a source of resistance to dominant ideologies in this era, Christian metal bands espoused a conservative brand of youth culture that sought to advance acceptance of, not resistance to, white middle-class values such as family, marriage, and "traditional" gender roles. The cultural work of evangelicals thus proves that the definition of such concepts as rebellion and alienation have no fixed meaning. In their work as "metal missionaries" to America's youth, Christian bands sought to spread God's message to young people in their own cultural idiom.

## BEHIND ENEMY LINES:
## SPIRITUAL WARFARE WITH THE SECULAR WORLD

In February 1985 the conservative evangelical magazine *Christianity Today* published an article about Stryper, a Southern California–based Christian heavy metal band. Regular readers perhaps flipped immediately to the article "What It Takes to Fight Pornography"—this was just a few months before representatives of the Parents' Music Resource Center would condemn the "pornographic content" of music before a Senate subcommittee. Stryper, however, was not among the PMRC's targets. On the contrary, the Stryper story revealed a different thread in white evangelicals' cultural engagement with American society. The article explained that, as a result of the popularity of heavy metal music, bands like Motley Crüe and Twisted Sister had successfully introduced the themes of "generalized rage, sexual abandon, drug abuse, violence, and despair" into millions of American homes.[11] Stryper's arrival meant that this assault would remain uncontested no longer, since the band had vowed to claim the heavy metal terrain—and its young fans—for God.

The hype in Christian media surrounding Stryper's advent fit perfectly within a longer history of evangelical rhetorical patterns. In his analysis of religious sects in American history, R. Laurence Moore suggests that Christians' accusations of subversion have often demonstrated their intense sense of dispossession from and antagonism toward the dominant culture.[12] Evangelicals' tradition of dissent has allowed them to approach American life as disfranchised populists, a status bearing considerable cachet, ironically, in both politics and popular culture. The rhetorical patterns persisted even after evangelicals came to reside in a suburban milieu rather than rural backwaters. During the late twentieth century, conservative Christians embraced outsider rhetoric as they condemned the nation's perceived moral decay evidenced by the U.S. Supreme Court decisions on abortion and school prayer, the spread of secular humanism, and the inroads made by the gay rights and women's rights movements. In 1992 Pat Buchanan delivered a speech at the Republican National Convention that encapsulated conservative believers' feelings of alienation. Declaring a "cultural war," Buchanan, a devout Roman Catholic, called on American voters to "take back our cities, take back our culture and take back our country."[13] The era's Christian political and cultural activists echoed Buchanan's call to arms as they urged fellow believers to end their exile (whether self-imposed or forced) from public life. Ralph Reed, executive director of the Christian Coalition, emphasized the political dangers encountered by believers when he famously invoked the guerilla warfare of the Vietnam War to describe his organization's successful "stealth tactics" in local elections.[14] But conservative believers were also aware of cultural dangers, a concern made evident when Christian novelist Frank Peretti published his first thriller, *This Present Darkness,* which depicts the spiritual warfare that ensues when a New Age cult attempts to take over a small town.

During the mid-1980s, Christian musicians likewise found that the evangelical language of dissent gave them an entry point into the linguistic styles of metal music, a genre that emphasized themes of power and struggle. Christian metal bands like Stryper viewed American music as a spiritual battleground in which they were the soldiers of God and secular bands were the forces of Satan. Whereas previous Christian bands had avoided the hostile world, the Christian metal bands of the 1980s believed they needed to engage the enemy because Satan dominated the arena of music. Viewing their endeavor as spiritual warfare, Christians used warrior rhetoric. In a letter to the magazine *Lightshine,* a reader described members of the Christian band Sardonyx as "a small army boldly marching into enemy territory." The reader lamented that for the previous thirty years, rock 'n' roll had been "Satan's domain" as Christian bands had "either stood outside the playing field, mimicking those inside, or played in their own field." The letter then praised bands like Sardonyx that were invading Satan's arena and "playing hardball with the pros!"[15] Musicians described their work in a similar manner. Singer Steve Shannon, whose band Idle Cure frequently played at juvenile halls, told *Heaven's Metal:* "Sometimes you have to go out on the battle lines. Sometimes you have to go out against Satan and use your shield of faith against him. Sometimes you need to go out in the world full-force, dressed in worldly garb, and be a light."[16] Although Shannon's "shield of faith" suggested a defensive posture for the band's sorties into the world, others seemed to expect more aggressive confrontations with the world.

In 1985 the cover of Stryper's *Soldiers under Command* album showed drummer Robert Sweet holding a Bible in one hand and a gun in the other. Sweet also liked to pose for publicity photos with swords.[17]

Christian bands possessed important allies. As the infamous metal band KISS commanded allegiance of the "KISS Army," so Christian bands counted fans as fellow combatants in tales about the moral front lines. Stryken guitarist Dale Streiker optimistically noted: "I think there's gonna be a big turnaround in America. It's starting, you can feel it. Kids are starting to stand up."[18] Perhaps not surprisingly, bands attributed their success not just to divine inspiration but also to divine intervention: God's firepower was greater than any earthly creation. David Bach of Guardian explained the divine hand supporting his band's work: "Marketing and all that stuff is important, but . . . it's gonna be secondary to what God's Spirit can do. He can just blow the walls out."[19] To underscore the role of divine providence in their mission, Christian artists compared themselves to such Old Testament figures as Joshua, who needed to maintain his vigilance after a victory over Ai, or such early Christians as Paul, who evangelized among the Gentiles in the early years of the church.[20]

While portraying themselves as warriors, Christians also devoted considerable energy demonizing their enemies; in interviews, they consistently portrayed themselves as underdogs in the fight against forces that had harnessed music for evil purposes. The language of subversion, with its suggestion that American music and morals had been corrupted by unjust methods, was perhaps the most powerful arrow in the musicians' rhetorical quiver. This sense of alienation justified the use of countersubversion: drastic tactics that righteous outsiders borrowed from the enemy to bring about its downfall. Christian bands employed this rhetoric to describe where and how they planned to wage their battles. Just as the forces of evil had used culture to subvert American values, righteous musicians planned to usurp the enemy's cultural power from within, through music. Bands accordingly focused on finding their way into dominant culture so they could change it from within. Vocalist Lary Dean of Trytan (To Reach Youths through the Almighty Nazarene) told *Heaven's Metal* that "the enemy" was "really running rampant . . . through music mediums" and that his band was "really committed to getting behind the enemy lines."[21]

While Trytan expressed a desire to take the battle into enemy territory, bands like RECON used the metaphor of countersubversion more explicitly. When asked about his band's name, Dion Hunter explained, 'recon' is a military term. We relate it to the fact that we are soldiers for the Lord Jesus. Recon is short for reconnaissance, and it means going behind enemy lines. What we're doing is going into the devil's territory and therefore we chose this name. . . . We are in that territory to win souls for the Lord Jesus Christ.

It had apparently not occurred to the band that their name could also mean "reconciliation," as the interviewer pointed out to them.[22] In another interview, George Ochoa offered a military model for the band's work among nonbelievers:

All the outfits of the Armed Forces have [reconnaissance units], but I like the Marines because they do the down and dirty work, such as when the enemy has one or several hostages, they will be sent in, and they sneak their way in and [are] very wise about it, and blast their way in there, destroy the enemy and get the hostages out. I like to look at it that way because I feel that's what we do basically spiritually—going behind enemy lines in enemy turf, the clubs . . . this world. We go there and proclaim the light of Jesus Christ and set the captives free. We are the soldiers and the Lord wins the battles . . . we get in there and get right back out. We don't hang around to get destroyed by the enemy.[23]

Ochoa's remarks demonstrate his band's hostility toward the world: the band needed to blast its way out of "enemy" territory, lest they be destroyed. Moreover, by suggesting that heavy metal fans were "captives" or "hostages" waiting to be rescued, the band conveniently managed to implicate secular bands as the sole source of problems in the music world. Finally, by comparing their work to military special operations, Ochoa suggested that the group's work in the world held strategic moral importance.

As they battled on the frontlines of the music world, some Christian bands, like Gardian (later Guardian) and Stryken, came dressed for war. Gardian bassist David Bach explained the band's name and its approach to stage theatrics, which included futuristic battle armor:

We see [all] Christian bands [as] guardians. Guardians of the truth: God's Word. Especially in a world of secular metal. . . . We do take our imagery from Ephesians 6:10–17—putting on the full armor of God.

The armor we wear is theatrical armor, but it's symbolic of the real spiritual armor we wear. When we speak of our warfare image, it's symbolic of the real spiritual warfare that's goin' on right now in this world.[24]

Unlike the aggressive rhetoric about reconnaissance missions or the visual use of guns employed by other bands, Gardian's armor suggested a defensive posture. Even so, their gear reflected combat readiness: certainly, the

same armor would not be necessary for a band that played exclusively
for Christian audiences. As the apostle Paul advised Christian disciples
in Ephesus, bands like Gardian asserted that they could perform a special function in American music, but they needed to equip themselves
appropriately. Yet Gardian also believed it had to reclaim its role from a
hostile world—one that, like the early Christianity of Paul, was unfairly
controlled by illegitimate powers: "the rulers," "the authorities," and
the "spiritual forces of evil in the heavenly places." The metal band
Stryken, which drew its costume imagery from the same chapter of
Ephesians, frequently moved the notion of spiritual warfare from a
metaphorical to a literal level, as when, in June 1986, band members
donned their stage costumes and joined Citizens Against Pornography
in picketing a Texas adult theater. The following year, *CCM* captured
the band's approach to evangelism when it remarked that Stryken was
"a band not for the pulpit but for the streets."[25] By confronting secular
America, bands like Gardian and Stryken reinforced the need for
Christians to protect themselves from the world with both literal and
figurative armor.

With such negative characterizations of the world, Christian bands
might be assumed to have avoided their secular counterparts. Such
separation would not have been impossible, since many cities had a
Christian club, a coffeehouse, or even a sympathetic church where
bands could have played. Yet many bands were eager to share the
stage with secular acts and frequently referred to this wish in interviews, as when Trytan vocalist Lary Dean told *Heaven's Metal* of his
desire to tour with Bon Jovi or Motley Crüe, groups he described as
"out there really roaring for the kingdom of darkness."[26] Bands
offered several explanations for these worldly associations. Aside
from spiritual warfare, which could be waged only on the enemy's
turf, Christian bands often claimed they were playing at nightclubs in
order to reach "the lost." Secular bands essentially functioned as bait
for the Christians' hook: since nonbelievers could not be counted on
to attend a religious revival, Christian bands responded by bringing
the revival into urban nightlife.

Jim LaVerde of Southern California's Barren Cross, which at one
point had refused to play in secular clubs, reasoned that the band
needed secular bands to open for them because "secular bands are
gonna draw the secular people. Those are the ones we need to minister
to. . . . What's gonna motivate a non-Christian to go to a Christian concert? I think the motivation to get a non-Christian to come is to see a

Figure 8. The Christian metal band Stryken wore futuristic battle armor that underscored members' desire to conduct spiritual warfare with the world. Photograph courtesy of Stryken.

secular band."[27] As LaVerde's comments suggest, Christian bands remained hopeful about secular fans, who were believed to need only a moral alternative to secular music. Roxalt drummer Jim Brandt explained that a heavy metal fan (also known as a headbanger) could be seduced by satanic messages offered by bands. According to Brandt, bands began "with the lyrics, then they promote the lifestyle and they work you into buying their albums, supporting their philosophy—to bring in anarchy and . . . total degeneration . . . from everything God has planned for humans." It was at this degraded level that Christian bands intervened: "We also want to be good, wholesome entertainment that Christians and non-Christians can come and listen to. If they don't believe our philosophy, that's fine, we're gonna entertain no matter what with our music. Hopefully they'll hear our philosophy and they'll say, 'Hey, I've never considered that.'"[28] At best, bands hoped to lead fans to salvation; if not, they would at least provide an entertaining counterbalance to sinful secular acts.

This form of evangelism contained an element of self-interest: by reaching the lost, bands made their work more significant. If they performed only for believers, their work could simply be labeled entertainment; however, if they reached nonbelievers, their efforts had a higher—indeed, Christ-like—purpose. Golgatha's Adam Alvarez explained that his band did not play at churches because "if we play in a church, anyone who wouldn't ordinarily go to a church won't be there. We can reach the backslidden Christian, though. We can help them. For the believer, all we are is entertainment, which is good. We give them good music to listen to." This justification extended to contracts with secular record labels. Golgatha, Alvarez continued, was "dealing with secular record people because they can get us out to the people who need to hear us. Whereas a Christian label will distribute us to people who already know the Lord."[29] To give their work religious significance, Christian musicians often compared it to Jesus' efforts among the unwashed of his time. Guitarist Michael Cutting of Holy Soldier, a band from Los Angeles that claimed to draw an average crowd of seven hundred fans per show, suggested that the biggest problem in Christian music was that bands refused to go into the world. His band, in contrast, was "in the world," but not "of the world." Cutting explained, "When Christ came, He didn't hang out with the righteous people. He went to the sinner and He ministered to them [sic]." Likewise, Cutting suggested, "it takes a special calling for a band to turn around and go right back into the muck and the garbage. The bars and clubs where people are just there to pick up on other people and get drunk and party."[30] Bands like Holy Soldier thus hoped to meet nonbelievers in their environment and on their terms, as Jesus had. In the 1980s this meant that bands needed to play heavy metal in secular venues.

To deliver a message of salvation to American youths, Christian bands needed to move beyond rhetoric about spiritual warfare to action. During the 1980s and early 1990s, Christian metal bands began to play at secular clubs; they also sought airplay on mainstream radio and MTV and coverage in print magazines such as *Hit Parader, Kerrang!* and *Circus*.[31] Although some Christian bands claimed to have made inroads among souls in these venues, others found that secular crowds remained unrepentant, even defiant, when confronted with the message of salvation.

Christian metal groups played all over the country, but a particularly strong community of bands was concentrated in Los Angeles during the 1980s. These bands—including Holy Soldier, Gardian, Stryper, and Barren Cross—viewed themselves as an important counterbalance to LA-based secular metal bands like Motley Crüe, Van Halen, W.A.S.P., and Ratt. Beginning in 1984, Christian metal bands began to perform at popular venues like the Whiskey, the Palace, and the Roxy. At least one promoter deftly turned the moral duality into a marketing opportunity when Holy Right played a "Heaven and Hell" night whose bill featured both Christian and satanic metal bands.[32]

When bands actually played at nightclubs, they found that, as in the demon possession stories in the New Testament, the devil was not easily exorcised from venues: although the bands claimed some success, unsaved fans received bands with indifference or even hostility. A band's message had something to do with its reception. Christian bands that met nonbelievers on their turf did not dilute their message, which drew a sharp, eternal division between saved and unsaved. Holy Soldier bassist Andy Robbins, whose band played at both Christian and non-Christian venues with such bands as Omen and Pandemonium, described for a Christian magazine his group's reception at secular bars: "You walk on stage in a bar with a Bible, and the place is going to empty out, or you're going to be wearing beer. You're just going to be getting obscenities." Maybe it was something he said? Robbins then explained that the band did not alter its spiritual message when it went into the clubs. Once, he mentioned, the band held an altar call—that is, an invitation to commit one's life to Jesus—during a performance at the Whiskey-a-Go-Go, a popular nightclub on the Sunset Strip. In an earlier interview, another band member optimistically said that while some people at shows threw things at the band, "the majority of the people really responded to what the Spirit was saying on their heart. There's a really neat revival going on out here. People are beginning to know Jesus."[33]

While Holy Soldier claimed partial success in changing hearts, other bands found that certain tactics could compel the devil's minions to abandon the field in full retreat. This too was considered a success, although for different reasons. In 1987 Gardian, a band that wore armor on stage, was invited to play at a show at the Palace called "New World Rock Playoffs," where the audience comprised mostly non-Christians. The band gleefully reported to *Heaven's Metal* that, while praying before the show, they decided to preach the gospel rather than perform their usual set. After they had played a few songs, the lead singer began to preach. Their efforts were not well received: patrons began "trickling back to the bar one-by-one," then "leaving by fives." "Some of the people," another band member added, "were givin' us the finger and shouting stuff at us, so it was definitely a night of warfare." He concluded that the fans "understood exactly what was being said. . . . A lot of 'em didn't like it, because God's Word can be very offensive, but they heard it. . . . A lot of people will react with hostility, but they heard it at least."[34] In this instance, the Christian band viewed itself as a holy messenger to an unrepentant crowd. On other occasions, Gardian tried to impress fans with its proficiency and style. One member told *Radically Saved* that the band tried to "just go crazy on stage" because audiences rarely expected to see a Christian band onstage. At the end of its show, the band revealed their Christian beliefs and offered to speak to the curious.[35]

Bands from outside Los Angeles also performed for secular audiences. Like Gardian, the Austin-based punk-and–hard-rock band One Bad Pig seemed to thrive on inciting non-Christian crowds at their shows, and they always made their Christian commitment clear to the fans. In an article entitled "Jerry Falwell's Revenge, or Johnny Rotten's Nightmare?" guitarist Paul Q-Pek explained the band's approach to performances:

> First of all, the lyrics are very, very up-front. By the first or second song, everybody in the whole place knows that we're a Christian band. . . .We [reveal our faith] to provoke a reaction. Sometimes, when we play in a secular club, they'll chant out things like, "Satan rules and Jesus sucks," and things like that, to try and get us to retort back at them. They want to react to something, somehow.
> Our first secular show that we did, we were scared to death. We went up there and played and the punks really started in on us. You know, with cussing out Jesus and twisting our lyrics around. After we'd sing a song, like "Anarchy is Prison": "Jesus will set you free." They'd go, "Satan will set you free. Satan is God, blah, blah, blah." Most of 'em didn't really believe it, you know? They were just playing around. They thought it was hilarious. They just wanted to say some hilarious things.[36]

One Bad Pig seemed to arrive at two conflicting conclusions about unsaved fans. The crowd's hostility seemed to affirm the band's mission: they intentionally sought a reaction, whether positive or not. Like the rhetoric of spiritual warfare, the audience's hostile reaction simply affirmed the Christian band's sense of outsider identity, which in turn meshed nicely with punk music's hatred of insiderdom and dominant culture. Perhaps as a result, the band did not seem offended by the crowd's rejection of its message; indeed, band members *expected* it from punk fans. The band seemed to consider the chants to be an almost good-natured joke—part of the interplay between punk performers and audience—but the members also later claimed that these same individuals frequently approached them after their set to talk.

Although many bands jumped at the chance to play secular venues, others refused to do so, arguing that it was inconsistent with their mission. Whitecross, which wanted to reach believers and nonbelievers, nonetheless avoided secular clubs because, in singer Rex Carroll's wise estimation, "People go to bars for other reasons than to hear the Gospel preached."[37] Another band, Barren Cross, stopped playing with secular bands (although they still played on all-Christian bills) because it feared it was exposing young fans to the "ungodly" behavior of the secular opening acts; nonetheless, band members thought that nonbelievers came to see them perform at churches.[38]

In addition to playing in nightclubs, Christian bands—particularly Stryper—also began to appear in secular fan magazines like *Kerrang!* and *Hit Parader,* on MTV, and on occasionally on *Billboard* pop charts. Album sales for Christian metal and punk acts are difficult to trace precisely. In the 1980s, crossover album sales remained low because most acts were affiliated with Christian labels, which primarily distributed products in religious bookstores rather than secular outlets; during these years, *Billboard* maintained a separate chart for the top-selling inspirational albums. But even if Christian metal bands achieved only a small market share, they nonetheless infused their beliefs into the discourse; despite the inflated claims implied in such mantles as "the Moral Majority," some Christian political activists believed that influencing 6 or 7 percent of voter turnout could make a difference in an election.[39] When Christian pop acts like Amy Grant and Michael W. Smith became widely popular in the late 1980s, mainstream labels decided to establish a foothold in the industry through distribution alliances or outright purchase. By the early 1990s, Sony/Word, Geffen/Reunion, and Capitol/Sparrow had joined forces; Warner had established a Christian division, Alliance; and *Billboard* predicted that Christian music could be "the Next Big Thing."[40] Also by then, Christian music products were more readily available in large retail outlets like Wal-Mart and Tower Records that used the SoundScan sales-tracking system and thus provided artists with a better chance at breaking into the *Billboard* 200. Record sales for punk and metal acts prior to the mid-1990s are difficult to track since Christian bookstores were not added to SoundScan until 1995.[41] While mainstream radio airplay remained beyond the grasp of most Christian metal artists, they could take solace in the knowledge that venerable metal groups Iron Maiden and Judas Priest had established their reputation through touring rather than Top 40 success.[42]

Industry obstacles to crossover success explained why Stryper signed with the secular label Enigma/Capitol in the early 1980s, but they also made Stryper's success difficult to replicate. Not every band wanted to follow Stryper's path. Just as bands disagreed whether Christians belonged in nightclubs, they were similarly divided over whether attention from secular media denoted important evangelistic work or concessions to the world. In particular, fear persisted that bands would betray their values and give in to worldly temptations, that in a sense, bands would sell out their Christianity for success.

While it never attained the popularity of Christian adult-contemporary artist Amy Grant, Stryper was by far the most popular Christian metal band. Founded in 1984 in Orange County, California, the band's first major release for Enigma, *Soldiers under Command,* spent more than forty weeks on *Billboard*'s Hot 200 album chart and eventually went gold. The band's second full-length work, *To Hell with the Devil,* was certified platinum in 1988, and the single "Honestly" reached the *Billboard* Top 40. The third album, *In God We Trust,* also went gold, but the band declined in popularity after the release of *Against the Law* in 1990 (an album with fewer overt references to God) and the subsequent departure of lead singer Michael Sweet. The band also received airplay on MTV for the videos of "Soldiers under Command" (1985), "Honestly" (1987), "Always There for You" (1988), and "Shining Star" (1991); and in a telling example of 1980s cultural success, it had a song ("The Rock That Makes Me Roll") included on a K-Tel release that also included metal bands Twisted Sister and Rush.[43] In the late 1980s, the band toured with White Lion, Jet Boy, and other secular bands, filling small auditoriums and, in at least one instance, drawing a crowd of nearly 12,000.[44] By 1989 Stryper had achieved enough notoriety to appear in *Rolling Stone.*

Articles in popular metal magazines like *Hit Parader* and *Kerrang!* that covered Stryper embraced the sacred/profane binary created by the disjuncture between the bands' religious faith and musical style. In 1987 drummer Robert Sweet appeared on the cover of the metal music magazine *Hit Parader* opposite Blackie Lawless of W.A.S.P. in an article entitled "Heaven and Hell: Stryper vs. W.A.S.P." The story highlighted the differences between the two Los Angeles–based bands: while W.A.S.P. was concerned with "delivering maximum impact at all times," Stryper thought bands should "convey an uplifting message to their followers"; while W.A.S.P.'s lyrics embraced hedonism, Stryper's focused on the power of God; and perhaps most strikingly, while W.A.S.P. ended concerts by throwing raw meat into the audience, Stryper threw Bibles to fans (about $1,000 worth each night). But Stryper and W.A.S.P. had a few things in common: photographs depicted Lawless striking a rebellious pose and Sweet holding a pair of swords, both men had long hair and wore eye makeup, and both bands had recording contracts with Capitol Records.[45]

Stryper made consistent reference to faith in its songs and videos, especially during its early years. The band claimed to draw its name from Isaiah 53:5, which reads, "By His stripes we are healed"; for much of the band's existence, members dressed in yellow and black stripes.[46] The band name was an acronym for "Salvation through Redemption Yielding Peace and Everlasting Righteousness." In interviews, the band spoke about God and emphasized that they were trying to bring a "positive message" to their fans.[47] When the band appeared in fan magazines, its message was placed beside the more hedonistic words of Motley Crüe, its lyrics were displayed on back pages beside those of the band Britny Fox, and its posters were sold beside those of Warlock, KISS, and Megadeth.[48] Although Stryper's songs included references to God, the lyrics were confident but not confrontational. For example, the lyrics of "Soldiers under Command" optimistically predicted that the band would help God achieve victory over evil: members were soldiers under God's command who fought sin with the Bible. Although the song alluded to war, it was an affirmation of submission to God's plan. Other songs that proclaimed the strength and power of God hardly contained even the militancy of "Battle Hymn of the Republic"—which Stryper included as the last track on the album.[49]

Despite Stryper's considerable success in combining metal and message, doubters questioned whether it softened its religious stance to gain access to secular audiences. Band members were not shy about talking about their faith, but they were not bold enough in their pronouncements for some believers. Even in the band's years, Robert Sweet told the secular metal magazine *Hit Parader:* "We're not religious fanatics who are trying to convert everybody we meet. We're not trying to shut down rock radio stations or make magazines go out of business. We honestly

Figure 9. During the 1980s, Christian metal bands attempted to cross over to mainstream audiences by appearing in popular magazines. Robert Sweet, the drummer for Stryper, appeared on the cover of *Kerrang!* in December 1985. The article proclaimed Stryper "avenging angels" who would "strike a chord with the increasingly straight-laced, God-fearing US populace." © Idols Licensing & Publicity Limited/Ross Halfin.

believe that Jesus Christ is the savior, but we're about the most unreligious Christian band you could imagine. Religion is real for us, but so is rock and roll."[50] Critics decried Sweet's remarks about "religious fanatics" and the band's "unreligious" Christianity. When the band discarded its yellow-and-black costumes and announced a "direction change" in 1989 that included fewer references to faith, rumors circulated that the band had "gone secular" in both music and lifestyle. When asked about these rumors by *Radically Saved,* Michael Sweet bristled at the suggestion that the band was no longer Christian:

> What is secular? What is Christian? Does it mean if you don't say the word Jesus in a song then it is secular? See I don't even know what's secular anymore and what's Christian. I know that we believe in Jesus and we love Jesus. Doesn't that make us Christians? We follow Christ. We're born again. What is a Christian? People are so screwed up now-a-days. . . . They freak out over the slightest things like stupid things like wearing jeans that are too tight or something. It's like you can't be a Christian and wear jeans that are too tight. Or like on stage I'll say, "Hey, we're happy to be partying with you people." A lot of people would probably freak out about that. . . . Our intentions when we say, "Let's party" is, "Let's have a good time" not "Let's smoke dope" and all this.[51]

Sweet's comments indicate dissatisfaction with Christian value judgments: he accused critics of judging the band not on its beliefs but rather its fashion and vocabulary. But to some believers such distinctions provided a critical boundary between the Christian self and the hostile world. By acknowledging the exchange of practices between Christianity and the world, Sweet failed to recognize a strict dividing line that other Christians held dear.

Other bands deemed themselves Christian by using an absolute rather than a relative scale. Sardonyx, a metal band formed in 1988 in Pennsylvania, used music primarily as an evangelizing tool, though it never approached Stryper's success; the band released a self-produced demo but never signed a recording contract. In fact, the band was an outreach program of Lightshine International Metal Ministries, and band members were unpaid volunteers for the organization (the ministry never generated enough money to pay salaries). Sardonyx did not rely on secular or Christian music magazines to promote its work: instead, the ministry sent a complementary newsletter, *Lightshine International,* to a mailing list that, at its peak in the early 1990s, exceeded 8,000 individuals and institutions.[52] Sardonyx was not prepared to compromise with the world—or with Christian bands that had so compromised.

*Lightshine* seized on the motto "Tolerant only to truth"—that is, biblical truth—and reinforced this mantra with band photographs taken on the battlefields of Gettysburg.[53] While worried about the state of the pagan souls of secular bands, Sardonyx regarded those worldly bands as dangerous and preferred to deal with them from afar. Thus *Lightshine* featured a "Prayer Focus," which directed readers to offer their prayers to a different group of sinners (i.e., a different band) identified in each issue, including Ozzy Osborne, Anthrax, and Metallica.

Despite these extraordinary efforts on behalf of the unsaved, it was the lack of purity in the Christian rock world that truly concerned Sardonyx. On its radio show, *The Thunder Zone,* the band maintained a policy that barred Christian bands that violated scripture. Sardonyx offered no specific examples of lyrical violations that would result in banishment, but bands that did not maintain "a godly personal lifestyle" would never be given air time.[54] Other issues of *Lightshine* offer further insight into what violated the band's policy. For example, when Stryper announced its new direction, Tom Denlinger, Sardonyx lead singer and primary columnist for the newsletter, expressed concern about Stryper's new "bad boy" image, complaining that the band used "questionable language" in popular magazines. He urged readers to pray that Stryper "does not compromise their faith in Jesus" and that each member "realizes that their [sic] actions will affect the integrity of all Christian metal bands."[55] Sardonyx also disapproved of success in the secular realm. In a later edition, Denlinger opined, "Every successful band that has experienced secular approval has hardened [itself] against ministry because they know it will not mix with secular success."[56] Denlinger believed that popular acceptance and truthful evangelism were mutually exclusive: indeed, he claimed that it was "biblically impossible" for bands "to be loved by the world and also be teaching the Good News that Jesus told us to."[57] In other words, Christian bands that actually did the Lord's work were doomed to failure. Sardonyx would be validated not by album sales but by persecution, which "drives the church into a deeper fellowship with one another and their Lord."[58]

## AUTHORITY IN MUSIC

Although bands often spoke of their gains in terms of clubs and coverage, the most prized terrain was the hearts and minds of young people. Christian artists assumed that because music influenced what young Americans believed and how they acted, recording artists bore a tremendous responsibility. According to this logic, young people who listened to immoral music were inevitably tempted to sin and rebel. Heavy metal was, according to Christians, brimming with immorality, so it was no wonder that America was experiencing a blight of social problems such as teenage pregnancy, drug abuse, and suicide. Christian artists wished to curtail the influence of secular artists, but they did not wish to eradicate the influence music had on American culture. Rather, they aimed, first, to limit the influence of secular rock musicians had on listeners. Second, Christian artists hoped to use the existing relationship between culture and social power to insert their ideas about authority into the minds of young people. By usurping the vaunted cultural position that secular artists already enjoyed, Christian bands believed they could inspire a return to submission to the authority of parents, God, and the church among their youthful fan base.

In interviews, Christian artists consistently expressed a desire to curb the influence that secular artists exerted on the listening public, because, they maintained, kids could not distinguish between music and lyrics. When asked whether it was possible to block out immoral words and listen only to a beat, Jim LaVerde of Barren Cross told *Gospel Metal*: "You start listening to the music and, before long, you're singing the words and there's no way you can decipher the words from the music. When the music goes in, so do the lyrics. Even if you don't think you're listening to the words, you are."[59] LaVerde argued that the words of secular music opened the doors to un-Christian behavior. Stryper's Michael Sweet, who claimed not to listen to secular music, explained that "most secular music, not all, but most secular music when you listen to it, it puts you in certain moods, and most of the time they're not Christian influenced."[60] Another musician, David Raymond Reeves of Neon Cross, compared music to food and argued that secular music, depending on its intensity, was at best junk food and at worst poison.[61] For these reasons, Christian bands generally advised believers to purge their record collections of all vestiges of secular music, lest it harm their moral well-being.

Despite their warnings about the hazards of secular music, many Christian artists admitted to listening to the music as a necessary evil of their job: they needed to understand the music, and the industry, in order to fight it. Gardian guitarist Paul Cawley summed up the necessity of listening to secular heavy metal: "I heard a guy say once that you don't have to lift up the sewer lid to know that the sewer stinks. But, if you have to get down in the sewer to stop the stench and repair it, then go for it."[62] While concerned that average listeners lacked the willpower to resist suggestive messages in secular music, Christian artists insisted that they possessed the necessary skills for discernment.

During the PMRC hearings, parent activists complained that rock musicians had supplanted parents as the source of authority in American households. As they surveyed American society, Christian artists echoed this sentiment and vowed they would be role models who solved social problems rather than demagogues who incited them. While Christians lamented the heroic status conferred on secular artists, they also wanted to capitalize on youth culture's willingness to put musicians on a pedestal. In interviews, Christian artists compared their behavior to that of secular artists. The Christian music world included a number of artists who had renounced their hedonistic past to join the white metal movement. They described their preconversion lives in the worst possible light, reinforcing the notion that secular musicians routinely charted a Sherman-like path through respectable American norms. The lead singer of Ransom described the secular band he had belonged to previously, Sweet Cheater, as "another Motley Crüe. Just girls, girls, girls, drugs, drinkin', the whole nine yards."[63] Secular bands like Motley Crüe welcomed—even cultivated—this reputation, which tended to reinforce the distance between artist and fan: artist lifestyles offered fans an escape from, but not an answer to, their everyday lives.[64] But Christian artists believed that musicians should offer listeners, not an escape, but rather models for moral living.

Guitarist Tony Rossi of the Daniel Band typified the Christian artist's ideal of living an exemplary life for fans. In an interview with *Heaven's Metal*, Rossi declared that secular musicians, who were "heroes" to the young, led "wanton, reckless lives" that contaminated America's moral climate. Rossi directed his complaint not so much at the heroic status of musicians in contemporary society as at their desire to use their cultural influence to defy social norms.[65] Christian metal bands, on the other hand, based their reputations on responsiveness to listeners; they boasted that they were more sensitive and more accountable to their fans' needs. Mike Lee of Barren Cross claimed that secular bands that endorsed a hedonistic lifestyle "forget that their fans are loaded with problems that they have to deal with day after day." In contrast, Lee claimed that his band was "trying to provide a solution."[66] Young Christian musicians therefore bore a heavy burden, since they had to resist temptation in order to be good role models.

In many ways, Christian bands felt the same alienation that the era's punk music expressed, but their explanation for the causes of that alienation and the necessary response to this issue certainly differed. While hardcore punks refused integration into family, school, work, or consumption, the Christian metal bands of the 1980s and early 1990s endeavored to reconcile young people to these institutions and practices through youth culture.[67] The Christian metal-punk band One Bad Pig typified the use of youth culture to induce young people to accept middle-class social norms. The band frequently offered altar calls, followed after the set by one-on-one counseling with band members. One Bad Pig particularly emphasized their concern for children of divorced parents, as when Paul Q-Pek told *Take a Stand:* "It's amazing the situations we run into; there are so many kids from broken homes coming for prayer and healing, confused kids that don't understand what's going on in their lives and don't feel they have any reason for living, or kids that have come to know the Lord, but have fallen away and keep sinning and they want to know how to change and become victorious over that."[68] Whereas hardcore punks fought the existential voids created by postsuburbia with what one historian has called "a violent, individualist, anti-political politics of refusal," One Bad Pig used religion to salve social wounds and create new beginnings.[69] Although it claimed to possess the same disappointment with the world as punk bands, One Bad Pig ultimately offered its listeners quiescence and acceptance, not refusal. In this instance, a hard-core band inverted the symbolic universe of punk, with its emphasis on dissent and negation. Metal bands, on the other hand, expressed concern for youth through the language of spiritual warfare. Lary Dean of Trytan explained the band's song "It's War" to *White Throne:*

> We see so much coming against the young people in this country. They're deceived, and they think no one cares about them and no one loves them. They are committing suicide at mind-boggling rates. They are turning to drugs, booze, and sex. All these things only sustain them for only a short period of time and then they're right back where they were. Eventually, it will destroy them. . . . [The song says] that the weapons the enemy uses are deception, suicide, and drug abuse. The weapons we use are simply one thing: Christ's love and His compassion for people.[70]

While Q-Pek, a punk rock musician, viewed social maladies like drugs, alcohol, and premarital sex as symptoms of youth alienation, Dean, a metal musician, saw an "enemy" deploying "weapons" including "deception, suicide, and drug abuse" that would ultimately "destroy" young people. The musicians agreed, however, that young people needed tools—or rather religion—to reintegrate themselves into society.

Rather than protesting social conditions or escaping them through suicide or drugs, young people could relieve their alienation religion.

Christian music also promised to help young people cope with peer
pressure. Tom Denlinger of Sardonyx reminded a reader who complained
about the shallowness of Christian music that "Christian teens are con-
stantly facing peer pressure from their non-Christian friends. They need
powerful music that stands up to the secular garbage you were talking
about. Just the fact that it is Christian metal gives them something to
stand on regardless of how shallow more spiritually mature Christians
think it is."[71] According to this logic, white metal became a substitute for
the immoral product consumed by a young person's age cohort. The music
may have been doctrinally tepid, but its conviction provided a spiritual
antidote for the kids who consumed it. Moreover, although Christian
music had long been presented as a "moral alternative," the bands maintained that their work helped kids who still existed in the world of
choices, rather than one of Christian separatism. As one member of the
band Thunder Calling said about those young people, "Most of them
think that Christian music is dull, drab, and boring, but now there's music
to listen to and it gives kids an alternative to secular music."[72] This thinking expressed a certain economic rationalism: when presented with two
otherwise identical products, the young consumer could now choose the
morally superior product without sacrificing musical credibility.

Christians were also aware that because secular youths had a range
of choices for role models, it was likewise necessary to cloak religious
role models in the idiom of youth culture to reach nonbelievers. A Trytan
bandmate told *Heaven's Metal:* "Billy Graham cannot go to *Kerrang!*
magazine and do an article. The kids won't even read it. But if [it's] some
cat like Michael Sweet, with long hair and a Jackson guitar hanging
from his shoulder, they're gonna listen to this guy and what he's doing
with his life. They're gonna receive the fact that he is a musician and he's
doing it for Jesus—and the Holy Spirit can take it from there."[73] People
like Michael Sweet, the lead singer of Stryper, could use the access they
had to the world of youth culture as an entry point to evangelize.

## "THIS IS A CONDOM NATION":
## THE MESSAGE IN CHRISTIAN MUSIC

Although Christian metal bands stretched across subgenres from glam
to death metal, they all claimed that their music contained an important
religious message for listeners. While they accused their mainstream

counterparts of debasing authority, these bands tended to use all aspects of their work—including interviews, lyrics, liner notes, album art, music videos, and live performances—to convey a "Christian" perspective. That message can be placed into two categories. First, Christian metal bands tried to impart not just the virtues of salvation but also the values of self-reliance and personal responsibility through their music. Christian bands usually approached such lessons through straightforward exhortations to faith in Jesus or through first-person narratives that involved salvation.[74] Despite a tradition of focusing on spiritual rather than social issues, Christian metal bands expanded their repertoire to include a second kind of message that included commentary on contemporary events. In these songs, bands explicitly addressed cultural and political topics such as abortion, drugs and alcohol, divorce, and national values.

Christian metal bands understood the importance of making their message of salvation clear to their audience. The liner notes for Sardonyx's demo *Majestic Serenity* offered listeners overviews to each song as well as scriptural information for further study.[75] Bands like Holy Soldier and Whitecross shared Sardonyx's concern about clarity; they told interviewers that their songs employed "upfront" language— no "Christian-ese" phrases like "born-again" or "saved"—making their work "accessible" to non-Christians.[76] Bands believed "explicit" lyrics appealed to young metal fans. Asked by *Heaven's Metal* what a "heathen headbanger" needed to know that a "heathen preppie" did not, Zion lead singer Rex Scott explained that his band, whose audience ranged from elementary school kids to young people in their twenties, tried to "hit [listeners] blunt in the face with what we have and make it very easily understandable. . . . I don't want to underestimate our audience at all. I know that they can get into lyrics that make people think. We do make 'em think, but it's not in an allegorical-sense necessarily."[77] The band Bloodgood shared this outlook and featured songs like "Crucify," which dramatized the story of Jesus' crucifixion, and "The Messiah," which told the resurrection story.[78]

Although metal bands devoted considerable energy to urging spiritual rededication, they also used their music to address social issues. These songs resembled the outlook of other conservatives in the 1980s who became involved in single-issue campaigns to combat "domestic corruption" in the form of pornography, gay rights, and abortion.[79] While the work of Jerry Falwell and Pat Robertson in mobilizing Christian conservatives for political activism is well documented, metal bands were also an integral part of the cultural work of the Christian Right. Whereas Robertson's 1988 presidential campaign built on civil rights–era practices of voter registration drives and voter guides, Christian rock bands used music to comment on contemporary society.

Like the testimony at the PMRC hearings that linked teenage suicide rates to heavy metal's lyrics and visual imagery, Christian metal's issue-based songs reflected Christian musicians' conviction that young fans listened to lyrics and used the meanings they discerned as guidelines for behavior.[80] As evangelicals, many band members felt that the solution to the nation's problems lay in a revival, but they could not rely on Americans to attend church to renew their religious commitments, nor could they rely on secular bands to bring the message of salvation to the lost. Christian bands often described their songs as important counterpoints to secular work and explained that listeners needed to understand the "Christian point of view" on topics like abortion and premarital sex. While narrowly focused, the issue-based songs reflected a concern about the fate of the family and of the nation following the civil rights, feminist, and gay rights movements of the 1960s and 1970s. Like other religious conservatives, Christian bands mourned what they perceived to be a post-1960s loss of stability in American society. They sought to restore that stability—and the values associated with it—using the very culture they blamed for destabilization in the first place.

Christian metal and punk bands tended to write about issues they believed affected young people: suicide, drug use, and sexual promiscuity. They wrote topical songs, bands typically explained, because they wanted to offer a "Christian" perspective that countered secular releases. During the 1980s, metal acts like Ozzy Osborne, AC/DC, and Judas Priest were accused of promoting suicide in songs.[81] In an effort to counteract this trend, Empty Tomb, Rapture, and Bloodgood each recorded a song about suicide.[82] The first three verses of Bloodgood's song "Alone in Suicide" are written from the perspective of a person contemplating suicide; however, both the final verse and the chorus offer the Christian perspective, counseling the individual to seek salvation and redemption. Here, once again, a Christian band addressed a familiar theme of metal music but altered the message to suit its religious viewpoint.[83]

Drug and alcohol abuse was another topic of concern for Christian bands, many of them including members who had used drugs before their conversion. The bands Bride ("No Matter the Price" and

"Whiskey See"), Gardian ("Good Life"), and Shout ("Shout") recorded songs about drugs or alcohol use. Philadelphia recorded a concept album, *Search and Destroy,* that chronicled the problems of a runaway named Bobby who experimented with drugs before becoming a Christian.[84] Like their secular counterparts, Christian bands occasionally gave benefit concerts in support of a favorite cause. Such was the case in Baltimore in 1988 when Bride, Believer, Torn Flesh, Souldier, and other bands performed at a free white metal concert called the RRAD Festival (Righteous Rock Against Drugs).[85] David Bach of Gardian, whose members included former drug users, explained the band's reasons for recording the antidrug song "Good Life": "I've had terrible experiences in my life with drug abuse. That's what this song is all about, the big lie of drugs. It goes on to explain how we, at one time, lived that way—enslaved by our various passions. Now we know what the good life truly is."[86] While it was common for musicians to refer to drug use in songs, the approach of Christian bands differed in that they offered religion as an alternative. Still other bands registered songs on hot Christian topics such as evolution (One Bad Pig's song "Let's Be Frank"), cults (Barren Cross's "Cultic Regimes"), gay rights (Torn Flesh's "Gay Rights?" and Seraiah's "Carnival World"), and abstinence versus premarital sex (Zion's song "Sold You a Lie" and Lust Control's "Virginity Disease" and "Get Married").[87]

When it came to addressing social issues in songs, Christian metal bands most often focused on abortion. Groups that expressed their views were uniformly pro-life. During the 1980s and 1990s, several bands wrote at least one song that addressed abortion: REZ ("Fiend or Foul"), Barren Cross ("Killers of the Unborn"), King's X ("Legal Kill"), Holy Danger ("Don't Slaughter Your Daughter"), Hellfire ("Abolish Legal Murder"), Guardian ("World without Love"), and Lust Control ("Planned Parenthood" and "Operation Rescue").[88] Holy Soldier made abortion a theme in its video for "See No Evil" (1990). The video, which MTV rejected, depicted a teenage boy wandering alone, which, according to the band, represented "the spirit of an aborted child."[89] This concept followed from the song's lyrics, written from the fetus's point of view.[90] By giving an aborted fetus a voice and life, the lyrics and video made an emotional appeal against abortion. Other bands, such as Exodus II ("Choose Life"), featured booths at concerts offering antiabortion literature and stickers (echoing similar efforts for progressive causes by secular bands); according to *Heaven's Metal,* the booth referred pregnant young women to "a nearby pro-life crisis pregnancy center" for assistance.[91] The issue even inspired Christian musicians to produce a benefit song in the vein of Band Aid (British musicians' mid-1980s effort), and USA for Africa. In 1985 Christian artists ranging from pop music's Debby Boone to heavy metal's Barren Cross recorded the anti-abortion song "Fight the Fight" to benefit Americans Against Abortion, the pro-life wing of Texas-based folksinger Keith Green's organization, Last Days Ministries.[92]

While Christian artists of all genres recorded pro-life songs, the punk-thrash band Lust Control offered one of the most strident condemnations of abortion. Founded in 1988 by *Heaven's Metal* publisher Doug Van Pelt with help from Paul Q-Pek and a few other established Christian metal musicians, the band performed in masks to conceal their identities. Spring Arbor, the major distributor for Christian bookstores across the country, initially banned Lust Control's first album, *This Is a Condom Nation*.[93] Van Pelt, the band's only permanent member, later explained that he started it as a ministry because he "realized we could meet some real needs . . . by addressing some issues that most people in the church, unfortunately, ignore. God was not silent on these issues, so we screamed out some answers."[94] The band's 1992 release, *We Are Not Ashamed,* included two songs that directly addressed abortion. "Planned Parenthood" begins by praising "godly" parents, teachers, and preachers but quickly condemns Planned Parenthood—"Your answers for kids lead to their destruction"—before moving to the chorus: "Planned parenthood, you ain't no good / Your only plan: To brainwash the nation / Planned parenthood, you ain't no good / You justify murder and fornication." In subsequent verses the song draws other eternal battle lines and connects Planned Parenthood to another contemporary movement, gay liberation: "You are pro-abortion / You are pro–gay rights / I know one thing that you're against / You are anti-Christ!!!"[95] Lust Control viewed Operation Rescue more favorably and even wrote a song about the movement. In contrast to the accusative "you" of "Planned Parenthood," the lyrics for "Operation Rescue" were written from the perspective of someone within the movement. The second verse begins by warning onlookers of God's wrath: "Won't you lift a hand? / For some it's too late / God will smite our land / We can't sleep away our fate." Then the verse describes the plight of activists: "We crawl and cry / And end up in jail / Want no babies to die / And end up for sale / There's no room for pride / I've done nothing too long / To feel that way inside." The song ends by asking, "Operation Rescue—What if they were killing you?"[96]

Bands were not satisfied to allow such lyrics to speak for themselves; they frequently expounded on social themes in interviews. Jim LaVerde of Barren Cross explained his politically minded band's music: "We don't promote violence, drug traffic, sex, etc. We promote something very positive, something that would get the family back together as a unit."[97] Whereas the themes of secular music allegedly contributed to increased levels of violence, drug use, and sexual promiscuity, bands like Barren Cross believed they promoted "family values." Besides, the band believed, converts needed guidance regarding complicated contemporary issues that arose in the lives of even the most devout believers. Singer Mike Lee told an interviewer:

> I'm a very politically minded person, and I regard [Barren Cross] as a very socially conscious band. There's a lot more to life than just "Jesus saves." I mean, what do you do after you become a Christian? What about all the aspects of life that people go through? I think a lot of bands are on top of the world and forget their fans down here and that they go through struggles. We try to meet people's needs in areas like suicide, drug abuse, children of alcoholic parents, abortion; we touch on a lot of issues and try to be as encouraging as we can.[98]

To be a "socially conscious band," Barren Cross believed it needed to write about more than faith and salvation. Yet when the band addressed the issue of family and abortion, it clearly aimed much of its message at young women. Members suggested that their song "Killers of the Unborn," for example, offered "God's view" on abortion.[99] Although Barren Cross hoped that the song would reach a heavy metal fan who might not otherwise have cared about the issue, the band was particularly concerned about reaching women. Member Steve Whitaker claimed the song had a profound effect on female audience members: "Some women and other people have been really touched. We played San Francisco a few weeks ago and a girl came up after the show and said, 'Will you sign an autograph for my unborn child?' She's pregnant. She wasn't planning an abortion, but it touched my heart that she even said that."[100] In this anecdote, Whitaker suggests that the song strengthened a bond between mother and "unborn child"; the girl acted on behalf of the fetus by securing an autograph. In other interviews, the band spoke about confrontations with abortion supporters. Jim LaVerde remembered a pro-choice audience member who approached him after a show. LaVerde said he told the woman about "a beautiful baby, a precious little girl who was baptized at church last Sunday only because her mother who heard that song had decided to go ahead and have that child rather than abort it." According to LaVerde, the woman "stood in front of me and couldn't say a word after that"; he believed the story "may have convicted her really hard, but God will use that and maybe down the road another child will be saved because of it."[101]

The abortion issue often led Christian metal bands and magazines to discuss electoral politics. During the 1992 presidential campaign, Dale Thompson of Bride surprised the audience during his acceptance speech at an awards show by endorsing the Bush-Quayle ticket; he later explained that the Republican candidates' stance on abortion was the key factor in earning his support.[102] The band Sardonyx used its newsletter, *Lightshine*, to publish anti-abortion materials, including a photograph of an aborted fetus with the caption "freedom of choice???" When a reader wrote in to complain about the band's pro-life stance, Tom Denlinger's published response stated, "Pro-Abortion people are self centered killers and must be outlawed."[103] In the next newsletter, the band published a "fact sheet" entitled "Abortion: The Human Factor" and accompanied by an editorial from Sardonyx member Kevin Bradley, who wrote: "People cringe when they see the horror of the Nazi Holocaust. . . . How much more of a disgrace when a country and a people condone abortion and allow it to remain legal."[104] In a later issue, Bradley's wife shared the couple's story of the death of their twins, born premature. The editorial closed by challenging "anyone who has lost a child and remains Pro-Choice (Pro-Death)" to write to them.[105] In addition to emotional appeals against abortion, *Lightshine* also had an eye on political developments regarding the issue. Denlinger attacked Bill Clinton's position on abortion, claiming that Clinton was "bowing to the radical women's organizations of the liberal politically correct."[106]

Just as Christian bands divided on the issue of secular crossover, there was also division over whether bands should address social issues in their work. Many bands believed that simply singing about social issues failed to address the real problem. Paul Cawley told *The Pendragon* that Gardian wanted to reach "those in need," including the children of divorce, runaways, and drug addicts; they did not, however, address social issues in song, because, according to one band member, the band wanted to provide fans "with hope, not tell them the problem."[107] A reviewer for the same magazine found fault in the music of Barren Cross, which prided itself on addressing social themes. According to the reviewer, "rather than attacking the root of the problem"—sin—the band focused on the symptoms. "What good is it," the reviewer asked, "to prevent someone from committing suicide, or from getting an abortion, if you fail to present them with the real problem, their sin, and their need of a savior from that sin? Without that, they will end up in hell anyway."[108] Since only the Gospel provided answers to social problems, the band needed to direct its energy toward bringing God's message to sinful audiences. Although they claimed to disavow politics, those who called for a focus on "biblical" values in fact took a rather political stance, since they were suggesting that the answers to society's problems depended on individual Americans renewing their religious commitment.

Besides specific political issues, Christians also worried more generally about rebellion. In their work as "metal missionaries" to America's youth, bands often attempted to redefine rebellion: in a "post-Christian" (and post-1960s) world, true rebellion was resistance to sin and obedience to parental, church, and divine authority. In this sense of the word, Christians were those truly in opposition to prevailing social norms. When asked what he wanted to say to *Heaven's Metal* readers, singer Steve Camp said: "Metal music is a very radical form of music. It's a very aggressive form. Adults that do not understand it say that 'it's just used to cause rebellion.' I'd say to them, 'Use it to cause rebellion against hell. Use it to cause rebellion on the world that's trying to conform people against Jesus Christ.'"[109] In once sense Camp was reiterating a generational refrain: adults just didn't understand. But his meaning diverged from the old message when he suggested that conformity to contemporary society's will rested in sin, not prayer. In this interpretation, obedience was the true transgression.

Other Christians who identified connections between rebellion and rock music tried to carefully refine its usage. In an article he wrote, "What's Wrong with Christian Music," musician Michael Bloodgood focused on clothing, rebellious attitude, and idolatry. Discussing the "rebellious attitude" of Christian music, Bloodgood explained, "There has traditionally been an underlying attitude of rebellion" in music, particularly in the hard rock and heavy metal genres. Bloodgood continued:

> Now I'm all for rebellion: rebellion against the world's eroding values and morals (i.e., legalized abortion, pornography, etc.); rebellion against the violations of our fellow man's rights; rebellion against any authority who tries to suppress my freedom to worship as I choose (and we're getting dangerously close to that even in this country); and rebellion against any world system that goes against the Bible and the things of God. However, the attitude of rebellion that I'm talking about must be centered in agape (God's)

love; not in uncontrolled emotionalism or with disrespect for those who might not agree with us. The latter group might include our teachers, parents, pastors, etc., who might not share your enthusiasm for rock and roll. Remember that even Jesus, God in the flesh, was submitted to His earthly parents; that is, as long as He lived with them He was submitted to their authority.[110]

"Permissible" rebellion, according to Bloodgood, included either taking specific stands against issues such as abortion or pornography, or exercising the freedom of religion guaranteed by the Constitution. Significantly, Bloodgood vaguely blamed the world for curtailing values and rights: one may surmise that he advocated rebellion against society—for eroding values—or possibly against the government—for legalizing abortion and pornography. It is less clear whom Bloodgood would have fingered for suppressing worship or violating the rights of his fellow man. But Bloodgood warned specifically that rebellion should not include "undue emotionalism" or "disrespect" for embodied authorities like teachers, parents, and pastors. He even gave readers biblical passages that warned of the consequences of disobedience, and he reminded readers that even Jesus submitted to his earthly parents.

While Michael Bloodgood focused on rebellion permissible for teenagers, other bands concentrated on their responsibilities as Christian musicians in a secular musical universe. Stryper's Michael Sweet suggested that bands could rebel by offering a different kind of role model to teenagers. When asked why secular metal bands were popular with teenagers, Sweet ventured that kids found bands' "rebellious attitude" appealing because kids "tend to have a spirit of rebellion in life, against their parents, against their school, against anything that tries to stand in their way. Most kids like to rebel." When asked by the interviewer if Stryper used its music as "rebellion against evil," Sweet was cautious: "I don't think we should use that term because automatically we'll be known as a 'rebellious group.' . . . I'll tell you what we are . . . we are a band that is trying their hardest to get rid of the Devil in rock 'n' roll. That means getting rid of drugs in rock 'n' roll, sex outside of marriage in rock, those things, out of rock."[111] Thus, while unwilling to embrace the term "rebellion," Sweet nevertheless placed his band as the exception to accepted norms of rock music.

While Stryper seemed reluctant to accept the word "rebellion" in relation its work, the members of One Bad Pig, the punk–hard rock band from Austin, enthusiastically embraced the word in discussing their band's place in the punk music industry. A major record label had rejected their album, they claimed, because of the group's Christian beliefs. Yet rejection by secular punks merely served to authenticate their punk identity. Paul Q-Pek explained:

> Even in a movement that has as its very purpose to be offensive, to break rules, being just anti-whatever else there was, here we were: a band with a hardcore sound speaking about Jesus. What could be more controversial and offensive than that? It just seems like the message of the Gospel will offend even the ones who have a goal to offend people.[112]

More than a decade before Q-Pek made his remarks, Johnny Rotten of the Sex Pistols had roiled audiences by declaring "I am an antichrist" in the song "Anarchy in the U.K.," only to see his band's record label cease production and distribution of its album—effectively banning the band from British airwaves—after members misbehaved on national television.[113] Now, Christian bands asserted that they could offend audiences for God. One Bad Pig rested its claim to rebellion upon songs that suggested "anarchy is prison," upon religious testimonies that proclaimed the Gospel, and upon rejection by secular record labels. The band even incorporated this rebellion into its first independent release, *A Christian Banned*. At times the sense of rebellion in the Christian rock world achieved aphoristic pith, as when magazine editor Tyler Bacon concluded a column by urging readers, "If you're going to choose to sin, commit a hedonist's sin and obey God!"[114]

## JUSTIFYING METAL TO THE CONSERVATIVE CHURCH

Although the secular world greeted them somewhat incredulously, Christian musicians received some of their harshest criticism from their conservative brethren in the church. Members of secular bands had it easy: they had to negotiate only the perils of sex, drugs, and rock 'n' roll, whereas Christian bands had to worry about the pitfalls of theology and doctrine, as well as condemnations from outraged ministers who asserted that "Christian rock" was a contradiction in terms. Bands confronted a dilemma that had vexed conservative Protestants since the Scopes Trial in 1925: they could remain "separate" from the world and play only to religious audiences—the path fundamentalists had chosen through much of the twentieth century—or they could engage with the world while taking care to avoid internalizing its values—the choice favored by evangelicals. By selecting the evangelical route and seeking secular audiences, Christian metal groups faced the difficult task of explaining to believers how they had successfully replicated secular rock 'n' roll (evidence of their role "in the world") without becoming corrupted (evidence of being "of the world").[115]

Jimmy Swaggart was one of Christian rock music's most ardent critics. His southern gospel albums appeared with Christian metal albums on *Billboard*'s inspirational album charts, but Swaggart and Christian metal bands were certainly not on the same page when it came to Christian rock.[116] In a 1986 pamphlet, Swaggart repeated an argument that had been used by ministers against rock 'n' roll for thirty years when he declared that Satan was using the genre "to destroy an entire generation of young people" by incrementally introducing youths to drugs, alcohol, sex, and Satan worship. Swaggart argued that, regardless of lyrical content, secular and Christian rock were indistinguishable; the problem with Christian rock was that "it strives to make Christ acceptable to man rather than man acceptable to Christ."[117] Given these criticisms, it is not surprising that when the newsletter *Take a Stand* asked Bloodgood members about the kinds of people who attacked them, guitarist David Zaffiro identified the "Satanic church" and the "very conservative religious church."[118]

In describing their work, Christian bands were careful not to provoke their Christian critics, instead calling for unity in the church. To mollify conservatives, Christian bands characterized their work as a mission among young Americans. They insisted they were on the same side as other Christians; they had merely developed a different—and more effective—way of reaching young people. Rex Carroll of Whitecross tried to explain the difference between his band and preachers like Jimmy Swaggart and Billy Graham. According to Carroll, Christian bands were "ambassadors" or "special messengers." Unlike musicians, ministers "simply can't reach a certain crowd . . . they just don't have the vocabulary, connection, communication," but, Carroll said, "God wants to reach those people still."[119] Bands thus insisted that although they used a more extreme medium, their message of salvation remained the same. They also claimed that their music was sanctioned by God. Tom Denlinger wrote:

> [God] gives us the ability to create good music and we have. We praise Him with our best. We praise Him with our metal and we make disciples with our metal. God commanded us to tell the world about Jesus' love for them. Metal is our mission field. As musicians we skillfully build the vehicle that introduces the creation to its Creator. . . . He also lets us enjoy this life of service to Him. Metal is our life. Evangelism is our mission.[120]

According to Denlinger, musicians were using their God-given talents not only to praise God but also to recruit new disciples. The music was not an end in itself; rather, musicianship was a life in service to God.

As they struggled to justify their music to conservatives, Christian bands sometimes emphasized their intentions to evangelize, but at other times measured their results. As Christian bands defended their work to conservatives, they occasionally echoed the secular artists at the PMRC Senate hearings who complained that listeners had misinterpreted their intentions. Thus, conservatives who criticized the "worldliness" of Christian metal were ignoring the bands' goal of merely trying to spread the Gospel in the most effective manner possible. Christian bands frequently turned to the Bible to justify their efforts, as when Glenn Kaiser of REZ, one of the oldest and most respected Christian rock bands, told *Heaven's Metal* that there were "380 verses in Scripture that speak to music: 40 in the New Testament and 340 in the Old."[121] Kaiser argued that although musical styles had changed, the importance of music to Christianity had not. Bands also used the Bible to emphasize that believers should not prejudge potential converts based on their appearances; rather, they needed to look at the person's heart. Steve Valdez of Sanctuary defended long hair, asking *Gospel Metal*, "What is a 'worldly look?' Is it a physical appearance or an attitude of the heart?" Valdez then used King David to illustrate the importance of the right "attitude of the heart": "God chose David to be king of Israel because of his heart. His brothers were very elegant looking and masculine, but God chose this young shepherd boy to be king. . . . We're saying that our standard is greater than God's. God isn't bound by culture or dress codes or particular styles. A lot of people that we reach and evangelize [have] long hair. We need to reach everybody."[122]

Yet even as bands emphasized the importance of intentions, they also stressed their success in reaching secular audiences. Specifically, bands cited the gospel story in which Jesus cast a demon out of a man, only to have the Pharisees suggest that the exorcism occurred through the aid of Beelzebul, ruler of demons.[123] The bands downplayed the conflict inherent in the story of Jesus lashing out against his elders even as they positioned themselves as the inheritors of Jesus' actions and identified their conservative elders as latter-day Pharisees.

While Christian bands complained about their burden of self-discipline, they also allowed some rather worldly practices to define their notion of professionalism. Indeed, as much as the bands defined themselves *against* secular bands in terms of morality and discipline, they strove to emulate their adversaries in sound quality, live performance, and appearance. Because Christian bands so closely mimicked their secular counterparts, they felt compelled to explain why these similarities were necessary, lest they be accused of becoming part of the world. Ultimately, the issue of professionalism can be explained by a simple division in Christian thought over whether metal music should be a tool or a lifestyle. If metal was a tool, Christians could clothe themselves in the culture's accoutrements without sullying their faith; as missionaries, they were simply using the medium for its broad appeal and practicality. On the other hand, metal as a lifestyle presented Christians with a broad set of problems, as it suggested that lifestyle took precedence over faith. Therefore, as bands tried to explain their actions to potential conservative critics, they emphasized that their intentions, or motivations, were the most important factor in the creative process. And, as they consistently explained in interviews, their intention was to create a professional-sounding and professional-looking band in order to bring glory to God.

During the 1980s, many Christian bands emphasized the importance of quality in both lyrical content and sound. Bands complained that fans would not take them seriously unless record labels provided them with a recording budget equal to those for secular bands. In interviews, bands such as Bride, Whitecross, and Judea all expressed the need for more generous recording budgets; without the funds, these bands argued, Christians could not be expected to set the standard in production quality.[124]

As bands sought to enhance their work with styles from the secular world, they had to be careful to maintain their religious focus. Perhaps the most controversial syncretism lay in costume and hairstyle. In the metal world, artists often used clothing and hair as a means of transgressing conventions of gender (especially masculinity) and sexuality; as Robert Walser suggests, approaches have included misogyny, "exscription" of the feminine, and androgyny.[125] Many Christian bands favored glam rock, which featured ornate costumes and hairstyles as well as a sound that emphasized melody rather than aggression. But for conservative Christians, clothes and hair were important indicia of gender roles: long hair on men suggested effeminacy, and conservatives were as likely to denounce this cultural challenge to "traditional" gender norms—regardless of its prevalence in the mainstream—as they were political affronts like the Equal Rights Amendment. Moreover, some Protestant translations of the Bible used "effeminacy" and "sodomy" interchangeably, so the challenge to "manliness" presented by long hair and glam makeup posed a further threat to heterosexual norms at a time when Christian conservatives blamed gay men for the AIDS epidemic, applauded the 1986 U.S. Supreme Court decision in *Bowers v. Hardwick* upholding sodomy laws, and lobbied for anti–gay rights ordinances in local communities.

In the Christian world, where artists sought to reinforce traditional gender roles, however, long hair and clothes needed to be based on professional obligation or biblical directive. When asked about costume and stage makeup in interviews with Christian magazines, bands consistently explained that they needed to use props to look professional. They distanced themselves from the clothes by insisting the items were "stage makeup," "costumes," or "uniforms." About makeup, Michael Bloodgood said, "There's a lot of Christian bands that get washed out because they don't really act or look like a professional band."[126] Other bands emphasized that their stage costumes were for the benefit of their fans, who judged them by standards set by secular bands. Bassist Mike Grato of Eternal Ryte explained that the band was "picky" about costumes because fans were concerned about them. Fashion was particularly important when Eternal Ryte played with secular bands, because "when we're out there and we're preaching the gospel, we need to be a step ahead of [secular bands]. We need [to be] even better. We're going out there representing God." Later in the interview, guitarist Bob Smith assured readers that the band's stage appearance was just an act: "All the stuff we use on stage as far as what we wear and how we look and what we do to our hair; when we leave that stage, it all stays there. We don't take that off [*sic*] and wear it around the streets either. When we're offstage, we're not anything like what we are onstage."[127] Similarly, Jim LaVerde claimed that secular fans wanted a spectacular show: "It's the dress that attracts the secular crowd. . . . If you don't have a good stage show, people say, 'Yeah, they were a good band but, they don't look that great. No pyrotechniques, no light show, no fog machines, or cool costumes.' It's like a dramatic presentation."[128] In order to win souls for Jesus, bands reasoned, they needed to impress fans with a visual display; thus, their stage shows could be justified as professional necessity rather than personal extravagance.

Hairstyles proved particularly difficult to justify, since, unlike a costume, long hair could not be removed when not on stage. For conservative Christians, long hair on men suggested effeminacy. To strengthen their arguments about hairstyle, bands scoured the Bible for a verse that

justified their position. An interviewer asked Jim LaVerde of Barren
Cross about a biblical passage (1 Corinthians 6:9–10) that suggested
that "effeminates won't inherit the kingdom of God" and the common
notion that "guys with long hair are effeminates." LaVerde responded
by claiming that Jesus and the apostles had long hair, as did Samson.
But he also countered the author's reading of the verse by quoting from
later in the same book (1 Corinthians 11:13–15) and arguing that Paul's
letter simply talked about "neat, clean hair."[129] At other times, bands
dismissed the controversy over long hair as cultural, as when a member
of the band Gardian, which offered a biblical verse as the basis of its
stage costumes, nonetheless told *Gospel Metal*, "Long hair is a cultural
attitude."[130]

## "IF STRYPER HAD ONE FAN, IT WOULD BE ME": EFFECTIVENESS

Although bands tried to avoid discussing the implications of their imi-
tation of secular styles, the issue of masculinity persistently arose when
magazines discussed current problems in Christian metal. Christians
bands were vulnerable to such questions in ways that secular bands
were not: as the PMRC had complained, secular bands like Motley Crüe
and W.A.S.P. sang about their (hetero)sexual conquests, gave interviews
in which they discussed their sexual exploits, and made videos that featured scantily clad women fawning over them. Christian publications,
in contrast, suggested that Christian beliefs and metal lifestyles could
coexist. In "Rock 'n' Roll Wives," for example, *Take a Stand* offered a
three-part interview with the wives of the members of Barren Cross in
order to show readers "the importance, responsibility, and balance of
family in a music ministry."[131] Similarly, *Lightshine* frequently published pictures of band members and their children; it also updated fans
on family news, as when it reported that vocalist Tom Denlinger and his
wife were expecting their first child in 1992. The item added, "When we
say we are family oriented metal, that's what we mean. To all you musicians out there who fear getting married and having children, well let's
just say, yeah right! It all depends on your priorities."[132] Unmarried
Christian artists, as well, assured fans they lived according to biblical
guidelines. In interviews with secular fan magazines, members of
Stryper contrasted their behavior with that of secular bands. When
asked how they dealt with flirtatious female fans, Robert Sweet told *Hit
Parader:* "A lot of times girls . . . who want to go back to the hotel with

us" would approach the band backstage. Sweet added, "We're only too happy to oblige—but not for the reason you probably think. We want to talk to them about the power of Jesus. They probably come to us for sex, but we try to tell them we've found something even better than sex—the word of Jesus Christ."[133]

Despite such reassurances that musicians were leading heterosexual lives that conformed to conservative Christian precepts, bands and fans worried that their clothing suggested otherwise. For example, when an interviewer asked Zion lead singer Rex Scott about costume and effeminate appearance, he cited the need to look a certain way to be convincing: "We wear real flashy stuff too and a little bit of makeup, but it's pretty much theater-style. It's rock theater. It's not to look effeminate or anything. A lot of people would say certain bands look effeminate, where, in the eyes of another person, they don't."[134] Yet other musicians were less convinced that costumes did not undermine gender roles. David Raymond Reeves explained that he had left Neon Cross because he saw "some of the choices that we made . . . as compromising, like going glam, dressing glam (glamorous). . . . With the makeup, I felt that I was dressing as a girl, which I was not at all happy with."[135] Fans were at times similarly unnerved by the gender-bending tendencies of Christian metal, as demonstrated in a 1987 *Heaven's Metal* readers' poll that asked fans to name the "biggest problem in Christian rock." While top concerns were the lack of promotion, the quality of the music, and "lack of Christ-centered lyrics," the "effeminate appearance by many Christian metal artists" registered as the sixth-greatest concern among fans. One reader even rebuked fellow fans for "getting hung up on the heavy metal image and look," thereby forcing bands to emulate secular bands.[136]

When Christian artists dressed in a sexually ambiguous manner, fans reacted angrily. In 1992 *White Throne* ran a photograph of Cross, the male singer for the band Virginia Creeper, who had a decidedly glam—that is, "feminine"—appearance. In the picture, Cross was seductively posed wearing white boots, fishnet stockings, a belt with feathers, leather gloves, and an off-the-shoulder shirt; he also wore bracelets, a rhinestone choker, and large hoop earrings, had long feathered black hair, and wore mascara and lipstick.[137] Readers were outraged. One, who claimed to have used the magazine to evangelize among nonbelievers, wrote: "This poor deceived gentleman is dressed like a woman. It's bad enough for men to dress like women but this Virginia Creeper guy is dressed like an immoral woman. I wouldn't feel comfortable dating a woman dressed like that, and this is a man. . . . This kind of stuff destroys the line of definition between what is sin and what is right-eousness and brings confusion to people who don't know God." Another letter commented, "I realize that Christian music has broken ground in all areas, but I refuse to accept a Transvestite Christian Band. I fail to see how anyone (male or female) who dresses like that can hon-estly call [himself or herself] Christian. Not only is it unscriptural (Romans 1:24–32), but it's completely immoral."[138] In the following issue, the editor admitted that he had disapproved of Virginia Creeper's appearance and that he had run the photograph to provoke a reaction; he also added that, following the outcry, the band had informed the magazine of its decision to tone down its look.[139]

Stryper also received attention for dressing in a manner that imitated secular groups. Although the band provided an interesting counterbal-ance to secular acts whenever it appeared in fan magazines like *Kerrang!* and *Hit Parader,* the band's ambiguity was certain to make Bible believ-ers uncomfortable. The same December 1985 issue of *Kerrang!* that fea-tured Robert Sweet in a cover article ran pictures of musicians celebrating the holidays: Motörhead's Lemmy posed with a young woman wearing stiletto heals, garters, a short skirt, and a gift tag read-ing "to Lemmy"; members of RATT posed with bottles of champagne and, according to the caption, "an address book containing the names of every eligible gal in the States"; and female members of bands Girlschool and Rock Goddess were featured in a centerfold with the banner headline "Christmas Tarts" (notably, the back cover showed Ozzy Osborne holding his children in front of a mantel adorned with stockings.) On the same issue's cover, Robert Sweet holds a Bible; with feathered blond hair and an unzipped leather shirt, he wears eyeliner, bracelets, an earring, a crucifix, and legwarmers. The article informs readers that Sweet was a "quiet, unassuming, self-effacing fellow," but also described him as "extremely pretty" with "a mane of beautifully flowing blond hair framing oh-so delicate, almost girlish features."[140] Christian magazines occasionally drew attention to the issue, as when *Heaven's Metal* suggested the resemblance between Sweet and long-haired actress Farrah Fawcett.[141]

Critics who worried that metal fashion caused confusion about gender roles also worried that it provoked heterosexual desire in both fans and musicians. In his article "What's Wrong with Christian Music," Michael Bloodgood cited clothing of both bands and fans as a top issue to be addressed. He chastised readers for tempting one another, asking,

"Does any Christian want to attract a potential boyfriend/girlfriend that way? Should a Christian man or woman be attracted to someone who dresses seductively?"[142] *Take a Stand* editor Christy Arnold echoed these sentiments when, after attending the HIS II metal festival in Fontana, California, she lamented the worldliness of fans' style choices. Arnold reminded readers, "Being a Christian does not give you the right to cause your brother or sister in the Lord to stumble."[143] Clothing thus remained an important distinction between the world and the Christian.

While Christian musicians believed their work should serve God, their actions themselves—particularly their clothing—frequently attracted attention. As Michael Bloodgood wrote in his critique of Christian music, "Anything that takes the rightful place of our attention away from God is idolatry."[144] Whenever Christian bands' styles and practices distracted fans—particularly female fans—from worshipping God, the bands faced a dilemma. After a fan chastised him for bearing his chest and wearing tight pants, thus drawing the attention of young girls, Tom Denlinger explained that when he went to minister to the flock, he always made sure "as much attention goes to Jesus as possible and not to my body."[145] When asked about groupies, some bands claimed they resisted them through the power of the Holy Spirit. For example, when *Gospel Metal* asked Sacred Warrior how its members dealt with "the lust of the flesh, the lust of the eyes, and the pride of life while on stage," they responded that they looked people in the eyes, "which is where the Spirit will bite them harder."[146] Other bands expressed disgust at fans who idolized them. A member of the band Deliverance told *Heaven's Metal:* "It's mostly girls I talk to and it's, 'Oh they're so cute. They're this and that.' You never hear any ministry comments or where, 'They're so into the Lord.' That's where I have a problem. As long as they're idolizing the right thing about them. I think Christ has to be portrayed through us and if they're idolizing Christ through us, fine. But if they're idolizing the band, I have problems with it."[147] Deliverance worried that fans had merely substituted a Christian rock idol for a secular idol and that, while the band had reached the flock, the flock had not heard the message.

A fan letter sent to *Metal,* a mainstream fan magazine, suggests that bands' fears about idolatry may have been well founded. After a reader had disparaged Stryper in an earlier issue, Miss Jane Ann Evans of Henrietta, Texas, jumped to the band's defense. As one might expect, the fan cited the band's musical accomplishments ("I've seen Stryper live four times and they kick some serious rock 'n' roll") and its Christian perspective (the band had "the sweetest, most loving personalities" in rock, and if the critics wanted "to see them disappear from the face of the earth you'll get your wish. When the rapture occurs they'll disappear and so will I."). But the letter writer also professed a physical attraction to the band, arguing that "Stryper is the best looking band and Robert Sweet is the most GORGEOUS babe I've ever laid eyes on!" Admitting to having over one hundred pictures and posters of the band on her wall, she concluded: "If [Stryper] had one fan it would be me" (God loving all his children, He couldn't choose favorites).[148] While Stryper assumed it could blur the line between Christianity and the world without implications for its fans, it was clear that fans also mixed secular and Christian behaviors: while the letter writer was a professing Christian, she was also a fan who idolized her favorite band much as secular fans did.

The popularity of Christian heavy metal between 1984 and 1994 occurred during a period of heightened rhetorical hostility from and political activism among conservative activists. Activists battled over elections, public space, and language. High points included the early success of Jerry Falwell's Moral Majority, Pat Robertson's 1988 presidential bid, his subsequent establishment of the Christian Coalition, the rise of Operation Rescue in the late 1980s, and Patrick Buchanan's "culture wars" speech at the 1992 Republican National Convention. Discussion of Christians' cultural work during this period was generally limited to televangelist scandals. Indeed, critics often scoffed at the idea that consumption could serve as a political act. In 1996 the *New Republic* snickered, "Just as it was being rebuilt politically by Jerry Falwell and Pat Robertson, the conservative Christian community was reborn as a marketing demographic."[149]

However, viewing white evangelicals' political potency as separate from their emergence as a consumer bloc overlooks the cultural politics of enterprises like Christian heavy metal. In their altered (and activist) stance toward American culture, Christian heavy metal musicians demonstrated evangelicals' hope of providing a basis for national renewal. Tom Denlinger of Sardonyx urged readers to take action against divorce, abortion, and the gay rights movement by giving unsaved friends a cassette made by a "good Christian band."[150] Christian metal artists of the late 1980s believed that their work offered a starting point for "returning" America to solid biblical values. Such activities demonstrate an improved coordination among artists, spiritual leaders, and the fans who published and read punk and metal zines, coordination that contributed to an increased evangelical political momentum.

The theatrics associated with Christian metal bands—the armor, the premeditated confrontations with secular bands, the epic rhetoric— matched the hard-charging tactics of the period's conservative political activists. Yet even as evangelicals invoked outsider rhetoric to describe their marginalized position in American society, they laid claim with increasing ease to a range of cultural styles and spaces—metal and punk, as well as nightclubs, baseball stadiums, and amusement parks. Indeed, as evangelicalism gathered strength in the suburbs—and as the Christian music industry became more widespread—believers showed they could position themselves as cultural insiders. That is, evangelicals increasingly mourned the decline of "family values" in America from a position of strength and comfort in suburbia and exurbia.

CHAPTER 4

# "An MTV Approach to Evangelism"

*The Cultural Politics of Suburban Revivalism*

There is nothing unusual about a crowded baseball stadium on a summer night in the United States. But the 37,000 people—plus the 12,000-person overflow crowd seated in the parking lot—who packed into Anaheim Stadium on August 16, 1997, were not watching America's favorite pastime. Rather, they were attending the Harvest Crusade, an annual evangelical revival meeting. The four-day event not only featured an updated version of old-time fire-and-brimstone sermons urging believers to recommit but also aimed to bring the "unchurched" to God. In the months preceding the Crusade, organizers had saturated Orange County with flyers, posters, and bumper stickers that heralded the event, and they had urged attendees to bring non-Christian acquaintances.[1] On this particular night the Crusade took what a spokesman for the event called "an MTV approach to evangelism" by appealing to local high school and college students with a bill featuring Christian rock 'n' roll bands Audio Adrenaline, Big Tent Revival, and The Kry.[2] As the event's youth ministry coordinator explained, the kids "arrived for the music, but we want them to leave with the message of Jesus ringing in their ears. . . . All those songs and riffs are just an avenue for them to come out and hear God's word." Bob Herdman, a member of Audio Adrenaline, agreed: "You can have fun and discover Christ at the same time. We're just a regular rock band—except we use our God-given gifts to explore our faith and inspire others to do the same."[3] At the end of the evening, 5,000 people attested to the

154

Figure 10. At the 1998 Harvest Crusade, held at Anaheim Stadium, audience members stream onto the field during the "altar call." Held after the evening's sermon, the altar call included volunteers ready to speak to would-be converts in a variety of languages; a sign bearing the word "ESPAÑOL" is just visible at the left field fence. According to the Crusade website, 4,940 made "decisions for Christ." Photograph courtesy of Nathan Hayden.

Crusade's effectiveness by responding to the nightly altar call, when evangelist preacher Greg Laurie—in a sermon translated into Spanish, Korean, Chinese, Japanese, Vietnamese, and sign language—invited participants to come onto the field and dedicate their lives to Jesus.[4]

To some nonbelievers in the 1990s, events like the Harvest Crusade represented an isolated Christian subculture known only to its adherents. Others used these events to reject evangelicalism as crassly commercial; as historian Colleen McDannell has noted, observers have routinely charged that contemporary syncretism like that exhibited at the Harvest Crusade indicates "how a commercial American mentality has invaded the inner sanctum of religion."[5] Yet the importance of the Harvest Crusade rests neither in its invisibility to nonbelievers nor in its commodification of religion but rather in its power to evangelize the suburbs. The Crusade demonstrated how religious conservatives mastered the cultural formulas of consumerism as they adjusted their witnessing practices to a suburban landscape where civic life increasingly occurred in commercially owned spaces. Event organizers prided themselves on their ability to mix current cultural styles with religious content while still fostering "traditional values" among audience members, particularly young people. Yet beneath the crusade's relaxed atmosphere—the ballpark, contemporary music, and casual dress— there remained a very conservative message about self-reliance, personal responsibility, and obedience to authority. The Crusade shunned the confrontations and softened the rhetoric of conservative politics while still embracing themes that dovetailed with the era's conservative grassroots campaigns.

At the close of the twentieth century, evangelical cultural events like the Harvest Crusade surpassed faith-based political campaigns as the preferred method for simultaneously celebrating and protecting normative values and traditional authority in American exurbia. The evangelical cultural activism perfected in Orange County, California—postliberal America's quintessential consumer exurb—provides an opportunity to examine the suburbanization of evangelicalism and the "Christianization" of popular culture. Through these simultaneous processes, the public spaces of Orange County, ranging from city parks to amusement parks to ballparks, became critical sites of contestation for evangelicals, who justified their campaigns by claiming they needed to shield children and adolescents from gay rights and abortion rights activists.

During the 1990s, Christian conservatives vigorously contested local elections, and the Christian Coalition and other organizations mobilized to elect "Christian" leaders to all levels of public office in order to, in the words of Coalition executive director Ralph Reed, "take back this country, one precinct at a time, one neighborhood at a time, and one state at a time."[6] Although organizations such as the Christian Coalition focused specifically on grassroots politics, Christians' efforts involved cultural as well as political contestation. Some of these engagements are well known: the obscenity cases involving rap artists 2 Live Crew and the organizers of an exhibition of photographs by artist Robert Mapplethorpe received national media attention in 1989 and 1990, and Christian advocates such as Pat Robertson of the Family Channel and radio's James Dobson of Focus on the Family continued to reach millions through media outlets around the country, even after the televangelist scandals that exploded in the late 1980s. While these matters received national attention, however, little attention was paid to the ways that Christians deployed popular culture locally in response to threats against the family, or how these cultural efforts related to political activism.

Historically American religious revivals have flourished in areas with mobile populations whose social positions were respectable but slightly precarious.[7] At the turn of the previous century, migrations into southern California created a burned-over district featuring "every religion, freakish or orthodox, that the world ever knew."[8] Later, preachers such as Aimee Semple McPherson and Bob Shuler were particularly successful in Los Angeles.[9] According to journalist Morrow Mayo, in 1925, "no people shouted louder . . . for William Jennings Bryan to scotch the Devil" than Angelenos following the Scopes Trial from within their congregations, women's clubs, and civic organizations. After the trial's conclusion and Bryan's death, religious conservatives placed before California voters a ballot initiative to amend the state constitution to mandate that a copy of the Bible be placed in every public school classroom and library, where it could be read by any teacher "without comment as a part of the daily school exercises." Although supported by voters in Southern California by a three-to-one margin, the so-called "Bible Bill" was defeated by voters in central and Northern California.[10] Depression- and World War II–era migrations from the Southwest added to the area's revivalist inclination, and the Jesus Movement that sprouted among countercultural youth in local beach communities solidified the area's reputation as a religious hothouse.

The Harvest Crusade, however, adhered to a respectable standard by addressing itself to a white, middle-class audience—or to those aspiring to that status. Like his revivalist predecessors Charles Grandison Finney and Dwight Moody, Greg Laurie emphasized the impossibility of social, political, or economic reform without personal moral and spiritual regeneration. During the 1990s the message of self-reliance and responsibility were important to a Crusade audience that believed that worldly permissiveness and government programs had encroached upon national standards of morality and freedom. The Crusade's message and medium were also in line with earlier revivals, as Laurie's theology blurred denominational and theological distinctions and instead emphasized the personal experience of being born again. In fact, the Harvest Crusade drew so heavily—and successfully—on the evangelistic traditions of its predecessors that the *New York Times* mentioned its organizer, Greg Laurie, as a possible successor to Billy Graham in the "unofficial role as national evangelist."[11]

The Crusade was quite at home among the area's political and cultural conservatives. As Lisa McGirr has shown in her social history of Orange County conservatism, the area had been a grassroots stronghold for both fiscal and normative conservatives since the early 1960s. During this period, Orange County conservatives transformed themselves from marginalized (even "radical") political novices to a respectable and powerful voting bloc. They rallied behind a series of economic and cultural initiatives in the 1960s and 1970s: Proposition 16, an anti-pornography measure that failed but nonetheless received majority support from Orange County voters in 1966; Proposition 13, which limited property taxes throughout the state in 1978; and Proposition 6 (sponsored in 1978 by John Briggs, state senator from Fullerton), which would have made it illegal for public schools in California to hire gay teachers and would have prohibited heterosexual teachers from depicting homosexuality in a positive light (defeated in Orange County, though by a lower margin than in the rest of the state).[12] Of course, the crowning achievement of Southern California conservatives occurred when Ronald Reagan, first championed by conservatives during his successful run for governor in 1966, was elected president in 1980.

Orange County remained a national symbol of conservatism into the 1990s. Two of the most conservative congressmen in the country, Robert K. Dornan (R–Garden Grove) and William Dannemeyer (R-Fullerton), represented the area. Moreover, the county was home to several conservative political action groups, including the Costa Mesa–based Citizens for Excellence in Education, which aimed to elect conservatives to school boards, and Lou Sheldon's Anaheim-based Traditional Values

Coalition (TVC), which supported candidates for local offices and battled against local gay rights efforts.[13] National organizations such as the Christian Coalition relied on the county's churches as a distribution network for its voter guides, and for good reason: in 1996 the *Los Angeles Times* estimated that religious conservatives made up about 20 percent of Republican voters in the county.[14]

In addition to their continued political strength, white evangelical Christian churches constituted an entrenched tradition in Orange County culture by the 1990s. In the late 1960s and early 1970s, Orange County's Calvary Chapel helped ignite the Jesus Movement. The area was home to some of the nation's largest and most conservative churches, including not only Chuck Smith's Calvary Chapel of Costa Mesa but also Chuck Swindoll's First Evangelical Free Church in Fullerton (until 1994, when he became president of the conservative Dallas Theological Seminary), Robert Schuller's Crystal Cathedral in Garden Grove, Ralph Wilkerson's Melodyland Christian Center in Anaheim, and Rick Warren's Saddleback Christian Church (another church that participated in the annual Crusade). The churches were augmented by Christian schools and colleges such as Calvary Chapel High School and Southern California College (later renamed Vanguard University), which was affiliated with the Assemblies of God.

A number of cultural organizations and businesses catered to the area's conservative Christian population. In 1975 Orange County's KYMS became one of the first radio stations in the nation to switch from a secular to a Christian music format; a few years after the station's mid-1990s demise, KFSH ("the Fish") emerged to fill the county's airwaves with the latest contemporary Christian rock.[15] Calvary Chapel purchased KWVE in 1985, a 50,000-watt station in Costa Mesa that featured preaching and spoken-word programs, and seven other religious stations dotted the radio dials of Los Angeles and Orange County by 1997.[16] And while Nashville remained Christian music's recording capital, Orange County contributed to the genre popular bands such as Stryper and the OC Supertones, at least one prominent record label (Frontline), and a slew of underground magazines devoted to Christian rock bands. At the end of the decade, sales figures showed that the area was the nation's second-largest market for Christian music.[17] The cultural influence of evangelicalism extended to print media: the area boasted an independent Christian newspaper, the *Christian Times* (established in 1983), as well as a Christian phone directory, the *Christian Times Yellow Pages* (established in 1987).[18] Believers could also choose from a range of Christian coffeehouses and bookstores that dotted the area. The county's traffic in souls even spilled into rush hour, as thousands of believers seized on freeway gridlock to witness to other drivers with *icthus* (fish) emblems, antenna balls, and Christian-themed bumper stickers—including tens of thousands that advertised the annual Harvest Crusade. The Crusade's audience was so reliably conservative that, in August 2003, Mel Gibson offered concertgoers an exclusive four-minute preview of his blockbuster *The Passion of the Christ*.

Despite the appearance of white evangelical dominance in Orange County political and cultural life, the region underwent dramatic demographic changes during the late twentieth century that challenged its reputation as a bastion of white home owners. Cities such as Westminster and Santa Ana became known for their Vietnamese- and Spanish-speaking populations whose faiths ranged from Catholicism to Buddhism to storefront Pentecostalism. At the same time, Anglos in Orange County were sharply divided by class. With the end of the Cold War looming, the county's economic base started to transition from manufacturing to information and service businesses.[19] Evangelicals who attended churches such as Calvary Chapel were not executives at aerospace corporations but the lower- and mid-level employees of those firms.[20] The churches that sprouted in Orange County in the 1980s were in the county's older, northern cities such as Anaheim, Santa Ana (Calvary Chapel Costa Mesa's actual location), and Fullerton, not the wealthier coastal cities of Newport Beach or Laguna. At the same time, the latter cities had become more liberal—at least relative to other parts of Orange County. Laguna elected the first publicly gay mayor in 1983, and both Laguna and Irvine, the site of a University of California campus, passed human rights ordinances protecting gay rights. Perhaps the most telling sign of the area's shifting demographics came in 1996, when Democrat Loretta Sanchez edged the incumbent Bob Dornan in a closely contested election for the seat in Congress representing central Orange County.

In addition to these racial, economic, and electoral shifts, Orange County saw significant cultural changes that made it an even likelier site for religious activism. In their study of evangelical political activism in congressional campaigns between 1978 and 1988, political scientists John Green, James L. Guth, and Kevin Hill note that "Christian Right activism occurred predominantly in rapidly growing—and relatively prosperous—suburban areas in the South, Southwest, and Midwest" where conservative Protestants confronted "direct challenges to their values."[21] Despite persistent campaigns centered on issues such as school curricula, pornography, and abortion, the area's Christians suffered several setbacks during the late 1980s and early 1990s. In fact, some of the most emotionally charged political confrontations in Orange County during these years occurred between Christian conservatives and gay rights and abortion rights groups. Latino and Vietnamese communities organized campaigns, for example, against Proposition 187, which would have denied social services to illegal immigrants, and against the Clinton administration's normalization of diplomatic relations with Vietnam. The county's gay rights and abortion rights activists, however, confronted white evangelicals more directly.

When Christian conservatives contested gay rights and abortion rights activists over the uses and meaning of public space in Orange County, they triggered some of the most compelling battles in the county's late-twentieth-century "culture wars." By taking to Orange County's public spaces, gay and abortion rights activists disrupted the heterosexual order that had structured both the county's ethos and its built environment. With their alternative vision of affluent whiteness, the county's gay rights activists posed significant challenges every evangelical facet of the concept "family values": whiteness, middle-class respectability, gender normativity (especially regarding masculinity), and sexuality. Abortion providers at women's health clinics similarly antagonized pro-life Christian conservatives, who viewed the facilities as an extension of the Left's campaign against children. Christian conservatives responded by vilifying these groups as "special interests" anxious to gain access to children through public demonstrations, educational curricula, government office, and consumer products. These counteractions forced evangelicals to articulate their assumptions about "family values" and public laws, space, and culture.

Yet because some Christian conservatives emphasized the importance of changing hearts rather than votes, an interrogation of political interventions over public space tells only part of the story of how believers sought to protect their surroundings. The full story of evangelical resurgence in the suburbs should also encompass how Christian conservatives tried to solve the moral crisis they perceived through religion. In this process, Christians engaged with contemporary popular culture both to foster group identity and reach out to nonbelievers. The religious revival served as both a recreational event that could bolster family values and a religious event that would provide public affirmation of evangelical beliefs and behavioral standards. As in previous eras, revival meetings were intended to touch, among those who attended, neophytes, dedicated believers, and backsliders.[22] The Harvest Crusade—one of at least twenty multiday religious festivals nationwide—shows how evangelicals claimed both suburban space and suburban culture in a message that simultaneously sought to evangelize young people and foster the "traditional values" embraced by Republican and Democratic politicians alike.[23]

When contrasted with struggles over the Gay Pride Festival in Santa Ana, Measure N in Irvine, and ACT UP protests outside Calvary Chapel, the cultural politics of the Harvest Crusade—with its blatant advocacy of a white, suburban, middle-class, and heterosexual sensibility— come into greater relief. Through its message of self-reliance, family, and individualism, the Harvest Crusade provided justification for the era's dominant political and cultural ethos—a period when the Reagan, Bush, and Clinton administrations rolled back New Deal and Great Society programs aimed at economic redistribution, a period when conservatives linked the nation's fate to restoration of patriarchal authority after the feminist and gay rights movements had challenged that prerogative.

Although Harvest Ministries, the organization that sponsored the Harvest Crusade, did not venture directly into electoral politics, the event's cultural politics endorsed a decidedly conservative view of society as it attempted to proselytize young people. The Crusade's politics had three main characteristics. First, the Harvest Crusade, like the gay rights and abortion rights movements, located its roots in the 1960s and thus claimed to offer a counternarrative of—not a reaction to—the decade. Second, in its effort to avoid a second "great refusal" by young adults to be put in predetermined roles of class, gender, or sexuality, the Crusade sought to empower youth through popular culture. Unlike the anti–gay rights and anti-abortion campaigns, in which Christian activists undertook public campaigns in the name of children and families, the Harvest Crusade directly addressed young people through popular culture. Having experienced the power of consumer culture during their own youth, organizers attempted to channel its impact toward religious belief. As a result, rather than condemning popular culture, the Crusade suggested that a contributing source of the "loosening" of society—youth culture—could be used to support traditional authority. Third, the Crusade was an important act of sacralization whereby evangelicals claimed public space for Christ.

Public space and consumer culture reveal the ways in which evangelicals' race, class, gender, and religious identities converged. Historian

Lizabeth Cohen has shown how post–World War II suburban development wove consumer culture into public space and helped privately owned and operated marketplaces and entertainment centers replace downtown shopping areas.[24] No area surpassed Orange County in realizing this idealized "variation on a theme park."[25] Critics worried that consumerism, the nuclear family, and the built environment were so intertwined that too little public space was left through which to contest prevailing notions about normativity.[26] Despite these factors, both public space and consumer culture formed a terrain of significant struggle during the 1990s for gay rights, abortion rights, and Christian activists. Although Christian conservatives frequently criticized popular culture, consumer culture, as a centerpiece of white suburban existence, became a locus around which they could form a religious group identity. It also served as ground zero for Christians' conversion mission for American society. Pointing to the problems among American teenagers—not just kids in the cities but those in the *suburbs* too—Christians declared that society had lost its values and that it was their duty to help the nation recover its Judeo-Christian sensibilities. Within this mission, events like the Harvest Crusade became a form of activism for Christ—a way of witnessing God's message to suburbia. Christian conservatives used not just political campaigns but also public space and consumer culture both to establish a community of believers and to reinforce a white, middle-class, heterosexual cultural sensibility.

## CONSERVATIVE CHRISTIAN RESPONSE TO GAY RIGHTS ACTIVISM IN ORANGE COUNTY

Gay rights became one of the most polarizing issues of the late-twentieth-century "culture wars." The reaction to gay rights in Orange County was no exception. During the late 1980s, gay activist groups such as ACT UP (AIDS Coalition to Unleash Power) and the Gay Visibility League organized chapters in Orange County. Religious conservatives, in turn, viewed gay rights campaigns as an unwelcome disruption in suburban space that threatened the nuclear family. Conservative efforts to deny gays access to public space followed three paths: through anti–gay rights initiative campaigns at the ballot box; through campaigns designed to deny gay rights groups access to local public spaces; and through campaigns aimed at pressuring corporations to exclude gays from employee benefits and to deny them access to semipublic spaces such as amusement parks.[27]

Anti-discrimination laws became an issue important to conservatives almost as soon as they were passed in the years after the Stonewall riot in 1969. In the most famous standoff, former Miss America Anita Bryant led a successful campaign in 1977 against a gay rights ordinance in Dade County, Florida. Despite such early resistance, over the next several years, eight states and 130 local jurisdictions passed ordinances that offered legal protection to homosexuals, a development that inspired intensive countermobilization by Christian conservatives, including statewide initiatives in Colorado and Florida in the early 1990s to prevent such local legislation.[28] Some of the tactics deployed in the statewide anti-ordinance measures were developed during a 1988–89 campaign in Orange County. Despite estimates that about one-fifth of California voters could be considered part of the Religious Right, Christian political organizations struggled to achieve results in statewide elections during the 1990s, in part because of the state's population of moderate voters.[29] Although Christian conservatives' statewide campaigns failed to meet expectations, they frequently succeeded in local campaigns, especially in Orange County. While the anti-gay ordinance campaigns were local, Christian conservatives found that their organizing strategies and rhetorical appeals resonated in a range of communities around the nation.

In local campaigns against gay rights, Christian conservatives developed a two-pronged rhetorical strategy: first, they framed themselves as the guardians of "traditional morality" who were protecting solidly American values rather than advancing partisan or religious doctrine; second, they labeled their opponents in the gay rights movement as "special interests" that were pursuing advantages and representation incommensurate with their numbers and incompatible with American democratic values.[30] As political scientist Kenneth Wald suggests, this strategy allowed Christians to frame their argument within the "secular language of American individualism" and thus mask the extent to which religious belief informed their activism.[31]

The backlash in Irvine developed shortly after the city council, in June 1988, passed a human rights ordinance that prohibited discrimination by race, color, religion, national origin, sex, age, sexual orientation, marital status, or physical disability in workplaces, housing, public places, or educational institutions.[32] As the ordinance went into effect in August 1988, a group calling itself the Irvine Values Coalition (IVC) organized a drive to put a citywide initiative on the ballot to remove homosexuals from the list of groups protected by the ordinance, and to bar the council from defining "sexual orientation as a fundamental human right" in the future without the consent of a two-thirds majority of the electorate.[33] Members of the coalition argued that, rather than guaranteeing equal rights, the ordinance extended "special rights" to homosexuals. Supported by the county's conservative politicians, the group gathered enough signatures to place the issue on the November 1989 ballot. Aside from the statewide Briggs initiative (Proposition 6) of 1978, Measure N marked the first time that voters in Orange County cast ballots directly on a gay rights issue.[34] On November 7, Measure N passed by a vote of 53 percent to 47 percent, removing from the ordinance the clause that protected homosexuals.

In explaining the importance of Measure N's passage, conservatives made their ideas about values explicit. Although the Irvine Values Coalition had sought in the campaign's latter stages to associate itself with democratic ideals by changing its name to Citizens for Equal Rights, its activists frequently suggested that their cause was a defense of family.[35] Just as national conservatives condemned the federal government as they appealed to nationalism, patriotism, and morality, local activists distinguished between Irvine's (liberal) city government and the community's "traditional" values, a set of beliefs interchangeable with the heterosexual family.

While condemning "special rights" for homosexuals, it was clear that activists believed family should occupy a privileged place in Irvine's city policies. As literary critic Linda Kintz has argued, by deploying such simple, emotional, and seemingly universal terms as "family," "nation," and even "childhood," religious conservatives shifted the focus of public discourse to an emphasis on the "families who count."[36] Initiative supporters' use of the word "promote," for example, shows how word choice helped privilege one family structure over another. In an interview, activist Scott Peotter stressed that he did not want homosexuality "promoted in Irvine" because he believed that protection amounted to endorsement or even preference. The gay lifestyle, Peotter explained, "doesn't lend itself to the traditional family. I don't think Irvine should be in business to promote the alternative family. . . . Obviously, the city's interest and promotion of day care shows Irvine really wants to be a pro-family type of community. That's not to say homosexuals aren't welcome, but the promotion of their life style is not in the same line as being pro-family."[37] Another organizer for the Irvine Values Coalition simply explained that homosexuals should not be given legal protection "in a family community."[38] In this view, protection of "family" precluded protection of homosexuals' housing rights.

When it came to describing homosexuals, Measure N organizers spoke as if they were beating back an invading army from Sodom and Gomorrah. Their comments indicate their belief that "the family" was the source of Irvine's social order, suggesting that a set of simultaneously observed private values and actions, not a civic orientation to community, should be the basis of public life in the city. While proclaiming their desire to protect children, campaign organizers worked vigorously to frighten adult voters with incendiary direct mail. In the weeks leading up to the election, mailings described the "gay lifestyle" with meticulous detail and warned of Irvine's possible fate as another "Gay Mecca" like San Francisco, suggesting that the purveyors of urban vice, having sacked the nation's cities, were at the gates of the planned suburbs.[39]

Organizers vehemently objected to allowing homosexuality in public discourse or space. Shortly after the measure passed, one of the IVC's founding members, Christina Shea, linked the ordinance to homosexual behavior in public (and in public view of children), explaining, "I'm a mom with three kids and I don't want gay pride festivals or public sex in bathrooms in my city." She then elaborated: "I'm not on a huge crusade to wipe out homosexuals. But I'll fight again if they want to bring homosexuality into the public arena. I believe (sexuality) belongs in the home, in the privacy of one's own domain."[40] Even as Shea established her ethos as a public speaker (and activist) and a heterosexual mother of three, she argued that homosexuality did not belong in the "public arena." It was clear that organizers believed that heterosexuality needed protection in public: other activists suggested that the city should take a more "pro-family" stance on issues such as traffic, taxes, and day care.[41] Yet removing legal protection of homosexuality was only the first measure to ensure sexual order within the city. Some members of the IVC wanted to expand the group's policing of sexuality to include monitoring sex education in schools, boycotts of video stores that rented pornography, and "helping" homosexuals who were unhappy with their sexuality to "get out of the lifestyle."[42]

Like other conservative activists in the culture wars, the IVC's leaders sought to defend not just law and space but also public memory. When organizers spoke of their beliefs, they argued that they were defending universal American values. They traced their beliefs to the American Revolution and the nation's founding, as when Scott Peotter told the *Los Angeles Times:*

> When we say traditional values, what we're referring to are traditional
> values that come from the Founding Fathers, that are repeated and shown
> throughout the Declaration of Independence and U.S. Constitution—God-
> given, inalienable rights. So it refers to the Judeo-Christian set of values,
> and that's the background that we're coming from.[43]

Peotter attributed his coalition's origins to earthly as well as heavenly
fathers; the group claimed to defend both national "values" as well as
Judeo-Christian "rights." But while the sources were linked, there was
an important divergence. On the one hand, the "traditional values"
invoked by the coalition were passed down from the Founding Fathers
through documents such as the Declaration of Independence and the
Constitution. On the other hand, "inalienable rights"—those sought
also by homosexuals through anti-discrimination ordinances—were
"God-given." But the Bible made it pretty clear to conservatives how
God felt about homosexuality. And while there were to be no "special
rights" for homosexuals, Christian conservatives nonetheless claimed
the mantle of special protectors of the nation's values.

The struggle over Measure N was one instance in which Orange
County voters and local governments determined the rights, protec-
tions, and acknowledgment of homosexuals in the legal code or educational curriculum. The passage of Measure N followed on the heels of
the defeat of a countywide ordinance banning discrimination against
AIDS victims in housing, employment, and public services. In June 1988
supporters of the Traditional Values Coalition had organized a flyer and
phone bank campaign aimed at persuading the Board of Supervisors to
reject the ordinance. The board indeed rejected the ordinance in a 3–2
vote; similar ordinances had passed in Los Angeles, Riverside, San
Diego, San Francisco, and Alameda counties.[44] In Corona del Mar,
school officials required that a high school psychology teacher discon-
tinue inviting homosexuals to speak to his class after at least seventy
parents expressed opposition to the nineteen-year-old practice.[45]

Over the next decade, gay rights continued to be an important issue
in local and state politics and education. In 1991 Governor Pete Wilson
vetoed Assembly Bill 101, which would have extended protection from
job discrimination to gays and lesbians. In 1993 students at Fountain
Valley High School in the Huntington Beach Union High School District
invoked a school-board policy (backed by the U.S. Supreme Court's
1990 *Mergens* decision) that allowed extracurricular groups (including
Bible study groups) equal access to school facilities to establish a support group for gay teenagers, the Student Alliance.[46] In response, a

conservative student group that called itself the Future Good Boys of America organized a daylong protest at the school for students and parents. At a public meeting, a student pleaded with the board to close the campus to the group's meetings because school "is not the place to discuss homosexual acts. Our school adopted a zero tolerance of disruptive behavior such as violence, drugs and graffiti. Homosexuality is also such a behavior." Parents complained that the policy of allowing unofficial student organizations failed to recognize parental rights in school activities. The club continued to meet on school grounds.[47] The idea that homosexuality disrupted heterosexual identity persisted into the next decade. In 2000, Orange County voters favored Proposition 22, which would have permitted the state to recognize marriages only between men and women, by a margin of 69 to 31 percent.[48]

At the same time that Irvine voters were deciding whether homosexuals would receive legal protection from discrimination under city law, another struggle over gay rights erupted in nearby Santa Ana. In this case, gay rights activists and Christian activists battled over access to public parks and facilities after a local organization, Orange County Cultural Pride, sought to hold the county's first-ever gay pride festival in Santa Ana's Centennial Park. Throughout the seven-month campaign, conservatives maintained that allowing the festival to take place in the park would harm children by exposing them to explicit acts and nonnormative lifestyles.

In February 1989 the organization Orange County Pride received approval to use Santa Ana's Centennial Park for a pride festival in September of the same year. Vocal opposition immediately arose to persuade the city government to withdraw the permit.[49] In mid-May, some three hundred gay rights and Christian activists filled the Santa Ana City Council's chamber to watch a debate about the permit, during which Mayor Daniel H. Young charged the city manager and city attorney with researching and reporting on two questions: "Does the city have a right or responsibility to be concerned with the content of a cultural festival?" and "How would the Gay Pride festival affect the community that lives near Centennial Park?"[50] In mid-June it appeared as though the two opposing sides would compromise. It was proposed that the festival would change its venue from Centennial Park, which was surrounded by residences, to the downtown confines of the city's civic center (located where a barrio had been until "civic renewal" cleared it in 1977). Here, it was thought, children were less likely to see the event. In return, fundamentalists groups would cease opposing the event.[51]

The TVC, however, continued its opposition, so Orange County Pride maintained its plans for the Centennial Park venue.[52] The controversy energized both sides: a hearing in July drew over 550 protesters.[53] A few weeks earlier, more than one hundred city workers (including nearly all park maintenance workers) had joined the fray by submitting a petition stating that the festival "would constitute a compromise" of workers' moral values.[54]

As the festival date drew closer, opponents tested other measures aimed at banning the event, including an ordinance that would have limited festivals to 5,000 people and barred for-profit groups from charging fees to enter festivals.[55] The city attorney, aware of a possible lawsuit, continued to insist that any emergency ordinance against gay pride could be proposed only in the event that "public peace, health, or safety" was jeopardized.[56] These terms infuriated conservatives, who viewed the festival as an intrinsic violation of public peace, health, *and* safety. When the city council failed to pass a "pro-family" resolution that would ban the festival, the Traditional Values Coalition served recall notices on three council members who had voted against the resolution (two other council members were already up for reelection).[57]

With the city attorney maintaining that there was no legal basis for revoking the permit, the event proceeded as planned in early September—but with heightened political significance. The festival drew about 10,000 attendees—about one-fifth the size of the gay pride festival in West Hollywood. On the first day, tacks were placed in the parking lot, and some shouting and shoving occurred between protesters and attendees, but no arrests were made. On the second day, police arrested six gay festivalgoers and Christian protesters after a fight began outside the gates.[58] The event was otherwise peaceful.

For conservative Christian activists, allowing Orange County Cultural Pride access to public parks—with their historical link to Victorian ideas about the middle-class family, leisure, and morality—bestowed legitimacy on homosexual identity.[59] Don Richardson, a pastor at Calvary Church of Santa Ana, declared that the use of a public park could not be neutral: "This event is not just about the use of facilities; it is about the promotion of the homosexual life style."[60] As with the Measure N campaign, "promotion" became the operative word. Richardson suggested that public space and facilities could not be "used" without endorsing a particular viewpoint. Mayor Young linked the issue to safety, complaining that he was "real unhappy about the parks that are there for quiet time and recreation becoming a focal point for controversial issues. . . . The issue is the health and welfare of our community. . . . That park happens to be in the middle of a quiet residential neighborhood."[61] Young thus invoked the original reason for public parks, designed as a means for quelling urban working-class disorder and urban disease by providing fresh air and encouraging recreation. Presumably, Young favored family picnics, not civic celebrations or parades, for the city's parks. With its emphasis on celebration and spectacle and the association of homosexuality with AIDS, the festival could not possibly fit within this understanding of parks as a source for order and contemplation. At one city council meeting, anti-parade coalition member John Turner accused the council of letting "the homosexual lobby bully them into allowing gays and lesbians nationwide to come to our neighborhood to 'parade' their life style. This includes such activities as live marriages, body painting, gay games, massages and kissing booths, all in public view."[62] Turner suggested that event participants would be intruders, outside agitators with no claim to public space who for one day trespassed on "our neighborhood" to "parade" their lifestyle in "public view." After the festival, some residents criticized the council for allowing the festival; one, who was also circulating a recall petition, told the *Los Angeles Times:* "The issue is sex in the park. I don't care if you're heterosexual or homosexual, sex does not belong in a public park. This is our park, and we don't like this one bit."[63]

Gay activists, well aware of the politics of public space, organized several counteractions against Christian conservatives. While conservative evangelicals protested homosexuals' access to residential parks, gay activists resented evangelicals' repeated attempts to turn them from the "gay lifestyle." In early 1991, a few months after ACT UP/Orange County was established, several activists were arrested in Anaheim for trying to disrupt a symposium sponsored by Lou Sheldon, founder of the Traditional Values Coalition, entitled "The Preservation of the Heterosexual Ethic." A few weeks later, several ACT UP protesters left 170 pounds of steer manure outside Lou Sheldon's headquarters.[64]

While Lou Sheldon was a clear target for protests, activists also confronted Calvary Chapel, which prided itself on its avoidance of both politics and headlines. On Friday nights in 1990 and 1991, several young evangelicals from Calvary Chapel ventured into West Hollywood to proselytize the gay men who frequented the neighborhood's bars and restaurants. In response to these weekly sorties into Los Angeles's most visibly gay neighborhood, several gay activists decided to reciprocate.

On September 8, 1991, approximately eighty Queer Nation activists picketed a Calvary Chapel Costa Mesa service; three gay men were arrested after they disrupted the 11:15 A.M. service by yelling "Stop crucifying queers!" Outside, other protesters addressed the fear of gay spectacle by picketing in drag as they distributed pamphlets designed to resemble Calvary's Sunday program. Several pro-choice activists joined the pickets to protest fundamentalists' opposition to abortion.[65]

Amid the battles for access, even Disneyland, "the happiest place on earth," became a site of contestation. This struggle reflected a third strain of confrontation between homosexuals and Christian conservatives. Although area amusement parks such as Disneyland and Knott's Berry Farm were not "public" in the same sense as municipal parks, the emergence of "gay nights" at the parks demonstrates how access became intertwined with consumerism. During the 1970s corporations had increasingly sought to market their products to market segments defined by age, race, class, and sexual orientation. As historian Lizabeth Cohen has shown, corporations generally attempted to market to homosexuals using a "dual marketing approach" that avoided specific reference to homosexuality. But Disney drew criticism from Christian conservative groups for promoting gay nights in its parks, including Disneyland in Anaheim.[66]

During the postwar era, Disneyland and Knott's Berry Farm, a nearby amusement park established by conservative and "Freedom Center" founder Walter Knott, came to symbolize the confluence of family togetherness, nationalism, and consumerism.[67] Disneyland provided a space where adults could examine the world from a child's perspective, making the park an appealing place for family amusement, even among Christians.[68] It didn't hurt, either, that the companies filled park schedules with Christian events. Each Christmas season, Disney hosted a celebrity reading of the Christmas story. A few miles away, Knott's opened its park to Christian music events ranging from Calvary Chapel's Love Song Festival in 1971 to its descendents, Maranatha Night, Jubilation, and Praise, held at various times—including New Year's Eve—during the 1970s, 1980s, and 1990s. According to one leader of the Jesus Movement, these events were important to California youths who "were accustomed to the fun and flash of entertainment." While there were no Bible teachings or baptisms at the events, the leader recalls that the "amusement park Jesus festivals"—as well as revivals held on campgrounds—"became church for many young people—outdoor sanctuaries with the sky as a canopy."[69]

Despite Christians' efforts to sacralize the amusement park landscape, their monopoly on park events did not last. In May 1978—just
months before voters rejected the Briggs initiative—a representative for
the Los Angeles Bar and Restaurant Association, an association of
mostly gay-clientele businesses, organized the first "gay day" at
Disneyland. Over 20,000 visitors—accompanied by forty to fifty church
group protesters—descended on Disneyland, which had taken the pre-
caution of closing the dance floors, mandating a dress code, and banning the distribution of pamphlets.[70] Over the next decade, gay nights at
local amusement parks became regular occurrences. Not all local parks
welcomed their visitors with open arms: in 1986 a gay rights group won
a lawsuit against Magic Mountain in the San Fernando Valley, about sixty
miles from Orange County, after the park refused to host "Gay Pride
Night"; the park maintained that the parents of its teenage workers had
complained about the previous such event in 1979.[71] While controversial,
the events were certainly successful: Knott's Berry Farm held its first gay
night in 1988, and in 1989 drew 13,000 to the park. Gay Day, an unofficial event when gays showed up at Disney theme parks in red shirts,
also became popular beginning in 1991 in Orlando, Florida.[72]

Although open to organized group events at the park, Disney policed
the actions of visitors to keep its "family" visitors shielded from "offensive" behaviors. For example, Disneyland maintained its ban on same-
sex dancing—first established in 1957 (two years after the park
opened)—until the park lost a lawsuit in 1984 filed by a gay couple who
had been removed from the park for dancing in 1980.[73] The men said
that guards ejected them by saying, "This is a family park. There's no
room for alternative life styles here."[74] Disney claimed it changed its
policy in response to requests from customers at Videopolis, an outdoor
dance and music venue, rather than to the outcome of the lawsuit. But
the company confronted a second charge of discrimination in 1988
when three UCLA students claimed that a security guard informed them
that "touch dancing is reserved for heterosexual couples only" as they
danced at the Videopolis. A little more than a year later, the lawsuit was
dropped after the park promised not to discriminate based on sexual
orientation.[75]

Disney's altered policies toward gay groups—not just the popular gay
nights at the park but also health benefits to partners of gay employees,
which the company began to offer in 1996—did not go unnoticed by religious conservatives. For these believers, the company was so intertwined
with the category of childhood that any tolerance of homosexuality

seemed like an attack on children. Radio host Warren Duffy of the Orange County–based Christian station KKLA frequently attacked Disney on air for the content of its products as well as its annual Gay Day, and in 1997 he led a march to the Disney offices in Burbank.[76] A year earlier, the Southern Baptist Convention struck back over what it called "family-values issues," calling for a boycott of the company's products, theme parks, and movies.[77] In 1997 the church instituted a formal boycott with the help of a Buena Park–based pastor.[78]

As early as 1978, when the Briggs initiative appeared on the statewide ballot, religious conservatives had sought to limit the public rights and activities of homosexuals. During the late 1980s, the battle over homosexual rights in Orange County intensified as gay rights groups openly challenged conservative mores. While some of these struggles took place within the context of political campaigns, others unfolded on the very terrain, such as amusement parks, that had defined white middle-class heterosexual suburban identity. While not every campaign against gay rights succeeded, the expansion of anti-gay mobilization proved significant because it showed evangelical activists mobilizing voters based on "quality of life" issues that focused on protecting the local community. Conservatives would need to rely on cultural as well as political tactics to defend the concepts of marriage and family.

## ABORTION PROTESTS

The protests over gay rights in Orange County during the 1980s and 1990s were largely about white male normativity. Yet there was a public debate over normative femininity during these years as well. These debates and protests, contested largely by middle-class white women at the local level, centered on the issue of abortion. To pro-life activists, abortion represented a threat to motherhood as well as the family, as it threatened to upset social and biological roles of men and women.[79] Christian conservatives, of course, linked these roles to divine authority, making abortion seem like an attack on their religious beliefs as well. In this sense, Christians conservatives viewed abortion as yet another example of the assault on Christian belief systems stemming from the political environment and social movements of the 1960s and early 1970s—in this case, the Warren Court and the women's movement.

While marches on the national mall received more attention, the abortion debate became a routinized and ritualized contest between pro-life and pro-choice sides at the local level. Abortion foes around the country pursued a variety of organizing efforts over the years, including education and counseling sessions, lobbying efforts aimed at legislators, and campaigns to elect pro-life officials. Abortion opponents also staged protests at abortion clinics, which brought them into direct confrontation with pro-choice activists. As historian Lisa McGirr has shown, abortion—along with pornography law and sex education in schools—was among the single-issue campaigns embraced by normative conservatives in Southern California as they broadened their mobilization beyond anti-communism during the late 1960s. During the 1970s, the county became home to pro-life organizations such as Crusade for Life, whose founder also had a hand in producing the anti-abortion film *Silent Scream*.[80] The activism continued during the late 1990s, when pro-life organizers, including many Christian conservatives, vehemently—and sometimes violently—claimed public space in an effort to protect the sanctity of motherhood, family, and the home.

During the 1980s and 1990s, conservatives protested against abortion, holding vigils in public parks, protests outside clinics, and picket lines on sidewalks outside private homes in residential neighborhoods. Anti-abortion protesters picketed the Feminist Women's Health Center in Santa Ana twice a week for several years beginning in the mid-1980s; pro-choice volunteers served as escorts for patients.[81] Every January both pro-life and pro-choice groups hosted several hundred people at Centennial Park, the Civic Center Plaza, and other sites in Santa Ana to mark the anniversary of the Supreme Court's 1973 *Roe v. Wade* decision.[82] To mark the anniversary in 1990, 12,000 anti-abortion activists formed a human cross that extended through parts of Buena Park, Anaheim, Stanton, Garden Grove, and Westminster. The "human chain of life," as organizers called it, stretched five miles north to south on sidewalks along Beach Boulevard and two miles east to west on Katella Avenue.[83]

Clinics were heavily contested sites throughout the year. On some occasions, they were targeted by violence. Just before Christmas 1984, the OC Planned Parenthood clinic in Santa Ana was firebombed; a few months later, another fire was investigated at a nearby clinic.[84] Pro-life activists also held vigils at local clinics. In 1985 an Orange County Superior Court commissioner issued a restraining order against anti-abortion groups to keep them from physically touching or obstructing patients entering the Feminist Women's Health Center.[85]

During the late 1980s, Operation Rescue, which first achieved notoriety for its "siege of Atlanta" at the Democratic National Convention in 1988, began protesting at clinics around the nation. The group and its founder, Randall Terry, were blamed generally for the escalation of violence at abortion clinics, especially after a Florida doctor, David Gunn, was shot to death outside his clinic in 1993.[86] Operation Rescue first took action in Orange County in the spring of 1989, when it staged a "Holy Week of Rescue," three days of protests at clinics providing abortions. The protests drew about six hundred pro-life demonstrators as well as more than one hundred pro-choice advocates.[87] Police made 373 arrests, including Randall Terry, after demonstrators at a clinic in Cypress refused to disperse and thereby violated a federal court injunction against protesting within fifteen feet of a clinic doorway. Police also arrested protesters for blocking entrances to clinics in Long Beach and Los Angeles; in all, 771 protesters were arrested. The protests continued in late April with coordinated events in seventy cities across the country.[88] On a weekend morning in July, shortly after the U.S. Supreme Court's ruling in *Webster v. Reproductive Health Services,* approximately 1,000 abortion protesters and supporters took part in a confrontation outside a Tustin medical clinic.[89] During Easter week 1990, 350 Operation Rescue supporters blocked a Tustin clinic's entrances for nine hours, resulting in forty-eight arrests including a Tustin city councilman. The protest also drew two hundred pro-choice activists.[90] In December, a protest at a Santa Ana clinic drew another four hundred people.[91]

While Operation Rescue attempted to block access to facilities, other abortion protesters sought access to parking lots and other open spaces in order to distribute pro-life literature. As with many of the issues surrounding abortion, the courts were left to decide what constituted public space. In April 1989, at the end of a two-week trial, a judge banned all protesters from the parking lot of a Cypress clinic, finding that protesters, who had targeted the facility for twelve years, had hampered patients' right to seek medical services. Whereas another judge's injunction in 1987 had simply limited the number of protesters to the number of the cars in the parking lot plus one person for the entrance, Orange County Superior Court judge Linda H. McLaughlin barred picketers from the parking lot altogether, finding that protesters had infringed on patients' right to medical services and could adequately make their point from a public sidewalk.[92] According to the *Los Angeles Times,* the court found "that abortion clinics are essentially private properties that are not subject to the same public access as shopping malls, grocery stores and other frequent targets of picketers."[93] The trial placed abortion protesters in the unusual position of basing their right to demonstrate on the First Amendment, as they sought to prove that a clinic was a "quasi-public facility" open to everyone.

During this period, anti-abortion protesters further tested the boundaries of public and private space by protesting at the homes of abortion providers. In 1988 the U.S. Supreme Court ruled that protesters could enter residential areas but could not invade a person's privacy by targeting his or her home. In Orange County the pickets quickly became a NIMBY (not in my backyard) issue that required action from local city councils. In response to repeated pickets at the homes of clinic workers, as well as the death of David Gunn in Florida, the city of Tustin passed an ordinance in 1993 that banned pickets from targeting specific homes; the neighboring city of Santa Ana already had a law in place to protect council members from protests over the gay pride parade in 1989.[94] Just ten days after Tustin enacted the ban, forty anti-abortion protesters tested the ordinance by demonstrating in the neighborhood where a clinic director lived, resulting in three arrests.[95] A few weeks later, Huntington Beach became the seventh local government in California and the third in Orange County to ban picketing in front of homes when it too passed an emergency ordinance.[96] Two years later, twenty anti-abortion activists protested outside a physician's home in Santa Ana, although they dispersed when the police ordered them to leave.[97]

Orange County's anti-abortion activists pursued a variety of strategies in attempting to protect motherhood and family. Like the anti-gay protesters, anti-abortion protesters supplemented their legislative efforts with direct-action demonstrations that politicized local spaces and highlighted competing understandings of femininity in the post-1960s era.

## WITNESSING SUBURBIA: A NEW FORM OF CULTURAL ACTIVISM

Although many Christian conservatives employed direct political intervention to stave off the advances of the gay rights and feminist movements, some white evangelicals maintained that it was more important to change hearts than votes. These campaigns held political significance as well. As Paul Apostolidis has explained in his analysis of James Dobson's *Focus on the Family* radio program, the political significance of the Christian conservatives' culture rested not just in its direct relationship to political activism but also "in its expression, reinforcement, and contestation of contemporary, social-structural relations of power."[98]

This expanded understanding of political action—one that encompasses the cultural activism of events like the Harvest Crusade—better captures how evangelicals sought to address through religion the moral crisis they perceived. This approach suited the political outlook born of a decade of economic restructuring and governmental retreat from the safety net programs established during the New Deal and the Great Society. According to this logic, self-control and respect for traditional authority would obviate the need for government welfare programs by replacing them with "family values."

In the context of the culture wars, the Harvest Crusade demonstrated evangelicals' desire to reclaim both space and culture for "Christian" beliefs, and it reveals how culture was mobilized in response to threats against "the family" represented in Orange County by gay activism, abortion clinics, and youth alienation. While mirroring much of the explicitly "political" activism associated with this era, cultural activities like the Harvest Crusade localized politics by taking issues out of Washington corridors (or even city hall) and out of the polling place and inserting them into immediate, everyday contexts such as the home, the neighborhood, and the airwaves. These activities, in turn, were linked to the fate of the nation. The greater immediacy of issues made it easier for Christians to view themselves as "citizen activists" deputized to protect the local community.

The Crusade expressed its cultural message in three critical ways, each perfectly synchronized with Orange County's suburban consumerism. First, while other conservative organizations condemned the events of the 1960s, the Harvest Crusade emphasized its roots in the 1960s counterculture. The event and its organizers claimed to offer a counternarrative—not a reaction—to the decade. Second, while the Harvest Crusade defended a conservative worldview, its methods were far from old-fashioned: rather than denouncing popular culture for its role in the decline of Western Civilization, evangelicals tried to buttress conservative values by making consumer culture—from bumper stickers to contemporary music to a ballpark atmosphere—a starting point for restoring biblical values to the suburbs. This allowed Crusade organizers to address young people directly rather than simply undertaking public campaigns on their behalf. Third, the Crusade was an important act of sacralization in which public space was claimed for Christ. Evangelicals believed they had a special role to play in American society, and the Crusade offered them a position of cultural leadership through which to model "family values." At a time when gay rights protests, gay pride celebrations, and abortion clinics were staking a claim to public space, the Crusade represented a way to carry God's message into the suburbs.

Gay rights and abortion rights groups are widely acknowledged as including within their movements' identities foundational events such as the Stonewall riot of 1969 and the *Roe v. Wade* decision of 1973. The Harvest Crusade located its origins in the 1960s, when thousands of countercultural youths were reintegrated into mainstream society through the religious faith of the Jesus Movement. Event organizers rarely failed to note this connection in interviews. Greg Laurie, the event's organizer, was initiated into the ministry by Chuck Smith Sr. of Calvary Chapel Costa Mesa, who, beginning in the late 1960s, began what one author called an "evangelical rescue mission to the troubled youths of the 1960s."[99] Smith told a reporter in 1970, "Dope addicts, panhandlers, and just regular kids who were confused have come through here and accepted Christ."[100] As a result of his work among young people, Smith's ministry became renowned for its mass baptisms in Corona del Mar and its acceptance of contemporary musical forms.

In 1972 Smith asked Laurie (who was then nineteen years old) to preside over a youth Bible study in Riverside. Laurie was so successful with the youth group that in 1974 Smith bought an abandoned church for Laurie in Riverside and affiliated it with Calvary Chapel. By 1994 the Harvest Christian Fellowship, Laurie's congregation, was one of the ten largest Protestant churches in the country, with approximately 12,000 members.[101] The ties between Smith and Laurie endured. Laurie continued to lead a weekly Bible study at Smith's Costa Mesa headquarters, Smith's Calvary Chapel sponsored the first two Harvest Crusades before it became a separate nonprofit ministry, and Laurie appeared at the "Jesus People Reunion" hosted by Smith at Arrowhead Pond in 1999.

While accepting young people's cultural styles, Smith practiced an iconoclastic brand of fundamentalism that, sociologist Donald E. Miller argues, "reformed" American Protestantism in the United States. According to Miller, Calvary Chapel represented a "new paradigm" in American Protestantism that changed how Christianity looked and was experienced.[102] Miller credits the high growth rates of churches like Calvary Chapel to their worship patterns: their music appealed to the middle class, they avoided aspects of organized religion that alienated young people, and their programming emphasized "well-defined moral values" not available in secular culture.[103] By following these concepts— and by downplaying appeals for financial contributions—Calvary

Chapel Costa Mesa became one of the largest churches in the nation. When the church celebrated its twenty-fifth anniversary in 1990, it boasted a weekly attendance of 12,000 at its Costa Mesa location and a 1989 budget of $9.5 million. The church expanded its affiliations to include 386 churches in the United States, Canada, Europe, and Asia; its religious programs aired on 140 radio stations across the nation, including KWVE, the church-owned station in Orange County.[104]

While Chuck Smith and Calvary Chapel ministered to the Jesus People, Greg Laurie evangelized to both baby boomers and their children through the Harvest Crusade. The Crusade arose during the late 1980s out of the increased interest in the baptisms that Calvary Chapel held at Corona del Mar. On August 17, 1990, between five hundred and one thousand people, many of them attendees of the first Harvest Crusade at the nearby Pacific Amphitheater, were baptized at Pirate's Cove.[105] By the second year of its existence, the Crusade had become popular enough to move its final night to Anaheim Stadium; by the third year, the Orange County Crusade was held entirely in Anaheim, and Laurie took the show on the road to stadiums in Honolulu, Seattle, San Diego, Long Beach, Riverside, and Phoenix, with total attendance—according to the Crusade's website—reaching more than 228,000. By the end of the decade, again according to numbers posted to the Crusade's website, attendance at its events had surpassed 2 million, with over 160,000 concertgoers making "decisions for Christ."[106] In some years the Crusade was the hottest ticket in town; in 1995 an *Orange County Register* columnist observed that the free five-day Crusade in mid-July outdrew baseball's California Angels for the entire month of June.[107]

Harvest Crusade organizers staked their claim to the historical memory of Orange County by offering a seamless narration of religion's vital role in quelling youthful rebellion, from the Vietnam era's days of rage through contemporary concerns about the disappearance of family values. With its roots in the 1960s, moreover, the Crusade claimed legitimacy in that decade: for the Harvest Crusade, the "unfinished revolution" of the 1960s lay not in its campaigns against war or social injustice but rather in the failure to claim more souls for Jesus. But there was still time. Alluding to his earlier work among the youth who came of age during the sixties, Chuck Smith attributed interest in the early Crusades to a new generation: "These are the children of the Jesus People. It's happening to them just like it happened to their parents."[108] The 1960s continued to haunt Orange County, as church officials located the existential crises of aging baby boomers and their teenage children in the counterculture "rebellion" rather than in social and economic problems associated with life in the 1980s and 1990s. A spokesman for the crusade, citing the prevalence of drug use and rebellious attitudes among young people, concluded, "Many of the same conditions prevail now which prevailed at the time of the original movement."[109]

At the same time that Crusade organizers reinforced their connection to the religious revival of the 1960s, they were not afraid to harness countercultural impulses for their religious purposes. In particular, organizers emphasized the decade's call for personal experience and fulfillment. Whereas conservatives such as William J. Bennett criticized the counterculture of the late 1960s and early 1970s, the Crusade proudly showcased converts from secular music. In 1997 the Crusade invited singer Ritchie Furay, the former Buffalo Springfield singer who had performed at the Monterey Pop Festival in 1967, to sing the Neil Young song "On the Way Home" at a night devoted to remembering the thirtieth anniversary of the Summer of Love.[110] Organizers saw no contradiction in repurposing the LSD-laced summer of 1967 in Haight-Ashbury for a nostalgic call for spiritual renewal; redemption was available to baby boomers as well as to historical memory. In organizers' minds, the dissidence witnessed during the decade was an eternal yearning for salvation rather than an earthly youth revolt. Any search for authenticity in the 1960s that had not led to Jesus had been (or would be, in the eternal sense) subsequently discredited. Referring to Furay's appearance at the Crusade, Greg Laurie told an interviewer, "The fulfillment of the ideals of the '60s—the peace, joy, and innocence of purpose—could not be found in drugs, sex, and rock 'n' roll." Underscoring Furay's song, Laurie said that the ideals could only be reached "in coming home to God."[111] Chuck Smith echoed these comments when he reminisced about 1960s revivals at the Jesus People Reunion in 1999, an event that drew former Jesus People together to recapture some of the old spiritual magic. According to Smith, Jesus—not "LSD or heroin" and "not sexual promiscuity"—was "the single answer" to young people's disenchantment with the world.[112] In this version of events, the tumult of the 1960s—the civil rights movement, student movement, riots of 1965 and 1968, Vietnam War, and Great Society—receded in importance behind the impact of a great revival that brought order to a lost generation through religious belief.

To Greg Laurie and other Crusade organizers, the youth of the 1960s and of the 1990s shared similar worlds. In the minds of these evangelicals, the incomplete spiritual renewal of the sixties and early seventies had significant ramifications. By the 1990s, the belief that rising single parenthood, high crime rates, drug use, gang membership, and other inner-city pathologies had infected suburban harmony quite literally put the fear of God into many middle-class white parents. Adolescents seemed particularly vulnerable to social maladies, as parents worried they would end up adrift and unattached to families. The Crusade's youth-focused message appeared at what seemed a critical time for suburban parents, especially because Laurie expressed these same concerns. Although Laurie claimed that "the No. 1 violent criminal today is the teenager," he also believed that "these young people must be reached, and the only thing that will turn them around will be a change of heart."[113] Referring back to his own youth, Laurie told the *Orange County Register:* "Look at the challenges youths confront today. The world they are growing up in is even more radical than my tumultuous heyday of the '60s. . . . Everything has escalated: broken families, drugs, suicide, gangs, freewheeling sex, violence by 8-year-olds. And, amid this chaos, Christ, the only eternal solution, is nowhere to be seen."[114] In particular, Laurie, whose own parents were divorced, tried to reach out to youths from "broken" families. "We want to bring the gospel," Laurie said, "to the new generations that were raised in single-parent households, let them know that there is purpose and meaning in life through a relationship with God."[115]

Laurie's acceptance of the accoutrements of youth culture gave him a tremendous advantage in addressing young people. By continuing Calvary Chapel's tradition of suturing "countercultural" styles—casual dress, long hair, contemporary music—to a fundamentalist, Bible-believing religious message, Laurie signaled his willingness to meet youth on a cultural middle ground. But in contrast to its secular counterparts, the Crusade's religiously inspired youth culture would secure, rather than sever, family bonds, and would inculcate self-discipline and self-control in suburban kids. The interconnection between consumer culture and family values was particularly visible in two aspects of the Harvest Crusade: Laurie's sermons to the audience and the event's play-by-play Internet broadcasts.

To teach kids how to negotiate the perils of mainstream culture, Laurie had to show his familiarity with it. Accordingly, Laurie's sermons at the "youth jams" were infused with references to popular culture. Celebrity, fame, and his own youthful experimentation were the sources for Laurie's cautionary parables. He mentioned Tupac Shakur's death at the Los Angeles youth jam in 1996. Although

Shakur had been murdered, Laurie noted the sense of doom in his
work, saying that Shakur often "sang of his hopeless and empty condi-
tion." Laurie also drew on his early, preconversion years when he was
both "in the world *and of* the world." Talking about his experimentation with drugs, he confided:

> People get into drugs, drinking, sex, partying, even joining gangs because
> they are empty inside. Jesus says 'I love you.' He'll fill that void inside you.
> Before I became a Christian, I thought using drugs would make me more
> aware. Well, I was aware, but what I was aware of was how empty I was![116]

Returning to current cultural events, Laurie criticized the Smashing
Pumpkins song "Bullet with Butterfly Wings" for its lyrics ("Despite all
my rage, I'm still just a rat in a cage / And I still believe that I cannot be
saved"). He told the audience: "But that is wrong! You can be saved!
God can save you. Maybe you feel like a rat in a cage. Maybe you are
out there right now, searching for answers. Christianity is not just some
brand of toothpaste, you know! You have a choice!"[117] Laurie's 1996
talk typified his Harvest Crusade sermons. Rather than lecturing against
gang membership, sexual activity, and drug use, the sermons stressed
that teenagers were capable of making the right choice. No age was too
young to be saved, either: kids who were not old enough to understand
references to Madonna or Tupac could instead attend a children's program featuring puppet shows and "Psalty, the Singing Psalmbook,"
who urged youngsters to demonstrate their devotion and "make Jesus
your forever friend."[118] The notion of choice and spiritual autonomy, in
turn, fit the consumerist and neoliberal rhetoric that permeated
American society.

Teenager Joe Zannettino could have been the Harvest Ministry's
poster child. An *Orange County Register* reporter spoke to Zannettino
and a few other teenagers in 1995 about their conversion experience at
a pre-Harvest rally. Zannettino echoed many of the fears voiced by
Laurie, telling the *Register*, "I used to steal from my family, worry about
the police and gangs and stuff," before a friend invited him to summer
Bible camp. Now, however, Zannettino assured the paper, "I'm strong.
I cut my bad friends off." This new self-control extended to his attitude
toward girls, as Zannettino explained: "It was all lust before. Now that
I have Christian girlfriends, it's 'Let's go to Bible study.'" Perhaps most
important, Zannettino's change of heart had improved his relationship
with his mother, who said her son was "100 percent different since he
committed to Jesus. He has respect for everyone; he comes home on

time; he studies." After his conversion experience, Zannettino started to make the right kinds of choices. According to the article, mother and son had started to study the Bible together, and they were planning to attend the crusade.[119]

For those unable to attend the event in person, the Crusade recreated the powerful religious assembly through radio and Internet broadcast. In 1996 Warren Duffy, the KKLA radio personality who had vocally criticized Disney for its attacks on family values, broadcast the Crusade's Fourth of July concert. Perhaps more significant than the radio broadcast, however, were the Internet broadcasts. Users could not listen and view the events live on the Web until 1998, but transcripts were available online beginning in 1995, when 2,000 visitors to the website followed the event. In 1996, 8,000 virtual concertgoers followed the event via a transcript and slide show that attempted to convey the excitement and action of the event.[120] The transcript of the July 1996 Anaheim Crusade emphasized the crowd's enthusiasm, even during the early parts of the concert:

> 7:50—The Kry has the crowd on its feet clapping and praising the Lord to "Let's Stand Together." The Stadium is now almost completely filled. This is the best attendance of any Harvest Crusade to date. Praise God! The boom camera pans in and captures close-ups of the musicians. . . . The image is displayed on the big JumboTron . . . it's like being on stage! The Kry just reminded all of us that, all that is being said here, all that's being done here, it's all for the purpose of glorifying JESUS CHRIST!!! Praise God![121]

Broadcasters frenetically described features that enhanced the evening's experience: the band, the attendance, even the exciting camera shots that, through the JumboTron, brought the crowd closer to the action on stage. While celebrating the evening's agenda, however, The Kry warned participants to keep God at the center of their experience. They were witnessing through the event, and the success of the event would be proportional to its spirit.

Online staff members made it clear that God's presence made the event different—perhaps even better—than others held at the stadium. They even quoted a Crusade volunteer who had attended baseball games at the stadium. The volunteer "commented on the difference between the spirit we feel here tonight and the secular world spirit of the ball games." The broadcaster then elaborated on the volunteer's comments: "Looking throughout the crowd, there are all ages, all races, all sizes here to hear the message of the gospel . . . the people of God and

Figure 11. Organizers of the 1998 Harvest Crusade in Orange County made
sure that audience members understood vocalist Mark Stewart of Audio
Adrenaline by displaying his lyrics on the JumboTron. Photograph courtesy of
Nathan Hayden.

those who do not yet know the Lord are gathering."[122] On other
summer nights, the entertainment provided by baseball's Anaheim
Angels brought generations and races together. Organizers believed they
had improved the experience by combining religion with consumer culture to transform Angel Stadium into a revival tent. The broadcaster's
remarks suggested that the most important difference within the crowd ·
remained that between the saved and—at least before the nightly altar
call—the unsaved.

Historian Colleen McDannell has argued that the values of white,
politically conservative, fundamentalist Christians depend not just on
believing but also on identifying themselves as Christian If this is the
case, then while Laurie's sermons were an event cornerstone for their
efforts at shoring up belief, the other parts of the concert are equally
important to understanding concertgoers' identities.[123] Although
Laurie's sermons debated aspects of popular culture, other parts of the
Crusade represented a nearly seamless combination of consumer culture and values. Concertgoers were politely reminded to sit quietly and
listen while Greg Laurie and other speakers delivered their sermons, but

every other aspect of the Crusade involved more active forms of participation. The Crusade used music, friendly ushers, crowd interaction (including section-versus-section cheers of "We love Jesus, yes we do, we love Jesus, how 'bout you?"), fireworks, and even the JumboTron to help concertgoers not just *think* about but also *practice* their religion.[124]

In addition to providing a language with which to address young people and families, the Harvest Crusade provided white evangelicals with an opportunity to assume a position of cultural leadership. In a 1994 editorial in *CCM* magazine, a Christian critic urged believers to lead by example in their cultural choices. Christians had to regulate their appropriation of popular culture, the critic argued, because, "everything we do is a witness to what we believe. The clothes we wear, the cars we drive, the homework we do and the music we buy are all witnesses to our basic values. We tell other people what we believe by everything that we do."[125] The Great Commission called on Christians not only to produce the best possible culture but also to lead others by consuming the best products. According to this logic, even attending a concert became a form of witnessing, since Christians were "telling others what music is worthwhile and of value" and "casting [their] cultural allegiance with particular groups, artists, or companies."[126] In a sense, Christians' "God-centered spending" is analogous to the "family-centered spending" described by Elaine Tyler May in *Homeward Bound*: like middle-class white Americans during the 1950s, middle-class white Christians believed their purchases "were intended to foster traditional values."[127] By attaching the notion of witnessing to their purchases, Christians also emphasized their role as cultural leaders. If consumers in the 1950s used family-centered spending to ease their consciences about overconsumption, Christians believed that their God-centered spending might actually *change* consciences.

On a few occasions, Harvest Ministries took its message to other areas of Orange County. In May 1996, before the Southern Baptist Convention staged a formal boycott that Harvest Ministries observed in solidarity, the organization held a one-day event at Disneyland. The result was a perfect synergy of religion and consumerism. The organization's website aptly captured the organization's embrace of consumer culture as a means for conversion when it described the event as a day when "the good news of God's kingdom was proclaimed in the magic kingdom."[128] Due to a change in sales strategy for private parties, the park had ceased to hold Christian concerts in 1987.[129] But in May 1996 Greg Laurie brought the Crusade to Disney for a day of evangelizing.

Joined on stage by The Kry, Lou Gramm, and other musicians, Laurie delivered his message from the Rivers of America on Tom Sawyer's Island to an estimated evening crowd of 12,000 (there were a reported 51,000 visitors earlier that day). The previous week, in the *Harvest Christian Fellowship Bulletin,* Pastor Rick Myers had written with great anticipation about the event's significance:

> One of the exciting things to do as a kid growing up was going to Disneyland. . . . Truly, Disneyland was the happiest place on earth; a place where you could escape the real world. . . . In the early years of Disneyland the tickets were sold in packets with each packet having a certain amount of letter tickets, A, B, C, D, and E. These would get you into the park and onto the various rides. Of course, the best rides were the E ticket rides. . . .
>
> Well, here we are in May of 1996 and before us is an opportunity to have an E ticket day at Disneyland. Never before has any group gone into the Magic Kingdom with the express purpose to preach the gospel. So ask an unsaved family member or friend to Harvest Day at Disneyland, and who knows they may have an E ticket ride into God's kingdom. On second thought, I think the E ticket stands for "Eternity!" And the happiest place on earth is in the heart of a new believer.[130]

While some might see the event as evidence of secularization or even sacrilege, event organizers viewed it as a significant act of sacralization of both time and space. Clearly, Myers was not one of those who believed consumer culture was intrinsically evil. By eagerly melding the cheerful atmosphere of the "magic kingdom" with the message of "God's kingdom"—and by skirting the negative connotation that the word "magic" denoted to some Christian believers—the Crusade afforded one an opportunity to turn a one-day park pass into an eternal commitment. Rather than robbing religion of its meaning, organizers believed that they were adding import to what would otherwise be a fun—but spiritually empty—outing.

Neither the music nor the sermons at the Crusade urged audience members to get involved in politics; instead, the sermons called on listeners to re-examine their morals and beliefs. In his sermons, Laurie addressed suburban fears of gangs, drugs, crime, and the absence of personal responsibility, but told listeners that the answers to society's problems rested in the renewed religious commitment of individuals. Rather than emphasizing a public culture of civic action, these evangelicals preferred to celebrate the private nature of families in public space. As a result, while celebrating the emotionally powerful categories of family and nation, the Crusade avoided mundane ones such as government. The Harvest Crusade, which began just as the struggle over gay rights and abortion clinics intensified in Orange County, therefore offers a glimpse of what Christian conservatives believed civic life in a culture of "family values" would look like.

Clearly, Laurie believed revivals were capable of inspiring greater change. In a letter to the editor written in response to a critique of the Harvest Crusade in 1993, Laurie argued, "Throughout history, revivals have done more good for society than any moral reform or social campaign ever did." This was the case, Laurie maintained, because the revivals have "dealt with changing the person before trying to change the person's environment. To do it the other way around is to place the proverbial cart before the horse."[131] A few weeks earlier, Laurie had told the *Orange County Register,* "I'm striking at the root of the problem. Instead of dwelling on social issues I try to get to the heart of the matter by helping people establish a personal relationship with God."[132] Laurie's claims seem a bit disingenuous given that Calvary Chapel, the church where he still conducted weekly Bible classes, actively supported conservative causes during the same period. During the 1990s, Pastor Chuck Smith endorsed a "pro-family" school board candidate, and a few years later Calvary Chapel raised a furor by becoming the first local church to measure political candidates' positions on moral issues when it sent over six hundred surveys to candidates running for county and city elections.[133] The church distributed copies of the Christian Coalition's voter guides in 1994 and 1996.[134] In 1994 Calvary Chapel members conducted an additional survey of local candidates on issues such as abstinence-only sex education, parental consent for presenting "questionable materials" in the classroom, abortion, and condom distribution. Although the church backed away (under a challenge to its tax-exempt status) from sponsoring the guides, members printed 10,000 copies for distribution at the church and did so under the name "Concerned Parents of Orange County."[135]

Organizers denied that the Crusade contained a political message. Although the event's message of family values avoided the rhetoric of "spiritual warfare" that inflected the language of Christian metal bands, it nonetheless revealed a conservative cultural sensibility. Indeed, both revivalists and politicians sounded similar calls for values in American society during the 1980s and 1990s. The resemblance did not go unnoticed by political operatives such as Elizabeth Dole or religious leaders such as Franklin Graham, the head of the Christian relief agency Samaritan's Purse and the son of evangelist Billy Graham. In August 1992 concertgoers heard a prerecorded message from President George

H. W. Bush. While the original plan called for Bush to "speak and pray" with Chuck Smith, attendees ultimately listened to the address as the president's picture flickered on the JumboTron and television monitors at the stadium. Preacher Greg Laurie later suggested that "politicians don't have the answers to man's deepest questions," because "those are questions of the heart." But Bush's campaign managers knew the demographic he was reaching at the Crusade.[136] One adviser explained Bush's decision to speak to the gathering: "It will be the Judeo-Christian, traditional family values coalition that gets Bush elected. And this is probably the largest Christian gathering in California each year."[137] With the "family values" debate raging on the national scene, Bush assured the crowd of his stand on the issue: "There are four principles that inspire us: freedom, family, faith, and fellowship."[138] In this equation, family provided the necessary link between freedom, faith, and fellowship. The four principles represented the positive statement of the "values" message: on the surface, who would dare oppose the broadly stated combination of "freedom, family, faith, and fellowship"? The message, when stated in exclusionary terms, had disastrous political implications. Within the month Bush presided over the Republican National Convention in Houston, during which Pat Buchanan, in a speech that condemned the recent riots in Los Angeles, declared a "cultural war" and urged American voters to "take back our cities, take back our culture and take back our country."[139]

The Crusade showed a consistent concern for the plight of the American nuclear family. Laurie's sermons on the topic were unmistakable jeremiads, but he delivered them with a sunny demeanor that avoided the harshly militaristic rhetoric voiced by politicians like Buchanan. Crusade sermons, like those routinely delivered in megachurches, conveyed a therapeutic message that focused on individual well-being and avoided specific condemnations of sin.[140] Laurie highlighted societal failures, especially surrounding the family, but also offered the possibility of amelioration through religious belief rather than through the violent seizure Buchanan had suggested. At the Crusade's Fourth of July concert in 1996, Laurie urged: "With the breakdown of the society, crime on the street and the dissolution of the American family, we're going to have to turn back the clock. Only through changing people's hearts through God's promise are we going to get America back on track."[141] These few sentences identified the "breakdown" and "dissolution" of society and the family but also provided the way to repair these broken institutions: religion. After Bush gave his speech in 1992, Laurie, a registered Republican, in his own sermon downplayed the political impact of Bush's message, but nonetheless reaffirmed the president's emphasis on the interconnection between religion, freedom, and family. Laurie told the *Orange County Register:* "The family can survive without the nation, but the nation can't survive without the family." Earlier in 1992, Dan Quayle's condemnation of the "lawless social anarchy" exhibited in the Los Angeles riots of that year established conservatives' toughened approach to social amelioration. The Crusade, in contrast, avoided specific recriminations while echoing conservative sentiment about the cause of social unrest. While not directly mentioning current events, Laurie stated that many of the country's problems were "directly connected to the breakdown of the family."[142]

Laurie's religious remedy for improving "family values" abetted a conservative ethos that substituted calls for increased "self-control" and "respect" for reform of the nation's economic structure. Sermons gave participants a sense of agency in both personal and religious matters. The national "breakdown of the family" had both local implications and local solutions. While much of the Harvest Crusade's message focused on reinforcing the bonds of individual family lives, organizers believed that a return to "family values" could have a larger social effect. In this part of its message, not addressed to youth, the Crusade called on evangelicals to become "social parents" who would infuse American suburbs with Christian witness.[143] This seemingly achievable prescription for social ills offered concertgoers a sense of agency that fit within their everyday lives. It valued parenthood—a social role established by God—above earthly political activism.

Shortly after the shootings at Columbine High School in the suburban town of Littleton, Colorado, in 1999, Greg Laurie sent a letter to Harvest Crusade supporters in which he criticized media accounts that asked what went wrong with the two teenage boys and, furthermore, who should be blamed for their actions. For Laurie, the real question was, "Why should we be so surprised?" He pointed to the attitudes that an amoral culture and government had instilled in children:

> [H]ere is a generation that has been raised to believe that we are all products of the evolutionary process. They've been told that there is no God—and therefore no absolute values. The Ten Commandments are passé. We make up the rules as we go. Moral relativity rules the day. Life is what we make it.[144]

To remedy this national "moral relativity," Laurie urged Christian believers not only to pray for a revival in America but he also to undertake a greater degree of activism. As a blueprint, Laurie evoked the "effective witness" of the first-century church, whose believers shared their faith with "a hurting and often hostile world." These early believers, he wrote, "didn't leave the world the way they found it"; on the contrary, according to the Acts of the Apostles, they "turned the world upside down" for the sake of Jesus Christ.[145]

Laurie emphasized the need for similarly committed and coordinated action by Christians in the present day. As in his "youth jam" sermons, witnessing had to begin by bringing kids into sound nuclear families. Therefore, if believers saw "troubled kids" running around their neighborhoods, they should invite them into their homes because "a lot of them don't have moms and dads—or if they do, the parents just don't care." Christian adults needed to take such kids under their wing by bringing them into a "stable Christian home" and showing them "what Christian parents are actually like." Because the Columbine shooters had both come from intact nuclear families, "Christian" became a necessary addendum to achieving a stable, loving home. If negligent parents refused to discipline their children, Christian parents—who had established proper parental authority in their homes—would step in as surrogates.

Much attention has been paid to the way Christian conservatives sought to inject American politics with faith-based values in the late twentieth century, but Christians' efforts to engage with consumer culture were just as significant and as ambitious. The community of believers established at the Harvest Crusade had a mission to pursue beyond the confines of Anaheim Stadium. To repair suburbia's disrupted spaces—evident in the continued success of gay and abortion rights activists—it was not enough for Christians to be "speakers" at revivals like the Harvest. Instead, concertgoers had to continue this role in their neighborhoods and communities because everything they did was a witness to what they believed. Like members of the early church, present-day Christians had to be willing to turn the world—including its consumer culture—"upside-down" through their daily engagement with it. In a sense, then, the Harvest Crusade's cultural activism was more ambitious and radical than its counterparts in single-issue political campaigns, which were more narrowly delimited in both tactics and objectives. Christians traced their beliefs to the Bible and linked these values to the fate of the nation—as when Laurie told believers their activism was "the only hope for America." In mobilizing against the gains of identity politics in the 1990s, Harvest Crusade organizers used the defining idiom of the suburbs, consumer culture, to witness to America's youth.

# Epilogue

In the first issue of *Contemporary Christian Music,* published in the summer of 1978, critic Don Cusic doubted that Christian music would ever be a "dominant . . . force" in the industry. If Elvis could not popularize gospel music, Cusic reasoned, then the genre was perhaps "destined always to be a minority." Cusic's discussion of Elvis's gospel recordings provided white evangelicals with a precedent—or rather a usable past—for engagement with the mainstream music industry. But Cusic yearned for the day when a Christian would "[cross] into the secular field instead of a secular performer reaching into the Christian field."[1] Twenty-five years later, another Christian critic, Mark Joseph, published an analysis of Christians in the music industry in which he praised the efforts of bands such as POD (Payable on Death), a San Diego–based hard rock band with nonreligious fans that had appeared on the cover of *Hit Parader* and on Howard Stern's morning radio show. Unlike Cusic, who was skeptical of Christian music's ability to succeed, Joseph envisioned a level of engagement in which 80 percent of believers would "[rejoin] the mainstream of American pop cultural life" while the other 20 percent "[continued] to perform in a church-based subculture."[2]

By 2003 the youth-oriented culture that white evangelicals had begun crafting in the late 1960s had matured into a formidable industry. By Joseph's account, Christians were prepared to enter mainstream culture on an equal footing with secular bands. Yet Joseph's desire to delineate the ways that Christians influenced the mainstream demonstrates that white evangelicals continued to fluctuate between two extreme attitudes in their dealings with the secular world: they lamented their marginalization from unregenerate society while simultaneously noting the special role they were destined to play in redeeming American culture. Christian popular culture did more than help young evangelicals develop their beliefs. The increasingly widespread culture facilitated evangelicals' entrance into American cultural conversations.

The suburbanization of evangelical Christianity allowed conservative believers to "Christianize" the broader culture, especially the entertainment industry. These Christians embraced the outlook of producer Bob Briner, who suggested that Christians should become "roaring lambs" who, rather than calling for boycotts or protests, attracted nonbelievers "through lives of excellent, selfless service" within the media and entertainment industries.[3] Mark Joseph agreed with Briner. In fact, Joseph was so confident of Christians' contributions to the music industry that he objected to the system by which Christian music sales were measured, arguing that it allowed nonbelievers to dismiss bands with Christian beliefs as part of a "subculture." He also argued that the key difference between bands in the "mainstream" and bands in the "church-based subculture" lay in its members' willingness to use the term "Christian" as a noun rather than an adjective.[4]

Joseph's claim had merit. Christian music was not monolithic; in fact, some of it was not even "Christian." A number of devout white musicians—including indie-rock denizens such as Sufjan Stevens, Pedro the Lion, Danielson Famile, and Cold War Kids, as well as mainstream artists like U2—forswore the "Christian" label while including spiritual themes in their work. Other bands, perhaps hoping to boost sales among secular fans, avoided the militant posturing once embraced by flamboyantly evangelical metal bands.[5] While potentially opportunistic, the new, low-key approach more likely mirrored a general decline in rock star antics as well as a change in tone among evangelicals who felt less alienated from the so-called mainstream consumer society. While not abandoning a "Christian" worldview, these bands sought to provide a "positive" message to youths, a strategy that mirrored earlier attempts by evangelical leaders like Ralph Reed to "cast a wider net" in finding potential alliances for faith-based organizations like the Christian Coalition.[6] But just as organizations like the Christian Coalition built their influence on strong grassroots organizing, so did Christian bands benefit from the cultural infrastructure nurtured by the Jesus Movement. Even as bands sought to downplay the importance of their

Christian beliefs to their music, the sense that evangelical believers had a redemptive role to play in American culture remained. Joseph, for example, praised POD for emulating "cultural confrontationalists like Daniel, Shadrach, Meshach, and Abednego," who were "Jewish captives in ancient Babylon who stood tall for their faith amidst a culture of degradation and wild excess, and never used their belief in God as an excuse to withdraw from a culture in which they had been divinely placed."[7] Echoing the hopes of earlier generations of Christian bands, one punk band member explained to the *New York Times* that the goal of his group was not to "mimic" the mainstream but rather "to lead"— a belief-inflected claim to leadership that was rarely, if ever, expressed by secular artists.[8]

The mainstreaming of Christian musician reflected a broader assimilation of evangelical Christians into American exurbia. In the years following George W. Bush's election, middle-class Christian culture flourished. Once considered cultural rubes, white evangelical Christians had, as media critic Heather Hendershot has suggested, become respectable consumers.[9] There was no doubt that white evangelical Christians—especially families—were a powerful consumer demographic. In the year 2000 alone, Christian merchandise produced $4 billion in sales of books, videos, music, and other items. While books and Bibles accounted for 43 percent ($1.7 billion) of this total, Christian music accounted for 19 percent—or $747 million. In 2001 Christian music generated $920 million in sales.[10] Christian music may not have become a "dominant" force, but with 49.6 million gospel music albums sold in 2002 and 47.1 million sold in 2003, the genre's growth in an otherwise struggling industry was impressive. In fact, Christian and gospel music sales grew about 80 percent between 1995 and 2005.[11] This surge in popularity of Christian music garnered considerable attention from mainstream media sources, including the *New York Times, Newsweek,* the *Village Voice,* and the *Christian Science Monitor.*[12]

Like Christian musicians, Christian consumers were demonstrating their influence outside the traditional evangelical subculture. Christian consumer merchandise became available at suburban retail outlets as well as specialized Christian stores. The Christian Booksellers Association reported that about 63 percent of Christian products were sold at religious stores in 2000, but evidence showed that Christian products were increasingly purchased at big-box stores like Target and Wal-Mart. An executive for Zondervan, a Michigan-based Christian book publisher purchased by HarperCollins in the late 1980s, reported

that as recently as 1993, 85 percent of the company's sales had been at
Christian bookstores, but by 2001 sales were split evenly between religious and secular outlets.[13] Retailers who opened stores in suburban,
exurban, and rural areas considered white evangelicals a desirable marketing demographic. As historian Nelson Lichtenstein has explained,
Wal-Mart and the megachurch fit within the same "Christian ethos"
that linked "personal salvation to entrepreneurial success" and "social
service to free enterprise."[14] This ethos carried a moralistic attitude
toward consumer goods as well as labor practices. Retailers eagerly
catered to "traditionalist" customers, who bought items such as Tim
LaHaye's Left Behind fiction series or copies of the animated video series
VeggieTales. The stores also narrowed their selection of materials considered controversial by refusing to stock the music releases of controversial artists such as rappers 50 Cent and Eminem as well as racy men's
magazines such as *Maxim*.[15] This elimination of "controversial" merchandise, achieved not through boycotts but through the purchasing
power of consumers who wanted a family-friendly shopping experience,
represented a long-term victory for parent-advocates who had begun
lobbying for morality-based consumerism in the 1980s. Christian consumers also drew the attention of national advertisers. In 2002
Chevrolet agreed to be title sponsors of the sixteen-city Come Together
and Worship tour, which featured artists Third Day and Michael W.
Smith (among others), the sermons of Texas-based Pastor Max Lucado,
and distribution of evangelical literature.[16] Ultimately, however, the coalescence of exurban consumerism and religious belief could find no
greater expression than the August 2004 opening of a Calvary Chapel
on the grounds of a former Wal-Mart Superstore in St. Petersburg,
Florida. The floor plan for the megachurch included a playground, a
skate park, nurseries, a "kids zone," a children's worship center ("kids
live"), a bookstore, classrooms, a café, a banquet hall, a commercial
kitchen, and a 1,500-seat auditorium.

Many evangelicals downplayed the conservative ideological label
placed on their culture. Christian musicians were among those who
tried to avoid ideological associations. In 1996 Audio Adrenaline lead
singer Mark Stuart spoke of the church's need to "re-market itself" and
his hope that Christian music could be part of the transformation.
According to Stuart, "If you ask someone what a Christian is, they say,
'Republican, conservative, anti-abortion'—not love or forgiveness or
joy. The Bible clearly states the greatest commandment is to love God
first and then the people around him. That's as far from a Rush

Limbaugh show as you can get."[17] Nonetheless, Christians' desire to contest the categories of youth, family, and nation were embedded in the culture, even if the rhetoric did not replicate Limbaugh's controversial language. In the immediate aftermath of 9/11, Christian music experienced a spike in sales, which industry executives attributed to a reevaluation of goals. Frank Breeden, president of the Gospel Music Association, cited a survey of priorities and argued that while "career and money" had previously trumped other goals, in the wake of the disaster, people would place "faith and family" at the top.[18] Describing the same phenomenon in the radio industry, a Christian network executive explained, "People are flocking to the format just like they're flocking to church and family and everything else that represents conservative values."[19] Executives were confident that Christian culture would be an important part of a general reassessment of the American way of life.

The increased integration of Christian consumerism in exurbia paralleled the increased integration of conservative evangelicals in the political process. Between 2000 and 2004, conservative Christian activists made inroads into politics, particularly at the national level; on the other hand, politicians attempted to maximize their electoral advantage among white evangelicals by mobilizing institutions as well as culture. Although Bill Clinton was raised a Southern Baptist, his political orientation and perceived moral shortcomings infuriated white Christian conservatives. Al Gore, who was raised in the same church, perhaps suffered among white evangelicals as a result of his connection to the Clinton administration and despite his wife's involvement in the PMRC. George W. Bush, on the other hand, was a Republican and a born-again Christian who deployed evangelical rhetoric with the zeal of the post–Damascus Road Paul. His speeches, especially those describing America's role in the world after 9/11, were filled with language that resonated with evangelicals. Moreover, Bush supported the political agenda favored by many Christian conservatives. During his first term, Bush endeared himself to religious conservatives by signing a ban on partial-birth abortion and by supporting faith-based initiatives and school vouchers. The president's call for a constitutional amendment to ban gay marriage also energized Christian conservatives, as did his repeated pleas for bans on euthanasia and stem cell research. Rather than state these beliefs in oppositional terms, however, Bush often spoke of a "culture of life," a phrase originated by Pope John Paul II that stated his position as positively worded moral objectives (while skirting his support for the death penalty and preemptive war).[20]

In 2004, Bush campaign officials clearly believed that Bush's reelection hinged on their ability to cooperate with and mobilize conservative evangelical voters. White evangelical Protestants represented approximately 50 million voters, which translated into 20 to 25 percent of the electorate.[21] Newspapers teemed with details of Bush adviser Karl Rove's plans to maximize the number of evangelical voters through anti-gay marriage initiatives in thirteen key states and get-out-the-vote drives, especially in conservative counties. To Republican operatives, the megachurch represented a contact point for reaching conservative voters concerned with the plight of the white middle-class home and morals. Liberals were infuriated when it was revealed that the campaign had sought to enlist evangelicals who worshiped at "friendly congregations."[22] The suburban megachurch—and the evangelical culture that had grown up alongside it—became the focus of Republican mobilization efforts. The campaign requested that each church's "coalition coordinator" perform tasks such as sending church directories to campaign headquarters, referring other churches to the campaign, recruiting church members to participate in voter registration, talking to senior or "20–30 something" groups, holding a "citizenship Sunday" to encourage voting, distributing "voters' guides" in the church, and posting reminders of the duty of "'Christian citizens' to vote."[23] According to the *Washington Post,* even Rick Warren—the author of *The Purpose Driven Life* who was often cited as part of the "new generation" of independent-minded evangelical ministers not associated with the Christian Right—sent a letter to 136,000 pastors asking them to compare candidate positions on five "'non-negotiable' issues: abortion, stem cell research, same-sex marriage, human cloning and euthanasia."[24] The list did not include the issues often listed by progressives as possible points of agreement between Democratic politicians and moderate evangelicals—debt relief, foreign aid, and the environment—although in a separate message Warren urged the network to put pressure on Bush to address these issues.[25]

After Bush's victory, Rove repeatedly cited his candidate's appeal among "churchgoers" as the reason for victory, even as analysts questioned the validity of the claim. Nonetheless, according to exit polls, 23 percent of voters (about 26.5 million) in 2004 identified themselves as white "evangelicals or born-again" Christians; of these voters, nearly four in five (78%) supported Bush.[26] Ralph Reed, the former Christian Coalition executive director who coordinated the Bush-Cheney campaign's Southeast region, crowed that 2004 marked the first time that "the effort to get out the socially conservative faith community has been fully integrated into the presidential campaign," a sign that Christian conservatism had become mainstream within the GOP.[27]

Christian organizations, aware of the earthly political benefits to be reaped from gatherings of young and conservative believers, tapped into evangelical culture for political gain. Just a few weeks before the 2000 presidential election, several Christian organizations and media outlets sponsored "Votopia," a concert at the University of California, Irvine's Bren Events Center to benefit Rock for Life and Food for the Hungry. The flyer for the event included links for the Traditional Values Coalition, the American Center for Law and Justice, and Rock for Life—an organization that viewed itself as the pro-life foil for organizations such as Rock for Choice.[28] Just as George H. W. Bush's campaign staff had attempted to reach conservative voters at the Harvest Crusade, the Votopia organizers mined Christian concerts for young conservative voters.

In 2004 concerts and benefits became part of a broader infrastructure for locating conservative voters. Randy Brinson, a gastroenterologist from Alabama, established Redeem the Vote as a Christian counterpart to Rock the Vote. A spokesman for the organization noted that while it would not endorse any political candidates, it sought to "reach kids of faith because we know how kids of faith are going to vote. They're going to vote for those issues that support Judeo-Christian values."[29] With the help of the same PR firm that ran the publicity for Mel Gibson's movie *The Passion of the Christ*, the organization partnered with the American Tract Society, the Christian Broadcasting Network, the Gospel Music Association, American Family Radio, Charles W. Colson's Wilberforce Forum, FOX News, Trinity Broadcasting Network, the Southern Baptist Convention's FamilyNet, Homemakers for America, and bands such as Jonah33. Brinson explained, "Music influences the culture. . . . We're just trying to influence people on the other side."[30] The Redeem the Vote's efforts included attempts to stir voter turnout in Ohio with six concerts in five cities, Mansfield, Zanesville, Mt. Gilead, Dayton, and Findlay. The organization also helped distribute voter turnout information to 125 churches and twenty-one radio stations across the state and booked airtime for cooperating artists who encouraged listeners to vote. Jim Caveziel, who played Jesus in *The Passion of the Christ*, appeared in an e-mail video that the organization sent to 650,000 people throughout the state.[31] Around the country, public service announcements recorded by thirty-five

Figure 12. This flyer for a Christian concert "in support of Rock for Life and Food for the Hungry" was distributed before the 2000 election. The reverse side urged young people to REGISTER TO VOTE and offered Web links for organizations including the Traditional Values Coalition.

Christian musicians aired on 2,500 religious radio stations, and the organization set up registration tables at Christian concerts—including a few in battleground states like Ohio, Pennsylvania, Wisconsin, and Florida. The organization eventually registered 78,000 young evangelicals to vote.[32]

After the 2004 election, many progressives maintained that the Democratic Party needed to court evangelical voters, who composed 26 percent of the electorate in 2004.[33] Political scientist John Green, among others, suggested that 41 percent of those evangelical voters in 2004 were moderates who might respond to Democratic overtures on issues such as education, health care, and the environment.[34] In an article posted to his organization's website, Brinson spoke of his meetings with the centrist Democratic Leadership Committee. Like evangelical musicians who maintained they had to proselytize among all genres, Brinson argued that conservative Christians "must foster and nourish Christian values within both parties, not to the exclusion of those ideals that differ from our own positions or convictions. We cannot have one political party seen as taking the Christian vote for granted and one party writing it off."[35] Democratic politicians infused religious rhetoric into their messages. And although the war in Iraq represented a clear-cut ethical issue to many liberals, it seemed likely that "cultural issues" that focused on the sentimentalized white suburban family would remain an important part of American political debate.[36] Democrats could well become part of that debate—Jesse Jackson had organized Operation PUSH and Tipper Gore had spearheaded the PMRC—but only to the extent that they deployed the rhetoric of values defined for so long by conservative believers. Democrats' increased willingness to frame policy using religious language in order to draw moderate evangelical votes demonstrated the extent to which conservative religious believers have influenced the cultural conversation of postliberal American society.

The GOP worked diligently to garner evangelical votes with political rhetoric expressed in moral terms. This does not mean, however, that suburban evangelicals were destined to remain steadfast GOP voters. To draw this conclusion would be to suggest that evangelicalism does not change and to reduce conservatism to party allegiance. The generation of evangelicals documented in this book consistently demonstrated a commitment to a program of engagement with suburban consumer culture that represented a renewal of their reformist impulse. Their morality-based cultural criticism shed Old Right fears about global communism, internal subversion, and the intrinsic immorality of popular culture in order to focus on personal piety and the sentimental family. But engagement alters the evangelizer as well as the evangelized. Christian parent-activists and the Harvest Crusade organizers softened the angriest edges of fundamentalism while creating an idealized vision of "family values" centered on the home rather than the church. Conservative parent and political organizations occasionally found ways to co-opt youth religious networks, but expressions of youth religiosity—which often demonstrated steadfast generational independence—also evolved in unexpected directions. The youth activism pursued by metal bands and zine writers signaled that evangelicals were unwilling to cede even the farthest reaches of the music world to either secular or satanic control. Christian musicians also helped redefine evangelicals' understanding of acceptable models of "Christian" behavior. In this light, engaged Christian consumerism—devout Protestant believers' desire to witness God's message to suburbia in its own idiom—transformed the American religious, political, and cultural landscape of the late twentieth century.

# Acknowledgments

My interest in conservatism dates to the 1992 Republican National Convention, when Pat Buchanan used his prime-time speaking slot to declare a domestic "cultural war" in the aftermath of the international Cold War. As an undergraduate at Williams College, I became fascinated with the inclusive and exclusive connotations of "family values," as well as with the political culture that developed around the concept.

After I wrote an undergraduate thesis and worked for a time in politics in Washington, D.C., my interest in "family values" took a cultural turn at the University of California, Irvine. The school's location in Orange County provided a perfect vantage point for observing conservative evangelicalism, and its graduate program fostered my belief in the explanatory power of cultural politics. My adviser, Jon Wiener, was the first and most critical reader for each segment of the dissertation. I am fortunate to have had his writing as a model for connecting music and American politics; in addition, working on his public affairs program deepened my knowledge of the history of popular music. Dickson D. Bruce made sure I knew the historiography of American revivalism and shared his thoughts on contemporary religious ephemera. Heidi Tinsman helped me envision a research project that brought youth culture and conservatism into dialogue. Mike Davis has been an enthusiastic supporter of the project, and his suggestions provided the basis for revising the dissertation into a manuscript. Several faculty members at UC Irvine made suggestions on pieces of the dissertation: Alice Fahs,

Thelma Foote, Lynn Mally, Vicki Ruiz, and Ulrike Strasser. Dave Johnson, Mike Masatsugu, Tracy Sachtjen, and Marc Kanda also assisted with segments of the project. The UC Irvine History Project provided me with employment during my graduate and early postgraduate career. Nicole Gilbertson, Rob Vicario, and Stephanie Reyes-Tuccio work hard to improve history teaching in K–12 classrooms, but they actively supported my research efforts.

Chapter 3 contains a slightly revised version of "Metal Missionaries to the Nation: Christian Heavy Metal Music, 'Family Values,' and Youth Culture, 1984–1994," originally published in *American Quarterly* 57, no. 1 (March 2005). I was unable to reprint some primary source materials from albums and magazines. This made me more appreciative of the following people, who allowed me to reproduce lyrics, photographs, and original illustrations from their albums and magazines: Alexis Colbert and John DiDonna, Joey Knight, Duane Pederson, Dave Simmons, and Doug Van Pelt. The lyrics to "Panned Parenthood" and "Operation Rescue" appear courtesy of Lust Control (Captive Thought/ASCAP). All verses of the Bible not taken from quotations are derived from the New Revised Standard Version Bible, copyright 1989, Division of Christian Education of the National Council of Churches of Christ in the United States of America. I'd also like to thank Nathan Hayden, who provided photographs from our group field trip to the Harvest Crusade in 1998. I located many of the Christian punk and heavy metal zines at the Center for Popular Music at Middle Tennessee State University in Murfreesboro, Tennessee.

Thanks to the Kevin Starr Fellowship in California Studies, I was able to spend a full year revising the manuscript. At the University of California Humanities Research Institute, Philomena Essed and the rest of the Cloning Cultures research group welcomed me into their discussions and provided helpful comments for revisions to the manuscript's final chapter. I'd like to thank Hamza Walker for inviting me to talk about my project at the Renaissance Society at the University of Chicago. I also benefited from comments provided by audiences at the American Studies Association meeting, the American Historical Association/Pacific Coast Branch meeting, and the History and Theory Conference at UC Irvine. At the California State University, Long Beach, my reduced teaching load as a new faculty member provided needed time for final revisions. I am fortunate to have such supportive colleagues in the Department of History; in particular, I'm indebted to Sarah Schrank for her advice on the process of completing a first manuscript.

At UC Press, Niels Hooper, Rachel Lockman, and Caroline Knapp helped guide the project toward completion, and Steven Baker greatly enhanced its clarity. Two anonymous readers for UC Press also provided useful comments for revision. I'm grateful to Bob Johnson and Adam Wemmer for reading the entire revised manuscript and offering their insights as the project neared completion.

I've been nattering for several years about "family values" as an issue in American culture and politics. Many friends have humored my preoccupation by listening to me describe my project; others have enabled it by gamely accompanying me on field trips, participating in film festivals, or sending me articles, websites, recordings, and other artifacts. Thanks to Steven Dean, Jennifer Wingate, Rachel Jones, Jack O'Brien, Sabrina Fève, Jessica Cross, Nick Poppy, and Sarah Gardam for enduring my ramblings.

As the youngest of thirteen children, I've been fortunate to have the support of a rather extensive family network. I'm grateful to Catherine Luhr, Florine Luhr, Jane Snyder, Margaret Brady, and Lidia Snyder for their interest in the project. Clay Marquardt and Betsy Snyder have regularly welcomed me into their house since I relocated to California; Adair Kearney and Mary Beth Johnson welcomed me back whenever I returned to Buffalo and called to check up on me when I didn't. Ann Luhr provided indispensable travel and tech support for many years, and Alfred F. Luhr carefully monitored the project's progress through his frequent calls. Finally, my biggest thanks belong to my selflessly devoted parents, George L. Snyder and Leah Luhr Snyder, for supporting me and for imparting their love of history.

# Notes

1. "Elvis—a Different Kind of Idol," *Life* (27 August 1956): 101–9. For a description of the controversy surrounding Elvis in the spring and summer of 1956, see Peter Guralnick, *Last Train to Memphis: The Rise of Elvis Presley* (Boston: Little, Brown, 1994), 277–324.

2. Thomas C. Ryan, "Rock'n'Roll Battle: Pat Boone vs. Elvis Presley," *Collier's* (26 October 1956): 109–11.

3. John Styll, "The Boones/*First Class Music*," *Contemporary Christian Music* 1, no. 1 (July 1978): 1.

4. Don Cusic, "Destined to Be a Minority," *Contemporary Christian Music* 1, no. 1 (July 1978): 15. Religious conservatives continued to debate the merits of Elvis as a Christian icon. On the twenty-fifth anniversary of Elvis's death, the evangelical family magazine *Charisma* published an article about Christian Elvis Tribute Artists (ETAs) around the world. Andy Butcher, "For the Love of Elvis," *Charisma*, August 2003, www.charismamag.com/a.php?ArticleID=7841. For analysis of the emergence of Elvis as an object of religious devotion among fans, see Erika Doss, *Elvis Culture: Fans, Faith, and Image* (Lawrence: University Press of Kansas, 1999).

5. Elvis continued to sing gospel music after he was no longer a teen idol. In 1967 he received a Grammy—a career first—for Best Sacred Performance for his second gospel album, *How Great Thou Art*. Elvis continued to incorporate spirituals in his live performances in Las Vegas and, ultimately, in his final television special in 1977. See Guralnick, *Last Train to Memphis*, 47, 379, 387.

6. Although some church leaders continued to resist the genre, gospel stations flourished across the South. For an explanation of the role of gospel music in African American churches and culture, see Brian Ward, *Just My Soul Responding: Rhythm and Blues, Black Consciousness, and Race Relations*

(Berkeley and Los Angeles: University of California Press, 1998), chapter 5; Peter Guralnick, *Dream Boogie: The Triumph of Sam Cooke* (New York: Little, Brown, 2005), 65–129; Milton Sernett, *Bound for the Promised Land: African American Religion and the Great Migration* (Durham, NC: Duke University Press, 1997), chapters 6–7.

7. Stan Cohen, *Folk Devils and Moral Panics: The Creation of the Mods and Rockers* (New York: St. Martin's Press, 1972).

8. For an overview of the contest over values in the late twentieth century, see James Davison Hunter, *Culture Wars: The Struggle to Define America* (New York: Basic Books, 1991). For a discussion of the connections between Christianity and modern consumerism, see Heather Hendershot, *Shaking the World for Jesus: Media and Conservative Evangelical Culture* (Chicago: University of Chicago Press, 2004), and Colleen McDannell, *Material Christianity: Religion and Popular Culture in America* (New Haven: Yale University Press, 1995), chapter 8; for a nonacademic discussion of evangelical consumer culture, see Carol Flake, *Redemptorama: Culture, Politics, and the New Evangelicalism* (Garden City, NY: Anchor Press, 1984); Sara Diamond, *Not by Politics Alone: The Enduring Influence of the Christian Right* (New York: Guilford Press, 1998); and Lauren Sandler, *Righteous: Dispatches from the Evangelical Youth Movement* (New York: Viking, 2006); for an analysis of the connections between fundamentalist politics and linguistic practices in the 1980s, see Susan Friend Harding, *The Book of Jerry Falwell: Fundamentalist Language and Politics* (Princeton, NJ: Princeton University Press, 2000).

9. Matthew Lassiter, *The Silent Majority: Suburban Politics in the Sunbelt South* (Princeton, NJ: Princeton University Press, 2006), 1; Kevin M. Kruse, *White Flight: Atlanta and the Making of Modern Conservatism* (Princeton, NJ: Princeton University Press, 2005); Robert O. Self, *American Babylon: Race and the Struggle for Postwar Oakland* (Princeton, NJ: Princeton University Press, 2003); Becky M. Nicolaides, *My Blue Heaven: Life and Politics in the Working-Class Suburbs of Los Angeles, 1920–1965* (Chicago: University of Chicago Press, 2002); Lisa McGirr, *Suburban Warriors: The Origins of the New American Right* (Princeton, NJ: Princeton University Press, 2001).

10. William Schneider, "The Suburban Century Begins," *Atlantic Monthly* (July 1992): 35.

11. Ronald Brownstein and Richard Rainey, "GOP Plants Flag on New Voting Frontier," *Los Angeles Times,* 22 November 2004, A1.

12. Donald E. Miller, *Reinventing American Protestantism: Christianity in the New Millennium* (Berkeley and Los Angeles: University of California Press, 1997); Charles Trueheart, "Welcome to the Next Church," *Atlantic Monthly* (August 1996): 37–58.

13. In 2004 the only age group that Democratic John Kerry won was the 18-to-24-year-old group. In 2006 an online survey by the Harvard Institute of Politics showed that 35% of 18-to-24-year-old Americans identified as Democrats, compared to 27% as Republicans and 39% as Independents. The GOP, though cognizant of the Democrats' advantage, sought to minimize the advantage by mobilizing young conservatives on campuses. In the months preceding the midterm elections in 2006, GOP pollsters cited a 7-percentage-point

"intensity advantage" in young voters who were already affiliated with a political party, which suggested that young Republicans were more motivated to vote. Gina Kim, "Young Voters Are Back," *Sacramento Bee*, 3 November 2006, sec. J, p. 1; Zachary A. Goldfarb, "Parties Scramble for Youth Vote," *Washington Post*, 16 July 2006, sec. A, p. 4.

14. Stephen A. Flanders, *Atlas of American Migration* (New York: Facts on File, 1998), 193.

15. Schneider, "Suburban Century Begins," 33.

16. Kevin Phillips, *The Emerging Republican Majority* (New Rochelle, NY: Arlington House, 1969), 38–39, 184, 442.

17. Mike Davis, *City of Quartz: Excavating the Future in Los Angeles* (New York: Vintage Books, 1990), 223, 227.

18. Robin D. G. Kelley, *Yo' Mama's DisFUNKtional! Fighting the Culture Wars in Urban America* (Boston: Beacon Press, 1997), 9. For an investigation of the urban conditions in the post–World War II era (especially in the North), see also George Lipsitz, *The Possessive Investment in Whiteness: How White People Profit from Identity Politics* (Philadelphia: Temple University Press, 1998), chapter 2; Stephen Nathan Haymes, *Race, Culture, and the City: A Pedagogy for Black Urban Struggle* (Albany: State University of New York Press, 1995); Thomas J. Sugrue, *The Origins of the Urban Crisis: Race and Inequality in Postwar Detroit* (Princeton, NJ: Princeton University Press, 1996); John T. McGreevy, *Parish Boundaries: The Catholic Encounter with Race in the Twentieth-Century Urban North* (Chicago: University of Chicago Press, 1996).

19. Centre for Contemporary Cultural Studies, *The Empire Strikes Back: Race and Racism in 70s Britain* (London: Hutchinson, 1982), 18–20.

20. Lizabeth Cohen, *A Consumers' Republic: The Politics of Mass Consumption in Postwar America* (New York: Alfred A. Knopf, 2003).

21. Elaine Tyler May, *Homeward Bound: American Families in the Cold-War Era* (New York: Basic Books, 1988), 16, 18.

22. For more on the Kitchen Debate and Cold War ideology, see ibid., chapter 1.

23. Peter La Chapelle, *Proud to Be an Okie: Cultural Politics, Country Music, and Migration to Southern California* (Berkeley and Los Angeles: University of California Press, 2007), 3.

24. See Thomas Byrne Edsall and Mary Edsall, *Chain Reaction: The Impact of Race, Rights, and Taxes on American Politics* (New York: W. W. Norton, 1992), chapter 6; and Mike Davis, "From Fordism to Reaganism: The Crisis of American Hegemony in the 1980s," in Ray Bush, Gordon Johnston, and David Coates, eds., *The World Order: Socialist Perspectives* (New York: Polity Press, 1987), 17–21.

25. Lewis Mumford, *The Culture of the Cities*, as cited in Robert Putnam, *Bowling Alone: The Collapse and Revival of American Community* (New York: Simon and Schuster, 2000), 211.

26. Andres Duany, with Elizabeth Plater-Zyberk and Jeff Speck, *Suburban Nation: The Rise of Sprawl and the Decline of the American Dream* (New York: Farrar, Straus and Giroux/North Point Press, 2000), 40; Schneider, "The Suburban Century Begins," 34. For a discussion of zoning laws and racial

covenants, see Lipsitz, *Possessive Investment in Whiteness*, 25–33, and Davis, *City of Quartz*, 158–69.

27. Edward J. Blakely and Mary Gail Snyder, *Fortress America* (Washington, DC: Brookings Institution, 1997), as cited in Duany et al., *Suburban Nation*, 43.

28. Eric Avila, *Popular Culture in the Age of White Flight: Fear and Fantasy in Suburban Los Angeles* (Berkeley and Los Angeles: University of California Press, 2004), 6.

29. Barbara Ehrenreich, *Fear of Falling: The Inner Life of the Middle Class* (New York: HarperCollins, 1989), 4; Barbara Ehrenreich, "The Silenced Majority: Why the Average Working Person Has Disappeared from American Media and Culture," *Zeta Magazine* (September 1989): 40–42. George Lipsitz, in his meditation on representations of ethnicity and class in early television sitcoms, mentions the "re-appearance of race, class, and ethnicity" in 1970s shows such as *All in the Family, Chico and the Man, Barney Miller,* and *Sanford and Son.* These portrayals promptly disappeared again in 1980s TV shows (except for *Roseanne* and *The Simpsons*). See George Lipsitz, *Time Passages: Collective Memory and American Popular Culture* (Minneapolis: University of Minnesota Press, 1990), chapter 3.

30. Davis, *City of Quartz*, 223–31; Mike Davis, *Ecology of Fear: Los Angeles and the Imagination of Disaster* (New York: Metropolitan Books, 1998), 363–68.

31. Keith Bradsher, *High and Mighty: SUVs—The World's Most Dangerous Vehicles and How They Got That Way* (New York: PublicAffairs, 2002), 96, 102–3, chapters 6 and 9.

32. Mike Davis, *Prisoners of the American Dream: Politics and Economy in the History of the U.S. Working Class* (New York: Verso, 1986), 170–171.

33. Phillips, *Emerging Republican Majority*, 470.

34. James Q. Wilson, "A Guide to Reagan Country: The Political Culture of Southern California," *Commentary* (May 1967): 37–45.

35. Peter Schrag, *Paradise Lost: California's Experience, America's Future* (New York: New Press, 1998), 172.

36. See Jon Wiener, "Working-Class Republicans and 'False Consciousness,'" *Dissent* (Spring 2005): 55–58. False consciousness is generally defined as workers' acceptance of ideologies that justify (and thereby prolong) their oppression. Religious beliefs, morality, nationalism, and ethnic and racial divisions have been suggested as examples of false consciousness that prevent workers from perceiving economic exploitation as the source of their problems. Although the characterization of conservatism as reactionary or delusional has waned recently, it characterized much of the academic research done on the Right between the 1950s and the 1980s, including Richard Hofstadter's *The Paranoid Style in American Politics.* For a discussion of the origins and legacy of the Cold War–era historiography on the "radical right," see Leo Ribuffo, *The Old Christian Right: The Protestant Far Right from the Great Depression to the Cold War* (Philadelphia: Temple University Press, 1983), 237–58, 270–71.

37. Edsall and Edsall, *Chain Reaction*, 131–32.

38. See Davis, "Preface," in *City of Quartz: Excavating the Future in Los Angeles* (New York: Verso, 2006), xviii.

39. McGirr, *Suburban Warriors*.

40. Alexis de Tocqueville, "Principal Causes Which Tend To Maintain The Democratic Republic In The United States," *Democracy in America* vol. 1, http://xroads.virginia.edu/~HYPER /DETOC/1_ch17.htm. For a discussion of Tocqueville and the issue of secularism versus public Christianity, see Connolly, *Why I Am Not a Secularist* (Minneapolis: University of Minnesota Press, 1999).

41. Lauren Berlant, *The Queen of America Goes to Washington City: Essays on Sex and Citizenship* (Durham, NC: Duke University Press, 1997), 1.

42. Ehrenreich, *Fear of Falling,* 168–69.

43. Paul Apostolidis, *Stations of the Cross: Adorno and Christian Right Radio* (Durham, NC: Duke University Press, 2000), 20, 92.

44. Thomas Byrne Edsall, "Blue Movie," *Atlantic Monthly* (January–February 2003): 36–37.

45. Stuart Hall, "The Great Moving Right Show," in Stuart Hall and Martin Jaques, eds., *The Politics of Thatcherism* (London: Lawrence and Wishart, 1983), 29.

46. Martin E. Marty, "The Revival of Evangelicalism and Southern Religion," in David Harrell, ed., *Varieties of Southern Evangelicalism* (Macon, GA: Mercer University Press, 1981), 13.

47. Whitney Cross, *The Burned-Over District: The Social and Intellectual History of Enthusiastic Religion, 1800–1850* (Ithaca, NY: Cornell University Press, 1950), 271. See also Paul Johnson, *A Shopkeeper's Millennium: Society and Revivals in Rochester, New York, 1815–1837* (New York: Hill and Wang, 1978); Mary P. Ryan, *Cradle of the Middle Class: The Family in Oneida County, New York, 1790–1865* (New York: Cambridge University Press, 1981); Christine Leigh Heyrman, *Southern Cross: The Beginnings of the Bible Belt* (Chapel Hill: University of North Carolina Press, 1997).

48. Catharine E. Beecher, *Treatise on Domestic Economy for the Use of Young Ladies at Home and at School* (Boston: Thomas H. Webb, 1842), as quoted in Dolores Hayden, *Building Suburbia: Green Fields and Urban Growth, 1820–2000* (New York: Pantheon Books, 2003), 35.

49. Stephanie McCurry, *Masters of Small Worlds: Yeoman Households, Gender Relations, and the Political Culture of the Antebellum South Carolina Low Country* (New York: Oxford University Press, 1995); Ted Ownby, *Subduing Satan: Religion, Recreation, and Manhood in the Rural South, 1865–1920* (Chapel Hill: University of North Carolina Press, 1990).

50. Donald G. Mathews, *Religion in the Old South* (Chicago: University of Chicago Press, 1977), 99.

51. Anthony Comstock, *Traps for the Young,* ed. Robert Bremner (Cambridge, MA: Belknap Press of Harvard University Press, 1967), 240.

52. Michael Kazin, *The Populist Persuasion: An American History* (New York: Basic Books, 1995), 43–44; Thomas Frank, *What's the Matter with Kansas? How Conservatives Won the Heart of America* (New York: Metropolitan Books, 2004), 15–16.

53. Michael Kazin, *A Godly Hero: The Life of William Jennings Bryan* (New York: Random House, 2006), 172–5.

54. Sydney Ahlstrom, *A Religious History of the American People* (New Haven: Yale University Press, 1972), 747.

55. Mrs. Charles Stewart Daggett, as cited in Carey McWilliams, *Southern California Country: An Island on the Land* (New York: Duell, Sloan, and Pearce, 1946), 249.

56. "Weird Babel of Tongues," *Los Angeles Times,* 18 April 1906, sec. 2, p. 1. On Los Angeles imagined as the City of the Future, see William Deverell, *Whitewashed Adobe: The Rise of Los Angeles and the Remaking of Its Mexican Past* (Berkeley and Los Angeles: University of California Press, 2005).

57. Willard Huntington Wright, "Los Angeles—The Chemically Pure," in Burton Rascoe and Groff Conklin, eds., *The Smart Set Anthology* (New York: Reynal and Hitchcock, 1934), 93.

58. For an account of how the Scopes Trial shaped American public opinion concerning fundamentalism and science, see Edward Larson, *Summer for the Gods: The Scopes Trial and America's Continuing Debate over Science and Religion* (New York: Basic Books, 1997).

59. H.L. Mencken, "William Jennings Bryan" (1925), in Lawrence E. Spivak and Charles Angoff, eds., *The American Mercury Reader* (Garden City, NY: Blue Ribbon Books, 1946): 34–37.

60. Sinclair Lewis, *Elmer Gantry* (New York: Harcourt Inc., 1927; repr., New York: New American Library, 1970). The rural-to-urban migration to the West celebrated by Aimee Semple McPherson didn't escape Sinclair Lewis' notice. In the novel's first chapter, the founders of Gritzmacher Springs, the location of Elmer Gantry's Baptist college, have moved to Los Angeles "to sell bungalows and delicatessen."

61. Wright, "Los Angeles," 102.

62. Harding, *Book of Jerry Falwell,* 21, 62. For more on the importance of the Scopes Trial for creating "fundamentalism" as a discourse of modernity, see Susan Harding, "Representing Fundamentalism: The Problem of the Repugnant Cultural Other," *Social Research* 58, no. 2 (Summer 1991): 373–93.

63. Marty, "The Revival of Evangelicalism and Southern Religion," 12–15. In writing of the "chopping up" of life, Marty quotes from John Murray Cuddihy's *The Ordeal of Civility: Freud, Marx, Levi-Strauss, and the Jewish Struggle with Modernity* (New York: Basic Books, 1974), 9–10.

64. It is perhaps no coincidence that the progressive evangelical most identified with social justice causes, Jim Wallis of *Sojourners,* lives in Washington, D.C. Similarly, Jesus People USA, a conservative evangelical community that grew out of the Jesus Movement of the 1960s, is located on Chicago's North Side.

65. Harrell, "Introduction," in *Varieties of Southern Evangelicalism,* 2.

66. Pat Robertson, *America's Dates with Destiny* (New York: Thomas Nelson, 1986), 252.

67. Russell Chandler, "God as Capitalist: Seminar Promotes Religion and Riches," *Los Angeles Times,* 10 June 1981, A3, as quoted in Kevin Phillips, *Post-Conservative America: People, Politics, and Ideology in a Time of Crisis* (New York: Random House, 1982), 141. Herbert Ellingwood, deputy counsel to Ronald Reagan, was the administration official quoted by Chandler.

68. *Gallup Opinion* Index, no. 57 (March 1970): 20.

69. Patrick Allitt, *Religion in America since 1945: A History* (New York: Columbia University Press, 2003), 74–76.

70. "The New Rebel Cry: Jesus Is Coming!" *Time* (21 June 1971): 56–63.

71. The Gallup Opinion Index, *Religion in America 1976*, no. 130, p. 3.

72. Christian Smith, with Melinda Lundquist Denton, *Soul Searching: The Religious and Spiritual Lives of American Teenagers* (New York: Oxford University Press, 2005), 176.

73. Christian Smith, with Michael Emerson, Sally Gallagher, Paul Kennedy, and David Sikkink, *American Evangelicalism: Embattled and Thriving* (Chicago: University of Chicago Press, 1998), 74.

74. Robert Wuthnow, *Restructuring American Religion: Society and Faith since World War II* (Princeton, NJ: Princeton University Press, 1988), 26; James Hudnut-Beumler, *Looking for God in the Suburbs: The Religion of the American Dream and Its Critics, 1945–1965* (New Brunswick, NJ: Rutgers University Press, 1994), 33–37.

75. Hudnut-Beumler, *Looking for God in the Suburbs*, 33–40, 79–80.

76. Ibid., 68.

77. Gibson Winter, *The Suburban Captivity of the Churches* (New York: Macmillan, 1962), 30, 33, 39, 93.

78. Smith et al., *American Evangelicalism*, 89.

79. Grant Wacker, "Uneasy in Zion: Evangelicals in Postmodern Society," in George Marsden, ed., *Evangelicalism and Modern America* (Grand Rapids, MI: William B. Eerdmans, 1984), 25–26; Mark A. Shibley, *Resurgent Evangelicalism in the United States: Mapping Cultural Change since 1970* (Columbia: University of South Carolina Press, 1996), 1. The spread of southern-style religion in the late twentieth century has been described as the "cultural diaspora of Southern evangelicalism" and the "southernization of American religion." The attributes of the style included a born-again experience, a literal interpretation of scripture, and a commitment to proselytizing, a greater emotional intensity in worship, a tendency toward sectarianism, and high expectations of individual piety. See Shibley, *Resurgent Evangelicalism*, 20.

80. James N. Gregory, *Southern Diaspora: How the Great Migrations of Black and White Southerners Transformed America* (Chapel Hill: University of North Carolina Press, 2005), 197–236; for a close examination of the process in California, see James N. Gregory, *American Exodus: The Dust Bowl Migration and Okie Culture in California* (New York: Oxford University Press, 1989), 191–221.

81. Shibley, *Resurgent Evangelicalism*, 28–29.

82. Nancy Tatom Ammerman, *Baptist Battles: Social Change and Religious Conflict in the Southern Baptist Convention* (New Brunswick, NJ: Rutgers University Press, 1990), 52–53; William M. Newman and Peter L. Halvorson, *Atlas of American Religion: The Denominational Era, 1776–1990* (Walnut Creek, CA: AltaMira Press, 2000), 72–75, 85–88.

83. Frances Fitzgerald, *Cities on a Hill: A Journey through Contemporary American Cultures* (New York: Simon and Schuster, 1986), 132–33, 137.

84. Wuthnow, *Restructuring of American Religion*, 101.

85. Smith et al., *American Evangelicalism*, 86–87.

86. Joel A. Carpenter, *Revive Us Again: The Reawakening of American Fundamentalism* (New York: Oxford University Press, 1997), 16; Wuthnow, *Restructuring of American Religion*, 101.

87. See Susan Faludi, *Stiffed: The Betrayal of the American Man* (New York: HarperCollins, 1999), chapter 5; Joel Garreau, *Edge City: Life on the New Frontier* (New York: Anchor Books, 1991), chapter 8; FitzGerald, "Liberty Baptist," in *Cities on a Hill*.

88. Robert D. Putnam and Lewis M. Feldstein, with Don Cohen, *Better Together: Restoring the American Community* (New York: Simon and Schuster, 2003), 126.

89. Francis A. Schaeffer, *A Christian Manifesto*, rev. ed. (Westchester, IL: Crossway Books, 1982), 136–37. See also Schaeffer, *Art and the Bible: Two Essays* (Downers Grove, IL: InterVarsity Press, 1973).

90. Smith et al., *American Evangelicalism*, 44.

91. Ibid., 37–38. Smith's findings derived from a study, the Evangelical Identity and Influence Project, conducted in 1995 and 1996. The survey, conducted in 1996, distinguished evangelicals from fundamentalists.

92. Jackson Lears, "From Salvation to Self-Realization: Advertising and the Therapeutic Roots of the Consumer Culture, 1880–1930," in T. J. Jackson Lears and Richard Wrightman Fox, eds., *The Culture of Consumption: Critical Essays in American History, 1880–1980* (New York: Pantheon Books, 1983), 4.

93. R. Laurence Moore, *Selling God: American Religion in the Marketplace of Culture* (New York: Oxford University Press, 1994), 6.

94. Robert F. Martin, *Hero of the Heartland: Billy Sunday and the Transformation of American Society, 1862–1935* (Bloomington: Indiana University Press, 2002), 63.

95. Morrow Mayo, *Los Angeles* (New York: Alfred A. Knopf, 1933), as cited in McWilliams, *Southern California Country*, 260; Tona J. Hangen, *Redeeming the Dial: Radio, Religion, and Popular Culture in America* (Chapel Hill: University of North Carolina Press, 2002), 63.

96. Lewis, *Elmer Gantry*, 204.

97. Ahlstrom, *A Religious History*, 747; Martin, *Hero of the Heartland*, 58–59.

98. A clip of the Nugrape Twins' song "I Got Your Ice Cold Nugrape" is available on the Internet Archive's open source audio page, www.archive. org/audio/audio-details-db.php?collectionid=Nugrape&collection=open-source_audio. Their work is also available on the Document Records compilation, *Sinners and Saints, 1926–1931* (DOCD-5106), *The Tofu Hut*, "glisten guzzle guzzle grape glory," June 27, 2005, http://tofuhut.blogspot.com/2005/06/tasty-glisten-guzzle-guzzle-grape.html.

99. Smith et al., *American Evangelicalism*, 40–42, as cited in Hendershot, *Shaking the World for Jesus*, 9.

100. Harding, *Book of Jerry Falwell*, 36–37.

101. Hendershot, *Shaking the World for Jesus*, 30–31.

102. Scott Leith, "Spreading the Gospel," *Atlanta Journal-Constitution*, 11 July 2001, 1a.

103. Smith et al., *Evangelicalism*, 51.

104. Hendershot, *Shaking the World for Jesus*, 37.

105. Rick Perlstein, "Who Owns the Sixties?" *Lingua Franca* (May–June 1996), 30–37.

106. Doug Rossinow, *The Politics of Authenticity: Liberalism, Christianity, and the New Left in America* (New York: Columbia University Press, 1998), 8. See also Stephen A. Kent, *From Slogans to Mantras: Social Protest and Religious Conversion in the Late Vietnam War Era* (Syracuse, NY: Syracuse University Press, 2001).

107. Thomas Frank, *The Conquest of Cool: Business Culture, Counterculture, and the Rise of Hip Consumerism* (Chicago: University of Chicago Press, 1997), 7.

108. George Will, "'Slow Growth' Is the Liberalism of the Privileged," *Chicago Sun-Times*, 30 August 1987, 12, as cited in Davis, *City of Quartz* (1990 edition), 158–59.

109. Kent, *From Slogans to Mantras*, chapter 3.

110. Connolly, *Why I Am Not a Secularist*, chapter 4; George Marsden, *The Soul of the American University: From Protestant Establishment to Establishment Nonbelief* (New York: Oxford University Press, 1994).

111. Leonard Sweet, "The 1960s: The Crises of Liberal Christianity and the Public Emergence of Evangelicalism," in Marsden, *Evangelicalism and Modern America*, 32–36.

112. Miller, *Reinventing American Protestantism*, 20–21.

113. Norman Cohn, *The Pursuit of the Millennium: Revolutionary Millenarians and Mystical Anarchists of the Middle Ages,* rev. and expanded (New York: Oxford University Press, 1970), 20–23.

114. R. Laurence Moore, *Religious Outsiders and the Making of America* (New York: Oxford University Press, 1986). See also Robert S. Ellwood Jr., *One Way: The Jesus Movement and Its Meaning* (Englewood Cliffs, NJ: Prentice-Hall, 1973).

115. Kazin, *Populist Persuasion*, 3. For more on the connections between religion and populism, see chapters 2 and 4 of Kazin's work.

116. Greil Marcus, *Lipstick Traces: A Secret History of the Twentieth Century* (Cambridge, MA: Harvard University Press, 1989), 90–94, 313. Marcus notes that the Situationists were fascinated by the revolutionary millenarian movements described in Cohn's *The Pursuit of the Millennium.*

117. Negativland actually had a history with conservative Christians as a result of its song "Christianity Is Stupid!" whose lyrics included the decontextualized words of a Baptist pastor, Estus Pirkle: "Christianity is stupid! Communism is good!" In 1988, after a teenager in Minnesota killed his family, the band sent out a bogus press release suggesting that authorities had implicated their song in the deaths. The prank, in turn, generated publicity for the band when media outlets did not thoroughly check the facts of the case. In a fall 2006 talk at the New School in New York, band member Mark Hosler explained that one of his bandmates had found Pirkle's sermon "If Footmen Tire You, What Will Horses Do?" on a record purchased at a thrift store. Of course, the sermon was actually an anti-communist jeremiad that warned of an impending communist takeover, after which Americans would be forced to enter reeducation camps and recite the line quoted in the song. In 1971 Ron Ormond, an exploitation film director turned born-again Christian, created a film that dramatized the sermon's message of an impending communist takeover that would result in torture, atheism, executions, and forced labor if Americans did

not stand up to the "footmen" of vice and secularism. Liz Berg, "Negativland: Illegal Art," *WFMU's Beware of the Blog,* http://blog.wfmu.org/freeform/2006/10/negativland_ill.html (accessed 9 October 2006).

118. British cultural studies scholars are widely known for their research on working-class youth culture as a source of resistance to dominant ideologies. See, among others, Stuart Hall and Tony Jefferson, eds., *Resistance through Rituals: Youth Subcultures in Post-war Britain* (London: Hutchinson, 1976); Stuart Hall et al., *Policing the Crisis: Mugging, the State, and Law and Order* (London: MacMillan Press, 1978); Paul Gilroy, *There Ain't No Black in the Union Jack: The Cultural Politics of Race and Nation* (Chicago: University of Chicago Press, 1987); Paul Willis, *Learning to Labor: How Working Class Kids Get Working Class Jobs* (Farnborough, UK: Saxon House, 1977; repr., New York: Columbia University Press, 1981); Dick Hebdige, *Subculture: The Meaning of Style* (London: Methuen, 1979).

## 1. HOME IMPROVEMENT

1. Dan Peters and Steve Peters, with Cher Merrill, *Why Knock Rock?* (Minneapolis: Bethany House, 1984), 50.

2. John Camp, "Ministers Try to Shake 'Devil Rock,'" *St. Paul Pioneer Press,* 27 November 1979, 1.

3. Peters and Peters, *Why Knock Rock?* 50.

4. The burning takes place in Acts 19:19–20.

5. For an account of some of the more spectacular record-burning bonfires, see Mark Sullivan, "'More Popular Than Jesus': The Beatles and the Religious Far Right," *Popular Music* 6 (October 1987): 313.

6. Al Menconi, "Whose Records Should I Burn? Alice's or Amy's?" *Media Update* 6, no. 3 (May–June 1987): 1–5.

7. Ibid., 1–5.

8. McGirr, *Suburban Warriors,* 150–51.

9. For an analysis of the ways parents tried to control or co-opt television during the postwar era, see Lynn Spigel, "Seducing the Innocent: Childhood and Television in Postwar America," in *Welcome to the Dreamhouse: Popular Media and the Postwar Suburbs* (Durham, NC: Duke University Press, 2001), 185–218; and Heather Hendershot, *Saturday Morning Censors: Television Regulation before the V-chip* (Durham, NC: Duke University Press, 1998).

10. McGirr, *Suburban Warriors,* 225–37. For more on the terrain of the culture wars, see Hunter, *Culture Wars,* 171–291.

11. Lassiter, *Silent Majority,* 7.

12. Berlant, *The Queen of America Goes to Washington City,* 11.

13. Ibid., 3, 76.

14. For an analysis of the significance of popular culture, particularly that of urban blacks (as opposed to curriculum debates and arts and humanities funding), to the nation's culture wars, see Kelley, *Yo' Mama's DisFUNKtional!* 8–9.

15. Errol Lawrence, "Just Plain Common Sense: The 'Roots' of Racism," in Centre for Contemporary Cultural Studies, *The Empire Strikes Back,* 47–94.

16. Cliff Schimmels, "Understanding Today's Teens," *Moody Monthly* (March 1992): 13.

17. Lawrence Grossberg, *We Gotta Get Out of This Place: Popular Conservatism and Postmodern Culture* (New York: Routledge, 1992), 198.

18. Black youth, of course, were widely demonized during the same decade.

19. For a description of how parents became involved in the anti-marijuana movement during the 1970s and early 1980s, see Michael Massing, *The Fix* (New York: Simon and Schuster, 1998), chapters 11 and 12.

20. Christian organizations that aimed to affirm traditional authority continued to be established over the next decade. For example, the Promise Keepers, a well-known Christian organization aimed at helping men build relationships with one another and with their families, began in 1990. See Faludi, *Stiffed,* chapter 5.

21. Steve Rabey, "Heavy Metal Mania," *Newsound* (Spring 1987): 11; Tipper Gore, *Raising PG Kids in an X-Rated Society* (Nashville: Abingdon Press, 1987), 178.

22. See Barry Glassner, *The Culture of Fear: Why Americans Are Afraid of the Wrong Things* (New York: Basic Books, 1999), introduction and chapter 3.

23. "Music, Media Glorify Drugs, Reagan Says," *Los Angeles Times,* 10 October 1985, A27.

24. "U.S. Panel Urges Citizens to Picket, Boycott Porn Stores," *Los Angeles Times,* 9 July 1986, sec. 1, p. 1; Jude Shiver Jr., "7-Elevens Act to Stop Adult Magazine Sales," *Los Angeles Times,* 11 April 1986, sec. 1, p. 1.

25. Stewart Powell, with Ronald A. Taylor and Kenneth T. Walsh, "What Entertainers Are Doing to Your Kids," *U.S. News and World Report* (28 October 1985): 46–49.

26. David Gates, "Networking to Beat the Devil," *Newsweek* (5 December 1988): 29.

27. George Will, "Americans Blush over 'Porn Rock,'" *San Francisco Chronicle,* 16 September 1985, http://factiva.com.

28. Allan Bloom, *The Closing of the American Mind* (New York: Simon and Schuster, 1987), 58–59.

29. James Gilbert, *A Cycle of Outrage: America's Reaction to the Juvenile Delinquent in the 1950s* (New York: Oxford University Press, 1986), 204.

30. For an analysis of market segmentation by age, race, and ethnicity, see Cohen, *A Consumers' Republic,* chapter 7 (especially 318–20).

31. Gilbert, *Cycle of Outrage,* 4–5.

32. Lewis, *Elmer Gantry,* 286.

33. Carpenter, *Revive Us Again,* 161–76.

34. Linda Martin and Kerry Segrave, *Anti-Rock: The Opposition to Rock 'n' Roll* (Hamden, CT: Archon Books, 1988; repr., New York: Da Capo Press, 1993), 251–55.

35. "New Crusade Dimension: Music," *CACC Newsletter* (October 1964), www.schwarzreport.org/ (accessed March 30, 2006). See also Ken Freedman, "Janet Greene, the Anti-Baez," *WFMU's Beware of the Blog* (19 January 2006), http://blog.wfmu.org/freeform/2006/01/janet_greene_th.html. For details on the School of Anti-Communism, see Lisa McGirr, *Suburban Warriors,* chapter 2.

36. "New Crusade Dimension: Music." Information about Janet Greene, including an interview with the singer, is available at CONELRAD, a website dedicated to Cold War–era culture, www.conelrad.com/media/atomicmusic/sh_boom.php?platter=26 (accessed March 30, 2006) and www.conelrad.com/greene/greene_research.php (accessed January 15, 2007).

37. The most controversial part of Lennon's interview came when the musician stated, "Christianity will go. It will vanish and shrink. I needn't argue about that; I'm right and will be proven right. We're more popular than Jesus right now; I don't know which will go first—rock 'n' roll or Christianity. Jesus was alright, but his Disciples were thick and ordinary. It's them twisting it that ruins it for me." Lennon's comments were reprinted on the cover of *Datebook,* an American magazine for teenagers (as cited in Sullivan, "'More Popular Than Jesus," 313–14).

38. David Bonner, *Revolutionizing Children's Records: The Young People's Records and Children's Record Guild Series* (Lanham, MD: Scarecrow Press, 2008), 10–11, 100–103, 170–74. For an account of the debate over the records, see Paul Coates, "Mary Had a Little Lenin, Its Fleece Was Red as Treason," *Los Angeles Times,* 17 June 1965, A6; and Paul Coates, "Menticide-Monger Has Diagnosis of What's Being Done to Children," *Los Angeles Times,* 18 June 1965, A6.

39. David Noebel, *The Beatles: A Study in Drugs, Sex and Revolution* (Tulsa, OK: Christian Crusade, 1969), 55.

40. David Noebel, *The Marxist Minstrels: A Handbook on Communist Subversion of Music* (Tulsa, OK: American Christian College Press, 1974), 2.

41. David Noebel, *Rhythm, Riots, and Revolution* (Tulsa, OK: Christian Crusade, 1966), as quoted in Chip Berlet and Margaret Quigley, "Theocracy and White Supremacy: Behind the Culture War to Restore Traditional Values," in Chip Berlet, ed., *Eyes Right! Challenging the Right Wing Backlash* (Boston: South End Press, 1995), 37.

42. Noebel, *Marxist Minstrels,* 196.

43. Ibid., 97–98.

44. Hugh F. Pyle, *Skimpy Skirts and Hippie Hair* (Murfreesboro, TN: Sword of the Lord, 1972), 25–27. Pyle quoted the work of another evangelist, Dr. Hal Webb, to make his arguments about the connection between long hair and communism, but he provided no citation.

45. David Bennett, *The Party of Fear: From Nativist Movements to the New Right in American History* (Chapel Hill: University of North Carolina Press, 1988; repr., New York: Vintage, 1990), 330.

46. Hunter, *Culture Wars,* 197–244. For a case study of conservative activists who tried to influence education at the grassroots, see McGirr, *Suburban Warriors,* 179–82.

47. Bob Larson, *Rock & Roll: The Devil's Diversion,* rev. ed. (McCook, NE: n.p., 1970), 96.

48. Ibid., 116.

49. Frank Garlock, *The Big Beat: A Rock Blast* (Greenville, SC: Bob Jones University Press, 1971), 12–13.

50. 2 Corinthians 6:17, New Revised Standard Version (hereafter NRSV).

51. Garlock, *Big Beat,* 13.

52. Bob Larson, *Rock and the Church* (Carol Stream, IL: Creation House, 1971), 9.

53. Bob Jones III, *Look Again at the Jesus People* (Greenville, SC: Bob Jones University Press, 1972), 5–6.

54. Ibid., 14.

55. Garlock, *Big Beat,* 48.

56. John R. McMahon, "Unspeakable Jazz Must Go," *Ladies Home Journal* 38 (December 1921): 116; and Beatrice Forbes-Robertson Hode, quoted in Kate W. Jamison and FC Lockwood, *The Freshman Girl: A Guide to College Life* (New York, 1925), 162–66, both as quoted in Paula S. Fass, *The Damned and the Beautiful: American Youth in the 1920's* (New York: Oxford University Press, 1977), 22.

57. Garlock, *Big Beat,* 22.

58. See Jeff Godwin, *Dancing with Demons: The Music's Real Master* (Chino, CA: Chick, 1988), 17; and Larson, *Rock & Roll,* 66.

59. Garlock, *Big Beat,* 25, 29–30. Garlock's contrast between musical genres bears a similarity to Anthony Comstock's description of reading materials. A "good reading," Comstock wrote, "refines, elevates, ennobles, and stimulates the ambition to lofty purposes. It points upward. Evil reading debases, degrades, perverts, and turns away from lofty aims to follow examples of corruption and criminality." Comstock, *Traps for the Young,* 5.

60. Lowell Hart, *Satan's Music Exposed* (Chattanooga, TN: AMG Publishers, 1981), 105.

61. Moore, *Selling God,* 17–35.

62. Larson, *Rock and the Church,* 28, and Larson, *Rock & Roll,* 117.

63. In particular, critics tried to show the connection between serial killer-rapist Richard Ramirez and the music of Australian metal band AC/DC, particularly its 1979 song "Night Prowler." Critics also blamed artists for suicides. In 1985 the parents of a deceased teenager sued Ozzy Osborne and CBS records for the song "Suicide Solution," which they argued encouraged their son to commit suicide. Martin and Segrave, *Anti-Rock,* 281–83.

64. Several authors made this claim. See Jacob Aranza, *Lord! Why Is My Child a Rebel? Parents and Kids in Crisis* (Lafayette, LA: Huntington House, 1990), 87; Eric Barger, *From Rock to Rock: The Music of Darkness Exposed!* (Lafayette, LA: Huntington House, 1990), 14; Godwin, *Dancing with Demons,* 25; and Bob Larson, *Rock: Practical Help for Those Who Listen to the Words and Don't Like What They Hear* (Wheaton, IL: Tyndale House, 1980), 107.

65. Larson, *Rock & Roll,* 6–7. In 1993, *Cornerstone,* an evangelical magazine associated with Jesus People USA, published an article that questioned many of the stories Bob Larson told to audiences, including information about his rock band. See Jon Trott, "Bob Larson's Ministry under Scrutiny," *Cornerstone* 21, no. 100 (1993): 18, 37, 41–42.

66. Jeff Godwin, *The Devil's Disciples: The Truth about Rock* (Chino, CA: Chick, 1985), 15.

67. Jimmy Swaggart, with Robert Paul Lamb, *Religious Rock 'n' Roll: A Wolf in Sheep's Clothing* (Baton Rouge, LA: Jimmy Swaggart Ministries, 1987), 31.

68. Godwin, *Dancing with Demons,* 14.

69. Barger, *From Rock to Rock,* 4.

70. Larson, *Rock: Practical Help,* 32.

71. Larson, *Rock & Roll,* 97.

72. Godwin, *Dancing with Demons,* 335–36.

73. Larson, *Rock & Roll,* 105, 126.

74. Ibid., 99–100.

75. Bob Larson, *Satanism: The Seduction of America's Youth* (Nashville: Thomas Nelson, 1989), 166.

76. Godwin, *Devil's Disciples,* 201.

77. Larson, *Rock: Practical Help,* 19.

78. Aranza, *Lord! Why Is My Child a Rebel?* 126.

79. Godwin, *Devil's Disciples,* 285.

80. Larson, *Rock: Practical Help,* 39.

81. Jimmy Swaggart, *Christian Rock and Roll* (Baton Rouge, LA: Jimmy Swaggart Ministries, 1986), 12.

82. Larson, *Rock & Roll,* 18, 22.

83. Peters and Peters, *Why Knock Rock?* 188.

84. Larson, *Satanism,* 19.

85. Ibid., 19–20.

86. Swaggart, *Religious Rock 'n' Roll,* 35.

87. Larson, *Rock & Roll,* 17–18. See also Godwin, *Devil's Disciples,* 8, and Garlock, *Big Beat,* 25, 32.

88. Godwin, *Devil's Disciples,* 9.

89. Godwin, *Dancing with Demons,* 11; Larson, *Rock & Roll,* 67–80.

90. Larson, *Rock & Roll,* 67–69.

91. Jacob Aranza, *Backward Masking Unmasked: Backward Satanic Messages of Rock & Roll Exposed* (Shreveport and Lafayette, LA: Huntington House, 1983), 1.

92. Swaggart, *Religious Rock 'n' Roll,* 42.

93. Ibid., 45. See also John Blanchard, with Peter Anderson and Derek Cleave, *Pop Goes the Gospel: Rock in the Church,* rev. ed. (Durham, UK: Evangelical Press, 1989), 115–25.

94. See Larson, *Rock and the Church,* 86, and Blanchard et al., *Pop Goes the Gospel,* 99.

95. Larson, *Rock: Practical Help,* 101.

96. Larson, *Rock and the Church,* 43.

97. Hart, *Satan's Music Exposed,* 18.

98. Blanchard et al., *Pop Goes the Gospel,* 93.

99. Ibid., 27.

100. Godwin, *Dancing with Demons,* 236.

101. Larson, *Rock and the Church,* 42.

102. James Chute, *Milwaukee Journal,* as quoted in Swaggart, *Religious Rock 'n' Roll,* 77.

103. Ibid.

104. Larson, *Rock and the Church,* 57.

105. Swaggart, *Religious Rock 'n' Roll,* 104.

106. Kenneth Woodward, "The New Christian Minstrels," *Newsweek* (19 August 1985): 70–71; William D. Romanowski, "Contemporary Christian Music: The Business of Music Ministry," in Quentin J. Schultze, ed., *American Evangelicals and the Mass Media* (Grand Rapids, MI: Zondervan, 1990), 143–69; Jeffrey K. Hadden and Anson Shupe, *Televangelism: Power and Politics on God's Frontier* (New York: Henry Holt, 1988), 292, as quoted in Hunter, *Culture Wars*, 229. According to Hadden and Shupe, in the mid-1980s, there were some thirteen hundred religious radio stations (not all of which played Christian rock), two hundred religious television stations, and three religious TV networks.

107. Steve Rabey, "What Do You Do with Secular Rock?" *Youthworker* (Summer 1988): 28–34; Terry Mattingly, "Ten Questions That Depict Your Kids' Culture," *Youthworker* (Winter 1994): 97–102.

108. Quentin Schultze, "Turning This Week's Pop Culture into Next Week's Curriculum," *Youthworker* (Winter 1995): 34–39; Steve Rabey, "Media and Culture: How the Cast of 'Beverly Hills, 90210' Can Help You Lead Your Youth Group," *Youthworker* (Summer 1995): 95.

109. Walt Mueller, "Youth-Culture Literacy," *Youthworker* (Fall 1992): 40–47.

110. For one evangelical Christian's analysis of the impact of film on children, see Ted Baehr, *The Media Wise Family: A Christian Family Guide to Making Morally and Spiritually Responsible Decisions about Movies, TV, and Multimedia* (Colorado Springs: Chariot Victor, 1998); for another evangelical Christian's analysis of the impact of television on children, see Don Wildmon, *The Home Invaders* (Wheaton, IL: SP Publications, 1985).

111. Jim Burns, "Teens in Trouble," *Moody Monthly* (March 1992): 21.

112. Billy Graham, preface to *The Jesus Generation* (Grand Rapids, MI: Zondervan, 1971).

113. Wayne Rice, foreword, in David S. Hart, *It's All Rock 'n' Roll to Me: Profiling Today's Popular Artists and Bands from a Biblical Perspective* (San Marcos, CA: New Song, 1996), 5.

114. Terry Mattingly, "Beyond Petra," *Youthworker* (Winter 1994): 90–96.

115. Aranza, *Lord! Why Is My Child a Rebel?* 23–24.

116. Cliff Schimmels, "Understanding Today's Teens," *Moody Monthly* (March 1992): 14.

117. Al Menconi, "Al's Analysis," *Media Update* 16, no. 3 (May–June 1997): 7.

118. Al Menconi, "A Wake Up Call for America!" *Media Update* 15, no. 5 (September–October 1996): 1.

119. Schimmels, "Understanding Today's Teens."

120. For more on parental entertainment habits, see Barger, *From Rock to Rock*, 179.

121. Dave Hart, "Insights and Oversights," *Media Update* 6, no. 6 (November–December 1987): 6, 13.

122. Hart, *It's All Rock 'n' Roll to Me*, 153.

123. Al Menconi, "Rock Music: Why Do Teens Listen?" *Moody Monthly* (March 1992): 18–20.

124. Burns, "Teens in Trouble," 20–21.

125. Al Menconi, "The Hot 100," *Media Update* 6, no. 1 (January–February 1987): 1–6.

126. Dave Hart, "Same Subject, Different Approaches," *Media Update* 8, no. 6 (November–December 1989): 5, 13. *Contemporary Christian Music (CCM)* took a similar approach when editor John Styll wrote an editorial criticizing rock critic John Todd and publisher Jack Chick for *Spellbound?* the Chick Publications pamphlet about satanic influences on rock music. John Styll, "Spellbound?" *CCM* (January 1979): 31–32.

127. Dave Hart, "Rock Talk," *Media Update* 6, no. 2 (March–April 1987): 8–16.

128. Dave Hart, "A Wave of New Wave" *Media Update* 5, no. 3 (May–June 1986): 5–6.

129. Hart, *It's All Rock 'n' Roll to Me,* 79.

130. Ibid., 120.

131. Dan Peters and Steve Peters, with Cher Merrill, *Rock's Hidden Persuader: The Truth about Backmasking* (Minneapolis: Bethany House, 1985), 43.

132. Peters and Peters, *Why Knock Rock?* 229–30.

133. Barger, *From Rock to Rock,* chapter 5. *This Is Spinal Tap* (1984; directed by Rob Reiner) is a mockumentary that chronicles the touring exploits of a fictitious British heavy metal band, Spinal Tap. The film's soundtrack, released by Polydor, included songs that traced the band's fictional history from sixties pop to eighties metal. It was this music that Barger saw fit to rate.

134. Dan Peters and Steve Peters, *Hit Rock's Bottom: Exposing to the Light the Real World behind the False Image of Rock* (North St. Paul, MN: n.p., 1984), 14.

135. Peters and Peters, *Rock's Hidden Persuader,* 82–83.

136. Peters and Peters, *Hit Rock's Bottom,* 138; Dana Key and Steve Rabey, *Don't Stop the Music* (Grand Rapids, MI: Zondervan, 1989), 45.

137. Al Menconi used a biblical verse (Colossians 2:8) to emphasize the importance of "Christ-centered" entertainment. Al Menconi, "What Should I Do If My Kid Listens to Rock Music?" *Media Update* 5. no.1 (January–February 1986): 2–3.

138. Al Menconi, "Should Christians Rock?! An Open Letter to Christian Rock Critics," *Media Update* 5, no. 4 (July–October 1986): 2.

139. For a history of religious and moral criticism of the movie industry, see William D. Romanowski, *Pop Culture Wars: Religion and the Role of Entertainment in American Life* (Downers Grove, IL: InterVarsity Press, 1996). Romanowski, a professor at Calvin College (Christian Reformed Church), collaborated on other works that assessed the impact of consumer culture on young people, including Quentin J. Schultze et al., *Dancing in the Dark: Youth, Popular Culture, and the Electronic Media* (Grand Rapids, MI: William B. Eerdmans, 1991).

140. Peters and Peters, *Why Knock Rock?* 201.

141. Dan Peters, Steve Peters, and Cher Merrill, *What about Christian Rock?* (Minneapolis: Bethany House Publishers, 1986), 93.

142. Ibid., 86.

143. Menconi, "Should Christians Rock?!" 2.

144. Peters and Peters, *What about Christian Rock?* 153.

145. Quentin J. Schultze, "The Crossover Music Question," *Moody Monthly* (October 1992): 30–32.

146. Calvin M. Johansson, *Music and Ministry* (Hendrickson, 1984), as cited in John Styll, "What Makes Music Christian?" *CCM* (June 1991): 22–23.

147. Mark Joseph, Dr. Patrick Cavanaugh, and Kerry Livgren, "Can 'Christian' Music Exist? The Sacred vs. Secular Debate Rages On," *CCM* (August 1995): 55–57.

148. Chuck Colson, *The Body,* as cited in Joseph, Cavanaugh, and Livgren, "Can 'Christian' Music Exist?"

149. Styll, "What Makes Music Christian?" 23. Within fifteen years, Styll's line about determining "Christian" culture would be challenged by the establishment of JC's Girls, a ministry formed by a former stripper who went to strip clubs and adult entertainment conventions to encourage female sex workers to attend church. An anti-porn ministry, xxxchurch.com, raised the ire of conservatives by ministering to porn addicts. Gaby Wood, "God Squad," *The Observer* (England), 12 February 2006, 43.

150. Peters and Peters, *Rock's Hidden Persuader,* 94–95.

151. Dan Peters, Jim Peters, and Steve Peters, *What the Devil's Wrong with Rock Music?* (St. Paul: n.p., 1980), 50.

152. Peters and Peters, *Why Knock Rock?* 236.

153. Baehr, *Media Wise Family,* 225.

154. Barger, *From Rock to Rock,* 178.

155. Romanowski, *Pop Culture Wars,* chapter 8.

156. Peters and Peters, *Hit Rock's Bottom,* 15.

157. Martin and Segrave, *Anti-Rock,* 270–71.

158. "American Graffiti," *Newsweek* (17 May 1982): 61; Martin and Segrave, *Anti-Rock,* 288.

159. Key and Rabey, *Don't Stop the Music,* 48.

160. Peters and Peters, *What the Devil's Wrong with Rock Music?* 50. The brothers claimed that United States law (Title 18, Section 1464 of the U.S. Code) already forbade the broadcast of "obscene, indecent, or profane language on public airwaves."

161. "The Art of Being James Watt," *New York Times,* 8 April 1983, sec. A, p. 30, as quoted in Martin and Segrave, *Anti-Rock,* 268–69.

162. Parents' Music Resource Center, *Let's Talk Rock: A Primer for Parents* (Arlington, VA: Parents' Music Resource Center, 1986), 7.

163. In a chapter dedicated to "Media and Arts" as a "field of conflict" in the "culture wars," James Davison Hunter reviews the key battles in music as well as art, film, publishing, and television. The section on music revolves around 2 Live Crew's 1990 album. Hunter, *Culture Wars,* 232–33. For another analysis of the 2 Live Crew controversy, see Berlant, *The Queen of America Goes to Washington City,* 55–81.

## 2. REBEL WITH A CROSS

1. Will Herberg, "Anarchy on the Campus," *Modern Age* 14, no. 1 (Winter 1970): 3, 7.

2. Will Herberg, "Conservatives and the Jesus Freaks," *New Guard* 11, no. 8 (November 1971): 15–16.

3. See "The Jesus Revolution," *Time,* 21 June 1971, 56–63; "The Jesus Movement Is upon Us," *Look,* 9 February 1971, 15–21.

4. Patricia U. Bonomi, *Under the Cope of Heaven: Religion, Society, and Politics in Colonial America* (New York: Oxford University Press, 1986), 126, 153; also see Rhys Isaac, *The Transformation of Virginia, 1740–1790* (Chapel Hill: University of North Carolina Press, 1982).

5. Heyrman, *Southern Cross,* 80–81.

6. See Paul Boyer, *Urban Masses and Moral Order in America, 1820–1920* (Cambridge, MA: Harvard University Press, 1978); Lillian Taiz, *Hallelujah Lads and Lasses: Remaking the Salvation Army in America, 1880–1930* (Chapel Hill: University of North Carolina Press, 2001).

7. Grant Wacker, *Heaven Below: Early Pentecostals and American Culture* (Cambridge, MA: Harvard University Press, 2001), 105, 305n48.

8. Nancy Ammerman, "North American Protestantism Fundamentalism," in Linda Kintz and Julia Lesage, eds. *Media, Culture, and the Religious Right* (Minneapolis: University of Minnesota Press, 1998), 84. Carpenter, *Revive Us Again,* 165–66. Carpenter also argues that fundamentalists had catered to young people through Bible institutes and summer Bible conferences long before the youth-friendly rallies became popular.

9. Moore, *Selling God;* R. Laurence Moore, *Touchdown Jesus: The Mixing of Sacred and Secular in American History* (Louisville, KY: Westminster John Knox Press, 2003).

10. McDannell, *Material Christianity,* 2.

11. Ibid., 246, 259.

12. Hendershot, *Shaking the World for Jesus,* 24, 30–34.

13. Smith, *Soul Searching,* 46.

14. Hunter, *Culture Wars,* 42.

15. Connolly, *Why I Am Not a Secularist.*

16. Harding, *Book of Jerry Falwell,* 79–80.

17. Ibid., 80.

18. Susan Harding, "Convicted by the Holy Spirit: The Rhetoric of Fundamental Baptist Conversion," *American Ethnologist* 14 (February 1987): 167–81.

19. Smith, *Soul Searching,* 36, 110, 149. Smith defines "most highly devoted" as the 8 percent of teens "who believe in God, who attend religious services weekly or more often, for whom faith is extremely important in their lives, who regularly participate in religious youth groups, and who pray and read the Bible regularly."

20. Herberg, "Conservatives and the Jesus Freaks," 16.

21. John H. Wigger, "Taking Heaven by Storm: Enthusiasm and Early American Methodism, 1770–1820," *Journal of the American Republic* 14, no. 2 (Summer 1994): 173.

22. Moore, *Religious Outsiders and the Making of America.* See also Ellwood, *One Way.*

23. Rossinow, *Politics of Authenticity,* 8.

24. Kent, *From Slogans to Mantras,* chapter 3.

25. Ellwood, *One Way,* 23.

26. Ronald M. Enroth, Edward E. Ericson Jr., and C. Breckinridge Peters, *The Jesus People: Old-Time Religion in the Age of Aquarius* (Grand Rapids, MI: William B. Eerdmans, 1972), chapters 2–3.

27. Steve Rabey, "Age to Age," *CCM,* July 1998, www.ccmmagazine. com/features/55.aspx?Page=1.

28. Ibid.

29. The notion of denying the devil dominion over music was not new. In early-nineteenth-century England, Methodist clergyman Rowland Hill expressed a similar sentiment, leading his biographer, E. W. Broome, to conclude, "He did not see any reason why the devil should have all the good tunes." See the *Oxford Dictionary of Quotations,* 5th ed., s.v. "Rowland Hill" (377:3).

30. Davin Seay, with Mary Neely, *Stairway to Heaven: The Spiritual Roots of Rock 'n' Roll: From the King and Little Richard to Prince and Amy Grant* (New York: Ballantine Books, 1986), 6–8.

31. "From the Editor," *Rock in Jesus* 1, no. 1 (December 1971): 2.

32. For a description of Calvary Chapel and its relationship to the Jesus Movement, see McGirr, *Suburban Warriors,* chapter 6.

33. McDannell, *Material Christianity,* 248.

34. Abe Peck, *Uncovering the Sixties: The Life and Times of the Underground Press* (New York: Pantheon Press, 1985).

35. For a more detailed description of the newspapers, see Enroth, Ericson, and Peters, *Jesus People,* chapter 3.

36. Paul Baker, *Why Should the Devil Have All the Good Music? Jesus Music: Where It Began, Where It Is, and Where It Is Going* (Waco, TX: Word Books, 1979), 23.

37. Ibid.

38. Ibid., 25. The term "underground church" came from a book published in 1971 by Edward Plowman.

39. Key and Rabey, *Don't Stop the Music,* 140–41.

40. See Steve Lawhead, *Rock Reconsidered: A Christian Looks at Contemporary Music* (Downers Grove, IL: InterVarsity Press, 1981), 93.

41. Arthur Blessitt, *Tell the World: A Jesus People Manual* (Old Tappan, NJ: Fleming H. Revell, 1972), 9.

42. Rich Schmidt, "Can You Dig It?" *Hollywood Free Paper,* as cited in Duane Pederson, *Jesus People* (Pasadena, CA: Compass Press, 1971), 30–33.

43. McDannell, *Material Christianity,* 189. For more on the range of reactions to Sallman's *Head of Christ*—from praise for its idealized depiction of Jesus' masculinity to scorn for its depiction of a feminized Jesus—see David Morgan, *Visual Piety: A History and Theory of Popular Religious Images* (Berkeley and Los Angeles: University of California Press, 1998), 116–20, 124–35.

44. McDannell, *Material Christianity,* 192–93.

45. Kent, *From Slogans to Mantras,* 137. In chapter 5, Kent includes a lengthy section on the use of Jesus as an antihero.

46. "Wanted: Jesus Christ," in *The Street People: Selections from "Right On!" Berkeley's Christian Underground Student Newspaper* (Valley Forge, Pennsylvania: Judson Press, 1971), 10–11. The same year, the poster appeared

in the first issue of the *Hollywood Free Paper* on October 7, 1969. See "We Love You, Call Collect," *Hollywood Free Paper* 1, no. 1, www.hollywoodfreepaper. org /archive.php?v=1&n=1.

47. Blessitt, *Tell the World,* 10. During the mid-1980s, Blessitt's evangelism reached someone who would later be a key political figure. A year before George W. Bush's visit with evangelist Billy Graham, which reportedly led to his conversion, Bush reportedly met and prayed with Blessitt at a West Texas Holiday Inn. Although Bush never discussed this meeting, author David Aikman confirmed the account with Bush adviser Karl Rove. Alan Cooperman, "Openly Religious, to a Point," *Washington Post,* 16 September 2004, sec. A, p. 1.

48. Arthur Blessitt, with Walter Wagner, *Turned on to Jesus* (New York: Hawthorn Books, 1971), 2.

49. Ibid., 14.

50. Kent, *From Slogans to Mantras,* 151, 182–84.

51. Nick Bromell, *Tomorrow Never Knows: Rock and Psychedelics in the 1960s* (Chicago: University of Chicago Press, 2000).

52. Seay and Neely, *Stairway to Heaven,* 136.

53. Ibid., 211.

54. Ellwood, *One Way,* 71.

55. For an explanation of the cultural importance of the moment when Dylan gave the Beatles their first joints, see Bromell, *Tomorrow Never Knows,* chapter 3.

56. Review of *Saved,* by Bob Dylan, *CCM* (July 1980): 23; Karen Marie Platt, "The Saving Grace of God," *CCM* (August 1980): 6; Davin Seay, "A Sovereign Act of God," *CCM* (August 1980): 7–8, 12.

57. Frank M. Edmondson Jr., "Deviation: Explo '72 Afterthoughts," *Rock in Jesus* (September–October 1972): 22–27.

58. McDannell, *Material Christianity,* 265–66.

59. Hendershot, *Shaking the World for Jesus,* 28, 30, 37.

60. Jim Long, "I Am What I Follow," *Campus Life* (July–August 1990): 11–13.

61. Ron and Karen Hutchcraft, "Person to Person," *Campus Life* (July–August 1990): 14–21.

62. Tim Stafford, "Love, Sex and the Whole Person," *Campus Life* (July–August 1990): 58.

63. Stephen Duncombe, *Notes from Underground: Zines and the Politics of Alternative Culture* (New York: Verso, 1997), 117–30.

64. Hebdige, *Subculture,* 111–12.

65. According to information I compiled, the Bible Belt states normally identified with religious fundamentalism—South Carolina, Alabama, Mississippi, and Georgia—produced a total of five fan magazines.

66. Given that the magazines were published on a relatively small scale, readership is difficult to discern. One fan magazine published a reader's poll that listed the average respondent's age as 24; the overwhelming majority (83%) of respondents were men. The same survey indicated that 25% of respondents listened to secular music and 62% did not. The editors did not indicate how many surveys were returned, so it is difficult to assess how

representative the results are. "Voter Survey Results," *Rizzen Roxx,* no. 22 (1988): 22.

67. Steve Rabey, "Satan," *CCM* (February 1992): 37; Steve Rabey, "Sexual Temptation: Learning to 'Just Say No,'" *CCM* (November 1991): 52; Steve Rabey, "Abortion," *CCM* (March 1992): 26.

68. *Take a Stand* (December 1987): 3; *Take a Stand* (December 1989): 3; *Take a Stand* (July 1989): 3.

69. "Correspondence Directory," *Take a Stand* (December 1987): 5.

70. "Jesus Saves: The Testimony of Mike Girard" and "The Testimony of Ruben Meza," *Rizzen Roxx,* no. 20 (March–April 1988): 3; Chad Potokar, "Personal Testimony," *The Narrow Path,* no. 2 (June–July 1995): 4.

71. Judd Harper, "Denomination Dance," *Rizzen Roxx,* no. 20 (March–April 1988): 4–5.

72. Chris Yambar, "Grass Roots (The Basics), Part One," *Different Drummer,* no. 4 (1989): 12–15.

73. Jeff McCormack, "Saving Faith?" *The Pendragon,* no. 2 (1988): 2; Jeff McCormack, "A Brief and Untechnical Statement of Faith," *The Pendragon,* no. 3 (1988): 2–4.

74. Jeff McCormack, *The Pendragon,* no. 4 (1988): 1.

75. People!'s label, Capitol Records, changed the name to *I Love You,* and Norman left the band shortly after the record was released.

76. "Eternal Life," *Rizzen Roxx,* no. 20 (March–April 1988): 2.

77. Shawn Finley, "RAD: Dealing with Temptation," *Rizzen Roxx,* no. 22 (1988): 30–31.

78. Keith Day, "Good News!" *Gospel Metal* (Fall 1987): 32–34.

79. Judd Harper, "Credits," *Rizzen Roxx,* no. 20 (March–April 1988): 2.

80. Shawn Finley, "A RAD Guide to Church Members," *Rizzen Roxx,* no. 20 (March–April 1988): 18–19.

81. Shawn Finley, "Tips on Witnessing," *Rizzen Roxx,* no. 21 (May–June 1988): 29–30.

82. Dan Kennedy, review of *Under a Blood Red Sky,* by U2, *Cutting Edge* 1, no. 2 (March 1984): 1; Stephen A. Horne, "Concert Review," *CCM* (May 1992): 35.

83. "Feedback: Good News/Bad News," *CCM* (April 1990): 4–6; "Feedback: Who Cares?" *CCM* (May 1991): 6.

84. This phrase is from the Last Supper, when Jesus tells the apostle Thomas, "I am the way, and the truth, and the life. No one comes to the Father except through me. If you know me, you will know my Father also. From now on you do know him and have seen him." John 14:6–7 NRSV.

85. Doug Van Pelt, "What Megadeth Sez," *HM* (1996), www.christianmusic. org/cmp/hmmag/archives/Megadeth.html. Mustaine was not entirely happy to discuss religious belief. Later in the interview, after Van Pelt quoted the Gospel of John ("I am the way, and the truth, and the life. No one comes to the Father except through me."), Mustaine asked, "So, is this a music interview, or is it not?" When Van Pelt assured him that it was, Mustaine replied, "So, why are you asking questions like that?" The interview, and the discussion of religion, then resumed.

86. Doug Van Pelt, "What Sammy Hagar Sez," *HM* (July–August 1997), www.christianmusic.org/cmp/hmmag/archives/SammyHagar.htm.

87. Ibid.

88. Hebdige, *Subculture,* 27–29, 62–66.

89. Ibid., 112.

90. Alexis Colbert, e-mail to author, 31 July 2007.

91. DC Talk, *Jesus Freaks: DC Talk and the Voice of the Martyrs—Stories of Those Who Stood for Jesus, the Ultimate Jesus Freaks* (Bloomington, MN: Bethany House, 1999). DC Talk was a pop, not a punk, band, and its best-known album and single both carried the title "Jesus Freak." In this instance their sense of persecution matches the rhetoric of their Christian punk brethren.

92. "The Reviews Are In!" *Slaughter House,* no. 4 (Fall 1990): 9.

93. "The Critics Have Spoken . . . Gee," *Thieves and Prostitutes,* no. 8 (1993): 11.

94. "We Don't Mind If People Read Our Mail . . ." *Thieves and Prostitutes,* no. 8 (1993): 3.

95. John A. DiDonna and Alexis Levy Neptune, "Who Done It?" *Thieves and Prostitutes,* no. 8 (1993): 7.

96. Alexis Levy Neptune, "Christian Punk?" *Thieves and Prostitutes,* no. 8 (1993): 8–9.

97. Ibid., 8–10.

98. Ibid., 10.

99. Cross, *Burned-Over District,* 271. Many youths in the "straight edge" movement, another music-influenced renunciatory youth phenomenon of the 1980s, lived by a strict code that shunned alcohol, drugs, and (occasionally) sex, caffeine, and meat. Some members of the movement, including the band Youth of Today, belonged to Hari Krishna and criticized those who did not observe straight-edge norms.

100. Keith Day, "What Is a Christian . . . Really?" *Gospel Metal,* no. 6 (1989): 23–25.

101. "That's 100 Issues Not 100 Years! An Interview with Dan Kennedy by David Clay," *The Cutting Edge* 9, nos. 3–4 (May–June 1992): 7.

102. Dave Johnson, "The Forefathers of White Metal," *White Throne,* no. 7 (1991): 14–15.

103. *Heaven's Metal* 2, no. 6 (1987): 15.

104. J. J. Julian, "K.C. News," *The Burning Bush,* 13 (January–February 1990): 18–19.

105. Mailbox, *Different Drummer,* no. 4 (1989): 3.

106. Day, "What Is a Christian . . . Really?" 21–22. For more on the Operation Rescue protests in Cypress in 1989, see the subsection entitled "Abortion Protests" in Chapter 4.

107. Rich Wilkerson, "Abortion Is Not the #1 Problem," *Radically Saved* 1, no. 4 (1989), 3–4.

108. Mark Hodges, "Human Sacrifice," *Rizzen Roxx,* no. 21 (May–June 1988): 24–25.

109. *Slaughter House,* no. 4 (Fall 1990): 2.

110. In 1992 Michael Bailey was a Republican candidate in a House (not Senate) election against Lee H. Hamilton in Indiana (not Illinois). During the

spring primary campaign, the FCC ordered several Kentucky and Indiana stations to air Bailey's anti-abortion ads after they had refused. After Bailey won the Republican nomination, he told the *Washington Post* he planned to run ads that featured photographs of aborted fetuses, Holocaust victims, Nazi swastikas, and American flags. See Thomas B. Rosenstiel, "TV Election Ad Airs Pictures of Dead Fetuses," *Los Angeles Times* (Home Edition), 21 April 1992, sec. A, p. 14; William Booth, "Antiabortion TV Ads Catch On in Campaigns," *Washington Post*, 20 July 1992, sec. A, p. 1.

111. For claims against police that resemble those alleged in this magazine, see Barbara Brotman, "Antiabortion Group, Police Have a Clash of Tactics," *Chicago Tribune*, 29 October 1989, 8.

112. "Surprise!!! More Hypocritical Facts on Abortion!!!" *Thieves and Prostitutes*, no. 8 (1992): 14.

113. See, for example, Isaac, *Transformation of Virginia*, 148–73.

114. Harding, *Book of Jerry Falwell*, 79–80.

115. Wuthnow, *Restructuring of American Religion*, chapter 9.

116. Gustav Niebuhr, "Conservatives' New Frontier: Religious Liberty Law Firms," *New York Times*, 8 July 1995, sec. 1, p. 1.

117. The number of Christian schools rapidly expanded during the 1970s. The *Washington Post* estimated that the number grew from several hundred in the 1960s to more than 10,000 schools in 1985. The growth of the Association of Christian Schools International reflected this trend: formed in 1980 with about 1,200 member schools, the organization had nearly 4,000 members (and over 800,000 students) by 1997. Between 1970 and 1980, a period of overall declining enrollments in public and private schools, enrollment in non-Catholic church schools expanded at impressive rates throughout the country, particularly in the South and West. See Barbara Vobejda, "Christian Schools Pray, Teach Bible, and Prosper," *Washington Post* (Final Edition), 3 February 1985, sec. A, p. 1; Rene Sanchez, Popularity Grows for Alternatives to Public School," *Washington Post* (Final Edition), 1 October 1997, sec. A, p. 1. For a brief review of fundamentalism as a social movement, see Ammerman, "North American Protestant Fundamentalism."

118. Christian Smith, *Christian America? What Evangelicals Really Want* (Berkeley and Los Angeles: University of California Press), 131–32, 137. In describing evangelical attitudes toward education (chapter 4), Smith maintains that evangelicals wish to provide a moral presence in public schools—but not to make fundamental changes.

119. Michael deCourcy Hinds, "Robertson Trying Again to Put Prayer in Schools," *New York Times*, 16 April 1993, sec. A, p. 12. In *Santa Fe Independent School District v. Doe* (2000), the Supreme Court ruled that student-led prayers at graduations and assemblies were unconstitutional; see David G. Savage, "High Court Bars Student Prayers at School Events," *Los Angeles Times* (Home Edition), 20 June 2000, sec. A, p. 1.

120. T. R. Reid, "House Prepares for 'Son of School Prayer,'" *Washington Post*, 14 May 1984, sec. A, p. 5.

121. See Jennifer Warren, "New U.S. Law Has Schools in a Quandary over Religious Clubs," *Los Angeles Times* (San Diego County Edition), 3 February 1985, sec. 2, p. 1.

122. For an example of the controversy surrounding support groups for gay students, see the subsection of chapter 4 titled "Conservative Christian Response to Gay Rights Activism in Orange County."

123. David G. Savage, "High Court Ends Term," *Los Angeles Times* (Home Edition), 30 June 1995, sec. A, p. 21. Confusion over the proper application of the Supreme Court decisions ultimately drew the attention of the Clinton administration, which in August 1995 ordered the Department of Education to issue a (nonbinding) set of guidelines that outlined legally permissible expressions of religious belief in schools. The document affirmed the right to religious expression in schools. Students had the right to pray individually or in informal prayer groups; they could read Bibles and other religious tracts, distribute religious pamphlets, proselytize (unless another student requested that they cease), and wear religious clothing as long as such practices were not coercive and did not disrupt school activities. Limits were placed only on organized prayer in classrooms and assemblies led by either students, teachers, or school officials. See Steven A. Holmes, "Clinton Defines Religion's Role in U.S. Schools," *New York Times*, 26 August 1995, sec. 1, p. 1.

124. David G. Savage, "Justices Back Religious Rights in School Cases," *Los Angeles Times* (Home Edition), 8 June 1993, sec. A, p. 1. A 1993 Supreme Court decision, *Lamb's Chapel v. Center Moriches Union School District* (91–2024), expanded access to public school facilities by finding that church groups were entitled to the same accommodations made available to civic groups, and that schools could not discriminate against a speaker because his or her message was religious.

125. Dennis Romero, "Faith on Their Time," *Los Angeles Times* (Home Edition), 7 December 1994, sec. E, p. 1.

126. Caryle Murphy, "At Public Schools, Religion Thrives," *Washington Post*, 7 May 1998, sec. A, p. 1; Steve McGonigle, "School Religious Debate Intensifies," *Dallas Morning News*, 18 December 1994, 1A; Laurie Goodstein, "At This School, Prayer Is a Popular Elective," *Washington Post*, 4 December 1994, sec. A, p. 3. Saddleback Valley Unified School District in Orange County, California had a Bible club case appear before the Supreme Court in 1988, but the Court let stand a lower-court decision that denied students the right to establish a club. David Savage, "Court Lets Religious Clubs Meet in Schools," *Los Angeles Times* (Orange County Edition), 5 June 1990, sec. A, p. 1. In a 2001 decision, *Good News Club v. Milford Central* (99–2036), the Court allowed religious groups access to elementary schools. The man who brought the suit, Rev. Stephen Fournier, had been prohibited from establishing a "Good News Club," part of a national evangelical group aimed at children, at a local school. David Savage, "Justices Allow Church Club to Meet in School," *Los Angeles Times* (Home Edition), 12 June 2001, sec. A, p. 1.

127. Some school districts, such as the Capistrano Unified School District, prohibited all extracurricular groups, so the chapter met off campus. Jessica Garrison, "O.C. High Schools Prove Fertile Ground for Christian Clubs," *Los Angeles Times* (Orange County Edition), 5 March 2001, sec. A, p. 1. Some critics argued that the NFCA used adults—specifically coaches—to recruit students, in violation of the Equal Access Act.

128. Goodstein, "At This School, Prayer Is a Popular Elective"; Enrique Lavin, "Prayers Raised," *Los Angeles Times* (Orange County Edition), 19 September 1996, sec. B, p. 1.

129. Adon Taft, "Teens to Gather at Flagpoles in Prayer Campaign," *Miami Herald* (Final Edition), 6 September 1991, 6E.

130. Tony Mauro, "Students 'Taking Stand' for Prayer in Schools," *USA Today*, 15 September 1993, 4A.

131. In Orange County, Florida, a school policy allowed students to leave materials in an office or library, but the items could not be handed out. Associated Press, "Newspaper Distribution Sparks Confrontation," *Sun-Sentinel* (Florida), 19 May 1990, sec. A, p. 17; Robert Perez, "Students Win Struggle to Give Out Fliers," *Orlando Sentinel* (Seminole Edition), 18 August 1990, sec. D, p. 1.

132. Thomas J. Billitteri, "Getting the Message Across," *St. Petersburg Times* (City Edition), 22 September 1990, 4E.

133. In issue 8, the editors quoted the verse as, "For even the thieves and prostitutes are entering the kingdom of heaven!" The New Revised Standard Version of the Bible uses the word "tax collectors" instead of "thieves." "Hey, Kids!!!" *Thieves and Prostitutes* no. 8 (1992): 2; Matthew 21:31 NRSV.

134. Jodi Mailander, "Suspension Puts Broward Teen in National Spotlight," *Miami Herald* (Final Edition), 8 January 1992, 2B.

135. Jodi Mailander, "Suspension Stirs Religious Outrage," *Miami Herald* (Broward Edition), 8 January 1992, 2B.

136. Herald Staff Editorial, "A Clash of Rights," *Miami Herald* (Final Edition), 13 January 1992, 10A.

137. Mailander, "Suspension Puts Broward Teen in National Spotlight."

138. This article, contained in a collage in issue 8 of *Thieves and Prostitutes*, appears to come from another article, by Todd McDonald, entitled "The School That Forgot the First Amendment." "The Censorship of Fascist Liberalism," *Thieves and Prostitutes*, no. 8 (1992): 4. Sekulow's television program aired weekly on nearly 350 stations and was affiliated with Jan and Paul Crouch's Trinity Broadcast Network. With Paul Crouch's help, Sekulow had also established a five-station religious network in the Southeast. Mark I. Pinsky, "Legal Weapon," *Los Angeles Times* (Home Edition), 2 September 1993, sec. E, p. 1.

139. Similar charges had been made against DeKalb County school officials in 1989, when Jay Sekulow alleged that students at Henderson High School had been harassed for having religious literature in school. "Bible-Carrying Students Not Harassed, DeKalb Says," *Atlanta Constitution*, 6 December 1989, sec. B, p. 2.

140. Jodi Mailander, "Board Policy to Change to Avoid Suit over Fliers," *Miami Herald* (Broward Edition), 25 February 1992, 1BR.

141. Ibid. In the aftermath of the DeBenedetto controversy, many Florida school districts sought to alter or clarify their policies on the distribution of religious materials in public schools.

142. Mailander, "Suspension Puts Broward Teen in National Spotlight."

143. "The Censorship of Fascist Liberalism," 4. At the time of publication, only school-sanctioned prayer was prohibited in schools, and abortion protesters were not altogether prohibited from clinics. Regarding both issues, the Supreme

Court had recognized believers' right to express their views but had prohibited expressions that would disrupt or infringe upon others' rights.

144. John W. Styll, "It's Time for a New Revolution," *CCM* (January 1991): 24.

145. Ibid. The Great Commission appears in the final verses of the Gospel of Matthew, in which Jesus tells the apostles: "All authority in heaven and on earth has been given to me. Go therefore and make disciples of all nations, baptizing them in the name of the Father and of the Son and of the Holy Spirit, and teaching them to obey everything that I have commanded you. And remember, I am with you always, to the end of the age." Matthew 28:18–20 NRSV.

146. "Feedback: You Say You Want a Revolution?" *CCM* (March 1991): 6.

## 3. METAL MISSIONARIES TO THE NATION

1. White Metal News, *White Throne* no. 3 (1987): 3. This chapter relies heavily on fan magazines produced by nonprofessionals. Many of these magazines had irregular publication schedules, and some altered their system for cataloging issues over the course of their publication history. I have given as much information about each issue cited as I have at my disposal. In some instances, the year of publication is a contextual guess.

2. Moore, *Selling God;* Taiz, *Hallelujah Lads and Lasses;* John M. Giggie and Diane Winston, eds., *Faith in the Market: Religion and the Rise of Urban Commercial Culture* (New Brunswick, NJ: Rutgers University Press, 2002).

3. This chapter addresses the relationship between contemporary music and religion among white evangelical Christians. During this period, *Contemporary Christian Music (CCM)* magazine divided Christian-influenced music into various categories. For example, according to *CCM*, "contemporary music by Christians," produced by bands such as U2, had "at least one believer in a key role, and therefore is affected by the point-of-view many Christians share about the world we live in, which in turn is reflected in the music." Then there was "gospel," or "contemporary Christian," music, which revolved "lyrically around the central theme of the Christian gospel." "Ask CCM," *CCM* (April 1991): 8.

4. Harding, *Book of Jerry Falwell,* 10.

5. Hunter, *Culture Wars,* 280.

6. Robert Walser, *Running with the Devil: Power, Gender, and Madness in Heavy Metal Music* (Hanover, NH: Wesleyan University Press, 1993), 14.

7. Deena Weinstein, *Heavy Metal: The Music and Its Culture,* rev. ed. (New York: Da Capo Press, 2000), 21–41.

8. Ibid., 35–43.

9. Jay R. Howard and John M. Streck, *Apostles of Rock: The Splintered World of Contemporary Christian Music* (Lexington: University of Kentucky Press, 1999).

10. John Clarke, Stuart Hall, Tony Jefferson, and Brian Roberts, "Subcultures, Cultures, and Class: A Theoretical Overview," in Hall and Jefferson, *Resistance through Rituals,* 9–74. See also Hall et al., *Policing the Crisis.*

11. Steve Rabey, "A Christian 'Heavy-Metal' Band Makes Its Mark on the Secular Music Industry," *Christianity Today* (15 February 1985): 45–47.

12. Moore, *Religious Outsiders and the Making of America.* See also Ellwood, *One Way.*

13. Patrick Buchanan, "The Election Is about Who We Are," *Congressional Quarterly Weekly Report,* 22 August 1992, 2544.

14. William Eaton and Connie Stewart, "Purist's Right: Upward, Christian Soldiers," *Los Angeles Times,* 21 August 1992, sec. A, p. 13.

15. Feedback, *Lightshine International Metal Magazine* 4, no. 1 (1993): 7.

16. "Idle Cure," *Heaven's Metal* 2, no. 4 (1987): 2.

17. Strype Hype, *Heaven's Metal* 1, no. 4 (1986): 8–9. According to *Heaven's Metal,* Robert Sweet's pose on the front cover could be explained scripturally: 2 Timothy 2:3–4 reads: "Share in suffering like a good soldier of Christ Jesus. No one serving in the army gets entangled in everyday affairs; the soldier's aim is to please the enlisting officer" (NRSV). The band insisted that the cover suggested a "spiritual war." Robert Sweet posed with a sword on at least two occasions: once on the cover of *Hit Parader* in February 1987 and again in the main photograph accompanying a *Kerrang!* cover article on the band. Rick Evans, "Heaven and Hell: Stryper vs. WASP" *Hit Parader* (February 1987): 38–41; Geoff Barton, "Avenging Angels" *Kerrang!* (12–25 December 1985): 12–15.

18. "Stryken," *Heaven's Metal* 2, no. 1 (1986): 2–3, 6.

19. Doug Van Pelt, "Looking at Guardian's Future," *Heaven's Metal* no. 20 (1988): 6–8.

20. For a comparison to Joshua, see "Bloodgood," *Heaven's Metal* 2, no. 3 (1986): 3; for a comparison to the apostle Paul, see Bob Hopkins and Doug Van Pelt, "Trytan," *Heaven's Metal* 2, no. 6 (1987): 16–18.

21. Hopkins and Van Pelt, "Trytan."

22. Roger Martinez, "LA Report," *White Throne,* no. 4 (1988): 6.

23. Roger Martinez, "Going behind Enemy Lines," *White Throne,* no. 5 (1988): 10–11.

24. "Gardian," *Heaven's Metal* 2, no. 5 (1987): 14–15, 23. Ephesians 6:10–17 reads: "Finally, be strong in the Lord and in the strength of his power. Put on the whole armor of God, so that you may be able to stand against the wiles of the devil. For our struggle is not against the enemies of blood and flesh, but against the rulers, against the authorities, against the cosmic powers of this present darkness, against the spiritual forces of evil in the heavenly places. Therefore take up the whole armor of God, so that you may be able to withstand on that evil day, and having done everything, to stand firm. Stand therefore, and fasten the belt of truth around your waist, and put on the breastplate of righteousness. As shoes for your feet put on whatever will make you ready to proclaim the gospel of peace. With all of these, take the shield of faith, with which you will be able to quench all the flaming arrows of the evil one. Take the helmet of salvation, and the sword of the Spirit, which is the word of God" (NRSV).

25. "Stryken," *Heaven's Metal* 2, no. 1 (1986): 2–3, 6; *CCM* (March 1987).

26. Hopkins and Van Pelt, "Trytan."

27. "Quotable Quotes," *Heaven's Metal* 3, no. 3 (1987): 29.

28. "Roxalt: From Being a Bunch of Kiss Freaks to Guitar-Wielding Jesus Freaks," *Heaven's Metal* 1, no. 5 (1986): 8–10.

29. Untitled interview with Adam Alvarez, *Heaven's Metal* 1, no. 3 (1985): 4–5.

30. "Holy Soldier," *Heaven's Metal* 2, no. 3 (1986): 14–16.

31. For an in-depth look at the meanings nonmetal acts attached to their music, see Howard and Streck, *Apostles of Rock*.

32. Metal Tracks, *Heaven's Metal* 2, no. 4 (1987): 15.

33. "Holy Soldier," *Heaven's Metal,* no. 33 (1992): 4–7; "Holy Soldier," *Heaven's Metal* 2, no. 3 (1986): 14–15.

34. "Gardian," *Heaven's Metal* 3, no. 2 (1987): 8–9, 11.

35. Tyler Bacon and Marty Hoeft, untitled interview with Guardian, *Radically Saved* 2, no. 5 (1990): 4–6.

36. "One Bad Pig: Jerry Falwell's Revenge, or Johnny Rotten's Nightmare?" *Heaven's Metal* 2, no. 4 (1987): 12–13.

37. Steve Schmutzer, "One on One with Whitecross," *Heaven's Metal* 3, no. 3 (1987): 3–5.

38. "Interview with Steve Whitaker of Barren Cross," *Heaven's Metal* 1, no. 4 (1986): 2–3, 5.

39. Joe Conason, "The Religious Right's Quiet Revolution," *The Nation*, 27 April 1992, 555.

40. Bob Darden, "In the Wings, Christian Music Readies for the Spotlight," *Billboard* 105, no. 13 (27 March 1993): 44–45.

41. Bob Darden, "Crossover Dreams: Christian Music Stars Are Finding Glory in the Mainstream, But What Are the Dangers?" *Billboard* 104, no. 15 (11 April 1992): 27–28; Darden, "In the Wings," 44–45. In 1995 Christian bands made more than $700 million in record and concert ticket sales. Eric Boehlert, "Holy Rock & Rollers," *Rolling Stone,* no. 744 (3 October 1996): 23–24. For a case study of crossover success and the transformation of the Christian music industry, see William D. Romanowski, "Move Over Madonna: The Crossover Career of Gospel Artist Amy Grant," *Popular Music and Society* 17, no. 2 (Summer 1993): 47–67.

42. Walser, *Running with the Devil*, 10.

43. Strype Hype, *Heaven's Metal* 2, no. 2 (1986): 8.

44. Strype Hype, *Heaven's Metal* 1, no. 6 (1986): 2.

45. Rick Evans, "Heaven and Hell: Stryper vs. W.A.S.P.," *Hit Parader* (February 1987): 38–41. In an article published the month before the "Stryper vs. W.A.S.P." feature, Robert Sweet told *Hit Parader* that the band sometimes spent $1,000 on Bibles to throw to audience members. Andy Secher, "Stryper: Angels with Dirty Faces," *Hit Parader* (January 1987): 56–7.

46. Strype Hype, *Heaven's Metal* 2, no. 1 (1986): 8–9. In the NRSV the verse reads, "By his bruises we are healed."

47. See Andy Secher, "Stryper: Knocking on Heaven's Door," *Hit Parader* (November 1986): 21.

48. Lyrics for "Always There for You," published in *Hit Parader* (November 1988): 86–87; RockTops advertisement in *Hit Parader* (November 1988): 87.

49. Stryper, "Soldiers under Command," *Soldiers under Command* (Enigma 1985), www.stryper.com/disc/lyrics/suc.shtml.

50. Secher, "Stryper: Knocking on Heaven's Door."

51. Tyler Bacon, "Stryper," *Radically Saved* 2, no. 8 (1991): 11–12.

52. Table of contents, *Lightshine International Metal Magazine* 4, no. 2 (1993): 2.

53. *Lightshine International Metal Magazine* 5, no. 1 (1994): 1.

54. *Lightshine International Metal Magazine* 4, no. 2 (1993): 3.

55. *Lightshine International Metal Magazine*, no. 1 (1989): 1, 3.

56. Tom Denlinger, "Feedback," *Lightshine International Metal Magazine* 6, no. 4 (Fall 1995): 3–4.

57. Tom Denlinger, "Feedback," *Lightshine International Metal Magazine* 4, no. 1 (1993): 13.

58. Jeff Zimmerman, "Lessons of Suffering and Pain," *Lightshine International Metal Magazine* 6, no. 2 (Spring 1995): 1–4.

59. "Barren Cross Interview," *Gospel Metal* (Fall 1987): 25–27.

60. Crash McNamara, "Stryper," *Take a Stand* 3, no. 1 (July 1989): 1–2.

61. "Neon Cross," *Gospel Metal* (Fall 1987): 15–18.

62. "Gardian," *Gospel Metal* (Fall 1987): 22–24.

63. "Ransom," *Heaven's Metal* 2, no. 6 (1987): 2–3, 5–6.

64. Weinstein, *Heavy Metal*, 84–91.

65. "The Daniel Band," *Heaven's Metal* 1, no. 3 (1985): 1–3, 5.

66. Marc Carpenter, "Tackling Issues with Barren Cross," *Heaven's Metal*, no. 21 (1989): 13–15.

67. G. Dewar Macleod, "'Kids of the Black Hole': Youth Culture in Postsuburbia" (Ph.D. diss., City University of New York, 1998), 5.

68. Ed Warner, "One Bad Pig Interview," *Take a Stand* 4, no. 4 (October 1990): 1–2.

69. Macleod, "'Kids of the Black Hole,'" 5.

70. Doug Peterson, "Trytan," *White Throne*, no. 4 (1988): 22–23, 25.

71. Tom Denlinger, "Feedback," *Lightshine International Metal Magazine* 3, no. 2 (1992): 12.

72. "Interview with Thunder Calling," *Gospel Metal* (Fall 1987): 7–10.

73. "Trytan," *Heaven's Metal* 2, no. 2 (1986): 4–5.

74. Jeff McCormack, "Guardian," *The Pendragon*, no. 2 (1988–89): 7–8.

75. J. Emerson H., review of *Majestic Serenity*, by Sardonyx, *White Throne*, no. 13 (1993): 26.

76. Randy Rocker and Ed Warner, "Interview with Holy Soldier," *Take a Stand* 3, no. 7 (January 1990): 1–3; Caroline Knox, "Taking It to the Limit with Whitecross," *Heaven's Metal*, no. 18 (1988): 4–6.

77. "Zion," *Heaven's Metal* 2, no. 3 (1986): 8.

78. For lyrics to the songs in Bloodgood's 1987 release from Frontline Records, *Detonation*, see www.bloodgood.org/discography/lyrics/detonation.html#10.

79. McGirr, *Suburban Warriors*, 226.

80. Paul Verden, Kathleen Dunleavy, and Charles H. Powers, "Heavy Metal Mania and Adolescent Delinquency," *Popular Music and Society* 13, no. 1 (Spring 1989): 73–82, as cited in Weinstein, *Heavy Metal*, 254.

81. For a more in-depth discussion of the accusations directed against metal acts, see Weinstein, *Heavy Metal*, 250–58.

82. See "To Whom It May Concern," by Empty Tomb, *Burning Bush*, no. 13 (1989): 11; unsigned review of *Vacation from Hell*, by Rapture, *Burning Bush*, no. 13 (1989): 12; "Bloodgood," *Heaven's Metal* 2, no. 3 (1986): 3–5, 11. Empty Tomb was a punk band from Oregon, not to be confused with the later punk band with the same name from Australia.

83. David Zaffiro (Bloodgood), "Alone in Suicide," *Detonation* (Frontline Records, 1987), www.bloodgood.org/discography/.

84. Untitled article, *Heaven's Metal* 1, no. 3 (1985): 10.

85. White Metal News, *White Throne*, no. 4 (1988): 5.

86. Doug Van Pelt, "Looking at Guardian's Future," *Heaven's Metal*, no. 20 (1988): 6–8.

87. *Heaven's Metal* noted that Torn Flesh received a number of phone calls to its "Mosh Hotline" from gay people angered by the band's song "Gay Rights?" In anticipation of this, the band set up its hotline to include a five-minute sermon explaining "what God thinks of the issue." Metal Tracks, *Heaven's Metal*, no. 25 (1989): 29.

88. Metal Tracks, *Heaven's Metal* 2, no. 4 (1987): 9; unsigned review of *Death to Death*, by Hellfire, *Heaven's Metal*, 3, no. 1 (1987): 17; Van Pelt, "Looking at Guardian's Future."

89. Metal Tracks, *Heaven's Metal*, no. 25 (1989): 29.

90. Holy Soldier, "See No Evil," *Holy Soldier* (Myrrh Records, 1990), www.holysoldier.com/hslyr.htm.

91. "Exodus II: Rock to Reach," *Heaven's Metal* 2, no. 4 (1987): 15.

92. Carpenter, "Tackling Issues with Barren Cross."

93. "Interview with Doug Van Pelt—lead singer of the controversial thrash/punk band Lust Control!!!" www.geocities.com/SunsetStrip/Lounge/4892/interview.html (accessed March 20, 2002).

94. Ibid.

95. Lust Control, "Planned Parenthood," *We Are Not Ashamed* (Captive Thought/ASCAP, 1992), www.geocities.com/ariel777.geo/WANA.html.

96. Lust Control, "Operation Rescue," *We Are Not Ashamed*.

97. "Interview with Jim LaVerde," *Gospel Metal* (Fall 1987): 25–27.

98. Randy Rocker, "Mike Lee Interview," *Take a Stand* 3, no. 4 (October 1989): 2.

99. Bob Hopkins and Doug Van Pelt, "The Mighty Sound of Barren Cross," *Heaven's Metal*, no. 16 (1988): 21–4.

100. Ibid.

101. "Barren Cross," *Take a Stand* (August 1988): 1–2.

102. Bob Darden, "Christian Acts Forthcoming about Their Support for Bush," *Billboard* 104, no. 44 (31 October 1992): 8–9.

103. Tom Denlinger, "Feedback," *Lightshine International Metal Magazine* 4, no. 1 (1993): 11. In the next issue, Denlinger denied that he advocated violence against doctors who provided abortion: "We are pro-life and that includes the life of any doctor. There are many wackos out there but pro-lifers are generally peaceful protesters." Tom Denlinger, "Feedback," *Lightshine International Metal Magazine* 4, no. 2 (1993): 12.

104. Kevin Bradley, "Abortion: The Human Factor," *Lightshine International Metal Magazine* 4, no. 2 (1993): 10.

105. Deanna Bradley, "Abortion: The Human Factor," *Lightshine International Metal Magazine* 5, no. 1 (1994?): 17.

106. Tom Denlinger, "Feedback," *Lightshine International Metal Magazine* 4, no. 2 (1993): 12.

107. "Guardian," *The Pendragon*, no. 2 (1988–89): 7–8.

108. Jeff McCormack, review of *State of Control,* by Barren Cross, *The Pendragon*, no. 2 (1988–89): 12–13.

109. "Steve Camp," *Heaven's Metal* 1, no. 6 (1986): 14–15.

110. Michael Bloodgood, "What's Wrong with Christian Music: The Fans and the Bands," *Heaven's Metal*, no. 18 (1988): 34–35.

111. Crash McNamara, "Stryper," *Take a Stand* 3, no. 1 (July 1989): 1–2.

112. Doug Van Pelt, "Pigs in Hog Heaven," *Heaven's Metal*, no. 25 (1989): 6–9.

113. For a description of the uproar caused by the Sex Pistols in 1976–77, see Marcus, *Lipstick Traces,* 1–152; and James Miller, *Flowers in the Dustbin: The Rise of Rock and Roll, 1947–1977* (New York: Simon and Schuster, 1999), 226–36.

114. Tyler Bacon, "The Latest Word in Metal," *Radically Saved* 2, no. 7 (1991): 2.

115. Hendershot, *Shaking the World for Jesus,* chapter 1.

116. See, for example, *Billboard's* Top Inspirational Albums for the week ending 11 January 1986, when Stryper's "Soldiers under Command" occupied the number 4 spot, seventeen slots above Jimmy Swaggart's album *Sweet Anointing.* "Top Inspirational Albums," *Billboard* 98 (11 January 1986): 59.

117. Swaggart, *Christian Rock and Roll,* 21–27.

118. Christy Arnold, "Bloodgood interview," *Take a Stand* (December 1987): 1–3.

119. Schmutzer, "One on One with Whitecross."

120. Tom Denlinger, "Power Chords for the Christian Metalhead," *Sardonyx* 4 (1988–89): 4.

121. Dean Ross, "Glenn Kaiser Speaks Out on Music," *Heaven's Metal,* no. 26 (1990): 28–30.

122. "Interview with Steve Valdez," *Gospel Metal* (Fall 1987): 28–31.

123. Carpenter, "Tackling Issues with Barren Cross." The story is found in Matthew 12:22–37 and Luke 11:14–28. In the Gospel of Matthew, the key passage reads: "Then they brought to him a demoniac who was blind and mute; and he cured him, so that the one who had been mute could speak and see. All the crowds were amazed and said, 'Can this be the Son of David?' But when the Pharisees heard it, they said, 'It is only by Beelzebul, the ruler of the demons, that this fellow casts out the demons.' He knew what they were thinking and said to them, 'Every kingdom divided against itself is laid waste, and no city or house divided against itself will stand. If Satan casts out Satan, he is divided against himself; how then will his kingdom stand? If I cast out demons by Beelzebul, by whom do your own exorcists cast them out? Therefore they will be your judges. But if it is by the Spirit of God that I cast out demons, then the kingdom of God has come to you. Or how can one enter a strong man's house and plunder his

property, without first tying up the strong man? Then indeed the house can be plundered. Whoever is not with me is against me, and whoever does not gather with me scatters. Therefore I tell you, people will be forgiven for every sin and blasphemy, but blasphemy against the Spirit will not be forgiven. Whoever speaks a word against the Son of Man will be forgiven, but whoever speaks against the Holy Spirit will not be forgiven, either in this age or in the age to come. Either make the tree good, and its fruit good; or make the tree bad, and its fruit bad; for the tree is known by its fruit. You brood of vipers! How can you speak against good things, when you are evil? For out of the abundance of the heart the mouth speaks. The good person brings good things out of a good treasure, and the evil person brings evil things out of an evil treasure. I tell you, on the day of judgment you will have to give an account for every careless word you utter; for by your words you will be justified, and by your words you will be condemned" (NRSV).

124. See Bob Felberg, "No More Showing Mercy," *Rizzen Roxx,* no. 23 (1988): 5–6, 8; "Judea," *Gospel Metal* no. 6 (1989): 11–13.

125. Walser defines "'exscription' of the feminine" as "total denial of gender anxieties through the articulation of fantastic worlds without women." Walser, *Running with the Devil,* 110–11.

126. "Quotable Quotes," *Heaven's Metal* 3, no. 3 (1987): 29.

127. "Eternal Ryte," *Heaven's Metal* 2, no. 2 (1986): 3.

128. "Barren Cross Interview," *Gospel Metal* (Fall 1987): 25–27.

129. 1 Corinthians 6:9–10 (NRSV) reads: "Do you know that wrongdoers will not inherit the Kingdom of God? Do not be deceived! Fornicators, idolaters, adulterers, male prostitutes, sodomites, thieves, the greedy, drunkards, revilers, robbers—none of these will inherit the kingdom of God." LaVerde probably equated "effeminates" with "sodomites." 1 Corinthians 11:13–15 reads: "Judge for yourselves: is it proper for a woman to pray to God with her head unveiled? Does not nature itself teach you that if a man wears long hair, it is degrading to him, but if a woman has long hair, it is her glory? For her hair is given to her for a covering." "Barren Cross Interview."

130. "Gardian," *Gospel Metal* (Fall 1987): 22–27.

131. Christy Arnold, Randy Rocker, and Tara Jensen, "Rock 'n' Roll Wives: Interview with Christine Whitaker and Lisa Lee of Barren Cross," *Take a Stand* (December 1988): 3–4.

132. Sardonyx, *Lightshine International Metal Magazine* 3, no. 1 (Spring 1992): 6–7.

133. Secher, "Stryper: Angels with Dirty Faces."

134. "Zion," *Heaven's Metal* 2, no. 3 (1986): 8–9.

135. "Neon Cross," *Gospel Metal* (Fall 1987): 15–18.

136. "Results of Readers' Poll," *Heaven's Metal* 3, no. 3 (1987): 20–21.

137. Dave Muttillo, review of *Power Down in the Fun House,* by Virginia Creeper, *White Throne,* no. 11 (1992): 61.

138. Sound Off, *White Throne,* no. 12 (1992): 9.

139. Dave Johnson, "Editorial," *White Throne,* no. 13 (1993): 5, 8.

140. *Kerrang!* 12–25 December 1985.

141. Doug Van Pelt, "Will Stryper Play Heavy Metal?" *Heaven's Metal,* no. 21 (1989): 16–18.

142. Bloodgood, "What's Wrong with Christian Music?"

143. Christy Arnold and Tara Jensen, "HIS II: Two Days of Heavenly Metal on Earth," *Take a Stand* (May 1988): 1–6.

144. Bloodgood, "What's Wrong with Christian Music?"

145. Tom Denlinger, "Feedback," *Lightshine International Metal Magazine* 6, no. 4 (Fall 1995): 3–4.

146. "Interview with Sacred Warrior," *Gospel Metal*, no. 6 (1989): 20–21.

147. Deliverance, "Quotable Quotes," *Heaven's Metal* 2, no. 6 (1987): 14.

148. Chain Mail Section, *Metal* (December 1988): 4.

149. Paul O'Donnell, "Rock of Ages," *New Republic* 215, no. 21 (18 November 1996): 14–15.

150. Tom Denlinger, "Power Chords for the Christian Metalhead," *Lightshine International Metal Magazine* 2, no. 2 (Spring 1991): 6.

## 4. "AN MTV APPROACH TO EVANGELISM"

1. In Orange County, the Harvest Crusade was known best by its ubiquitous bumper stickers. In 1994, sponsors distributed one million flyers, 120,000 bumper stickers, and 30,000 T-shirts in preparation for the event. Roy Rivenburg, "A Cool Crusader," *Los Angeles Times* (Orange County Edition), 10 July 1994, sec. E, p. 1. The bumper stickers were made out of a rubber material, not paper, and bore a sun-protectant glaze so that they wouldn't fade or damage the car. Elaine Gale, "No Bumper Crop? Harvest Crusade Stickers Aren't Reaping Attention of Years Past," *Los Angeles Times* (Orange County Edition), 14 June 1999, sec. B, p. 1.

2. Carol McGraw, "Harvest Crusade Begins Tonight," *Orange County Register*, 14 August 1997, sec. B, p. 1.

3. Hieu Tran Phan, "Message Is Music to their Ears," *Orange County Register*, 17 August 1997, sec. B, p. 1.

4. Harvest Crusades, "Past Crusades," www.harvest.org/crusades/past/1997/body.htm (accessed May 1, 1999).

5. McDannell, *Material Christianity*, 222–23.

6. Russell Chandler, "Robertson Moves to Fill Christian Right Vacuum," *Los Angeles Times*, 15 May 1990, sec. A, p. 5.

7. Charles Grandison Finney directed his "new methods" at the emerging middle-class in the "burned-over" district of the western New York frontier; Dwight Moody's city-wide revivals in Chicago urged middle-class strivers to exhibit thrift and sobriety in the face of secularization and industrialization; and Billy Graham's postwar crusades, which became an enduring part of American television and radio culture (he was given a star on the Hollywood walk of fame), addressed middle-class fears about communism and juvenile delinquency.

8. Hoffman Birney, as cited in McWilliams, *Southern California Country*, 250. For a discussion of Protestant missionary activities in California before 1900, see Kevin Starr, *Americans and the California Dream 1850–1915* (New York: Oxford University Press, 1973), 69–109.

9. Kevin Starr, *Material Dreams: Southern California through the 1920s* (New York: Oxford University Press, 1990), 131–44.

10. Mayo, *Los Angeles*, 304–16.

11. Gustav Niebuhr and Laurie Goodstein, "New Wave of Evangelists Vying for National Pulpit," *New York Times*, 1 January 1999, sec. A, p. 1.

12. For more on conservative activism in Orange County between the 1960s and the 1980s, see McGirr, *Suburban Warriors*, chapter 6.

13. Lynn Smith and Dave Lesher, "Christian Activists Assume Large Role in O.C. Politics," *Los Angeles Times*, 20 December 1991, sec. A, p. 1. Years earlier, the county had been home to the Christian Voice, the first national organization of the Christian Right. See McGirr, *Suburban Warriors*, 259.

14. Tracy Weber, "Christian Right Flexes Its Political Muscles," *Orange County Register*, 9 March 1992, sec. A, p. 1; Matt Lait and Gebe Martinez, "Republicans Reign," *Los Angeles Times*, 10 July 1996, sec. A, p. 12.

15. In 1988 KYMS came in 39th in the Arbitrends, which measured a three-month rolling average of listening in Los Angeles and Orange counties. It was the only Orange County station to appear in the report. Gary Lycan, "Program Changes Give KYMS a Ratings Blessing," *Orange County Register*, 10 June 1988, p. 46.

16. Dennis McDougal, "'Building Highways in the Skyways': Old-Time Religion Meets High-Tech Media World," *Los Angeles Times*, 9 February 1985, 5–1; Paul Brownfield, "A Topic of Conversation," *Los Angeles Times* (Orange County Edition), 25 November 1997, sec. F, p. 1. In 1997 there were 1,650 religious radio stations in the United States. Fifty-three gospel-format stations were based in California in 1985, making that state the second, behind North Carolina (54), in the nation in the number of religious stations.

17. Gary Lycan, "Christian Station Goes on the Air," *Orange County Register*, 27 August 2000, sec. F, p. 38.

18. Both the *Christian Times* and *Christian Times Yellow Pages* were owned by Keener Communications Group. The company also owned regional newspapers in Colorado and Washington State.

19. Rob Kling and Clark Turner, "The Information Labor Force," in Rob Kling, Spencer Olin, and Mark Poster, eds., *Postsuburban California: The Transformation of Orange County since World War II* (Los Angeles and Berkeley: University of California Press, 1991), 92–141.

20. For an analysis of white evangelicals' response to the restructured economy of the post–Cold War era, see Faludi, *Stiffed*, chapter 5.

21. John C. Green, James L. Guth, and Kevin Hill, "Faith and Election: The Christian Right in Political Campaigns, 1978–1988," *Journal of Politics* 55, no. 1 (February 1993): 85.

22. Ownby, *Subduing Satan*, 144, 148, 155. For another close reading of camp meetings as social events, see Dickson D. Bruce, *And They All Sang Hallelujah: Plain-Folk Camp-Meeting Religion, 1800–1845* (Knoxville: University of Tennessee Press, 1974).

23. In May 1992, *CCM* featured a list of summer festivals in the United States. Although the Harvest Crusade (only in its third year) was not listed, nineteen other events in the United States were. Anya Krause, "Festivals '92," *CCM* 14, no. 11 (May 1992): 20–21.

24. Cohen, *Consumers' Republic*, chapter 6.

25. Michael Sorkin, ed., *Variations on a Theme Park: The New American City and the End of Public Space* (New York: Noonday Press, 1992).

26. See, for example, Debra Gold Hansen and Mary P. Ryan, "Public Ceremony in a Private Culture: Orange County Celebrates the Fourth of July," in Kling, Olin, and Poster, *Postsuburban California*, 165–89.

27. Religious conservatives also sought to minimize the number of homosexuals by establishing ministries for gay (evangelical) men who sought to become heterosexual through religious conversion. For an ethnography of the "ex-gay" movement, see Tanya Erzen, *Straight to Jesus: Sexual and Christian Conversions in the Ex-Gay Movement* (Berkeley and Los Angeles: University of California Press, 2006).

28. In 1992 voters in Colorado passed Amendment 2, which would have banned local legislation recognizing or protecting the rights of homosexuals. In 1996 the U.S. Supreme Court ruled that the measure was unconstitutional. See Kenneth Wald, "Florida: Running Globally and Winning Locally," in Mark J. Rozell and Clyde Wilcox, eds., *God at the Grass Roots: The Christian Right in the 1994 Elections* (Lanham, MD: Rowman and Littlefield, 1995), 36–37.

29. J. Christopher Soper, "California: Christian Conservative Influence in a Liberal State," in Rozell and Wilcox, *God at the Grassroots*, 211–26.

30. For an analysis of how conservatives developed strategies for anti-gay ordinance campaigns, see Chip Berlet, "Who Is Mediating the Storm? Right-Wing Alternative Information Networks," in Kintz and Lesage, *Media, Culture, and the Religious Right*, 249–73.

31. Wald, "Florida," 20, 36–37.

32. "Preliminary OK Given Human Rights Law," *Los Angeles Times* (Orange County Edition), 30 June 1988, 2–2.

33. Jim Carlton, "Irvine Group Starts Anti-Homosexual Initiative Drive," *Los Angeles Times* (Orange County Edition), 10 August 1988, 2–3.

34. Lynn Smith, "Irvine Position Forces Action on Gay Clause in Bias Law," *Los Angeles Times* (Orange County Edition), 30 March 1989, 2–1.

35. Eric Lichtblau, "Emotions Rule Irvine Battle on Gay Rights," *Los Angeles Times* (Orange County Edition), 9 October 1989, 1–1.

36. Linda Kintz, "Culture and the Religious Right," in Kintz and Lesage, *Media, Culture, and the Religious Right*, 8.

37. Dana Parsons, "A Matter of Values, Political Semantics," *Los Angeles Times* (Orange County Edition), 4 May 1989, 9–1.

38. Lynn Smith, "Values and Victories," *Los Angeles Times* (Orange County Edition), 12 November 1989, sec. B, p. 1.

39. Lichtblau, "Emotions Rule Irvine Battle on Gay Rights."

40. Smith, "Values and Victories."

41. Lynn Smith, "Irvine Group Warns Gays: Don't Flaunt Your Ways," *Los Angeles Times*, 14 November 1989, sec. A, p. 25.

42. Marcida Dodson, "Group Looks beyond Goal of Excluding Gays from Law," *Los Angeles Times* (Orange County Edition), 6 October 1988, 2–1.

43. Parsons, "A Matter of Values."

44. Lynn Smith, "AIDS Law Opponents Work Fast," *Los Angeles Times* (Orange County Edition), 14 June 1989, 2–1.

45. Eric Lichtblau, "Crucial Debates Ahead: After Slow Start, O.C. Gays Making Inroads," *Los Angeles Times* (Orange County Edition), 30 July 1989, 1–1.

46. On the impact of the Supreme Court's *Westside Community Schools v. Mergens* decision on student religious groups, see "Mobilizing Moral Righteousness" in chapter 2.

47. Debra Cano, "School Still Debating Gay Rights Mores," *Los Angeles Times,* 13 January 1994, sec. B, p. 1; Denice A. Rios, "Gay-Support Group Debated," *Orange County Register,* 8 December 1993, B1; Denice A. Rios, "Students Protest Gay Group," *Orange County Register,* 23 November 1993, B1.

48. The only city where the initiative did not receive a majority of votes was gay-friendly Laguna Beach, where voters rejected the measure by a 57%-to-43% margin. Dana Parsons, "A Different Drumbeat in Laguna Beach," *Los Angeles Times,* 12 March 2000, sec. B, p. 3. In 2002 Mayor Gavin Newsom of San Francisco challenged the state's marriage law by issuing marriage licenses to over 4,000 gay couples, but the California State Supreme Court determined that the mayor did not have the power to issue the licenses. A May 2008 State Supreme Court decision struck down the same-sex marriage ban. Preponents of Proposition 8, set for a November 2008 vote, hoped to override the decision. In 2006, state senator Sheila Kuehl proposed, then withdrew, a bill that mandated positive portrayals of gays and lesbians in school textbooks.

49. Conservative activists were countered by groups such as the Orange County Visibility League, which claimed seven hundred local members. Eric Lichtblau, "Crucial Debates Ahead."

50. Kevin O'Leary, "Debate on Gay Festival Packs Chambers," *Los Angeles Times* (Orange County Edition), 16 May 1989, sec. 2, p. 3. In 1985 Lou Sheldon, one of the leaders who opposed the festival, had engaged in a similar (and unsuccessful) campaign to deny a two-day gay pride festival in nearby Long Beach, located in Los Angeles County. John Needham, "Foe of Gay Rights, Abortion Takes Fight beyond Pulpit," *Los Angeles Times,* 14 October 1985, 2–1.

51. George Frank, "Organizers OK Relocation of Gay Festival to City's Plaza," *Los Angeles Times* (Orange County Edition), 20 June 1989, 2–3.

52. George Frank, "Gay Festival Alternative Falls Apart," *Los Angeles Times* (Orange County Edition), 22 June 1989, 2–3.

53. Ted Johnson and Eric Lichtblau, "Gay Pride Festival Spurs Face-Off," *Los Angeles Times* (Orange County Edition), 18 July 1989, 2–1.

54. Bob Schwartz, "Group's Petition Cites 'Compromise of Moral Values,'" *Los Angeles Times* (Orange County Edition), 24 June 1989, 2–3.

55. Santa Ana eventually closed its parks to events that charged entrance fees, served alcohol, or needed fences. The Gay and Lesbian Festival moved to UC Irvine the following year. "City Considers Closing Parks to Large Events," *Los Angeles Times* (Orange County Edition), 3 October 1989, 2–2; Michael Ashcroft, "UCI Welcomes Gay-Lesbian Festival but Housing Still for Marrieds Only," *Los Angeles Times* (Orange County Edition), 10 February 1990, 2–6.

56. Lily Eng, "Festival Size Limit Would Not Affect Gay Festival," *Los Angeles Times* (Orange County Edition), 10 August 1989, 2–3.

57. Lily Eng, "Sheldon Gives Santa Ana Council until Monday to Ban Gay Festival," *Los Angeles Times* (Orange County Edition), 18 August 1989, 2–3; Lily Eng, "3 Santa Ana Officials Get Recall Notices over Gay Issue," *Los Angeles Times* (Orange County Edition), 22 August 1989, 2–1. The recall effort failed to gain the required number of signatures.

58. Lily Eng, "County's First Gay Pride Festival to Open," *Los Angeles Times* (Orange County Edition), 9 September 1989, 2–1; Lily Eng and Steven R. Churm, "6 Arrested in Melee at Gay Festival in Santa Ana," *Los Angeles Times,* 11 September 1989, 1–3.

59. This was hardly the first time access to public parks had been at the center of a debate about access: in 1963 the city of Birmingham had closed its parks rather than allow them to be integrated.

60. O'Leary, "Debate on Gay Festival Packs Chambers."

61. Bob Schwartz, "Gay Event May Be Inappropriate for Park, Mayor Says," *Los Angeles Times* (Orange County Edition), 12 May 1989, 2–3.

62. Eng, "3 Santa Ana Officials Get Recall Notices over Gay Issue."

63. Steven R. Churm, "Neighbors near Fracas Say City Council Is to Blame," *Los Angeles Times* (Orange County Edition), 11 September 1989, 1–3.

64. Rich Kane, "An Incomplete History of Gay & Lesbian OC," *OC Weekly,* August 13–19, 1999, www.ocweekly.com/printme.php?eid=7629.

65. Michelle Nicolosi, "Gays Protest at OC Church," *Orange County Register,* 9 September 1991, sec. B, p. 01; Scott Harris and Lynn Smith, "Gay Activists Disrupt Church Service," *Los Angeles Times* (Orange County Edition), 9 September 1991, sec. A, p. 1. A few years later, the protests were used as evidence of the need for stricter penalties for disruption of religious services. The California State Legislature increased the punishment to include up to a year in county jail and doubled the community service requirement for a first offense to eighty hours. Eric Bailey, "New Church Protest Law Bringing Quick Dissension," *Los Angeles Times* (Orange County Edition), 14 September 1994, sec. A, p. 1.

66. Cohen, *Consumers' Republic,* 331.

67. For a description of Walter Knott's political activism, see Lisa McGirr, *Suburban Warriors,* 98–102.

68. Spigel, *Welcome to the Dreamhouse,* 209.

69. Baker, *Why Should the Devil Have All the Good Music?* 148–49.

70. Kane, "An Incomplete History of Gay & Lesbian OC"; Steve Harvey, "Disneyland at 30: The Unofficial History," *Los Angeles Times,* 14 July 1985, Calendar sec., 3.

71. Dorothy Townsend, "Magic Mountain Accused of Gay Bias," *Los Angeles Times,* 18 October 1985, 1–31; Kim Murphy, "Court Says Magic Mountain Can't Deny Request for Gays-Only Night," *Los Angeles Times,* 11 July 1986, 2–1.

72. Kane, "An Incomplete History of Gay & Lesbian OC"; Harvey, "Disneyland at 30"; E. Scott Reckard, "New Disneyland Hours Put Twist in Private Parties," *Los Angeles Times* (Orange County Edition), 2 October 1998, sec. D, p. 1.

73. Kane, "An Incomplete History of Gay & Lesbian OC."

74. Townsend, "Magic Mountain Accused of Gay Bias"; Harvey, "Disneyland at 30." Disney asserted that the finding in the lawsuit applied only to the plaintiffs in the case.

75. Gregg Zoroya, "Disneyland Still Bars Gays from Dancing Together, Suit Charges," *Orange County Register,* 26 February 1988, sec. B, p. 1; "Gay Lawsuit Dropped," *Orange County Register,* 1 October 1989, sec. B, p. 1.

76. John Dart, "Group Touting Family Values Protests at Disney Offices," *Los Angeles Times,* 6 September 1997, sec. B, p. 4.

77. Carol McGraw, "Taking On Goliath," *Orange County Register,* 7 July 1996, sec. E, p. 1.

78. Carol McGraw, "Locals Endorse Boycott, Though It'll Be Hard to Do," *Orange County Register,* 19 June 1997, sec. A, p. 16. The SBC boycott ended in June 2005, when delegates passed a resolution that stated, "The boycott has communicated effectively our displeasure concerning products and policies that violate moral righteousness and traditional family values." "National Briefing Religion: Baptists End Disney Boycott," *New York Times,* 23 June 2005, sec. A, p. 17.

79. Faye D. Ginsburg, *Contested Lives: The Abortion Debate in an American Community* (Berkeley and Los Angeles: University of California Press, 1984), 6–7.

80. McGirr, *Suburban Warriors,* 231–35. For an analysis of the national debate on abortion, see Kristin Luker, *Abortion and the Politics of Motherhood* (Berkeley and Los Angeles: University of California Press, 1984).

81. Adrianne Goodman and Nancy Wride, "Abortion Anniversary: Clinics Tighten Security," *Los Angeles Times* (Orange County Edition), 20 January 1990, 2–1.

82. Ibid.; Lanie Jones, "Protest Rally Marks 13th Anniversary of Legalized Abortion," *Los Angeles Times* (Orange County Edition), 26 January 1986, 2–1.

83. Eric Lichtblau, "Protests Mark Roe vs. Wade Anniversary," *Los Angeles Times,* 22 January 1990, sec. A, p. 3.

84. Goodman and Wride, "Abortion Anniversary"; "Fires Probed at Santa Ana Abortion Clinic," *Los Angeles Times* (Orange County Edition), 26 April 1985, 2–1. According to a January 1985 article, Planned Parenthood estimated that thirty-five incidents of bombing, bomb threat, arson, or attempted arson occurred at Planned Parenthood clinics nationwide in 1984. Louise Woo, "Ruling That Gave Women Right to Abortion: Rallies to Mark Fateful Anniversary," *Los Angeles Times* (Orange County Edition), 17 January 1985, 2–5.

85. James S. Granelli, "Court Temporarily Restrains Anti-Abortionist Groups, *Los Angeles Times* (Orange County Edition), 30 January 1985, 2–3.

86. In 1994 Bill Clinton signed the Freedom of Access to Clinic Entrances Act, which made it a federal crime to interfere with anyone receiving or providing abortion services (the same protection a prior law afforded churches).

87. Organizers estimated that 85% of protesters were from LA or OC. Andrea Ford and Judy Pasternak, "200 Abortion Foes Seized as Protest Gets under Way," *Los Angeles Times,* 23 March 1989, sec. A, p. 1; Jack Jones and Andrea Ford, "350 Anti-Abortion Activists Arrested at Cypress Clinic," *Los Angeles Times* (Orange County Edition), 24 March 1989, sec. 1, p. 1.

88. Lynn Smith, "Operation Rescue Plans More Protests," *Los Angeles Times* (Orange County Edition), 22 April 1989, 2–3.

89. Victor Merina, "1,000 Take Part in Confrontation at Abortion Clinic," *Los Angeles Times* (Orange County Edition), 9 July 1989, 2–1.

90. The previous year, Kelly had proposed a Tustin resolution that called the clinic "morally reprehensible and ethically unconscionable," but the action failed by a 3–2 margin. Wendy Paulson, "Councilman among 50 Abortion Foes Arrested in Tustin," *Los Angeles Times* (Orange County Edition), 14 April 1990, sec. B, p. 1.

91. An Operation Rescue spokeswoman attributed the decline in protests to the trespassing citations that had led to jail terms for seven hundred activists over the summer. Gebe Martinez, "Protest Stymies Santa Ana Clinic's Abortion Activities," *Los Angeles Times* (Orange County Edition), 9 December 1990, sec. B, p. 3.

92. Erich Lichtblau, "1,000 Activists Lobby for Abortion Rights," *Los Angeles Times* (Orange County Edition), 11 April 1989, 1–1.

93. Ibid. In *Madsen v. Women's Health Center* (93–880), the U.S. Supreme Court found that a "buffer zone" which prevented protesters from picketing and chanting around an abortion clinic did not violate the First Amendment as long as it was necessary to preserve a patient's right to enter a clinic. The Court reversed parts of the lower court's decision, including its injunction against protesters stalking or "shadowing" clinic workers and its injunction against graphic signs and posters. The lower court's noise injunction and ban on "targeted residential picketing" were allowed to stand. The federal law signed by Clinton in 1994 had already addressed some of these issues. David G. Savage, "Abortion Clinic Buffer against Protest Upheld," *Los Angeles Times* (Orange County Edition), 1 July 1994, sec. A, p. 1.

94. Jodi Wilgoren, "Tustin Bans Activists from Targeting Homes," *Los Angeles Times* (Orange County Edition), 7 April 1993, sec. B, p. 1.

95. Bert Eljera, "Putting Picketing Law to Test," *Los Angeles Times* (Orange County Edition), 18 April 1993, sec. B, p. 1.

96. Bill Billiter, "Huntington Beach Council Bans Picketing in Front of Homes," *Los Angeles Times* (Orange County Edition), 21 April 1993, sec. B, p. 4.

97. Martin Miller, "Abortion Opponents Picket Santa Ana Doctor's Home," *Los Angeles Times* (Orange County Edition), 27 May 1995, sec. B, p. 12. The Supreme Court's *Madsen* decision banned picketing directly in front of a doctor's home but allowed neighborhood picketing. Savage, "Abortion Clinic Buffer against Protest Upheld."

98. Apostolidis, *Stations of the Cross*, 6.

99. Randall Balmer and Jesse T. Todd Jr., "Calvary Chapel, Costa Mesa, CA," in James P. Wind and James W. Lewis, eds., *American Congregations*, vol. 1, *Portraits of Twelve Religious Communities* (Chicago: University of Chicago Press, 1994), 663–98.

100. Richard Dalrymple, "Beach Baptism Helps Save the Young," *Los Angeles Herald-Examiner*, 24 October 1970, sec. A, p. 7, as quoted in Balmer and Todd, "Calvary Chapel," 678.

101. Rivenberg, "Cool Crusader."

102. Miller, *Reinventing American Protestantism*, 1, 9. Miller lists twelve characteristics that distinguish new paradigm churches: "(1) they were started after the mid-1960s (2) the majority of congregation members were born after 1945 (3) seminary training of clergy is optional (4) worship is contemporary (5) lay leadership is highly valued (6) they have extensive small group ministries (7) clergy and congregants usually dress informally (8) tolerance of different personal styles is prized (9) pastors tend to be understated, humble, and self-revealing (10) bodily, rather than mere cognitive, participation in worship is the norm (11) the 'gifts of the Holy Spirit' are affirmed (12) Bible-centered teaching predominates over topical sermonizing" (p. 20). See also Robin D. Perrin, Paul Kennedy, and Donald E. Miller, "Examining the Sources of Conservative Church Growth: Where Are the New Evangelical Movements Getting Their Numbers?" *Journal for the Scientific Study of Religion* 36 (March 1997): 71–80.

103. Miller, *Reinventing American Protestantism*, 3.

104. Sonni Efron, "Calvary Chapel Stands Tall on Fundamental Tenets," *Los Angeles Times* (Orange County Edition), 12 October 1990, sec. A, p. 1.

105. Donald E. Skinner, "A Spirited Surf," *Orange County Register,* 18 August 1990, sec. A, p. 1.

106. Harvest Crusades, "Harvest Crusade: Summary of Attendance and Commitments," http://web.archive.org/web/19990202093224/http://harvest .org/text/summary.html (accessed April 5, 2003).

107. Brad Stetson, "Crusades Reap a Political Harvest," *Los Angeles Times,* 27 July 1995, sec. B, p. 9.

108. Tracy Weber, "Revival Concert Offers Christianity as an Encore," *Orange County Register,* 16 August 1990, sec. A, p. 1.

109. Ibid.

110. Carol McGraw, "United in Faith at Harvest Crusade," *Orange County Register,* 15 August 1997, sec. A, p. 1.

111. Ibid.

112. Hieu Tran Phan, "10,000 'Jesus People' Fill Pond," *Orange County Register,* 25 April 1999, sec. B, p. 1.

113. John Dart, "Laurie, Evangelist to Baby Boomers, Plans L.A. Crusade," *Los Angeles Times* (Valley Edition), 11 May 1995, sec. B, p. 9.

114. Hieu Tran Phan, "Crusade Aims to Harvest Youths," *Orange County Register,* 29 August 1998, sec. B, p. 1.

115. McGraw, "Harvest Crusade Begins Tonight."

116. Harvest Crusades, "Live at the Harvest Crusades" (1996), www. harvest.org/crusades/11_19.html (accessed April 26, 1999).

117. Ibid.

118. Greg Hernandez, "Music, Puppets Bring Gospel to the Young," *Los Angeles Times* (Orange County Edition), 10 July 1994, sec. B, p. 1.

119. Carol McGraw, "Preparing for Harvest," Orange *County Register,* 9 July 1995, sec. E, p. 1.

120. While the Crusade relied on modern technology and highly trained personnel to staff its online operation, organizers nonetheless assigned a staff member to pray that the equipment did not crash during the event. Elaine Gale,

"Crusade Uses Web to Let Believers Attend in Spirit," *Los Angeles Times* (Orange County Edition), 23 July 1999, sec. B, p. 1.

121. Harvest Crusades, "Live at the Harvest Crusades: Thursday, July 4" (1996), www.harvest.org/crusades/thu.html (accessed April 26, 1999).

122. Harvest Crusades, "Live at the Harvest Crusades: Sunday, July 7" (1996), www.harvest.org/crusades/sun.html (accessed April 26, 1999).

123. McDannell, *Material Christianity,* 2.

124. Ibid., 222–23.

125. Quentin J. Schultze, "Witnessing with our Music," *CCM* (February 1994): 46–48.

126. Ibid.

127. May, *Homeward Bound,* 166.

128. Harvest Crusades, "Harvest Night at Disneyland" (1996), http://web.archive.org/web/19970104175607/harvest.org/crusades/harvestnight.html (accessed April 5, 2003).

129. John Dart, "Keeping the Faith at Disney," *Los Angeles Times* (Valley Edition), 15 December 1997, sec. B, p. 1. Knott's held Christian concerts on New Year's Eve until 1992.

130. Harvest Crusades, "Harvest Night at Disneyland."

131. "Religion Professor's Views on Revivals Challenged," Letters to the Editor, *Los Angeles Times* (Orange County Edition), 5 September 1993, sec. B, p. 13.

132. Venise Wagner, "Crusade Expecting Bountiful Harvest," *Orange County Register,* 23 July 1993, sec. B, p. 1.

133. Tracy Weber, "Christian Right Flexes Its Political Muscle," *Orange County Register,* 9 March 1992, sec. A, p. 1; Jodi Wilgoren, "Church in O.C. Polls Candidates on Moral Issues," *Los Angeles Times* (Orange County Edition), 29 September 1994, sec. A, p. 1. While technically not allowed to endorse candidates, churches were permitted to distribute educational information during political campaigns.

134. Edward Iwata, "Politics Packs Sunday Punch," *Orange County Register,* 7 November 1994, sec. B, p. 1; James V. Grimaldi, "Christian Group Aims to Guide Voters," *Orange County Register,* 23 October 1996, sec. B, p. 2.

135. Jodi Wilgoren, "128 Candidates Agree with All Points in Calvary Chapel's Election Survey," *Los Angeles Times,* 28 October 1994, sec. B, p. 1; Jodi Wilgoren, "Church Group Will Rename Voter's Guide Politics," *Los Angeles Times,* 14 October 1994, sec. B, p. 1.

136. "Topic Watch: Government," *Orange County Register,* 6 August 1992, sec. B, p. 3.

137. "Bush to Talk by Telephone Sunday with Crusade," *Orange County Register,* 1 August 1992, sec. B, p. 2.

138. The plan for Bush's message changed several times during the week before the Crusade. At first, the president's handlers proposed, then canceled, a live appearance. Then they proposed—and canceled—a satellite-TV broadcast. A spokesman revealed that Crusade organizers also had reservations when he said, "There were some discussions on this end whether it was appropriate to bring in politics, because this is basically a church service." Andrew Horan,

"A Song in Their Hearts," *Orange County Register,* 3 August 1992, sec. A, p. 1. As a presidential candidate, Ronald Reagan spoke to at least one gospel concert: he addressed the Western Deserts Gospel Sing in Victorville, California, in May 1980.

139. Buchanan, "The Election Is about Who We Are."

140. Alan Wolfe, *The Transformation of American Religion: How We Actually Live Our Faith* (New York: Free Press, 2003), 166–67.

141. Carol McGraw, "Join in Praise: A Fire and Brimstone Night," *Orange County Register,* 5 July 1996, sec. B, p. 1.

142. Tracy Weber, "Crusade Expected to Draw 90,000 to Anaheim Stadium," *Orange County Register,* 31 July 1992, sec. B, p. 1.

143. Berlant, *The Queen of America Goes to Washington City,* 76.

144. Greg Laurie to Harvest Crusade supporters, June 1999, letter in author's possession.

145. Ibid. In Acts 17:6, Paul and Silas are in Thessalonica. The hostile townspeople attack a house (owned by Jason) looking for Paul and Silas, but "when they could not find them, they dragged Jason and some believers before the city authorities, shouting 'these people who have been turning the world upside down have come here also'" (NRSV).

EPILOGUE

1. Cusic, "Destined to Be a Minority," 15, 19.

2. Mark Joseph, *Faith, God, and Rock & Roll: How People of Faith Are Transforming American Popular Music* (Grand Rapids, MI: Baker Books, 2003), 15.

3. Bob Briner, *Lambs among Wolves* (Grand Rapids, MI: Zondervan, 1995), 18.

4. Joseph, *Faith, God, and Rock & Roll,* 26.

5. Neil Strauss, "Christian Bands, Crossing Over," *New York Times,* 10 June 2003, sec. B, p. 1.

6. Michael Shanahan, "Religious Right Takes Over, Angers GOP Moderates," *Times-Picayune* (New Orleans), 12 June 1994, sec. A, p. 20.

7. Joseph, *Faith, God, and Rock & Roll,* 18.

8. Strauss, "Christian Bands, Crossing Over."

9. Hendershot, *Shaking the World for Jesus,* 30–34.

10. Scott Leith, "Spreading the Gospel," *Atlanta Journal-Constitution,* 11 July 2001, 1a.

11. Deborah Evans Price, "Gospel and Christian Music," *Billboard* (1 April 2006), http://lexis-nexis.com.

12. See David D. Kirkpatrick, "Shaping Cultural Tastes at Big Retail Chains," *New York Times,* 18 May 2003, sec. A, p. 21; Lorraine Ali, "The Glorious Rise of Christian Pop," *Newsweek* (16 July 2001): 38–44; Lauren Sandler, "God Save the Teens," *Village Voice* (5 June 2001): 49–53; Mary Beth McCauley, "Extreme Devotion," *Christian Science Monitor,* 7 May 2002, pp. 14–15, 20.

13. Leith, "Spreading the Gospel."

14. Nelson Lichtenstein, "Wal-Mart: A Template for Twenty-First-Century Capitalism," in Nelson Lichtenstein, ed., *Wal-Mart: The Face of Twenty-First Century Capitalism* (New York: New Press, 2006), 24.

15. Kirkpatrick, "Shaping Cultural Tastes at Big Retail Chains."

16. Stuart Elliott, "G.M. Gets Criticism for Backing Tour of Christian Music Performers," *New York Times,* 24 October 2002, sec. C, p. 1.

17. Eric Boehlert, "Holy Rock & Rollers," *Rolling Stone* (3 October 1996): 24.

18. Deborah Evans Price, "National Mood Fuels Music Sales," *Billboard* (November 3, 2001): 53.

19. Jesse Hiestand and Tamara Conniff, "Faithful Flock to Christian Music after 9/11," *Hollywood Reporter,* 15 November 2001.

20. Alan Cooperman, "Openly Religious, to a Point," *Washington Post,* 16 September 2004, sec. A, p. 1.

21. Alan Cooperman, "Evangelical Leaders Appeal to Followers to Go to Polls," *Washington Post,* 15 October 2004, sec. A, p. 6.

22. David D. Kirkpatrick, "Going to Church for Votes," *New York Times,* 6 June 2004, sec. 4, p. 2.

23. David D. Kirkpatrick, "Bush Appeal to Churches Seeking Help Raises Doubts," *New York Times,* 2 July 2004, sec. A, p. 15; "Southern Baptists Blast Bush for Efforts to Mobilize Churches," *Associated Press,* 2 July 2004.

24. Alan Cooperman and Thomas B. Edsall, "Evangelicals Say They Led the Charge for GOP," *Washington Post,* 8 November 2004, sec. A, p. 1.

25. Frances Fitzgerald, "The Evangelical Surprise," *New York Review of Books,* 26 April 2007, 34.

26. Twenty-two percent of voters in 2004 listed "moral values" as their top priority. Critics, however noted that 35% of voters, including a third of voters for Green Party candidate Ralph Nader, had chosen a similar item ("ethical/moral values") in a 2000 exit poll by the *Los Angeles Times*. James Rosen, "Bush Feeling Heat from Evangelicals," *Sacramento Bee,* 14 November 2004, sec. A, p. 1.

27. Cooperman, "Evangelical Leaders Appeal to Followers to go to Polls."

28. Rock for Life, "Rock for Life—A Project of the American Life League," www.rockforlife.org/# (accessed June 6, 2004). During the 2004 campaign, Rock for Life promised to have registration tables for concertgoers at events such as Pennsylvania's Creation Festival, western New York's Kingdom Bound, and the annual Cornerstone festival (where the organization also hosted its own performance stage).

29. Phil Kloer, "Saints, Sinners Hustle to Sign Up New Voters," *Atlanta Journal-Constitution,* 28 August 2004, sec. A, p. 1.

30. Julia Duin, "Christian Youths Targeted for Votes," *Washington Times,* 12 August 2004, sec. A, p. 1.

31. Evelyn Nieves, "A Rallying Try for Young Voters," *Washington Post,* 4 July 2004, sec. A, p. 1.

32. Duin, "Christian Youths Targeted for Votes"; Kristie A. Martinez, "Democrats Follow GOP in Using Faith to Attract Young Voters," *Cox News Service,* 17 August 2005; Rachel DiCarlo, "Rocking the Christian Vote," *Weekly Standard,* 21 October 2004.

33. See Amy Sullivan, "When Would Jesus Bolt?" *Washington Monthly* (July–August 2006), www.washingtonmonthly.com/features/2006/0604.sullivan.html.

34. John C. Green, Corwin E. Smidt, James L. Guth, and Lyman A. Kellstedt, "The American Religious Landscape and the 2004 Presidential Vote: Increased Polarization" (Washington, DC: Pew Forum on Religion and Public Life, 3 February 2005), 2.

35. Randy Brinson, "Is America's Culture War Becoming America's 'Cold War'?" Redeem the Vote, 30 July 2006, www.redeemthevote.com/rtv_in_the_news.html (originally published in the *Mobile [AL] Register*).

36. Jane Lampman, "A 'Moral Voter' Majority? The Culture Wars Are Back," *Christian Science Monitor,* 8 November 2004, p. 4.

# Bibliography

NEWSPAPERS AND PERIODICALS

*ACM (Alternative Christian Music) Journal*
*Atlanta Constitution*
*Billboard*
*Burning Bush*
*Campus Life*
*Chicago Tribune*
*Christianity Today*
*Christian Musicians United*
*Christian Science Monitor*
*Congressional Quarterly Weekly Report*
*Contemporary Christian Music* (CCM)
*Cornerstone*
*Cutting Edge (Rock Gospel Review*, issues 1–9)
*Different Drummer*
*Gospel Metal*
*Harvest Rock Syndicate*
*Heaven's Metal* (1984–1994; renamed *HM*, 1994–present)
*Hit Parader*
*Hollywood Free Paper*
*Kerrang!*
*Life*
*Lightshine*
*Los Angeles Times*
*Media Update*
*Metal*
*Miami Herald*

*Modern Age*
*Moody Monthly*
*More Music Helps*
*Narrow Path*
*New Guard*
*New Republic*
*Newsound*
*Newsweek*
*New York Times*
*Notebored*
*OC Weekly*
*Orange County Register*
*Orlando Sentinel*
*Pendragon, The*
*Radically Saved*
*Reality Rock*
*Right On!*
*Rizzen Roxx*
*Rock in Jesus*
*Rolling Stone*
*Slaughter House*
*Spin*
*St. Paul Pioneer Press*
*St. Petersburg Times*
*Take a Stand*
*Thieves and Prostitutes*
*Time*
*True Tunes News*
*U.S. News & World Report*
*Village Voice*
*Vortex*
*Washington Post*
*White Throne*
*Tabooed*
*Youthworker*

## ARTICLES AND BOOKS

Ahlstrom, Sydney. *A Religious History of the American People.* New Haven, CT: Yale University Press, 1972.

Alfonso, Barry. *The Billboard Guide to Contemporary Christian Music.* New York: Billboard Books, 2002.

Allitt, Patrick. *Religion in America since 1945: A History.* New York: Columbia University Press, 2003.

Ammerman, Nancy Tatom. *Baptist Battles: Social Change and Religious Conflict in the Southern Baptist Convention.* New Brunswick, NJ: Rutgers University Press, 1990.

———. "North American Protestantism Fundamentalism." In Kintz and Lesage, *Media, Culture, and the Religious Right*, 55–113.

Anderson, Robert Maps. *Vision of the Disinherited: The Making of American Pentecostalism*. New York: Oxford University Press, 1979.

Apostolidis, Paul. *Stations of the Cross: Adorno and Christian Right Radio*. Durham, NC: Duke University Press, 2000.

Appadurai, Arjun, ed. *The Social Life of Things: Commodities in Cultural Perspective*. New York: Cambridge University Press, 1986.

Applebee, Peter. *Dixie Rising: How the South Is Shaping American Values, Politics, and Culture*. New York: Times Books/Random House, 1996.

Aranza, Jacob. *Backward Masking Unmasked: Backward Satanic Messages of Rock & Roll Exposed*. Shreveport and Lafayette, LA: Huntington House, 1983.

———. *Lord! Why Is My Child a Rebel? Parents and Kids in Crisis*. Lafayette, LA: Huntington House, 1990.

Asad, Tala. *Genealogies of Religion: Discipline and Reasons of Power in Christianity and Islam*. Baltimore: Johns Hopkins University Press, 1993.

Avila, Eric. *Popular Culture in the Age of White Flight: Fear and Fantasy in Suburban Los Angeles*. Berkeley and Los Angeles: University of California Press, 2004.

Azerred, Michael. *Our Band Could Be Your Life: Scenes from the American Indie Underground, 1981–1991*. Boston: Little, Brown, 2001.

Baehr, Ted. *The Media Wise Family: A Christian Family Guide to Making Morally and Spiritually Responsible Decisions about Movies, TV, and Multimedia*. Colorado Springs: Chariot Victor, 1998.

Baker, Paul. *Why Should the Devil Have All the Good Music? Jesus Music: Where It Began, Where It Is, and Where It Is Going*. Waco, TX: Word Books, 1979.

Baker, Paula. "The Domestication of Politics: Women and American Political Society, 1780–1920." *American Historical Review* 89 (June 1984): 620–47.

Balmer, Randall. *Mine Eyes Have Seen the Glory: A Journey into the Evangelical Subculture in America*. 3rd ed. New York: Oxford University Press, 2000.

Balmer, Randall, and Jesse T. Todd, Jr. "Calvary Chapel, Costa Mesa, CA." In James P. Wind and James W. Lewis, editors. *American Congregations*, vol. 1, *Portraits of Twelve Religious Communities*, 663–98. Chicago: University of Chicago Press, 1994.

Barger, Eric. *From Rock to Rock: The Music of Darkness Exposed!* Lafayette, LA: Huntington House, 1990.

Bennett, David. *The Party of Fear: From Nativist Movements to the New Right in American History*. Chapel Hill: University of North Carolina Press, 1988; reprint, New York: Vintage Books, 1990.

Bercovitch, Sacvan. *The American Jeremiad*. Madison: University of Wisconsin Press, 1978.

Berlant, Lauren. *The Queen of America Goes to Washington City: Essays on Sex and Citizenship*. Durham, NC: Duke University Press, 1997.

Berlet, Chip. "Who Is Mediating the Storm? Right-wing Alternative Information Networks." In Kintz and Lesage, *Media, Culture, and the Religious Right*, 249–73.

Berlet, Chip, ed. *Eyes Right! Challenging the Right Wing Backlash.* Boston: South End Press, 1995.

Blanchard, John, with Peter Anderson and Derek Cleave. *Pop Goes the Gospel: Rock in the Church.* Revised ed. Durham, UK: Evangelical Press, 1989.

Blessitt, Arthur. *Forty Days at the Cross.* Nashville: Broadman Press, 1971.

———. *Tell the World: A Jesus People Manual.* Old Tappan, NJ: Fleming H. Revell, 1972.

Blessitt, Arthur, with Walter Wagner. *Turned on to Jesus.* New York: Hawthorn Books, 1971.

Bloch, Ruth. *Visionary Republic: Millennial Themes in American Thought, 1756–1800.* New York: Cambridge University Press, 1985.

Bloom, Allan. *The Closing of the American Mind.* New York: Simon and Schuster, 1987.

Bloom, Nicholas Dagen. *Suburban Alchemy: 1960s New Towns and the Transformation of the American Dream.* Columbus: Ohio State University Press, 2001.

Bonner, David. *Revolutionizing Children's Records: The Young People's Records and Children's Record Guild Series.* Lanham, MD: Scarecrow Press, 2008.

Bonomi. Patricia U. *Under the Cope of Heaven: Religion, Society, and Politics in Colonial America.* New York: Oxford University Press, 1986.

Boyer, Horace Clarence. *The Golden Age of Gospel.* Montgomery, AL: Black Belt Press, 1995; reprint, Urbana and Chicago: University of Illinois Press, 2000.

Boyer, Paul. *Urban Masses and Moral Order in America, 1820–1920.* Cambridge, MA: Harvard University Press, 1978.

———. *When Time Shall Be No More: Prophecy Belief in Modern American Culture.* Cambridge: Harvard University Press, 1992.

Bradsher, Keith. *High and Mighty: SUVs—The World's Most Dangerous Vehicles and How They Got That Way.* New York: PublicAffairs, 2002.

Bright, Bill. *Come Help Change the World.* Old Tappan, NJ: Fleming H. Revell, 1970.

Briner, Bob. *Lambs among Wolves.* Grand Rapids, MI: Zondervan, 1995.

———. *Roaring Lambs.* Grand Rapids, MI: Zondervan, 2000.

Brinkley, Alan. "The Problem of American Conservatism." *American Historical Review* 99, no. 2 (April 1994): 409–29.

Bromell, Nick. *Tomorrow Never Knows: Rock and Psychedelics in the 1960s.* Chicago: University of Chicago Press, 2000.

Bruce, Dickson D. *And They All Sang Hallelujah: Plain-Folk Camp-Meeting Religion, 1800–1845.* Knoxville: University of Tennessee Press, 1974.

Butler, Jon. *Awash in a Sea of Faith: Christianizing the American People.* Cambridge, MA: Harvard University Press, 1990.

Cantwell, Robert. *When We Were Good: The Folk Revival.* Cambridge, MA: Harvard University Press, 1996.

Carpenter, Joel A. *Revive Us Again: The Reawakening of American Fundamentalism.* New York: Oxford University Press, 1997.

Carter, Dan T. *The Politics of Rage: George Wallace, the Origins of the New Conservatism, and the Transformation of American Politics.* New York: Simon and Schuster, 1995.

Centre for Contemporary Cultural Studies. *The Empire Strikes Back: Race and Racism in 70s Britain.* London: Hutchinson, 1982.

Cohen, Lizabeth. *Making a New Deal: Industrial Workers in Chicago, 1919–1939.* New York: Cambridge University Press, 1990.

———. *A Consumers' Republic: The Politics of Mass Consumption in Postwar America.* New York: Alfred A. Knopf, 2003.

Cohen, Stanley. *Folk Devils and Moral Panics: The Creation of the Mods and Rockers.* New York: St. Martin's Press, 1972.

Cohn, Norman. *The Pursuit of the Millennium: Revolutionary Millenarians and Mystical Anarchists of the Middle Ages.* Revised and expanded. New York: Oxford University Press, 1970.

Comstock, Anthony. *Traps for the Young.* Edited by Robert Bremner. Cambridge, MA: Belknap Press of Harvard University Press, 1967.

Conkin, Paul. *The Uneasy Center: Reformed Christianity in Antebellum America.* Chapel Hill: University of North Carolina Press, 1995.

Connolly, William. *Why I Am Not a Secularist.* Minneapolis: University of Minnesota Press, 1999.

Cross, Whitney. *The Burned-Over District: The Social and Intellectual History of Enthusiastic Religion, 1800–1850.* Ithaca, NY: Cornell University Press, 1950.

Cuddihy, John Murray. *The Ordeal of Civility: Freud, Marx, Levi-Strauss, and the Jewish Struggle with Modernity.* New York: Basic Books, 1974.

Davis, Mike. *City of Quartz: Excavating the Future in Los Angeles.* New York: Vintage Books, 1990.

———. *City of Quartz: Excavating the Future in Los Angeles.* New ed. London: Verso, 2006.

———. *Ecology of Fear: Los Angeles and the Imagination of Disaster.* New York: Metropolitan Books, 1998.

———. "From Fordism to Reaganism: The Crisis of American Hegemony in the 1980s." In Ray Bush, Gordon Johnston, and David Coates, editors. *The World Order: Socialist Perspectives,* 7–25. New York: Polity Press, 1987.

———. *Prisoners of the American Dream: Politics and Economy in the History of the U.S. Working Class.* New York: Verso, 1986.

DC Talk. *Jesus Freaks: DC Talk and the Voice of the Martyrs—Stories of Those Who Stood for Jesus, the Ultimate Jesus Freaks.* Bloomington, MN: Bethany House, 1999.

Deckman, Melissa M. *School Board Battles: The Christian Right in Local Politics.* Washington, DC: Georgetown University Press, 2004.

Deverell, William. *Whitewashed Adobe: The Rise of Los Angeles and the Remaking of its Mexican Past.* Berkeley and Los Angeles: University of California Press, 2005.

Diamond, Sara. *Not by Politics Alone: The Enduring Influence of the Christian Right.* New York: Guilford Press, 1998.

Di Sabatino, David. *The Jesus People Movement: An Annotated Bibliography and General Resource.* Westport, CT: Greenwood Press, 1999.

Dobson, James, and Gary Bauer. *Children at Risk: The Battle for the Hearts and Minds of Our Kids.* Dallas: Word Publishing, 1990.

Dorsett, Lyle W. *Billy Sunday and the Redemption of Urban America*. Grand Rapids, MI: William B. Eerdmans, 1991.

Doss, Erika. *Elvis Culture: Fans, Faith, and Image*. Lawrence: University Press of Kansas, 1999.

Duany, Andres, with Elizabeth Plater-Zyberk and Jeff Speck. *Suburban Nation: The Rise of Sprawl and the Decline of the American Dream*. New York: Farrar, Straus and Giroux/North Point Press, 2000.

Duncombe, Stephen. *Notes from Underground: Zines and the Politics of Alternative Culture*. New York: Verso, 1997.

Echols, Alice. *Daring to be Bad: Radical Feminism in America, 1967–1975*. Minneapolis: University of Minnesota Press, 1989.

Edsall, Thomas Byrne. *The New Politics of Inequality*. New York: W. W. Norton, 1984.

————. "Blue Movie." *Atlantic Monthly* (January–February 2003): 36–37.

Edsall, Thomas Byrne, and Mary Edsall. *Chain Reaction: The Impact of Race, Rights, and Taxes on American Politics*. New York: W. W. Norton, 1992.

Ehrenreich, Barbara. *Fear of Falling: The Inner Life of the Middle Class*. New York: HarperCollins, 1989.

————. "The Silenced Majority: Why the Average Working Person Has Disappeared from American Media and Culture." *Zeta Magazine* (September 1989): 40–42.

Ellwood, Robert S., Jr. *One Way: The Jesus Movement and Its Meaning*. Englewood Cliffs, NJ: Prentice-Hall, 1973.

Enroth, Ronald M., Edward E. Ericson Jr., and C. Breckinridge Peters. *The Jesus People: Old-Time Religion in the Age of Aquarius*. Grand Rapids, MI: William B. Eerdmans, 1972.

Erzen, Tanya. *Straight to Jesus: Sexual and Christian Conversions in the Ex-Gay Movement*. Berkeley and Los Angeles: University of California Press, 2006.

Evans, Sara. *Personal Politics: The Roots of Women's Liberation in the Civil Rights Movement and the New Left*. New York: Vintage Books, 1979.

Faludi, Susan. *Stiffed: The Betrayal of the American Man*. New York: Harper Collins, 1999.

Fass, Paula S. *The Damned and the Beautiful: American Youth in the 1920's*. New York: Oxford University Press, 1977.

Findlay, John M. *Magic Lands: Western Cityscapes and American Culture after 1940*. Berkeley and Los Angeles: University of California Press, 1992.

FitzGerald, Frances. *Cities on a Hill: A Journey through Contemporary American Cultures*. New York: Simon and Schuster, 1986.

Flake, Carol. *Redemptorama: Culture, Politics, and the New Evangelicalism*. Garden City, NY: Anchor Press, 1984.

Flanders, Stephen A. *Atlas of American Migration*. New York: Facts on File, 1998.

Flory, Richard W., and Donald E. Miller, eds. *GenX Religion*. New York: Routledge, 2000.

Forbes, Bruce David, and Jeffrey H. Mahan, eds. *Religion and Popular Culture in America*. Berkeley and Los Angeles: University of California Press, 2000.

Frank, Thomas. *The Conquest of Cool: Business Culture, Counterculture, and the Rise of Hip Consumerism*. Chicago: University of Chicago Press, 1997.

———. *One Market Under God: Extreme Capitalism, Market Populism, and the End of Economic Democracy*. New York: Doubleday, 2000.

———. *What's the Matter with Kansas: How Conservatives Won the Heart of America*. New York: Metropolitan Books, 2004.

———. "What's the Matter with Liberals?" *New York Review of Books* 52, no. 8 (May 12, 2005), www.nybooks.com/articles/17982.

Furniss, Norman. *The Fundamentalist Controversy, 1918–1931*. New Haven, CT: Yale University Press, 1954; reprint, Hamden, CT: Archon Books, 1963.

Gallup Report. *Religion in America, 50 Years: 1935–1984*, no. 236 (May 1985). Princeton, NJ: Gallup Report.

George H. Gallup International Institute, *The Religious Life of Young Americans: A Compendium of Surveys on the Spiritual Beliefs and Practices of Teen-Agers and Young Adults* (with commentary and analysis by George H. Gallup Jr. and Robert Bezilla). Princeton, NJ: George H. Gallup International Institute, 1992.

———. *The Spiritual Life of Young Americans approaching the Year 2000*. Princeton, NJ: George H. Gallup International Institute, n.d.

Garlock, Frank. *The Big Beat a Rock Blast*. Greenville, SC: Bob Jones University Press, 1971.

Garreau, Joel. *Edge City: Life on the New Frontier*. New York: Anchor Books, 1991.

Giggie, John M., and Diane Winston, eds. *Faith in the Market: Religion and the Rise of Urban Commercial Culture*. New Brunswick, NJ: Rutgers University Press, 2002.

Gilbert, James. *A Cycle of Outrage: America's Reaction to the Juvenile Delinquent in the 1950s*. New York: Oxford University Press, 1986.

Gilroy, Paul. *There Ain't No Black in the Union Jack: The Cultural Politics of Race and Nation*. Chicago: University of Chicago Press, 1987.

Ginsburg, Faye D. *Contested Lives: The Abortion Debate in an American Community*. Berkeley and Los Angeles: University of California Press, 1989.

Ginzberg, Lori D. *Women and the Work of Benevolence: Morality, Politics, and Class in the Nineteenth Century United States*. New Haven, CT: Yale University Press, 1990.

Gitlin, Todd. *The Sixties: Years of Hope, Days of Rage*. New York: Bantam Books, 1987.

Glassner, Barry. *The Culture of Fear: Why Americans Are Afraid of the Wrong Things*. New York: Basic Books, 1999.

Godwin, Jeff. *Dancing with Demons: The Music's Real Master*. Chino, CA: Chick, 1988.

———. *The Devil's Disciples: The Truth about Rock*. Chino, CA: Chick, 1985.

———. *What's Wrong with Christian Rock?* Chino, CA: Chick, 1990.

Gordon, Linda. *The Great Arizona Orphan Abduction*. Cambridge, MA: Harvard University Press, 1999.

Gore, Tipper. *Raising PG Kids in an X-Rated Society*. Nashville, TN: Abingdon Press, 1987.

Graham, Billy. *The Jesus Generation*. Grand Rapids, MI: Zondervan, 1971.

Green, John C., James L. Guth, and Kevin Hill. "Faith and Election: The Christian Right in Political Campaigns, 1978–1988." *Journal of Politics* 55, no. 1 (February 1993): 80–91.

Green, John C., Corwin E. Smidt, James L. Guth, and Lyman A. Kellstedt. "The American Religious Landscape and the 2004 Presidential Vote: Increased Polarization." Washington, DC: Pew Forum on Religion and Public Life, 3 February 2005.

Gregory, James N. *American Exodus: The Dust Bowl Migration and Okie Culture in California*. New York: Oxford University Press, 1989.

———. *Southern Diaspora: How the Great Migrations of Black and White Southerners Transformed America*. Chapel Hill: University of North Carolina Press, 2005.

Grossberg, Lawrence. *We Gotta Get Out of This Place: Popular Conservatism and Postmodern Culture*. New York: Routledge, 1992.

Guralnick, Peter. *Careless Love: The Unmaking of Elvis Presley*. Boston: Little, Brown, 1999.

———. *Dream Boogie: The Triumph of Sam Cooke*. New York: Little, Brown, 2005.

———. *Last Train to Memphis: The Rise of Elvis Presley*. Boston: Little, Brown, 1994.

Hall, Stuart. "The Toad in the Garden: Thatcherism among the Theorists." In Cary Nelson and Lawrence Grossberg, editors. *Marxism and the Interpretation of Culture*, 35–57. Urbana: University of Illinois Press, 1988.

Hall, Stuart, and Tony Jefferson, editors. *Resistance through Rituals: Youth Subcultures in Post-war Britain*. London: Hutchinson, 1976.

Hall, Stuart, Chas Critcher, Tony Jefferson, John Clarke, and Brian Roberts. *Policing the Crisis: Mugging, the State, and Law and Order*. London: MacMillan Press, 1978.

Hall, Stuart, and Martin Jaques, editors. *The Politics of Thatcherism*. London: Lawrence and Wishart, 1983.

Hangen, Tona J. *Redeeming the Dial: Radio, Religion, and Popular Culture in America*. Chapel Hill: University of North Carolina Press, 2002.

Hansen, Debra Gold, and Mary P. Ryan. "Public Ceremony in a Private Culture: Orange County Celebrates the Fourth of July." In Kling, Olin, and Poster, *Postsuburban California*, 165–89.

Harding, Susan. "Convicted by the Holy Spirit: the Rhetoric of Fundamental Baptist Conversion." *American Ethnologist* 14 (February 1987): 167–81.

———. "Representing Fundamentalism: The Problem of the Repugnant Cultural Other." *Social Research* 58 (Summer 1991): 373–93.

Harding, Susan Friend. *The Book of Jerry Falwell: Fundamentalist Language and Politics*. Princeton, NJ: Princeton University Press, 2000.

Harrell, David E., editor. *Varieties of Southern Evangelicalism*. Macon, GA: Mercer University Press, 1981.

Harris, Michael W. *The Rise of Gospel Blues: The Music of Thomas Andrew Dorsey in the Urban Church*. New York: Oxford University Press, 1992.

Hart, David S. *It's All Rock 'n' Roll to Me: Profiling Today's Popular Artists and Bands from a Biblical Perspective.* San Marcos, CA: New Song, 1996.

Hart, Lowell. *Satan's Music Exposed.* Chattanooga, TN: AMG, 1981.

Hayden, Dolores. *Building Suburbia: Green Fields and Urban Growth, 1820–2000.* New York: Pantheon Books, 2003.

Haymes, Stephen Nathan. *Race, Culture, and the City: A Pedagogy for Black Urban Struggle.* Albany: State University of New York Press, 1995.

Hebdige, Dick. *Subculture: The Meaning of Style.* London: Methuen & Co. Ltd, 1979.

Hendershot, Heather. *Saturday Morning Censors: Television Regulation before the V-chip.* Durham, NC: Duke University Press, 1998.

———. *Shaking the World for Jesus: Media and Conservative Evangelical Culture.* Chicago: University of Chicago Press, 2004.

Heyrman, Christine Leigh. *Southern Cross: The Beginnings of the Bible Belt.* Chapel Hill: University of North Carolina Press, 1997.

Hine, Robert V. *California's Utopian Colonies.* San Marino, CA: Huntington Library, 1953.

Howard, Jay R., and John M. Streck. *Apostles of Rock: The Splintered World of Contemporary Christian Music.* Lexington: University Press of Kentucky, 1999.

Hudnut-Beumler, James. *Looking for God in the Suburbs: The Religion of the American Dream and Its Critics, 1945–1965.* New Brunswick, NJ: Rutgers University Press, 1994.

Hunter, James Davison. *Culture Wars: The Struggle to Define America.* New York: Basic Books, 1991.

Isaac, Rhys. *The Transformation of Virginia, 1740–1790.* Chapel Hill: University of North Carolina Press, 1982.

Jeffords, Susan. " 'Debriding Vietnam': The Resurrection of the White American Male." *Feminist Studies* 14, no. 3 (Fall 1988): 525–43.

Johnson, Paul. *A Shopkeeper's Millennium: Society and Revivals in Rochester, New York, 1815–1837.* New York: Hill and Wang, 1978.

Jones, Bob, III. *Look Again at the Jesus People.* Greenville, SC: Bob Jones University Press, 1972.

Jorstad, Erling. *That New-time Religion: The Jesus Revival in America.* Minneapolis: Augsburg, 1972.

Joseph, Mark. *Faith, God, and Rock & Roll: How People of Faith Are Transforming American Popular Music.* Grand Rapids, MI: Baker Books, 2003.

———. *The Rock & Roll Rebellion: Why People of Faith Abandoned Rock Music and Why They're Coming Back.* Nashville: Broadman and Holman, 1999.

Judis, John B. *William F. Buckley, Jr.: Patron Saint of the Conservatives.* New York: Simon and Schuster, 1988.

Jurinski, James John. *Religion in the Schools: A Reference Handbook.* Santa Barbara, CA: ABC-Clio, 1998.

Juster, Susan. *Disorderly Women: Sexual Politics and Evangelicalism in Revolutionary New England.* Ithaca, NY: Cornell University Press, 1994.

Kaminer, Wendy. *Sleeping with Extra-terrestrials: The Rise of Irrationalism and the Perils of Piety.* New York: Vintage Books, 1999.

Kant, Immanuel. *The Conflict of the Faculties.* Translated by Mary J. Gregor. Lincoln: University of Nebraska Press, 1979.

Kazin, Michael. *A Godly Hero: The Life of William Jennings Bryan.* New York: Random House, 2006.

———. *The Populist Persuasion: An American History.* New York: Basic Books, 1995.

Kelley, Robin D. G. *Yo' Mama's DisFUNKtional! Fighting the Culture Wars in Urban America.* Boston: Beacon Press, 1997.

Kent, Stephen A. *From Slogans to Mantras: Social Protest and Religious Conversion in the Late Vietnam War Era.* Syracuse, NY: Syracuse University Press, 2001.

Key, Dana, and Steve Rabey. *Don't Stop the Music.* Grand Rapids, MI: Zondervan, 1989.

Kintz, Linda. "Culture and the Religious Right." In Kintz and Lesage, *Media, Culture, and the Religious Right,* 3–20.

Kintz, Linda, and Julia Lesage, editors. *Media, Culture, and the Religious Right.* Minneapolis: University of Minnesota Press, 1998.

Klatch, Rebecca. *A Generation Divided: The New Left, the New Right, and the 1960s.* Berkeley and Los Angeles: University of California Press, 1999.

Klein, Naomi. *No Logo.* New York: Picador, 2000.

Kling, Rob, Spencer Olin, and Mark Poster, editors. *Postsuburban California: The Transformation of Orange County since World War II.* Berkeley and Los Angeles: University of California Press, 1991.

Klosterman, Chuck. *Fargo Rock City: A Heavy Metal Odyssey in Rural North Dakota.* New York: Simon and Schuster, 2001.

Kozol, Wendy. *Life's America: Family and Nation in Postwar Photojournalism.* Philadelphia: Temple University Press, 1994.

Kramnick, Isaac, and R. Laurence Moore. *The Godless Constitution: A Moral Defense of the Secular State.* New York: W. W. Norton, 1996.

Kruse, Kevin M. *White Flight: Atlanta and the Making of Modern Conservatism.* Princeton, NJ: Princeton University Press, 2005.

La Chapelle, Peter. *Proud to Be an Okie: Cultural Politics, Country Music, and Migration to Southern California.* Berkeley and Los Angeles: University of California Press, 2007.

Larson, Bob. *Rock and the Church.* Carol Stream, IL: Creation House, 1971.

———. *Rock & Roll: The Devil's Diversion.* Rev. ed. McCook, NE: n.p., 1970.

———. *Rock: Practical Help for Those Who Listen to the Words and Don't Like What They Hear.* Wheaton, IL: Tyndale House, 1980.

———. *Satanism: The Seduction of America's Youth.* Nashville: Thomas Nelson, 1989.

Larson, Edward. *Summer for the Gods: The Scopes Trial and America's Continuing Debate over Science and Religion.* New York: Basic Books, 1997.

Lassiter, Matthew. *The Silent Majority: Suburban Politics in the Sunbelt South.* Princeton, NJ: Princeton University Press, 2006.

Lawhead, Steve. *Rock Reconsidered: A Christian Looks at Contemporary Music.* Downers Grove, IL: InterVarsity Press, 1981.

Lawrence, Errol. "Just Plain Common Sense: The 'Roots' of Racism." In Centre for Contemporary Cultural Studies, *The Empire Strikes Back,* 47–94.

Lears, T. J. Jackson. "From Salvation to Self-Realization: Advertising and the Therapeutic Roots of the Consumer Culture, 1880–1930." In T. J. Jackson Lears and Richard Wrightman Fox., editors. *The Culture of Consumption: Critical Essays in American History, 1880–1980,* 3–38. New York: Pantheon Books, 1983.

Lewis, Sinclair. *Elmer Gantry.* New York: Harcourt Inc., 1927; reprint, New York: New American Library, 1970.

Licthtenstein, Nelson, editor. *Wal-Mart: The Face of Twenty-first Century Capitalism.* New York: New Press, 2006.

Lienesch, Michael. *Redeeming America: Piety and Politics in the New Christian Right.* Chapel Hill: University of North Carolina Press, 1993.

Lindsay, Hal. *The Late Great Planet Earth.* Grand Rapids, MI: Zondervan, 1970.

Lipsitz, George. *The Possessive Investment in Whiteness: How White People Benefit from Identity Politics.* Philadelphia: Temple University Press, 1998.

———. *Rainbow at Midnight: Labor and Culture in the '40s.* Urbana and Chicago: University of Illinois Press, 1994.

———. *Time Passages: Collective Memory and American Popular Culture.* Minneapolis: University of Minnesota Press, 1990.

Low, Setha. *Behind the Gates: Life, Security, and the Pursuit of Happiness in Fortress America.* New York: Routledge, 2003.

Luker, Kristin. *Abortion and the Politics of Motherhood.* Berkeley and Los Angeles: University of California Press, 1984.

Macleod, G. Dewar. "'Kids of the Black Hole:' Youth Culture in Postsuburbia." Ph.D. diss., City University of New York, 1998.

Marcus, Greil. *Lipstick Traces: A Secret History of the Twentieth Century.* Cambridge, MA: Harvard University Press, 1989.

Marsden, George. *Fundamentalism and American Culture: The Shaping of Twentieth-Century Evangelicalism 1870–1925.* New York: Oxford University Press, 1980.

———. *The Soul of the American University: From Protestant Establishment to Establishment Nonbelief.* New York: Oxford University Press, 1994.

Marsden, George, editor. *Evangelicalism and Modern America.* Grand Rapids, MI: William B. Eerdmans, 1984.

Martin, Linda, and Kerry Segrave. *Anti-Rock: The Opposition to Rock 'n' Roll.* Hamden, CT: Archon Books, 1988; reprint, New York: Da Capo Press, 1993.

Martin, Robert F. *Hero of the Heartland: Billy Sunday and the Transformation of American Society, 1862–1935.* Bloomington and Indianapolis: Indiana University Press, 2002.

Marty, Martin E. "The Revival of Evangelicalism and Southern Religion." In Harrell, *Varieties of Southern Evangelicalism,* 7–22.

Massing, Michael. *The Fix.* New York: Simon and Schuster, 1998.

Mathews, Donald G. *Religion in the Old South*. Chicago: University of Chicago Press, 1977.

May, Elaine Tyler. *Homeward Bound: American Families in the Cold-War Era*. New York: Basic Books, 1988.

Mayo, Morrow. *Los Angeles*. New York: A. A. Knopf, 1933.

McCurry, Stephanie. *Masters of Small Worlds: Yeoman Households, Gender Relations, and the Political Culture of the Antebellum South Carolina Low Country*. New York: Oxford University Press, 1995.

McDannell, Colleen. *Material Christianity: Religion and Popular Culture in America*. New Haven, CT: Yale University Press, 1995.

McFadden, Michael. *The Jesus Revolution*. New York: Harrow Books, 1972.

McGirr, Lisa. *Suburban Warriors: The Origins of the New American Right*. Princeton, NJ: Princeton University Press, 2001.

McGreevy, John T. *Parish Boundaries: The Catholic Encounter with Race in the Twentieth-Century Urban North*. Chicago: University of Chicago Press, 1996.

McLoughlin, William G., Jr. *Billy Graham: Revivalist in a Secular Age*. New York: Ronald Press Co., 1960.

———. *Modern Revivalism: Charles Grandison Finney to Billy Graham*. New York: Ronald Press, 1959.

———. *Revivals, Awakenings, and Reform: An Essay on Religion and Social Change in America, 1607–1977*. Chicago: University of Chicago Press, 1978.

McWilliams, Carey. *Southern California Country: An Island on the Land*. New York: Duell, Sloan, and Pearce, 1946.

Mencken, H. L. "William Jennings Bryan." In Lawrence E. Spivak and Charles Angoff, editors. *The American Mercury Reader*, 34–37. Garden City, NY: Blue Ribbon Books, 1946.

Micklethwait, John, and Adrian Wooldridge. *The Right Nation: Conservative Power in America*. New York: Penguin, 2004.

Miller, Donald E. *Reinventing American Protestantism: Christianity in the New Millennium*. Berkeley and Los Angeles: University of California Press, 1997.

Miller, James. *Flowers in the Dustbin: The Rise of Rock and Roll, 1947–1977*. New York: Simon and Schuster, 1999.

Moen, Matthew. *The Christian Right and Congress*. Tuscaloosa: University of Alabama Press, 1989.

Moore, R. Laurence. *Religious Outsiders and the Making of America*. New York: Oxford University Press, 1986.

———. *Selling God: American Religion in the Marketplace of Culture*. New York: Oxford University Press, 1994.

———. *Touchdown Jesus: The Mixing of Sacred and Secular in American History*. Louisville, KY: Westminster John Knox Press, 2003.

Morgan, David. *Visual Piety: A History and Theory of Popular Religious Images*. Berkeley and Los Angeles: University of California Press, 1998.

Morgan, Edmund. *The Puritan Family*. New York: Harper and Row, 1944.

———. *Visible Saints: The History of a Puritan Idea*. Ithaca, NY: Cornell University Press, 1963.

Myers, Kenneth A. *All God's Children and Blue Suede Shoes: Christians and Popular Culture*. Westchester, IL: Crossway Books, 1989.

Newman, William M., and Peter L. Halvorson. *Atlas of American Religion: The Denominational Era, 1776–1990.* Walnut Creek, CA: AltaMira Press, 2000.

Nicolaides, Becky M. *My Blue Heaven: Life and Politics in the Working-Class Suburbs of Los Angeles, 1920–1965.* Chicago: University of Chicago Press, 2002.

Noebel, David. *The Beatles: A Study in Drugs, Sex and Revolution.* Tulsa, OK: Christian Crusade Publications, 1969.

———. *The Marxist Minstrels: A Handbook on Communist Subversion of Music.* Tulsa, OK: American Christian College Press, 1974.

———. *Rhythm, Riots, and Revolution.* Tulsa, OK: Christian Crusade, 1966.

Oppenheimer, Mark. *Knocking on Heaven's Door: American Religions in the Age of Counterculture.* New Haven, CT: Yale University Press, 2003.

Orsi, Robert, editor. *Gods of the City: Religion and the American Urban Landscape.* Bloomington and Indianapolis: Indiana University Press, 1999.

Ownby, Ted. *Subduing Satan: Religion, Recreation, and Manhood in the Rural South, 1865–1920.* Chapel Hill: University of North Carolina Press, 1990.

Palms, Roger C. *The Jesus Kids.* Valley Forge, PA: Judson Press, 1971.

Parents' Music Resource Center. *Let's Talk Rock: A Primer for Parents.* Arlington, VA: Parents' Music Resource Center, 1986.

Peck, Abe. *Uncovering the Sixties: The Life and Times of the Underground Press.* New York: Pantheon Press, 1985.

Pederson, Duane. *Jesus People.* Pasadena, CA: Compass Press, 1971.

Perlstein, Rick. *Before the Storm. Barry Goldwater and the Unmaking of the American Consensus.* New York: Hill and Wang, 2001.

———. "Who Owns the Sixties?" *Lingua Franca* (May–June 1996): 30–37.

Perrin, Robin D., Paul Kennedy, and Donald E. Miller. "Examining the Sources of Conservative Church Growth: Where Are the New Evangelical Movements Getting Their Numbers?" *Journal for the Scientific Study of Religion* 36 (March 1997): 71–80.

Peters, Dan, and Steve Peters. *Hit Rock's Bottom: Exposing to the Light the Real World behind the False Image of Rock.* North St. Paul, MN: n.p., 1984.

Peters, Dan, Steve Peters, and Jim Peters. *What the Devil's Wrong with Rock Music?* St. Paul, MN: n.p., 1980.

———. *Documentation, Part II: Rock Music Research.* St. Paul, MN: Zion Christian Life Center, 1981.

Peters, Dan, and Steve Peters, with Cher Miller. *Rock's Hidden Persuader: The Truth about Backmasking.* Minneapolis: Bethany House, 1985.

———. *Why Knock Rock?* Minneapolis: Bethany House, 1984.

Peters, Dan, Steve Peters, and Cher Miller. *What About Christian Rock? What About Christian Rock?* Minneapolis: Bethany House Publishers, 1986.

Phillips, Kevin. *The Emerging Republican Majority.* New Rochelle, NY: Arlington House, 1969.

———. *Post-Conservative America: People, Politics, and Ideology in a Time of Crisis.* New York: Random House, 1982.

Putnam, Robert D. *Bowling Alone: The Collapse and Revival of American Community.* New York: Simon and Schuster, 2000.

Putnam, Robert D., and Lewis M. Feldstein, with Don Cohen. *Better Together: Restoring the American Community*. New York: Simon and Schuster, 2003.

Pyle, Hugh. *Skimpy Skirts and Hippie Hair*. Murfreesboro, TN: Sword of the Lord, 1972.

Rabey, Steve. *The Heart of Rock and Roll*. Ada, MI: Fleming H. Revell, 1986.

Ribuffo, Leo. *The Old Christian Right: The Protestant Far Right from the Great Depression to the Cold War*. Philadelphia: Temple University Press, 1983.

Rice, John R., editor. *The Best of Billy Sunday: 17 Burning Sermons from the Most Spectacular Evangelist the World Has Ever Known*. Murfreesboro, TN: Sword of the Lord, 1965.

Robertson, Pat. *America's Dates with Destiny*. New York: Thomas Nelson, 1986.

Romanowski, William D. "Contemporary Christian Music: The Business of Music Ministry." In Schultze, *American Evangelicals and the Mass Media*, 143–69.

———. "Move Over Madonna: The Crossover Career of Gospel Artist Amy Grant." *Popular Music and Society* 17, no. 2 (Summer 1993): 47–67.

———. *Pop Culture Wars: Religion and the Role of Entertainment in American Life*. Downers Grove, IL; InterVarsity Press, 1996.

Rossinow, Doug. *The Politics of Authenticity: Liberalism, Christianity, and the New Left in America*. New York: Columbia University Press, 1998.

Rozell, Mark J., and Clyde Wilcox, editors. *God at the Grass Roots: The Christian Right in the 1994 Elections*. Lanham, MD: Rowman and Littlefield, 1995.

Ryan, Mary P. *Cradle of the Middle Class: The Family in Oneida County, New York 1790–1865*. New York: Cambridge University Press, 1981.

Sandler, Lauren. *Righteous: Dispatches from the Evangelical Youth Movement*. New York: Viking, 2006.

Schaeffer, Francis A. *Art and the Bible: Two Essays*. Downers Grove, IL: InterVarsity Press, 1973.

———. *A Christian Manifesto*. Revised ed. Westchester, IL: Crossway Books, 1982.

Schlosser, Eric. *Fast Food Nation: The Dark Side of the All-American Meal*. New York: Houghton Mifflin, 2001.

———. *Reefer Madness: Sex, Drugs, and Cheap Labor in the American Black Market*. Boston: Houghton Mifflin, 2003.

Schneider, William. "The Suburban Century Begins." *Atlantic Monthly* (July 1992): 33–44.

Schrag, Peter. *Paradise Lost: California's Experience, America's Future*. New York: New Press, 1998.

Schulman, Bruce J. *The Seventies: The Great Shift in American Culture, Society, and Politics*. Cambridge, MA: Da Capo Press, 2001.

Schultze, Quentin J., ed. *American Evangelicals and the Mass Media*. Grand Rapids, MI: Zondervan, 1990.

Schultze, Quentin J., Roy M. Anker, James D. Bratt, William D. Romanowski, John William Worst, and Lambert Zuidervaart. *Dancing in the Dark: Youth, Popular Culture, and the Electronic Media*. Grand Rapids, MI: William B. Eerdmans, 1991.

Seay, Davin, and Mary Neely. *Stairway to Heaven: The Spiritual Roots of Rock 'n' Roll—From the King and Little Richard to Prince and Amy Grant*. New York: Ballantine Books, 1996.

Self, Robert O. *American Babylon: Race and the Struggle for Postwar Oakland*. Princeton, NJ: Princeton University Press, 2003.

Sernett, Milton C. *Bound for the Promised Land: African American Religion and the Great Migration*. Durham, NC: Duke University Press, 1997.

Shibley, Mark A. *Resurgent Evangelicalism in the United States: Mapping Cultural Change since 1970*. Columbia: University of South Carolina Press, 1996.

Smith, Christian. *Christian America? What Evangelicals Really Want*. Berkeley and Los Angeles: University of California Press, 2000.

Smith, Christian, with Michael Emerson, Sally Gallagher, Paul Kennedy, and David Sikkink. *American Evangelicalism: Embattled and Thriving*. Chicago: University of Chicago Press, 1998.

Smith, Christian, with Melinda Lundquist Denton. *Soul Searching: The Religious and Spiritual Lives of American Teenagers*. New York: Oxford University Press, 2005.

Smith, Suzanne E. *Dancing in the Street: Motown and the Cultural Politics of Detroit*. Cambridge, MA: Harvard University Press, 1999.

Soper, J. Christopher. "California: Christian Conservative Influence in a Liberal State." In Rozell and Wilcox, *God at the Grassroots*, 211–26.

Sorkin, Michael, editor. *Variations on a Theme Park: The New American City and the End of Public Space*. New York: Noonday Press, 1992.

Spigel, Lynn. *Make Room for TV: Television and the Family Ideal in Postwar America*. Chicago: University of Chicago Press, 1992.

———. *Welcome to the Dreamhouse: Popular Media and the Postwar Suburbs*. Durham, NC: Duke University Press, 2001.

Stacey, Judith. *Brave New Families: Stories of Domestic Upheaval in Late Twentieth Century America*. New York: Basic Books, 1990.

———. *In the Name of the Family: Rethinking Family Values in the Postmodern Age*. Boston: Beacon Press, 1996.

Starr, Kevin. *Americans and the California Dream 1850–1915*. New York: Oxford University Press, 1973.

———. *Material Dreams: Southern California through the 1920s*. New York: Oxford University Press, 1990.

Sullivan, Mark. "'More Popular Than Jesus': The Beatles and the Religious Far Right." *Popular Music* 6 (October 1987): 313–26.

Sugrue, Thomas J. *The Origins of the Urban Crisis: Race and Inequality in Postwar Detroit*. Princeton, NJ: Princeton University Press, 1996.

Swaggart, Jimmy. *Christian Rock and Roll*. Baton Rouge, LA: Jimmy Swaggart Ministries, 1986.

Swaggart, Jimmy, with Robert Paul Lamb. *Religious Rock 'n' Roll: A Wolf in Sheep's Clothing*. Baton Rouge, LA: Jimmy Swaggart Ministries, 1987.

Taiz, Lillian. *Hallelujah Lads and Lasses: Remaking the Salvation Army in America, 1880–1930*. Chapel Hill: University of North Carolina Press, 2001.

Thompson, John J. *Raised by Wolves: The Story of Christian Rock & Roll*. Toronto: ECW Press, 2000.

Tocqueville, Alexis de. *Democracy in America*. From the Henry Reeve translation, revised and corrected, 1899. http://xroads.virginia.edu/~hyper/detoc/home.html.

Truehart, Charles. "Welcome to the Next Church." *Atlantic Monthly* (August 1996): 37–58.

Turner, Steve. *Hungry for Heaven: Rock and Roll and the Search for Redemption*. Downers Grove, IL: InterVarsity Press, 1988.

———. *Imagine: A Vision for Christians in the Arts*. Downers Grove, IL: Intervarsity Press, 2001.

Wacker, Grant. *Heaven Below: Early Pentecostals and American Culture*. Cambridge, MA: Harvard University Press, 2001.

———. "Uneasy in Zion: Evangelicals in Postmodern Society." In Marsden, *Evangelicalism and Modern America*, 17–28.

Wald, Kenneth. "Florida: Running Globally and Winning Locally." In Rozell and Wilcox, *God at the Grass Roots*, 19–46.

Walser, Robert. *Running with the Devil: Power, Gender, and Madness in Heavy Metal Music*. Hanover, NH: Wesleyan University Press, 1993.

Ward, Brian. *Just My Soul Responding: Rhythm and Blues, Black Consciousness, and Race Relations*. Berkeley and Los Angeles: University of California Press, 1998.

Weinstein, Deena. *Heavy Metal: The Music and Its Culture*. Rev. ed. New York: Da Capo Press, 2000.

Wiener, Jon. "Working-Class Republicans and 'False Consciousness.'" *Dissent* (Spring 2005): 55–58.

Wigger, John H. "Taking Heaven by Storm: Enthusiasm and Early American Methodism, 1770–1820." *Journal of the American Republic* 14, no. 2 (Summer 1994): 167–94.

Wilcox, Clyde. *God's Warriors: The Christian Right in Twentieth Century America*. Baltimore: Johns Hopkins University Press, 1992.

Wildmon, Donald E. *The Home Invaders*. Wheaton, IL: SP Publications, 1985.

Wilkerson, David, with Claire Cox. *Parents on Trial: Why Kids Go Wrong—or Right*. New York: Hawthorn Books, 1967.

Willis, Paul. *Learning to Labor: How Working Class Kids Get Working Class Jobs*. Farnborough, UK: Saxon House, 1977; reprint, New York: Columbia University Press, 1981.

Wilson, James Q. "A Guide to Reagan Country: The Political Culture of Southern California." *Commentary* (May 1967): 37–45.

Winter, Gibson. *The Suburban Captivity of the Churches*. New York: Macmillan, 1962.

Wolfe, Alan. *The Transformation of American Religion: How We Actually Live Our Faith*. New York: Free Press, 2003.

Wright, Willard Huntington. "Los Angeles—The Chemically Pure." In Burton Rascoe and Groff Conklin, editors. *The Smart Set Anthology*, 90–102. New York: Reynal and Hitchcock, 1934.

Wuthnow, Robert. *The Restructuring of American Religion: Society and Faith since World War II*. Princeton, NJ: Princeton University Press, 1988.

# Index

Page numbers in italics indicate illustrations.

Text: 10/13 Sabon
Display: Sabon
Compositor: International Typesetting and Composition
Printer & Binder: Sheridan Books, Inc.